WHITE SKINS/BLACK MASKS

The fascination with exotic cultures and the crossing of cultural boundaries provides some of the most striking ways in which a colonising culture articulates its self-identity and asserts its authority. *White Skins/Black Masks* examines the representational dynamics of coloniser versus colonised in the African and Indian writing of Henry Rider Haggard and Rudyard Kipling – exploring the interface between the native 'Other' as reflection and as a point of address. Gail Ching-Liang Low employs recent thinking in psychoanalysis, anthropology and colonial discourse to analyse the manner in which fantasy and fabulation is caught up in networks of desire and power.

Low focuses on the early fictional and travel writing of Haggard and Kipling. Close friends, as well as prominent figures of imperial and colonial myth-making, Haggard and Kipling were praised for their presumed knowledge of and alleged ability to speak from within the native cultures of Africa and India. Their fiction attests to a persistent fascination with the visual image of the other in the imaginative reconstruction of costume and body-image. But significantly, their work also exhibits the Other's ambivalence as challenge and fortification of colonial and imperial narrative authority. Low addresses the psychic processes of negation, projection and reappropriation in the dynamics of pleasure versus displeasure and mastery versus defence found in the work of these two writers. She also provides a historical context for understanding how these forces emerged from and were played out in contemporary society.

Interdisciplinary in its approach, *White Skins/Black Masks* will be of value to all students and scholars interested in representation and colonialism in cultural and literary studies.

Gail Ching-Liang Low lectures at Staffordshire University and has published articles in *New Formations* and *Women: A Cultural Review.*

WHITE SKINS/BLACK MASKS

Representation and colonialism

Gail Ching-Liang Low

London and New York

First published 1996
by Routledge
11 New Fetter Lane, London EC4P 4EE

Simultaneously published in the USA and Canada
by Routledge
29 West 35th Street, New York, NY 10001

© 1996 Gail Ching-Liang Low

Typeset in Baskerville by
Ponting–Green Publishing Services, Chesham, Bucks
Printed and bound in Great Britain by
Biddles Ltd, Guildford and King's Lynn

British Library Cataloguing in Publication Data
A catalogue record for this book is available from
the British Library

Library of Congress Cataloging in Publication Data
Low, Gail Ching-Liang
White Skins/Black Masks : Representation and Colonialism /
Gail Ching-Liang Low.
p.   cm.
Includes bibliographical references and index.
1. English fiction–19th century–History and criticism.
2. Colonies in literature.   3. Literature and anthropology–
Great Britain–Colonies–History–19th century.   4. Haggard,
H. Rider (Henry Rider), 1856–1925–Political and social views.
5. Kipling, Rudyard, 1865–1936–Political and social views.
6. Travelers' writings, English–History and criticism.
7. Cultural relations in literature.   8. Body, Human, in
literature.   9. Imperialism in literature.   10. Costume in
literature.   11. Race in literature.   12. South Africa–In
literature.   13. India–In Literature
I. Title
PR868.C6L69   1996
823'.809355–dc20   95–8889

ISBN 0–415–08147–5 (hbk)
ISBN 0–415–08148–3 (pbk)

CONTENTS

List of illustrations   vii
Acknowledgements   ix
Note on spellings   xi

INTRODUCTION   1

Part I

1 BODY/BORDER LINES   13
2 THE DOMINION OF SONS   36
3 MIMESIS OF SAVAGERY   66
   TRANSITIONS   104

Part II

4 THE COLONIAL UNCANNY   113
5 THE CITY OF DREADFUL NIGHT   156
6 THE COLONIAL MIRROR   191
7 LOAFERS AND STORY-TELLERS   238
   CONCLUSION   264

Notes   269
Bibliography   277
Index   291

ILLUSTRATIONS

1 'Boy and Girl of the Earthmen tribe, from Port Natal',
   Illustrated London News, Nov 6, 1852.   26
2 'Zulu Kaffirs at St George Gallery, Knightsbridge',
   Illustrated London News, May 28, 1853.   27
3 'Lord Beresford's encounter with a Zulu in the
   reconnaisance across the Umvolosi, July 3', *Illustrated
   London News*, Sept 6, 1879.   56
4 'At Bay!: The battle of Isandula, Jan 22, 1879. The last
   order that we heard was "fix bayonets men and die like
   English soldiers do", and so they did – Extract from a
   letter by a survivor', *Graphic*, March 15, 1879.   57
5 'The Zulu War in South Africa: Cetewayo, the Zulu
   King', *Illustrated London News*, Feb 22, 1879.   92
6 'An Attack of Zulu Warriors', *Graphic*, May 3, 1879.   94
7 'The Zulu War: Embarkation of the 91st Highlanders at
   Southampton', *Illustrated London News*, March 1, 1879.   95
8 'Umslopogaas smote as he rushed, and the great blade
   of the great spear that was lifted to pierce him fell to the
   ground hewn from its haft', *Illustrated London News*,
   Feb 27, 1892.   97
9 'Then again Chaka speaks: "Charge! Children of the
   Zulu!"', *Illustrated London News*, Jan 16, 1892;
   serialisation of *Nada the Lily*.   100
10 'The Zulu War: General Lord Chelmsford reviewing the
   native contingent on the banks of the Tugela', *Illustrated
   London News*, May 10, 1879.   101
11 'The Zulu War: The Gallant Defence of Rorke's Drift by
   Lieutenants Chard and Bromhead and one hundred
   and thirty-seven men', *Graphic*, March 15, 1879.   102

12 'The Zulu War: Zulus Crossing a River', *Illustrated London News*, April 12, 1879.   103
13 'A Mohamedan' (from Coleman, 1899).   204
14 'The Rajputs of Telingana, India' (from Racinet, 1988).   205
15 'The Lama' (from Kipling, 1912).   208
16 'Richard Burton as "The Pilgrim"' (from Burton, 1893).   210
17 'Rae Doona Chund' (from Watson and Kaye, 1968–75).   222

ACKNOWLEDGEMENTS

Special thanks must go to Robert Clark, Roger Sales and Louis James who read and commented on my doctoral dissertation and encouraged me to publish, and to Ann Parry, Rhys Garnett, Ulrike Sieglohr and Hugh Marles who read sections of the manuscript and offered invaluable advice and criticism. My warmest thanks to Vanessa Lockwood, Peter Kramer, Ravi Vasudevan, Radhika Singha, Jane Rondot, Martin Brown and Clare Midgley for passionate and challenging discussions over the politics and poetics of Empire that help set the framework for this book. This book could not have been completed without a term's study leave from Staffordshire University and I am grateful for the support of my colleagues in the School of Arts who have helped not only with their ideas but also with their wit and good cheer.

I am grateful to The United Society for the Propagation of the Gospel and the Rhodes House Library for permission to quote from the SPG papers, and to Claire Brown for her painstaking help with the Bishop Colenso papers. I am also grateful to Studio Editions for permission to reproduce a black and white illustration of the 'Rajputs of Telingana' from their 1988 reprint of Albert Racinet's *Historical Encyclopedia of Costume*, to A. P. Watt and The National Trust for permission to quote from Rudyard Kipling's *From Sea to Sea*, *Kim*, *Plain Tales From the Hills*, *Wee Willie Winkle*, *Life's Handicap* and from the Kipling Papers at the University of Sussex. Thanks must also go to A. P. Watt and The National Trust for permission to reproduce John Lockwood Kipling's illustration of 'The Lama' in the 1912 Macmillan edition of *Kim*.

Finally, to my partner Stuart MacFarlane, who has had to take on the often awkward task of being critic, friend, parent, companion,

ACKNOWLEDGEMENTS

editor and proof-reader all rolled into one, I owe a very special debt of gratitude. Only you know how much.

x

NOTE ON SPELLINGS

I have adopted the modern spelling for Zulu names where they occur within my own text. Where Zulu names and words occur within nineteenth-century texts, I have kept assiduously to their original spelling and have not sought to standardise them. Thus Cetshwayo appears as 'Cetewayo' in the *Illustrated London News* and 'Cetywayo' in Haggard's prose; Shaka appears sometimes as 'Chaka'.

INTRODUCTION

> My reading of colonial discourse suggests that the point
> of intervention should shift from the identification of
> images as positive or negative, to an understanding of
> the processes of subjectification made possible (and
> plausible) through stereotypical discourse. To judge the
> stereotyped image on the basis of a prior political
> normativity is to dismiss it, not to displace it, which is
> only possible by engaging with its effectivity; with the
> repertoire of positions of power and resistance, domina-
> tion and dependence that constructs the colonial sub-
> ject (both coloniser and colonised).
>
> (Bhabha, 1983: 18–19)

'Difference', 'power' and 'pleasure' are all issues which must be
addressed in any critique of colonial representation. Yet these are
issues which are difficult to come to terms with in colonial and post-
colonial politics because they require an acknowledgement of the
ambivalences and complexities of political intervention, and because they forestall an easy appeal to epistemological certainty –
'the truth' – which authorises critical transparency and orthodoxy.
I begin this book with a quotation from Bhabha because his work
presents a clear challenge to rethink – in a self-reflexive way – the
whole politics and poetics of writing against the grain. In the
critique of the literature of Empire in general, and in my own study
of Henry Rider Haggard and Rudyard Kipling in particular, anger
at the subjugation and exploitation of other worlds often *dismisses*
these romances of imperialism as white patriarchal myths, which
attempt only to justify the conquest, occupation and destruction of
non-Western societies. They are, of course, all of these things.

1

INTRODUCTION

However, the easy negation of such writing does not address the power of their myth-making. If myth and fantasy touch on levels outside the conscious mind, then simply to point out the falsity of one's imagination leaves untouched the psychic investments which determine the formation of the fictions that sustain the world we live and act within. To recognise the instability of the divide between fantasy and reality, fiction and facts is to begin the difficult and painful task of constructing alternative futures. Walter Benjamin makes this clear in his outline of the (cultural) historian's task: the past 'manifests itself at any given time to a very specific epoch: that is, the one in which humanity, rubbing its eyes, suddenly recognizes the dream image as such. It is at that point that the historian takes on the task of dream interpretation' (Benjamin, 1983–4: 10).

The section of British literary history in the late nineteenth century that I shall be addressing is located within a period when Europe was beginning the serious task of discoursing on her non-European 'Others' in imaginative and scientific literature. The communal perception of other worlds, shaped and sustained through the mechanisms of textual production, turned on cultural difference (invariably racialised and sexualised). Investigations into European folklore, comparative philology, physical anthropology and the origins of civilisation produced the disciplinary rubrics of anthropology and ethnography, which focused on cultural and physical diversity. The period also saw the rise of the novel of adventure and the literature of Empire. Furthermore, boundaries between different forms of writing – travel narratives, adventure genres and scientific treatises – were more fluid than perhaps we have been accustomed to thinking. Explorers and travel writers wrote novels, while novelists produced imaginative imitations of explorers' exploits. Textual authority invoked by one form of writing finds its source in another and literary borrowings were not uncommon; travel writers produced narratives which relied heavily on the gothic and heroic paradigms of adventure genres while novelists produced 'ethnographic novels' which included the 'manners and customs' prototype of anthropological accounts.

Edward Said calls the maintenance of geopolitical divisions within scholarly and aesthetic texts 'Orientalist'. Linking the production of texts with the production of reality over time, Orientalism may be described as a form of 'radical realism' which seeks to institute Europe in 'flexible positional superiority' over its Others.

2

But even while it inhabits the apparatus of power by seeking to control, incorporate and domesticate 'manifestly different' and novel worlds, Orientalism must invoke, and inscribe the very pleasure and unpleasure contingent on that difference. Hence Orientalist discourse delivers an Other which is both an object of knowledge and surveillance and an object of libidinous impulses. Bhabha's theoretical analysis of this ambivalent vacillation between pleasure and unpleasure, mastery and defence provides a nodal point for my readings of colonial fiction.

The broad theoretical underpinnings of this book are taken from a psychoanalytically inflected understanding of imperial subjectivities produced at the interstices of power and desire. This book is an attempt to grapple with the complex dynamics of colonial desire and power which lie behind the persistent need to reappropriate the libidinous spaces imputed to non-Western cultures. Colonial subjectivities produced by the powerful divisions of self and Other seem paradoxically to be dogged by a relentless nostalgia and desire for the excluded Others. This is apparent in the fascination with 'native' culture and, particularly, with 'going native' even when the 'demarcating imperative'[1] of colonialism aims to divide 'white' from 'black', colonisers from colonised. This fascination was exemplified by the lives of figures such as Sir Richard Burton and T. E. Lawrence and is apparent in the fiction of writers such as Henry Rider Haggard, Rudyard Kipling, John Buchan and Joseph Conrad. My book will focus only on Haggard and Kipling in the 1880s and 1890s and will take for its object of inquiry a selection of Haggard's African romances and Kipling's short fiction and travelogue on India.[2]

Haggard was born into minor gentry in Norfolk; his father was a squire and his mother the wealthy daughter of a Bombay civil servant. At the age of nineteen, he sailed for South Africa to work on the staff of Sir Henry Bulwer, the new Lieutenant-Governor of Natal. Two years later in 1877, Haggard marched into Pretoria with Sir Theophilus Shepstone and hoisted the British flag over the Boer republic. He declared of the annexation of Transvaal, 'it will be some years before the people at home realise how great an act it has been, an act without parallel'. He worked first as an English Clerk to the Colonial Secretary of Transvaal and later as the peripatetic Registrar of Transvaal's High Court, writing the occasional article for publication. At the outbreak of the Anglo-Zulu war, Haggard joined a volunteer corps which was called upon to defend Pretoria from Boer agitation for independence. He left government service in May of 1879 and in the same year, he left South Africa for Britain. He returned to the Transvaal with his new wife in 1880 but soon grew disillusioned with Gladstone's foreign policy in South Africa, leaving for good in 1881. He published his first book, *Cetywayo and His White Neighbours* as a defence of Shepstone's policy in the Transvaal (Higgins, 1980: xii). When reading for the bar, he published two novels *Dawn* and *The Witch's Head*. *King Solomon's Mines*, his first African romance adventure, was published to great success in 1885; it was followed in quick succession by other novels set in Africa such as *She* (1887), *Jess* (1887), *Allan Quatermain* (1887), *Allan's Wife* (1889) and *Nada the Lily* (1892). He later served on various Royal Commissions, campaigned for agricultural reform and even contested unsucessfully for election as a Unionist. In 1912, he received a knighthood.

Kipling was born in Bombay in 1865 to John Lockwood Kipling, an artist and later museum curator and director of the School of Art in Lahore, and Alice Macdonald, the daughter of a Methodist minister. In 1871, just before his sixth birthday, he and his sister were fostered out to an old sea captain and his wife in Southsea. His stay with the Holloways was an unhappy one, alleviated only by holidays spent with family relations (the Burne-Joneses) in Fulham. From 1878 to 1882, Kipling was sent as a boarder to a new English public school founded by a group of Army officers. In September 1882 he sailed to India and found work as assistant editor for the *Civil and Military Gazette* (*CMG*), a provincial newspaper based in Lahore. His early days with the *CMG* consisted primarily of writing routine summaries of Government reports, home and foreign news, with the occasional chance to work on a special assignment, such as the meeting of Lord Dufferin and the Amir of Afghanistan. He was later allowed a weekly column of provincial news and views. Under the editor Kay Robinson, he was given a column and a half (about 2,000 words) or 'turnover' in which to write short stories, verses and sketches. Thirty-nine of these were later collected and published with Thacker Spink of Calcutta in 1888. Kipling moved to a sister newspaper, the all-India *Pioneer*, in November 1887. There he was installed as editor of a newly created supplement, *The Week's News*; there was a page of fiction reserved for him to fill and he was left relatively free to choose projects that took his fancy. The transfer also brought Kipling's first special assignment with the *Pioneer*, a travelogue on Rajasthan entitled 'Letters of Marque'.

During his six years work as a journalist in India, a collection of verse, *Departmental Ditties* and six volumes of short stories were issued under the imprint of the Indian Railway Library paperback series. In 1889 when he returned to Britain, the influential critic Andrew Lang had already reviewed *In Black and White* and *Under the Deodars* recommending them 'heartily' to the public (Green, 1971: 44). Kipling's rise to literary fame in Britain in the 1890s was 'meteoric' and he was soon compared by critics to Dickens (Green, 1971: 16). Soon after Kipling's arrival in Britain, Charles Carrington remarks, critics were praising him as the 'new literary star':

> Eighteen-ninety saw the publication or republication in England and America of more than eighty short stories from his pen, many ballads, and, at the end of the year, a novel. The market was flooded with his work in verse and prose. . . . A chorus of praise, not unmixed with astonishment, was the first reaction of the reviewers, and a judicious leading article in *The Times* assured Kipling's position as a star of the first magnitude.
>
> (Carrington, 1970: 24)

Although Haggard's and Kipling's work was dissimilar, and their contexts of production very different, both Haggard and Kipling were lauded for their alleged ability to speak from within the 'native' cultures of Africa and India. Contemporary critical reception in Britain alludes to their distinctive ability to cross cultures and spin stories of strange and exciting societies for British audiences. Haggard's speciality was the rendering of Zulu or African culture. Robert Stevenson admired in *King Solomon's Mines* the 'command of the savage way of talking', while Lang applauded Haggard's 'singular' 'natural gift of savagery' (Haggard, 1926 (vol 1): 235). Kipling received even more acclaim; Lang's review of *Plain Tales from the Hills* speaks of an 'Indian story-teller' and praises the author's 'freshness, wit, and knowledge of things little known – the dreams of opium smokers . . . the passions of Pathans and wild Border tribes, the magic which is yet a living force in India'; Kipling's tales will keep 'the English reader awake and excited' (Green, 1971: 48). Kay Robinson, Kipling's fellow journalist commends his wonderful insight into the 'strangely mixed manners of life and thought of the natives of India'. But if Haggard's and Kipling's authority are invoked on the same terms of authenticity that lie behind contemporary ethnography's textual delivery of foreign cultures, their work can also be said to dispense with narrative mediation of difference by presuming not only to speak on behalf of the Other, but also from the place of the Other.

Haggard in *Nada the Lily*, for example, aims 'to think with the mind, and speak with the voice of a Zulu of the old regime' while Kipling's *Kim* is narrated from the position of an Anglo-Irish boy who grows up virtually Indian and whose talent for disguise leads to his recruitment as an imperial spy. *Kim's* metamorphosis from young Anglo-Indian boy to spy projects a complex fantasy of surveillance and transgression while Haggard's Zulu-nation can be located within a long tradition of imaging the black body-politic as an idealised and nostalgic counterpart for the white reader. Both writers hold a distorted mirror which offers the Englishman a vision of himself transformed by the image of the Other.[3]

Haggard's popularity in the last fifteen years of the nineteenth century was chiefly due to the success of his African romances. *King Solomon's Mines*, published on September 30, 1885, after a massive publicity campaign mounted by Cassell, sold a total of 31,000 copies in the first year of its publication. It was followed by a string of equally popular novels. *She* was first serialised in the *Graphic* and then published by Longmans Green and Co. in January 1887 in a single volume, resulting in even more spectacular figures, selling 30,792 copies in June alone. *Allan Quatermain*, serialised in the *Longman's Magazine* from January to June, was published in book form on July 1, 1887. In June 1888, the Longman ledgers indicate a payment to Haggard for 29,403 copies. The distribution figures for *Nada the Lily* show a waning of the sales which had greeted his earlier novels. Only figures for the Silver Library edition are available and these show that 6,490 copies were sold after a month of publication and in January 1893, Haggard was given another cheque for the 8,368 copies sold of the smaller and cheaper Colonial edition, published in August of the preceding year.[4]

This book is divided into two parts. Haggard's representation of Africa is discussed in Part I and Kipling's India in Part II. Chapter one of this book details the crises of 'Englishness' – masculinity, militarism, patriotism and imperialism – which form the context of Haggard's African romances and focuses on the body as a privileged trope in the discourses of Empire and the nation. In many ways, his account of English adventurers' encounters with the Zulu (or Zulu prototype) represents an attempt to exploit and to answer these contemporary issues. Chapter two focuses on the ideological and psychic investment in the 'boy' in Haggard's fiction, and the imperialist nostalgia found in the pastoral preoccupations of the 'boy's adventure'. It addresses the heroic cult of English masculinity, formed through the romanticised image of Zulu politics and military prowess, that is available through the metaphor of the colonial mimesis of savagery. Chapter three interrogates the representational naturalism and symbolic capital obtained from the Anglo/Zulu mirror through the historical context of the Anglo-Zulu war. It also looks at Haggard's mentor Theophilus Shepstone, his creation of 'Locations' (native reservations sometimes referred to as the Shepstonian system), and argues that the temporal distancing and segregation that are built into the maintenance of the Locations are embodied within the narrative resolutions that appear in *King Solomon's Mines* and its sequel, *Allan Quatermain*.

Kipling has been portrayed as one of the most popular writers of the late nineteenth and early twentieth century, and is assumed to have attracted readers from all sections of society. Yet it is difficult to provide the hard evidence of book sales and royalties for the early part of Kipling's career with which to support this assertion. Scrupulous accounts are kept for the period 1910 to 1933 and 1937–8, but nothing in the present Macmillan archive nor in the Kipling archive at the University of Sussex gives any indication of earlier book sales. However, from the issue and re-issue of his work in the 1890s, one could reasonably assume that Kipling's books reached a large audience. Carrington argues that even after Kipling's literary fashionability had passed, and 'publicists no longer urged the public to acquire it', there was no lack of buyers and readers between 1890 and 1932 (Carrington, 1970: 24).

The Anglo-Indian context of Kipling's early work also makes it very different from Haggard's. Significantly, Haggard began writing fiction only after he had ceased to consider making a home in Southern Africa, whereas Kipling came to prominence during his time as a journalist working in India. Stories issued in the *Civil and Military Gazette* and in *The Week's News* were collected and published first in India and then later in Britain.[5] As Bart Moore-Gilbert points out, there is some justification in assuming that these early tales were directed solely at an Anglo-Indian readership (Moore-Gilbert, 1986). Kipling's early fiction registers the pull between different audiences and it is this division that I want to point up in my selection of Kipling's stories about Indians and Indian culture. If

Haggard's fiction is undeniably imperialist, in that it is meaningful in the context of metropolitan rivalries, Kipling's early writing seems more colonialist, in that it is more concerned with the relation between metropolis and colony, and with the impact of living and working in India on an English identity. Chapters four and five explore the contradictions of Anglo-Indian subjectivity split between Britain and India. This duality produces an ambivalence in Kipling's work which surfaces as what I have termed the 'colonial uncanny' (see chapter four) in 'Letters of Marque' and in gothic tales detailing the anxiety, alienation and horror of the Anglo-Indian experience. It also emerges in 'The City of Dreadful Night' where his writing portrays Calcutta in the satirical language and imagery of nineteenth-century London. Yet Kipling's derision presents problems: his desire to separate Anglo from Indian ends in a bewildered mockery of English culture. Chapter six begins with a more formal psychoanalytic account of the politics of identification in the colonial arena; it then proceeds to look, within a theory of fetishism, specifically at the Kipling characters who deliberately cross cultural boundaries in order to safeguard settler societies. It also argues that in *Kim* and the Strickland stories, the colonial policeman/spy is invested with extraordinary narrative energy by virtue of his knowledge and ability to pass as native – an investment which is matched by the contemporary critical reception of the writer himself. Chapter seven argues that this assumption of knowledge is a product of desire within the transferential dynamics of narrative and story-telling. In 'The Man Who Would Be King', the framed story of the loafers' rise and subsequent fall provides readers with a clear-sighted exploration of a colonial grammar and syntax of desire; but the text also teases us with the possibility that such a story may simply be a 'hoax' produced by vagabond story-tellers.

My book explores the ways in which desire is presented and channelled through fantasy in the fictions of Empire. It examines how Haggard and Kipling's narratives position the Other and the Other's body-image, and employs the metaphor of the colonial mirror, loosely based on a Lacanian account of mimesis and self-formation, for its mode of analysis. My reading of Haggard and Kipling is underpinned by the film theorist and critic Kaja Silverman's account of the relation between fantasy, ideology, body-image and desire (Silverman, 1992: 1–51). She asserts that there is no fault-line between fantasy and reality, the individual world of libidinal desires and the social world of politics and economics. Silverman argues for a 'libidinal politics' that will take on the political implications of the mutually defining matrix of desire and identification predicated on Lacan's mirror stage. To paraphrase her conclusions for my purposes: the imaginary relation to the real colonial world is promoted by a fantasmatic positioning of the imperial subject in a libidinal relation either to a past, present, or future mode of production. For even where the narcissism of Haggard's romantic appropriation of Zulu military culture diverges from Kipling's more ambivalent and sometimes unpleasurable rendering of Anglo and Indian culture, their fabulations still position readers in a libidinous relation to the theory and praxis of Empire. An examination of these two key story-tellers will enable us to trace a hidden English tradition where, in Michael O'Pray's words, 'romanticism merges with nostalgia . . . and an exoticism and quasi-mysticism that have a complex relation to the British Empire' (Parry, 1988: 57).

Part I

1

BODY/BORDER LINES

Haggard's African writing is preoccupied with racial bodies. This engagement is not unusual, for in the latter half of the nineteenth century, the body functions as a privileged trope in a variety of discourses ranging from the medical, anthropological and literary to the critical. The body's metaphoric standing renders it an exemplary historical map of social relations; the model of the physiologically healthy body was a common means of conceptualising psychological, national, literary and racial health. For not only are issues of sexuality, health and disease addressed physiologically but urban poverty, crime, race, nationality and literature also are discoursed upon via the figure of the body. This chapter will carve out four distinct thematic areas – health and the nation, the gendered body, the colonial body and the cultural body – with references to the culture and literature of the political Right in order better to situate the historical dimensions of the bodily fantasy surrounding white and black bodies.

HEALTH AND THE NATION

In their attempts to come to terms with previous historical versions of the late Victorian and Edwardian period as either a 'crisis age' or a 'golden age', contemporary historians have drawn attention to the centrifugal and centripetal tendencies in politics and society (Read, 1982). The former will be my focus, for such a narration of history echoes the paranoia and fears expressed by the forces on the pre-war Right and their attempts to reverse what they saw as Britain's decline (Kennedy and Nicholls, 1981; Searle, 1971; Colls and Dodd, 1986). Fears for Britain's vulnerability in the face of economic competition from the newly industrialised nations of

America and Germany were accentuated by the emergence of Italy and Germany as imperial powers (Robinson, Gallagher and Denny, 1981). German and American productivity was exceptional. For example, US steel production overtook Britain in the 1880s, while in the next decade German output surpassed that of Britain (Porter, 1975: 120). Sales of cotton goods showed signs, in a contemporary economist's words, of 'approaching something like stagnation'. Both US and German industrial development had reached a point where there was a marked decrease in foreign capital imports and in the sale of raw materials; both countries were also beginning to export capital and manufactured goods in large quantities. In 1894, statistics show Britain's exports valued at £216 million with US, German and French exports valued at £181m, £148m and £123m respectively. German and American industrialisation had the benefit of more highly developed technology, mass production and a more systematic management of labour, and the increase in the scale of economic enterprises through the concentration of production and ownership saw the formation of trusts, monopolies and oligopolies. Britain was slow to adopt all these new measures. Her policy of free trade met with the protectionist policies of Germany, Russia, France, Austria, Hungary; this meant that Britain would have to pay duties on her goods exported to these countries while her own market was open to commercial penetration. In the intensified competition for markets and raw materials, the 'official mind of imperialism', confronted with the increasing insecurity of having trade routes, supplies and markets cut off by rival colonial powers, 'concentrated on preserving authority' in the mad scramble for Africa. Haggard felt keenly the importance of Empire in Britain's declining fortunes. In 1882, he warned his readers that 'great as she [Britain] is, her future looks by no means sunny':

> Events in these latter days develop themselves very quickly; and though the idea may, at the present moment, seem absurd, surely it is possible that, what between the spread of Radical ideas, the enmity of Ireland, the importation of foreign produce, and the competition of foreign trade, to say nothing of all the unforeseen accidents and risks of the future, the Englishmen of, say, two generations hence, may not find their country in her proud present position.
>
> (Haggard, 1882: viii)

In the judgement of historians Gallagher and Robinson, this era of new imperialism was 'largely the work of men striving in more desperate times to keep to the grand conceptions of world policy and the high standards of imperial security inherited from the Mid-Victorian preponderance' (Robinson, Gallagher and Denny, 1981: 466). Moreover, the social consensus at home was being fragmented by the Irish question, a growing trade unionism and a more militant women's movement, producing, at least for the Right, a sense of an imperilled island.

The sense of threat from without was matched by an uneasiness within England as concern with the problems of urban poverty became enmeshed with an obsession with 'Darkest England'. This 'other' nation, the object of study by reformers, evangelists and sociologists, attested to the rapid growth of cities and fractured class relations which seem unbridgeable. The liberal Charles Masterman characterised relations between the rich and the poor as one of 'complete separation, not only in sympathy and feeling, but in actual geographical aggregation' (Masterman, 1901: iv). Discussions about conditions of poverty and deprivation among the labouring classes slide easily into discussions about different types of people. Henry Mayhew's introduction to *London Labour and the London Poor* published in 1861 had already begun to enmesh social practices with physical and cultural characteristics by situating his study within the disciplinary paradigm of contemporary anthropology. In his attempts to enhance the scientific status of his work, Mayhew's comparison of London's 'wandering tribes' to the 'Bushmen' and 'Hottentot Sonquas' reads like a catalogue of racial attributes (Mayhew, 1968: 1–2). Reverend Ross's 1854 investigation into the parish of St James with Pockthorpe describes an environment of 'large, low, populous districts' where poisonous miasmic odours from animal droppings and vegetable refuse generated disease and misery. The human occupants' 'continual contact with filth without has much to do in producing indifference to filth within doors, and in debasing the characters of those who inhabit there'. Metaphors of disease and disorder migrate from the environs to their occupants. These people have 'careless and dirty habits' and are a 'moral blight which infest' local parishes; they are effectively the 'heathens at home', the 'outcasts within . . . the pale of decency' (Ross, 1854: 4–5). Andrew Mearns's 1883 pamphlet, *The Bitter Cry of Outcast London*, reinforces the idea of two nations in his depiction of the 'vast mass of corruption' 'seething in the

15

very centre of our great cities, concealed by the thinnest crust of civilization and decency' (Keating, 1976: 92). Mearns's investigation into the living conditions of the urban poor begins with a comparison with the crowded horror of slave ships. His journey is a journey into the moral and physical abyss of 'pestilential human rookeries . . . where tens of thousands are [crammed] . . . together'. Guiding readers firmly through the maze of 'dark and filthy passages' and directing their attention to 'courts reeking with poisonous and malodorous gases' 'rotten and reeking tenements' which 'herd' both men and women together in long 'sleeping room[s]', Mearns's descriptions of the overcrowded conditions, destitution and exploitation which the urban poor had to endure is meant to provoke a sense of moral outrage. But his pamphlet draws on the rhetoric of bodily contagion and moral contamination which sets apart the slum dwellers from the middle class 'reliable explorer' and his readers (Keating, 1976: 94, 96). In its depiction of 'outcast London', Charles Dickens's slumming expedition, 'On Duty with Inspector Field', also registers outrage and fear. The shift in the 1880s from what Gareth Stedman Jones has called the language of 'demoralization' to that of 'degeneration' (Stedman Jones, 1971: 281–290, 313) is conspicuous in Dickens's presentation of the environs around St Giles Church and Ratcliffe Highway in London:

> How many people may there be in London, who, if we had brought them deviously and blindfold, to this street . . . would know it for not a remote part of the city in which their lives are passed? How many, who in amidst this compound of sickening smells, these heaps of filth, these tumbling houses, with all their vile contents, animate and inanimate, slimily overflowing into the black road . . . could look around on the faces which now hem us in . . . the lowering foreheads, the sallow cheeks, the brutal eyes, the matted hair, the infected, vermin-haunted heaps of rags – and say, 'I have thought of this'.
>
> (Dickens, 1899: 160)

Degeneration taps into a vein of writing on environmentalism and race. Victorian racial environmentalism draws on humoral theory which linked physiognomy, temperament and environment (Comaroff and Comaroff, 1992: 220; Haley, 1978: 30). Racial environmentalism details a paradigm in which external forces

16

(such as climate) mould the racial character and physical differences of the various human groups. Acclimatisation leads to racial traits over a period of time (Schiebinger, 1993: 136–139; Anderson, 1992: 512–513). Hence the ease with which Masterman's concern about rural–urban immigration slips into a biological discourse of gradual physical change. Being 'reared' in the crowded metropolis 'with cramped physical accessories, hot, fretful life, and long hours of sedentary or unhealthy toil', 'the second generation of immigrants' present a problem of some magnitude. This new 'physical type of town dweller' is 'stunted, narrow chested, easily wearied; yet voluble, excitable, with little ballast, stamina, or endurance' (Masterman, 1901: 7–8). Stedman Jones argues that specifically for the period between the 1880s and 1890s, the theory of 'hereditary urban degeneration' received support from eminent writers such as Charles Booth and Alfred Marshall (Stedman Jones, 1971: 128). Daniel Pick's findings lend support; he contends that the sustained cultural pessimism of the 1870s and 1880s recast the Victorian evolutionary theory within the biological rhetoric of degeneration; urban centres were especially targeted as 'literal breeding ground[s] of decay' as 'bodily degeneration was conflated with . . . social and urban crisis' (Pick, 1989: 180, 190). As Haggard's embittered narrator writes in the introduction to *Allan Quatermain*, 'we breed the sickly people' to fill modern hospitals.

An important strand of the 'condition of England' debate championed a bio-medical framing of urban degeneration and prophesied England's fall from the development of a new physical breed of people. Alfred Marshall wrote of increased bodily deterioration and the 'coming generation[s]' lower than 'average physique and . . . morality' (Stedman Jones, 1971: 128). The *Lancet* announced in 1888 that degeneration 'is undoubtedly at work among town-bred population as the consequences of unwholesome occupations, improper [diet], and juvenile vice'. As concern about the state of health in inner cities turned into a debate about racial degeneration, anxiety over the nation's development and defence became a question of healthy and unhealthy bodies. One respondent asked in the *Lancet*, 'how can the unhealthy semen of such produce healthy offspring' while another noted the 'overtaxing of the physical and mental energies of national life-blood' (Pick, 1989: 190–191). As Pick's survey of the work of Henry Maudsley and Francis Galton reveals, capital, the physical body and the body politic were inextricably linked in the rhetoric of degeneration;

'only by applying biological and medical truths to the body, the nation, and the empire, it was argued with increasing force, could the economy and society be sustained at all' (Pick, 1989: 201, 191, 197). The correlation between environment and health can be seen in Maudsley's formulation of a racial or socio-biological past (Pick, 1989: 207). Despite evidence to the contrary, there was widespread belief that the labouring poor in the countryside was inherently superior or healthier than its urban counterpart. Haggard, inspired by General Booth in *The Poor and the Land*, speaks scathingly of 'puny pygmies growing from towns or town bred parents' in contrast to the 'blood and sinew of the race' – the 'robust and intelligent' country-born English yeoman (Haggard, 1905: xix). Masterman remarked that whereas the 'England of the past . . . [had] been an England of reserved silent men', healthy and energetic for being 'reared amidst the fresh air and quieting influences of the life of the fields', the new generation of Englishmen were 'physically, mentally and spiritually different' and upon these 'depend the future of the Anglo-Saxon Race' (Masterman, 1901: 7–8). This appeal to England's rural past forms, of course, the basis of the 'pastoralisation' of England, an ideology which fostered the idea of England as an Edenic garden and elevated that ideal to the status of a national myth. It was directed at painting a picture of a simple, organic and classless society that, paradoxically, was England's true nature and that to which she should return. William Watson, Alfred Noyes, Henry Newbolt and Alfred Austen, all contributed to the myth of rural England as the place where 'home' was both memory and ideal. In this idyllic vision, the passing of the yeomanry signified the demise of what symbolised England's best – the traditional lifestyle of independent production, small estates and households bound by harmonious and customary ties of kinship and communal obligations (Thompson, 1963: 132; Comaroff and Comaroff, 1992: 191; Masterman, 1905: 304, 313). The pastoralisation of England cut across political parties with its dream of 'rural regeneration' and its rejection of urban alienation and disintegration (Pick, 1989: 213; Masterman, 1909: 14, 15, 190–191; Oldershaw, 1904: 58). But what was also striking about this idealisation of nature was the racialising of rural life as the national body.

The pastoral society presented in the rhetoric of nationalism tropes an autochthonous breed of epic heroes; in Haggard's words, 'the Englishmen of the past were land dwellers, and their deeds are written large in history' (Haggard, 1902: 553). The 'thews and sinews of her sons' are 'the foundation' of everything that has made Britain great. Haggard's reprint of Lord Walsingham's letter in *A Farmer's Year* reads, 'take the people away from their natural breeding and growing grounds . . . and the decay of this country becomes only a question of time. In this matter, as in many others, ancient Rome has a lesson to teach us' (Haggard, 1987: 466). The metaphors of masculinity inscribed in the 'thews and sinews' of the nation, and the references to the moral lessons of Roman history, narrate the attack against what was constructed as the decadence of *fin-de-siècle* culture. Edward Gibbon's depiction of Imperial Rome's decline sounded alarm bells for Britain's future demise and was framed within a rhetoric of bodily degeneration:

> the minds of men were gradually reduced to the same level, the fire of genius extinguished, and even the military evaporated . . . the Roman world was indeed peopled by a race of pygmies when the fierce giants of the North broke in and mended the puny breed.
>
> (Colls and Dodd, 1986: 65–66)

The linking of the healthy body and the healthy mind, or the use of the body as an expression of the spirit can be traced back to Thomas Carlyle's notion of 'perfect harmony' or a 'general law' of being which was to encompass man's physical, psychological, moral and social health (Haley, 1978: 70–73, 83–84). Charles Kingsley's reinterpretation of the Carlylean 'laws of nature' as 'healthy materialism' substituted a spiritual environment for a material one and emphasised the body as the source of national and individual health and disease. Accordingly, Kingsley's 'muscular Christianity' moralised on the disciplined male body. His manly hero acquired his virtues of daring, endurance, self-restraint and honour on the playing fields which taught not only physical but moral health and character-building. The principle of the healthy body was a national and racial imperative and Kingsley spoke of the need to 'increase the English race' and aid its development 'to the highest pitch . . . in physical strength and beauty' (Haley, 1978: 117–119). Thomas Hughes, an even greater supporter of manly virtues, located the 'muscular Christian' in the 'old chivalrous and Christian belief that a man's body . . . be trained and brought into subject'; this trained race of people should then be used 'for the protection of the weak, the advancement of all righteous causes, and the subduing of the earth which God has given to the children of men' (Girouard, 1981: 142). In the equation of body, racial and national health can be discerned the late Victorian fusing of Christian gentility, imperialism and social Darwinism. Manliness was seen as the natural characteristic of the British race. Garnet Wolseley argued in *Fortnightly Review,* that 'strength and fearlessness are natural characteristics of our race'. Furthermore,

> It is the nature of the Anglo-Saxon race to love those manly sports which entail violent exercise, with more or less danger to limb if not life. . . . This craving for the constant practice and employment of our muscles is in our blood, and the result is a development of bodily strength unknown in most nations and unsurpassed by any other breed of men.
>
> (Wolseley, 1888: 692)

His optimism in British manliness notwithstanding, Wolseley also warns readers of the urban sins of over-cultivation, refinement, the love of luxury and ease which were 'calculated to convert manliness into effeminacy', killing all the 'virile energy' that was vital to the 'greatness of the nation'. Lord Meath's contributions highlight the convergence of masculinity, race and the body politic (Meath, 1908). He asserts that the 'continuance of the British race as one of the dominant peoples of the world' is dependent on the sustained 'possession' of a

> virile spirit which makes light of pain and physical discomfort, and rejoices in the consciousness of victory over adverse circumstances, and which regards the performance of duty, however difficult and distasteful, as one of the supreme virtues of all true men and women.
>
> (Meath, 1908: 421)

Meath's view that contemporary society exhibited signs of 'a decadent spirit and of a lack of virility amongst portions of all classes of the community' was a warning that the 'pluck' and 'grit' of British 'forefathers' were in danger of being eroded. John Seeley's *Expansion of England* saw England as a 'living organism' forged out of the historical forces of race, language and moral authority' (Colls and Dodd, 1986: 44). But the problem was just how to preserve this dimension of national and racial character. The focus on discipline, education, the 'boy' and the public school system contained the solution. As J. A. Mangan observes, this focus promoted three distinct but interrelated ideologies: firstly, 'imperial Darwinism' and the belief in the white man's right to colonise and rule over other races; secondly, 'institutional Darwinism' and mental and physical schooling training as preparation for 'the rigours of imperial duty'; and finally, a 'gentleman's education' which cultivated leadership qualities (Mangan, 1981: 136). Building character in the British boy extended outside the public school system to the Scouts and Christian paramilitary movements directed at the working classes at the turn of the century (Springhall, 1977; Mangan, 1985).

THE GENDERED BODY

As is apparent in the focus on muscular Christianity and racial virility, the body politic was articulated against a concept of femininity and 'effeminacy'. Meath's attack on the softening and weakening of racial character in 'Have we the "Grit" of our Forefathers?' was directed at women. They were accused of not fulfilling the duties of self-sacrifice and childbirth. Unlike women who were previously 'taught that [their] . . . first duty in life was to marry and produce children' and 'carry on worthily the traditions of the family and of the race', modern women shirk the 'obligations of their sex'. They merely desire self pleasure and personal ease. Worse than that, the middle-class woman 'apes her fashionable sister' and 'vie[s] with her social superiors' in 'smartness and style'; her 'whims', frivolity, 'love of luxury, of excitement, and constant change' engender a climate that 'seriously militates against the development of the more stable traits of character' (Meath, 1908: 421–422). Meath's depiction of modern life and modern women's 'fever of an easy life and of equality in condition' is shared by Wolseley's militaristic equation of urban life with a degenerating softening of the masculine character. Wolseley's anxieties are starkly polarised into sexual opposites. 'Over-cultivation' breeds 'indolent habits which kill all virile energy' and 'converts manliness into effeminacy' while 'clap-trap sentimentality' converts a fearless nation into 'a nation of cowards' (Wolseley, 1888: 692). As the Anglo-Saxon breed is *naturally* virile, sexual perversity is signed by an unnatural, artificial and urban 'effeminacy'. Holding up the vanquished Zulu and the Ashanti nation as models of courage and bravery, Wolseley advocates a masculine savagery that is proper for an imperial nation.

The homophobic attack on Oscar Wilde, more than anything else, makes plain the equation between effeminacy, perversion, degeneration and urban(e) culture. Wilde was vilified in the wake of the trial's publicity; the London *Evening Standard* denounced him for attempting to undermine the 'wholesome, manly, simple ideals of English Life' while the *Daily Telegraph* set Wilde's intellectual powers against 'simpler ideas' and opted for the latter 'for fear of national contamination and decay' (Dollimore, 1991: 240). In these attacks, normality described in terms of nature, health, reason and 'unalterable standards of right and wrong' is paradoxically susceptible to Wilde's 'nerveless and effeminate' artifice. Jonathan Dollimore observes that press comment on Wilde linked sexual perversion with intellectual and moral subversion; Wilde represented cultural decay, 'vitiating regression' from '*within* an advance cultural sophistication' (Dollimore, 1991: 241).

Given the influence of Darwin's model of organic development, the growth of the biological sciences in the latter part of the century and the concern with population regulation, medico-psychological discussions of sexuality were framed within the parameters of biology and heredity. The mid to late nineteenth century was then to provide a discursive structure for isolating different kinds of pathological sexuality defined against what constituted 'normal' sexuality. Homosexuality was tied to bodily difference as various writers such as Karl Ulrich, Paul Moreau Krafft-Ebing and Havelock Ellis defined homosexuals as a 'third sex', 'congenital inverts' with 'organic dysfunction' (Weeks, 1981: 143–245; Bullough, 1976: 167–169; Krafft-Ebing, 1978; Ellis, 1933, 1936).

If effeminacy was a corruption of manly health, and homosexuality, the effect of perversion, cultural decay and/or sexual inversion, femininity was located firmly in the 'separate spheres' ideology. The Victorian ideology of separate spheres located women within the private and familial domain of home and hearth. In Ruskin's 'Of Queens' Gardens', the division is absolute. Man is 'eminently the doer, the creator, the discoverer, the defender'; his 'intellect is for speculation and invention; his energy for adventure, for war, and for conquest . . .' Woman, in contrast, is for 'sweet ordering, arrangement, and decision'; she must be 'enduringly, incorruptibly good' and by 'her office, and place . . . protected from all danger and temptation' (Hollis, 1979: 16–17). The separate spheres ideology was given scientific credibility by Charles Darwin, Herbert Spencer and Henry Maudsley. Darwin's 'natural' differences gave men energy, intellect and courage and women, intuition, 'characteristic of the lower races, and therefore of a past and lower state of civilisation', while Spencer argued that women's reproductive biology curbed their intellectual development (Showalter, 1987: 122). Maudsley asserted that women were tied to their reproductive function and 'cannot choose but to be women'. He warned against the unsexing of women:

> it is the plain statement of physiological fact . . . there is sex in mind as distinctly as there is sex in body . . . To aim, by means of education and pursuits in life, to assimilate the female to the male mind, might well be pronounced as unwise and fruitless a labour as it would be to strive to assimilate the female to the male body by means of the same kind of physical training and by adoption of the same pursuits.
>
> (Hollis, 1979: 24–25)

and argued that such unnatural activity would result in 'a puny, enfeebled, and sickly race'.

The construction of female sexuality as regressive or even pathological had a long history. Eighteenth-century naturalists' attempts to define the difference between man and the anthropoid apes referred to female anatomy (Schiebinger, 1993: 76). Whereas the faculty of reason and the use of language distinguished men from apes in the great chain of being, female sexual physiology became the border territory between humans and simians. Men were taken as iconic representatives of the race and women were defined primarily as sexual beings. Studies by Johann Blumenbach, a biologist, and Georges Buffon, a naturalist, aimed at differentiating female humans from animals concentrated on 'key sexual characteristics: menstruation, the clitoris, the breasts and the hymen' (Schiebinger, 1993: 89, 94). The case of Sarah Baartman illustrates the fine dividing line between woman and primitivity, as the black woman became a symbol of regressive sexuality and sexual promiscuity in the nineteenth century. Sander Gilman's discussion of the contemporary depiction of Baartman's exhibition and her subsequent dissection by Georges Cuvier, the comparative anatomist, rooted the lascivious and primitive nature of black women in physical difference (Gilman, 1985: 231). The black woman's '"primitive" sexual appetite' was bodily manifested in the possession of 'primitive' genitalia. Henri de Blainville and Georges Cuvier's descriptions of physical and sexual pathology as manifested in the 'Hottentot apron' and steatopygia represented Baartman's racial traits (Gilman, 1985: 235). A similar anatomy of difference was applied to European prostitutes as 'sexualized females'; A. J. B. Parent-Duchatelet, Cesare Lombroso and Adrien Charpy's discussion of the physiognomy of prostitutes manifests a racial trajectory of gender where atavism, degeneration, disease and corruption are embodied signs (Gilman, 1985: 240–250).

THE COLONIAL BODY

Johannes Fabian's critique of anthropology's temporal politics reminds us how the nineteenth-century naturalisation of geological and evolutionary time, whilst deceptively incorporative in its universal applicability, was in fact founded on difference and separation (Fabian, 1983). Anthropology's disciplinary object, 'the primitive', is a temporal category that institutes unbridgeable distance. Fabian argues that anthropology emerged and established itself as a 'science of other men in another time' (Fabian, 1983: 144). Within the context of imperialism, nineteenth-century anthropology produced a *taxonomy* of different cultures placed on a temporal scale of development. Nineteenth-century anthropology became a form of comparison between past and present time; geography and culture were reconstructed within a gradation of time and development based on Western civilization. Unlike its pagan–precursor in the sacred world, who is 'always already marked for salvation, the savage is not yet ready for civilisation' (Fabian, 1983: 26). The epistemic shift to a notion of primitivity after 1800 marked a shift in meaning from connoting merely 'nations' or 'peoples' to 'races' and organic evolution (Stocking, 1982: 121).

Like the naturalisation of time, the concept of 'generic human nature' allowed comparisons to be made, permitting the prototypical 'science of man' to 'contemplate man in all those various situations wherein he has been placed, [and] follow him in his progress through the different stages of society' (Stocking, 1987: 17). The disciplinary development of physical anthropology and ethnology reinforced by social Darwinism focused on the study of different races and their development (Brantlinger, 1985: 182–187). As Stocking observes, that civilization had definite boundaries was not a problem, the problem was 'to explain its development, and why it was that not all men had shared equally in the process' (Stocking, 1987:45). Nineteenth-century anthropology's temporal and spatial mapping transformed living peoples of the world into an exhibitionary complex and a living museum of time epochs (McGrane, 1989: 94). With a growing interest in mid-Victorian Britain in the newly established science of ethnology, the Englishman could play armchair traveller by reading the large output of travel writing and the journals of explorers and missionaries, and by visiting one of the live exhibitions of Africans and natives of foreign lands. The anthropological curiosities of these travelling exhibitions, variously labelled, 'earthmen' 'Aztec Lilliputians' and 'Zulus' were colourful spectacles of exotica; they were even given the honour of a Queen's command performance (van Wyk Smith and Maclennan, 1983). The *Illustrated London News* carried information and pictures of two such exhibitions 'Earthmen from Natal' (November 6, 1852) and 'The Zulu Kaffirs' (May 28, 1853) at the St George Gallery, Knightsbridge (Figures 1 and 2). Of the former, whose given name is a pun on both their peculiar status as humans and their distinctive habitat in burrows, the paper writes by way of an introduction to these grotesque curiosities:

> A few months ago rumours were current in the town of Croydon that two little savages from the Orange River had arrived at the Hare and Hounds Inn, at the little village of Waddon, half a mile from Croydon. They were said to be well-formed but of Lilliputian proportions, quick and active, and unable to express their wants save by a few guttural and uncouth sounds. When taken into an apartment they would climb the chairs, examine the looking-glasses and other objects with lively curiosity; but, if suddenly spoken to, they would crouch down upon the floor like half-tamed animals . . . these interesting little natives of the land of Bushmen, Hottentots and Kaffirs have been rescued from the lowest depths of barbarism and [are now] surrounded by the novel sights and sounds, and comforts of English civilisation.
>
> (*Illustrated London News*, November 6, 1852)

A list of physical attributes are given so that the potential viewer may locate for himself or herself what is so different about these earthmen. The superiority of caucasian features is the implicit point of reference:

25

Figure 1 'Boy and Girl of the Earthmen tribe, from Port Natal', *Illustrated London News*, Nov. 6, 1852.

The nose is the worst feature in the face. Between the eyes there is scarcely any projection; and the nose is so spread as to be confounded with the cheeks; until the nostrils appear. The lips are rather thick, and the mouth wide; the teeth, white as those of a sheep; the forehead, high and narrow; and the cheekbones broad. The hair is of remarkable colour and texture. It resembles the wool of black sheep, strong, short and coarse. It grows in stiff spiral lines, so that the scalp is everywhere seen.

Figure 2 'Zulu Kaffirs at St George Gallery, Knightsbridge', *Illustrated London News*, May 28, 1853.

A brief passage of descriptive ethnography – standardised within the 'manners and customs' mould – lists the earthmen's attributes and cultural practices and helps readers/viewers familiarise themselves with this strange display. The zoological approach was justified on the grounds that they 'may become fitting instruments, with missionary aid, for improving the habits, morals, and the religious feelings of their benighted country men'.

Traditional beliefs such as humoral theory, environmentalist explanations of physical types, the Great Chain of Being influenced explanations of human diversity. Southern climes were associated with 'heat, sensuality, depletion, and decay' while northern cooler climates produced the sanguine Anglo-Saxon (Comaroff and Comaroff, 1992: 220). Sir James Martin's *The Influence of Tropical Climates on European Constitutions* (1861) observes that while the people of India may be 'of Caucasian origin', their exposure 'during countless generations to the same succession of external influences of high temperature and corresponding habits of life and diet' renders them different 'widely, morally and physically, from Europeans'. These 'general causes' contribute to 'an excitability of the nervous system, diminished volume, enervation, and relaxation of the muscular system, as compared to Europeans . . .' (Martin, 1861: 415). Even after the turn of the century, the climatic theory of race can be seen in the advice on acclimatisation given by doctors. Medical experts argued, for example, that European bodies would not be able to adapt to equatorial regions which were so totally different from the temporal region in which the race evolved (Anderson, 1992: 511). Despite Martin's praise of the superior constitution of European bodies and its ability to adapt, his 1861 textbook insists that prolonged exposure leads to 'the injurious influence of tropical climate on European constitutions' (Martin, 1861: 48). And whilst there is some movement forwards on acclimatisation between the 1874 and 1883 edition of W. J. Moore's highly praised *Manual of Family Medicine for India*, Moore's 1883 edition still insists that 'as a rule' 'degeneration' and 'debilitation' will occur for the 'very large majority of Europeans living in India, notwithstanding frugality and care and exercise' (Moore, 1883: 650). Charles Woodruff, an influential American army surgeon, researched the effects of tropical light and produced a set of racial and bodily limits within 'natural selection': 'we are safe in saying that the black man should be 25 or 30 degrees of the Equator. The browns between 30 and 35 degrees. The olive . . .

flourished best at 35 to 45 degrees. The blond arose north of 50 degrees' (Woodruff, 1905: 271). The racial fault-line was embodied in a physical response to the environment. Andrew Balfour's paper on 'Hygiene and Minor Tropical Sanitation' in W. Byam and R. Archibald's standard work on tropical medicine argued that as a 'brown skin absorbs more heat than white skin, the point where perspiration shows itself is reached earlier in the case of the brown-skinned man, showing that his cutaneous heat-regulating apparatus is more sensitive than that of his white-skinned brother' (Byam and Archibald, 1921: 3). Illness, death and racial degeneration brought on by inhospitable tropical climes and poor sanitation preoccupied early colonial medicine and implied an urgent need to formulate strategies for acclimatisation. Clothes played a key role in strategies to minimise the adverse effects of climate in the tropics. Detailed and elaborate advice on the range and colour of textiles, underwear, the use of hats, flannel cholera belts, cummerbunds and shoes is given in medical and travel guides (Moore, 1874, 1883; Platt, 1923; King, 1976; Cohn, 1983).

The historians and anthropologists, John and Jean Comaroff, argue that the development of colonialism in Africa as a 'cultural enterprise' is 'inseparable from the rise of biomedicine as a science'. The image of Africa as an 'afflicted continent' shaped a European sense of social and bodily health and a European iconography of healing. With the formation of the colonial state, regulatory agencies of public health 'disciplined' and 'redistributed' communities 'in the name of sanitation and the control of disease' (Comaroff and Comaroff, 1992: 215–216). David Arnold's work on cholera and the plague shows that the same applies to tropical medicine in the Indian subcontinent (Arnold, 1987; Arnold, 1988). Arnold argues that the discipline of tropical medicine gave scientific support to the portrayal of the tropics as 'a primitive and dangerous environment' plagued by diseases that were banished from Europe. Just as with medicine, technological development was a 'hallmark of the racial pride', disease was part of Africa and Asia's backwardness (Arnold, 1988: 7). The association of the indigenous population with disease fostered fear and suspicion; the correspondences between dirt, bodily secretions and open pores in hot and humid climates produced a metaphoric connection between organic, climatic and moral degradation (Comaroff and Comaroff, 1992: 226; Douglas, 1984). It also meant that colonial sanitary and health reforms supported residential

29

segregation and regulated proper forms of contact between Europeans and the native population.

THE CULTURAL BODY

If colonial medicine had helped develop the iconography of disease and contamination, there was also a romanticising of healthy primitivity in the appreciation of what was deemed to be simple pastoral culture. This appreciation falls within the conventional opposition between an urban, effeminate and over-developed culture of consumption and domesticity, and the natural masculine outdoor life of sport and warfare. Ludlow's book on the Zulus, for example, applauds their 'spartan' and athletic lifestyles. Despite a negative assessment of their savage nature, and in spite of his support of the destruction of the independent Zulu kingdom, Ludlow is full of praise of their imputed lack of domestic ties:

> the king adopted the method of the Spartans in training his warriors, making them diet themselves, use certain herbs and roots to purify their bodies, and by means of all kinds of athletic exercises prepare to encounter dangers and hardships. . . . Love was deemed effeminate.
>
> (Ludlow, 1882: 121)

The *Morning Chronicle* review of the Zulu exhibition and performance at the St. George Gallery contains an erotic appreciation of their bodily beauty produced by their more healthy lifestyle; the men's muscular development is deemed 'magnificent, in chest, fore-arm, and calf while the fall in the back, and what the French call *svelte*, flexibility of the loins are no less remarkable. . .' (*Morning Chronicle*, 1853). Wolseley's piece discussed earlier, entitled 'The Negro as Soldier', contains a comparison of the cowardly Fantis and the fearless Ashanti and Zulu tribes. Wolseley suggests that the Fantis' cowardice is degenerative and due to the 'mildness' of the colonial administration under which they lived, which has changed them into 'lazy, good for nothing creatures' (Wolseley, 1888: 697, 702). Wolseley's tale of the Fantis is then a cautionary lesson within the present urban climate of luxury, decadence and excessive consumption. Mark Seltzer has recently called attention to the early American woodcraft movement's deliberate conjoining of the male body and the body of the nation. The movement's avowed desire to turn boys into healthy men is evinced in their founder's, Ernest

Seton, proclamation to 'combat the system that has turned such a large proportion of our robust, manly, self-reliant boyhood into a lot of flat-chested cigarette smokers, with shaky nerves and doubtful vitality' (Seltzer, 1992: 149). The British scouting movement shows a similar pedagogic desire to build character and improve physical health.

Seltzer labels these youth movements and their manuals of manly development 'the anthropology of boyhood', alluding to Seton's equation of boyhood with savagery. But the association of boyhood, anthropology, health and 'savagery' is also apt in another respect. Nineteenth-century ethnology's concern with the origin and development of European civilisation shared a common ancestry with the folklore movement; both possessed an antiquarian tradition which encompassed material artifacts and oral traditions. The folklore movement started in earnest in mid century with the collection of folktales, legends and ballads and the examination of their transmission and migration from one generation to another and from one country to another (Stocking, 1987: 53–54). The contemporary defences and manifestos of romance and adventure writing claimed kinship with folktales and medieval epics and sagas. Through folktales, fables and myths they posited a link with 'primitivity'; some, like Andrew Lang, Robert Stevenson and Rider Haggard, also resurrected the connection between primitivity and boyhood.

Lang, critic, anthropologist, poet and essayist, was perhaps the most articulate and committed spokesman for romance. His defence of romance lay in his interest in anthropology, myth and his belief in 'the ancestral barbarism of our [human] nature'; 'there is no more natural, true, and simple picture of human nature, human affections and passion than . . . from a savage tale' (Lang, 1887: 689, 692). He argued that all myth, sagas, epics and folklore come from a primitive unconscious and are a kind of racial memory of those early days:

> The natural people, the folk, has supplied us, in its unconscious way, with the stuff of all our poetry, law, ritual, and genius has selected from the mass, has turned custom into codes, nursery tales into romance, myth into science, ballad into epic . . . The student of this lore can look back and see the long-trodden way behind him, the winding tracks through marsh and forest and over burning sands. He sees the caves, the camps, the villages, the towns where the race has tarried

. . . . We have a foreboding of a purpose which we know not, a sense of will . . . . This is the lesson I think, of what we call folk-lore or anthropology.

(Green, 1946: 69)

Alfred Lyall's more evolutionary treatise on history and fable also supports the anthropological link with past cultures. Whereas in a previous and more primitive age, the 'marvellous and the miraculous' formed narratives of men's origins, history now emerges out of the 'sea of Fable' as 'youth of man' turns into civilisation. Yet delight in the 'spirit of imaginative fable' which nourished 'ancient legend and tradition' is also found in the contemporary reception of folklore and, to a lesser extent, the reading of romance (Lyall, 1894: 31–32). But for Lang, Stevenson and Haggard, romance also meant returning to one's boyhood. Haggard dedicated *King Solomon's Mines* to all the 'big boys and little boys who read it'. For Stevenson, real art 'that dealt with life directly was that of the first men who told their stories round the savage camp-fire'; delight in the novel of adventure was about returning to 'fondly imagined' and 'youthful daydreams'. Whereas intricate characterisation is a 'sealed book' for the boy, the novelist will find in bold plots of shipwreck, desperate ventures and treasure quests 'a readily accessible and beaten road to the sympathies of the reader' (Stevenson, 1925: 159, 161). Lang's esteem of the arts of childhood can be seen in the numerous children's story books he edited; he argued that the 'Odyssey' is loved because the 'barbaric element' in men's blood had not died out completely; they still possessed 'a childish love of marvels, miracles' (Lang, 1887: 689), and he praised Haggard's ability to create a good 'yarn' to charm 'the camp-fires of cattle-drivers in the bush as well as the holidays of schoolboys and the evenings of jaded literary persons in town' (Lang, 1888: 500).

The subjects for the writer of romance are 'heroic action[s] and marvellous enterprise[s]'; he is obliged to travel imaginatively backwards in time or to remote lands 'to preserve and hand down to us magnified figures of mighty men, or the pictures of great events' (Lyall, 1895: 533). Fictionalised violence should not be shirked despite critical disapproval, for 'the spectacle of valour and of high heart' is part of romance's appeal. Haggard's defence of the violence in his novels is modelled on romance and primitivity; 'man is a fighting animal' from the time of Homer and the Old Testament to the present day. Furthermore, Haggard adds, 'some of his finest qualities such as patriotism, courage, obedience to authority, patience in disaster, fidelity to friends and a noble cause . . . have been evolved in the exercise of war' (Haggard, 1926: 103). Lang's comments on Kingsley's fiction are revealing for they disclose a series of correspondences between primitivity, anthropology, boyhood and health integral to the contemporary genre of romance. The spectacle of masculinity (re)generates the health and innocence of boyhood as that of man's, 'to be at one with Kingsley one must be boys again, and that momentary change cannot but be good for us' (Lang, 1891: 188–189).

Lyall's division of contemporary fiction into the novel of adventure (romance) and the novel of manners (realism) is one upheld by contemporary criticism (Lyall, 1894, 1895; Lang, 1887; Haggard, 1887a; Stevenson, 1925). The latter 'confines itself to minute observation, whether of outward facts or inward feeling, and . . . is above all devoted to the close delineation of [the] contemporary society' of the domestic interior, the ballroom or the village (Lyall, 1895: 545). The contemporary novel of manners was seen to be largely moulded by women even when former practitioners like Dickens, Thackeray or Fielding were men; their current monopoly over this class of fiction extends 'to the degree that [it] threatens to evict men'. Stevenson refers to the novel of manners as 'the chink of teaspoons and the accents of the curate' (Stevenson, 1925: 145) while Lang and Haggard's metaphoric equation between this body of writing and feminine body spaces is directed at what they saw as the 'dovecotes of culture'. The 'modern Realist' with their 'Cousines Bettes', 'Misses Laphams' and 'minute portraiture of modern life' are 'limited in scope, and frequently cramped in style'. Lang accuses the novel of manners of unmanning both the novel form and its readers:

> If I were to draw up an indictment, I might add that some of them have an almost unholy knowledge of the nature of women. One would as lief explore a girl's room, and tumble about her little household treasures, as examine so curiously, the poor secrets of her heart and tremors of her frame. . . . Such analysis makes one feel uncomfortable in the reading, makes one feel intrusive and unmanly.
>
> (Lang, 1887: 688)

If in the manifestos of romance, the genre of realism and the wider contemporary cultural fears of urban softness and degeneration is unhealthily *feminine,* nation and narrative are intertwined in romance's natural and hearty male vitality. Romance is seen to represent more accurately a manly and healthy British morality against other imported continental genres like Naturalism. Foreign writers like Zola were lambasted for their continental decadence and for sexual explicitness: 'whatever there is that is carnal and filthy, is here brought into prominence, and thrust before the reader's eyes'. This wilful display, in Haggard's words, of 'Bacchanalian revellings' was unhealthy and detrimental to the moral fabric of the nation (Haggard, 1887a: 176). Another critic deplored the pessimism of French realism, arguing that it represented the 'literature of an exhausted race, the life-blood of which seems corrupted in its veins' (Barry, 1890: 87). While French and Russian Realism produced pessimism and morbidity, American writers like Henry James produced unmanly novels of 'silk and cambric' and emasculated heroes 'with culture on their lips'. In contrast to the swiftness, strength and directness of 'great English writers of the past', these works have a sickly atmosphere 'like that of the boudoir of a luxurious woman, faint and delicate, suggesting the essence of white rose'(Haggard, 1887a: 175). Coloured by the language of eugenics and the body, what was hailed as a relief to the novel of manners '"bred in and in" until the inevitable result of feebleness of strain has been reached' (Saintsbury, 1887: 415) was the appearance of romance of adventure. Extolling the invigoration and freshness of this new genre of fiction, George Saintsbury speculated: 'there is still too much healthy beefiness and beeriness (much of both as it has lost) in the English temperament to permit it to indulge in the sterile pessimism which seems to dominate Russian fiction' or the 'curious scholasticism of dull uncleanness' of the French novelists (Saintsbury, 1887: 412).

As is evident from the apologies for romance, patriotic, nationalistic and moral sentiments were expressed via a discourse of health and physiology. Haley notes that the Victorian literary critic operated like a 'medical diagnostician' looking for signs of disease or soundness, in the belief that man's moral and spiritual well being was manifested organically in the physical and social order (Haley, 1978: 46, 57–58). Evident in Haley's critical account of the contemporary homage to the healthy textual body is the implicit assumption that the body alluded to is a male body; this should come as no surprise, for the prevailing model of femininity in mid century was that of invalidism and consumptive affliction. The writer and artist is representative of all that is good and noble in man; Leslie Stephen praises Fielding's 'masculine grasp of fact' while Walter Bagehot praised Scott's 'manly mind' and his art's 'peculiar healthiness' (Haley, 1978: 49, 51). But what is perhaps also present and not as prominently addressed is the function that 'primitivity' is put to in the cultural discourses of health and in the sexual politics of manliness. Ruskin argued that the arts of the ancient world were healthier than those of modern times, for then people were 'full of animal spirit and physical power . . . incapable of every morbid condition of mental emotion'; his theory of gothic style emphasises an unfinished 'savageness or rudeness' (Haley, 1978: 66). The revival of folk studies led to rediscovery of rural Britain, which had important consequences for regional and sub-national identities. But again, the focus on the peasant and his customs represented an attempt to fuse together the discourses of masculinity, nationality and primitivity in a home-grown version of the colonial savage (Colls and Dodd, 1986: 47).

In the chapters that follow, I shall be exploring how both Haggard and Kipling depend on the body images of Africa and India to reconstitute their respective national and colonial identities. Haggard, dreaming of the Zulu nation, imagines an empowering world of masculinity and militarism, in order to rediscover the hidden English chivalric potential in a period of cultural decadence and effeminacy. Early Kipling, fitting much less easily into the terrain of romance than critics like Lang would like him to do, explores instead a colonial landscape which looks uncannily and alarmingly like *fin-de-siècle* Britain at home, despite all attempts to pretend otherwise. But in Kipling's fantasies of cultural metamorphosis we see how fully the colonial mirror of body-images penetrates the contemporary cultural Imaginary.

35

2

THE DOMINION OF SONS

In *The Burden of Time*, Hannah Arendt makes an intriguing connection between boyhood and the imperialist character (Arendt, 1951). Arendt observes that 'only those who had never been able to outgrow their boyhood ideals' make ideal candidates for enlistment in the colonial services; 'imperialism to them was nothing but an accidental opportunity to escape a society in which a man had to forget his youth if he wanted to grow up'. Arendt prefaces the small section she devotes to the imperialist character with the startling observation that imperialism guaranteed a 'certain conservation, or perhaps petrification, of boyhood noblesse which preserved *and* infantilised Western moral standards'. The infantilism of imperialism is a subject I would like to explore in this opening chapter on the writer Henry Rider Haggard and his contributions to the culture of masculinity in the late Victorian period. Because Arendt's analysis is essentially an attack on the totalitarian politics in Europe in the run-up to the Second World War, and because her argument is motivated by the desire to see the moral idealism of youth develop and mature into the good society (which, she argues, in the milieu of Empire they singularly failed to do), her deconstruction of imperialist ideology is framed against the 'plain insanity' of imperialism which turned moral idealism into the fraudulent conviction of inherent superiority. What is missing from her summation, although her own analysis shows a sensitivity to the complex workings of ideology and interpellation, is a sensitivity to the question of the fantasy and myth in the political unconscious. The issue is not one of knowledge (the fraudulent conviction of superiority) but one of desire – what is the cultural investment in the ideological figure of the 'boy' at the turn of the century? Why is the boy's story such a powerful myth? What kind of grammar and syntax of desire does the boy's story articulate for its readers? How desire is channelled (or lived through) in the boy's story will form the central motivation behind my reading of Haggard's African romances.

PASTORAL POLITICS

In the introduction to *Allan Quatermain*, the desire to escape the constraints of late nineteenth-century culture is a desire to escape defilement by what the narrator–character calls the 'sinks of struggling, sweltering humanity'. Quatermain's version of the civilised life is drawn directly from the changes in country–city relations brought on by nineteenth-century industrialisation, and by the *fin-de-siècle* perception of decadence and decline as quintessentially feminine. He can only escape contamination by his dreams of empowered masculinity in the wild open land of the African outback. The land Quatermain journeys to will be a land 'whereof none know the history' (Haggard, 1931: 12–15). Quatermain's aristocratic friend, Sir Henry Curtis, tired of playing the 'squire in a country sick of squires' shares his overwhelming dissatisfaction with contemporary society's modernity. Together with the former naval captain Good, they travel to the interior of Africa in search of a lost white civilisation. What they discover is a feudal monarchy based on an agricultural production that resembles Britain in the days before the Industrial Revolution. The Zu-Vendi people 'know nothing about steam, electricity, or gun powder, and mercifully for themselves nothing about printing or the penny post'; they are 'exceedingly conservative', and are not inclined to trade for profit, but produce enough to maintain their inherited status (Haggard, 1931: 177, 175). In short, they present a colonial pastoral idyll and mythic idealisation of a yeomanry no longer possible in Britain. The Englishmen's chivalric intervention in Zu-Vendi civil wars gives their lives a purpose and meaning absent in England. At the end of the tale, Curtis, the text's ideal knight, is rewarded with nothing less than a crown. If advancing from 'unknown wanderer' to king is perhaps the ultimate imperial fantasy, Haggard's beau-ideal can always be expected to play the part of a 'Christian [English] gentleman . . . called by Providence to a great and almost unprecedented trust' (Haggard, 1931: 302).

There are other, more domestic, variants of this colonial version of a rags-to-riches story. MacKenzie, the missionary and trader in *Allan Quatermain*, sets up in his personal fortress in a rural African station and makes it 'blossom like a rose in the wilderness'. He becomes a wealthy man and can tell Quatermain proudly, 'it is thirty thousand pounds I am worth to-day, and every farthing of it made by honest trade and savings in the bank of Zanzibar, for living here costs me next to nothing'(Haggard, 1931: 108). Haggard's farm novel *Jess*, begins on a happy and abundant note; nature 'unadorned' is beautiful enough 'to make the blood run in a man's veins, and his heart beat happily because he was alive to see it'. Even so, Silas Croft's house built of solid brown stone and covered with 'rich brown thatch' sits squarely in this pastoral domain and becomes its focal point:

> beyond was the broad carriage drive of red soil, bordered with busy orange-trees laden with odorous flowers and green and golden fruit. On the further side . . . to the right of the house grew thriving plantations of blue-gum and black wattle, and to the left was a broad stretch of cultivated lands, lying so that they could be irrigated for winter crops.
>
> (Haggard, 1887b: 20)

The presence of the white man domesticates the wild country into a safe pastoral one; here a man may live and work like an original Adam, creating and refashioning an Eden – trapped in a time warp – to his own image. Accordingly, Croft's pioneering parallels that of creation's tale:

> Twenty five years ago I rode up here and saw this spot. Look, you see that rock behind the house, I slept under it and woke at sunrise and looked out at this beautiful view and at the great veldt (it was all alive with game then), and I said to myself, 'Silas . . . you've never seen a fairer spot than this or healthier; now be a wise man and stop here.' And so I did. I bought the 3,000 morgen (6,000 acres), more or less, for 10*l.* down and a case of gin, and I set to work to make this place, and you see I have made it. Ay, it has grown under my hand, every stone and tree of it, and you know what that means in a new country.
>
> (Haggard, 1887b: 22)

This need to reproduce a European-style world in a foreign land also fuels the character, Squire Carson, in the story of Allan Quatermain's childhood and his marriage to Stella Carson. In *Allan's Wife*, Squire Carson is given another chance at happiness and dignity, after his wife's adulterous betrayal, when he emigrates to Africa (Haggard, 1915). Renouncing civilisation, he treks into virgin territory to impose his version of a perfect harmonious world on the barren wilderness. Here the colonial success story appears more properly as a farmstead pastoral; the land, domesticated and 'humanized when inscribed by hand and plough' (Coetzee, 1988: 7), is transformed in a more productive and wholesome marriage than Carson's previous union could ever be.

King Solomon's Mines, on the other hand, presents a more conventional narrative of adventure replete with treasure maps, hidden diamonds, unexplored regions, lost kingdoms and 'savage' tribes. The narrative is initiated by the desire of one of the four central characters to find his lost brother. But this motivation is soon superseded by the quest for the lost diamond mines of the biblical King. The treasure hunters find the famed Solomon Mines after much hardship and also help their Zulu companion, Umbopa/ Ignosi, to regain his rightful place as Kukuana chief. As reward for the Englishmen's aid, they are shown the diamond mines and exhorted to take as many diamonds they can carry. Initially, their attempts at removing the diamonds are foiled by the tribal shaman, but eventually all the Englishmen escape showing great courage and fortitude. Umbopa/Ignosi proposes a share of his kingdom but the three adventurers decline his offer. They journey back to civilisation and enroute stumble on the lost brother. Needless to say, they all return as rich men.

What unites *King Solomon's Mines*, *Allan Quatermain* and *Allan's Wife* is the presentation of African expedition as an empowering fantasy. This land 'whereof none know the history' is a fantasised place 'of a kind that help *make a man*'; a place in which 'it was possible for a man of moderate means to start his children in some respectable career ... and have a fair chance of getting on in the world' (Haggard, 1926: 88) [my emphasis]. This imagined empowerment had real-life correlations. Haggard's letter home on June 1877, recording his appointment as English clerk to the Colonial Secretary in the new Transvaal administration, speaks of the possibility of advancement in a country 'that must become rich and rising' (Haggard, 1926: 102). While such optimism was later to sour under the Gladstone administration, the connection between the colonial world and the pastoral form never ceased. Yet there is an ambivalence and contradictory movement in Haggard's version of the African pastoral. On the one hand, Africa is represented within the Judaeo-Christian myth of the garden as the place where the original perfection of man can be recovered; on the other, Africa is also presented as an anti-garden where man's presence in the landscape merely heralds impending corruption.

AFRICA AS GARDEN?

Haggard, writing his autobiography in 1926, remembers Natal as one of 'the most beautiful' parts of the world; he describes the visual panorama of its landscape from veldt to mountain thus:

> The great plains rising by the steps to the QuathLamba or Drakenburg Mountains, the sparkling torrential rivers, the sweeping thunderstorms, the grass-fires creeping over the veldt at night like snakes of living flame, the glorious aspect of the heavens, now of a spotless hue, now charged with the splendid and many coloured lights of sunset, and now sparkling with a myriad stars; the wine-like taste of the air upon the plains, the beautiful flowers in the bush clad kloofs or on the black veldt in spring.
>
> (Haggard, 1926: 52)

All of these things remain indelibly marked in his memory; 'were I to live a thousand years I never should forget them'. Such a passage is noteworthy for the absence of native life and for its naturalisation of human agency and vision. The grass fires creeping over the veldt, the wine-like taste of the air upon the plains naturalise the historical and material contexts which enabled the Western observer's presence and commentary on the African world. Instead, Africa is presented as a panorama which unfolds for the traveller. Metaphors appear in self-evident succession, in inverse proportion to the deliberate effacement of the human eye/I in the landscape.

The seeming absence of human life prior to the arrival of the European traveller is directly related to the colonial fantasy of virgin territory. In another classic passage of new world colonialism, Allan Quatermain describes sunrise on an empty South African veldt in *Allan's Wife*:

> Often and often I have crept shivering on to my wagon-box as the sun rose and looked out. At first one would see nothing but a vast field of white mist suffused towards the east by a tremendous golden glow, through which the tops of stony koppies stood up like gigantic beacons .... Presently this

great curtain would grow thinner, then would melt . . . and for miles on miles the wide rolling country, interspersed with bush, opened to view. But it was not tenantless as it is now, for as far as the eye could reach it would be literally black with game . . . . Here to the right might be a herd of vilderbeeste . . . . There, in front, a thousand yards away, though to the unpractised eye they looked much closer, because of the dazzling clearness of the atmosphere, was a great herd of springbok.

(Haggard, 1915: 49–50)

This passage follows a well trodden path where sunlight on the plains tropes the dawning of a cleaner and simpler new world made possible by the removal from the corrupt old. There is even an indication of divine blessing; the 'tremendous golden glow' and 'stony koppies' act as signs of celestial pleasure as the landscape opens to reveal the fruits of a paradisal inheritance. Just as the relation between Adam and nature may be read as the relation between man and a world which exists uniquely for his pleasure and sustenance, the African veldt, clear of all other men and populated only by African wildebeest and springbok, is here organised around one singular point of vision. The communion between man and nature is intimate and personal; a herd of springbok trek in a single file before this lone eye, the springbok who jumps over the wagon track performs joyfully for Quatermain's lone benefit. But just as the entry of man into paradise leads to the Fall, the presence of the white man in the veldt alters the delicate balance of natural forces. The presence of white men transforms Eden into a hunting ground; the entry of giraffes into Quatermain's field of vision sparks the cry 'there will be marrow-bones for supper tonight' (Haggard, 1915: 50). Yet if this passage recognises the violence that arrives with the figure of the hunter, it also attempts to naturalise violence by describing the harrying of a blesbock buck by a pack of wild dogs. The white hunter acts to save the buck by shooting two of the dogs; his intervention is life-saving and obtains shelter for the buck. A chain of canny displacements naturalises the image of white benevolent colonial rule over the African veldt. Indigenous Africans are displaced from the landscape. Instead, there is only abundant wildlife. The violence which heralds the arrival of three giraffes is displaced onto a voracious pack of wild dogs whose fur is 'draggled' and whose tongues loll. The hunter's destructive instinct is thereafter reconstituted as an act of protection; he cries out before shots ring out over the veldt, 'No. don't touch the buck, for he has come to us for shelter, and he shall have it' (Haggard, 1915: 51).

Yet, Haggard's novels return repetitively to the trauma of colonialism, expressed in the regretful sigh, 'Ah, how beautiful is nature before man comes to spoil it!' His novels are often preoccupied with justifying the white presence on African soil and deflecting a critique of the harm consequent on its presence. *Allan Quatermain* resolves this difficulty by transforming the kingdom of Zu-Vendi into a lost white feudal kingdom with more than a passing nod at more enlightened social practices. But even here, Sir Henry Curtis, the newly crowned king, is made to declare that he intends to bar all other foreigners from entering Zu-Vendi. The cautionary tale Curtis tells in justification of his exclusionist policies is that of the contemporary situation of Southern Africa. For that 'beautiful country' now 'torn and fought for by speculators, tourists, politicians, and teachers', simply reproduces the very 'greed, drunkenness, new diseases, gunpowder, and general demoralization' of the civilised world. Similarly, an open door policy to Kukuanaland in *King Solomon's Mines* would most certainly lead to an undesired cycle of greed, violation and violence. Such a process must be stopped in its tracks by demarcating the kingdom of the Kukuanas from the real historical Southern Africa. The newly installed black king decrees that other white men will in future be barred from entry:

> I will see no traders with their guns and gin . . . . I will have no praying men to put fear of death into men's hearts, to stir them up against the law of the king, and make a path for the white man to follow.
>
> (Haggard, 1940: 340)

SOME VERSIONS OF THE PASTORAL

The dedication in *Allan's Wife*, written partly in the style of a pastoral elegy combines two different moments of grief: a mourning for a lost youth – 'many a *boyish* enterprise and adventure' [my emphasis] – and a mourning for a natural and wild land of 'misty charm' now lost to development, civilisation and to Britain. That Haggard had never seen a Southern Africa without its diamond industry is irrelevant to the genre; as Northrop Frye discussing the genre of

romance remarks, 'the elegiac presents heroism unspoilt by irony
... [and] is often accompanied by a diffused, resigned, melancholic sense of passing time, of the old order changing and yielding
to a new one' (Frye, 1957: 36–37). The diurnal imagery which tracks
that passage of time makes it evident that the lost innocence and
freedom may never be regained. Yet the passage also reminds its
reader that the recall from memory secures an imperial inheritance
for future generations:

> [These further adventures of Quatermain] will remind you
> of many an African yarn ... perhaps they will do more than
> this. Perhaps they will bring back to you some of the long past
> romance of days that are lost to us. The country of which Allan
> Quatermain tells his tales is now, for the most part, as well
> known and explored as are the fields of Norfolk. Where we
> shot and trekked and galloped, scarcely seeing the face of
> civilised man, there the gold-seeker builds his cities. . . . the
> game is gone; the misty charm of the morning has become
> the glare of day. All is changed. . . . Still we can remember
> many a boyish enterprise and adventure, lightly undertaken,
> which now would strike us as hazardous indeed. . . . To you
> . . . in perpetual memory of those eventful years of youth
> which we passed together in the African towns and on the
> African veld, I dedicate these pages.
>
> (Haggard, 1915: 5–7)

I have quoted from the dedication at length because the pastoral
form, which suggests feelings of lost innocence and nostalgia (the
elegy), is a genre best suited to the poetics of Empire. It achieves
the twin tasks of disowning culpability for the destruction of
indigenous cultures, and of producing a gendered and, as I shall
make clear later, *infantilised* notion of culture, central to the
imperialist mythopoetics of the boy's story.

William Empson writes that the pastoral form was 'felt to imply
a beautiful relation between rich and poor' (Empson, 1950: 11),
while Kenneth Burke calls it a 'rhetoric of courtship between
contrasted social classes . . . a kind of expression which, while
thoroughly conscious of class differences, aims rather at stylistic
transcending of conflict' (Burke, 1962: 647, 648). Yet this hymn to
good relations between the colonised and the coloniser makes its
entrance only when the former is under threat of extinction. Mary
Pratt points out that in the case of the decimated Cape tribes, it is

only after their virtual extinction that the so-called 'Bushmen' became textualised as objects of ethnographic study – and as objects of pathos and guilt (Pratt, 1992). A similar nostalgia applies to the Zulus who achieved widespread fame as 'the noblest of savages' only after the destruction of their kingdom and their independence (Guy, 1979: xx). The pastoral is an 'elaborately conventional poem' which expresses an urban poet's nostalgic 'image of peace and the simplicity of the life of shepherds and other rural folk in an idealised natural setting' (Abrams, 1971: 120); shepherds and rural folk do not in any ordinary sense write the poem. Transposed into our version of the pastoral, the elaborate courtesy of the first pair, coloniser/city, to the second pair, colonised native/country, is made possible only by the ascendance of the former pair, and by the exercise of that power towards a transformation of the latter pair. The elegiac tone of Haggard's pronouncement often depicts the history of colonisation as an impersonal, ineluctable process. Written by the urban coloniser, the loss of organic simplicity is often expressed somewhat dishonestly as personal loss. The anthropologist, Renato Rosaldo, labels this seemingly innocent pose 'imperialist nostalgia' and argues that it conceals 'complicity with often brutal domination' (Rosaldo, 1989: 108).

The second strategic movement in Haggard's dedication is generated through an elision of the text of the boy-child and that of the adult man's inheritance. There is an enabling textual symmetry in this imbrication: the (recollected) innocence of the child is the (recollected) innocence of the land in a narrative where only the innocent may inherit the world, or find a new one. In the narrative resolutions of other frontier narratives such as the Western one of two positions is available to the hero. He may choose to marry and settle down to family life or he may seek the company of other men by riding away from domestic restraints. Mulvey argues that these two narrative resolutions are conventional in the Western and offer male readers and spectators two distinct generic pleasures. Both belong to the the male Oedipal drama: an adult acceptance of social integration which rewards 'individual impotence' with the promised inheritance of patriarchal power, or a narcissistic rejection of social integration which allows the male spectator a deliberately infantilised 'phallic' pleasure (Mulvey, 1981). What is apparent from my point of view is that these irreconcilable positions are elided in narratives of adventure, which

44

depend on a narcissistic childhood omnipotence for its vision of a new colonial world.

Conrad, in 'Geography and Some Explorers', evokes a long-established link between childhood, colonialism and geography. Conrad writes of his boyish fascination with maps based on the 'militant' geographer's map of 'open spaces and wide horizons built up on men's devoted work in the open air': 'My imagination could depict to itself there worthy, adventurous and devoted men, nibbling at the edges . . . conquering a bit of truth here and a bit of truth there'. But if blank spaces were especially compelling, the 'boyish boast' was to sour in 'the distasteful knowledge of the vilest scramble for loot that ever disfigured the history of human conscience and geographical exploration' (Conrad, 1926). Haggard's dedication, however, works towards reversing this movement in Conrad by privileging boyhood. This moment is absolutely crucial to the mystification of the adventure narrative. As I have already suggested, because childhood presents a world of innocence uncorrupted by age and civilisation; the boy child is necessarily the only figure capable of inheriting or founding, this blank new (colonial) world. The political implications of this conception of childhood innocence are clear. There are long-established links between children's fiction and colonialism which identify the new world with the infant state of men; Jacqueline Rose remarks that 'along the lines of what is almost a semantic slippage, the child is [here] assumed to have some special relation to a world which – in our eyes at least – was only born when we found it' (Rose, 1984: 50). Furthermore, these boyhood experiences are never written by the *child* as such, but by the adult man *remembering* himself as *a boy child*. The adult produces a childlike dream text as a narrative of enchantment, which may be read forwards as inheritance, or backwards as memory and history. This turning backwards which is simultaneously a turning forwards, both recovers childhood experiences and produces a dream which enables the boy/man and the man/boy to secure an inheritance of patriarchy and empire.

The publication of *Treasure Island* in the late nineteenth century opened the mythic space for Haggard's romances. *Treasure Island* was part of the tradition of adventure tales that specialised in the recreation of 'romantic boyhood'. The literary acceptance of Stevenson's book extended the possibility of adventure to older men precisely through its imaginative cathexis of the boy as hero. In the ideological mirror of adventure fiction, adult readers are captivated by the image of the child that they desire to be, and secure for themselves an inheritance of imperial continuity. As Rose argues, 'if children's fiction builds an image of the child inside the book, it does so in order to secure the child who is outside the book, the one who does not come so easily within its grasp' (Rose, 1984: 1–2). Haggard's dedication of 1887 expresses this fantasy of security and inheritance; he sincerely hopes that the tale may help 'all the big and little boys who read it' to reach what 'I hold to be the highest rank whereto we can attain – the state and dignity of English Gentlemen' (Haggard, 1931).

Yet in trying to secure the child that is outside the book, Haggard's writings give their strongest indication of the insecurity and instabilities which characterise the contradictory demands of imperial identities. This infantilising of culture testifies to the desire for safety and control *more as an adult fantasy*, than as a child's. The culture of the child, always reconstructed and already refashioned, provides the adult with a dream of its own origins. Such a fantasy of origins is ideally suited to the forms and conventions of the imperial romance; Northrop Frye suggests that 'the perennially childlike quality of romance is marked by its extraordinarily persistent nostalgia, its search for some kind of imaginative golden age in time or space' (Frye, 1957: 188) and his work on the genre may help unpick some major preoccupations (Frye, 1976).

Frye argues that romances promoted the ascendancy of the aristocratic section of medieval society. They form a means of expressing the aristocracy's 'dreams of its own social function', and legitimising its role through the ritualised and idealised portrayal of those social functions in the chivalric convention (Frye, 1976: 57). Tracing the link between identity, alienation and wish-fulfilment, Frye also argues that of all literary forms, romance comes closest to the functions of wish-fulfilment in dreams. But these dreams, rather than expressing the anarchic surfacing of unconscious desires, reflect a tightly controlled vision. For the die is cast from the very start; despite the trials which form the quest, identity and containment are always effected through the narrative's ending: 'Translated into dream terms, the quest-romance is the search of the libido or desiring self for fulfilment that will deliver it from the anxieties of reality but will still contain that reality' (Frye, 1957: 193). It is in this sense that Frye labels Haggard's adventures a 'kidnapped romance'; they represent the absorption and integration of the conventions of romance into the culture of imperialists abroad.

GENDER AND GENRE

The genre of adventure sits uneasily with the presence of women. In *King Solomon's Mines*, one of the major reasons cited for the telling of Quatermain's adventure is the suggestion that this 'strange' story contains no women. There are actually two women in Quatermain's tale, Foulata, the black companion of the English Captain Good, and Gagool, the ancient shaman or witch-doctor. Yet to the narrator's male eye, these women do not signify; he may 'safely say' in the introduction to the tale, 'there is not a *petticoat* in the whole history'. The transition from *King Solomon's Mines* to *Allan Quatermain* marks the termination of Quatermain's life. The community fashioned by the quest in *Allan Quatermain* is exclusively male until they reach the land of the Zu-Vendi peoples. But unlike the adventure pastoral, wherein the youthfulness of the new world coincides with the innocence of the boy-men, *Allan Quatermain* also tells a story about the adult responsibilities that come with marriage and sovereignty. The hunter Quatermain has no place in this inheritance. From the adventurers' first encounter with the Zu-Vendi queens, he warns of the fatal beauty of women: 'the beauty of a woman is like the beauty of the lightning – a destructive thing and a cause of desolation' (Haggard, 1931: 160). His steadfast Zulu companion, Umslopogaas, has a similar cautionary tale and remarks, 'woman will swim through blood to her desire, and think nought of it' (Haggard, 1931: 237). These two men stand above the storm that is unleashed through men's desire for the sister queens. Male friendship is the only form of friendship that is 'proof against any absence and evil conduct'. In *Nada the Lily*, ostensibly the story of a romance between Umslopogaas and Nada, an African Helen of Troy, women function as agents or catalysts to the fall of the Zulu nation. In contrast to the destruction caused by rival male suitors for Nada's hand in marriage, Haggard tells the story of partnership between two men who live a spartan existence in a forest away from civilisation. One character continually reproaches the other with the 'shame' of desiring women and warns his companion, 'from that source [can only] flow ... ills, as a river from a spring' (Haggard, 1933: 298). At his tragic death, his friend and companion responds mournfully, 'may we one day find a land where there are no women but war only, for in that land we shall grow great' (Haggard, 1933: 299).

Femininity in novels such as *Allan Quatermain* and *Allan's Wife* is affirmed as a positive quality only when referring to nature. *Allan Quatermain* begins with the description of a father's intense grief at the loss of his son, and an invocation to return to Africa, represented as that 'universal Mother' of Nature untouched by the civilised world:

> Who has not in his great grief felt a longing to look upon the outward features of the universal Mother . . . to let his poor struggling life mingle with her life; to feel the slow beat of her eternal heart, and to forget his woes, and let his identity be swallowed in the vast imperceptibly moving energy of her in whom we are, from whom we came.
>
> (Haggard, 1931: 15)

The deliberate gendering of the natural world as female, and all human agency as male, means that women who possess agency in Haggard are inevitably punished for it. The ideal unproblematic woman is not a human at all but is an emblem of either nature or man's spiritual condition. Nyleptha in *Allan Quatermain* is the angelic blonde queen, 'more an angel out of heaven than a living passionate mortal woman' (Haggard, 1931: 210). She comes from a long pedigree of literary womanliness manifested in the Victorian idealisation of the angel in the home. She is childlike, of 'dazzling fairness' with hair like gold 'clustered in short ringlets over her shapely head' (Haggard, 1931: 158). No artifice adorns her beauty; she wears no jewels, her dress is of 'pure white linen of excessive fineness, plentifully embroidered with gold and the familiar symbols of the sun' (Haggard, 1931: 159). In *Allan's Wife*, the good woman's virtues are those of the nature. As Quatermain's fond memories of his wife make clear:

> Often, I wonder now, if my fond fancies deceive me, or if indeed there are women as sweet and as dear as she . . . .. Was it solitude that had given such depth and gentleness to her? Was it the long years of communing with Nature that had endowed her with such peculiar grace, the grace we find in opening flowers and budding trees? Had she caught that murmuring voice from the sound of the streams which fall continually about her rocky home?
>
> (Haggard, 1915: 164)

Nature as invoked here by the male hero is not the primeval swamp, miasmatic mists and underground caverns of novels of aberrant sexual desire such as *She*. Instead, it is the clean, pastoral landscape of youth and innocence.[1] The conflation of woman and nature results in the slow but sure effacement of the human woman. Stella, in *Allan's Wife*, is defined by solitude and her long confinement within the natural environment, so much so that her movements bear the grace of 'opening flowers and budding trees' and her voice is like the sound of 'murmuring' streams. The human is gradually hollowed out in order that the height of mythification can be reached; her eyes become 'the light of the evening stars' and her tender expression that of the evening sky. The ideal woman is a woman whose presence least intrudes on her male partner. As the realisation of men's dreams, she presents the 'derealisation' of the real woman; Stella is most pure when she is the empty shell of the living woman, and most sought-after as the memory of a dead wife. Quatermain's wife belongs to the Victorian middle-class model of the 'conspicuous invalid' whose illnesses only enhance conventional notions of femininity as modest, spiritual, weak, delicate and completely passive.[2] On her death bed, she is depicted as 'gentle' 'patient' and 'resigned'; she smiles 'as an angel might smile'. The marriage is consummated finally with her final ghostly incarnation:

> *there on the rock sat the wraith of Stella, the Stella whom I had wed.*
> Aye! there she sat, and on her upturned face was that same spiritual look which I saw in the hour when we first had kissed.
> .... For a moment [her eyes] met mine, and their message entered into me.
>
> (Haggard, 1915: 253–254)

The association of women with nature in the Haggardian adventure has other manifestations and often the landscape of difficulty central to the genre of romance is feminised. The adventure story's displacement of woman returns in the form of the geography of the land. But in either case, male identity is forged at the expense of – and to the exclusion of – women. In *King Solomon's Mines*, adventurers are obliged to cross Sheba's breast to Kukuanaland to seek the treasure that remains buried in the caverns of this eroticised and feminised bodyscape:

> These mountains placed thus, like the pillars of a gigantic gateway, are shaped after the fashion of a woman's breasts,

and at times the mists and shadows beneath them take the form of a recumbent woman, veiled mysteriously in sleep. Their bases swell gently from the plain, looking at that distance perfectly round and smooth; and upon the top of each is a vast hillock covered with snow, exactly corresponding to the nipple on the female breast.

(Haggard, 1940: 89)

The quest for treasure is enacted upon the female body, so that the quest for treasure is erotically charged. In a reversal of the political and economic ravishing of Africa, it is the recumbent land that invites the adventurers' attention.

Acts of privation may be read as heroic acts necessary to effect the submission of the native land reluctant to offer up its secrets. They may also be read as the means by which the deliberate sexual eroticism of the plot attains a certain controlling sublimation; masculinity is confirmed through overcoming a feminised nature. The landscape of difficulty provides the opportunity for a narrative of the heroic performance of the male body under pressure. Associated with physical prowess, achievement, self-control and a regime of bodily discipline, physical pain becomes the means by which these ideals may be attained, and a ritual process by which an exclusively male community is created. The close of the day is invariably secured by 'yarns' – histories of travel and heroism – told around the campfire as (outdoor/male) substitute hearth: 'We ate our simple meal by the light of the moon . . . then began to smoke and yarn, and a curious picture we must have made squatting there round the fire' (Haggard, 1940: 53). The psychic investment in this ideological mirror is clearest when sympathisers like Andrew Lang cite its genre characteristics as an extra-textual defence of its form (Lang, 1888: 500).

THE ORIENTALIST GAZE

Mastery is not only achieved at the level of story but also at the level of discourse. Knowledge of the land, climates and peoples underscores narrative authority by reinforcing its privilege, possession and its science; maps enable the white adventurers, like Conrad's geographical militant whose knowledge represents the reach of his power, to discover hidden treasure. Descriptions of native culture fall into 'manners and custom portraits' which situate these romances within a loosely ethnographic frame of reference. *King*

Solomon's Mines, Allan Quatermain and *Allan's Wife* are narrated by the hunter Quatermain. In all three texts, the privileged status of the narrator is represented through the knowledgeability of his pronouncements; his authority is ratified by other characters in the text. The structure of the text enables the unreflexive and authoritative white voice to scrutinise, define and pin down its black subjects; thus Quatermain may say with absolute certainty that the Hottentot Ventvogel's affinity to drink is 'common with his race' or that 'being a Hottentot, the heat had no particular effect'. The same applies to the omniscient narrator of Haggard's African farmstead novel *Jess* where Jantje the Hottentot's home is described as 'very dirty, as was to be expected of a Hottentot's den.' Here the omniscient narrator's comments place the particularity of Jantje's action into the homogenised, collective and subdued other of his race:

> Jantje was lurking about the stems of the trees in the peculiar fashion that is characteristic of the Hottentot, and which doubtless is bred into him after tens of centuries of tracking animals and hiding from foes. There he was, slipping from trunk to trunk . . .. There was absolutely no reason why he should be carrying on in this fashion; he was simply indulging his natural instincts where he thought nobody would observe him. Life at Mooifontein was altogether too tame and civilised for Jantje's taste, and he absolutely needed periodical recreations of this sort.
>
> (Haggard, 1887b: 110)

The discursive strategy sets up the speaker/author in a position of superiority, possessing more knowledge than the object he scrutinises. What may conceivably be a cultural practice of hunting animals is here converted into a natural instinct; rational and historical purposefulness converted into thoughtless biology. The temporal categories which separate the subject from object bear no signs of cultural shock; instead, the irrationality of difference is subdued, interpreted for the reader and made meaningful by the controlling figure of author as ethnographer. Jantje is simply caught in the act of regressing into primitive man by the objective/objectivising eye of the narrator. But often, the neutralising discourse of science breaks down to reveal its textual double. In *Allan Quatermain*, the inventory of objects and precise measurements which form Haggard's description of the native warrior sit oddly with the emotional hysteria of the paragraph's concluding sentence:

51

To begin with the man was enormously tall . . . and beautifully though somewhat slightly shaped; but with the face of a devil. In his right hand he held a spear about five and a half feet long, the blade being two and a half feet in length, by nearly three inches in width, and having an iron spike at the end of a handle that measured more than a foot. On his left arm was a large and well-made elliptical shield of buffalo-hide . . . Round the ankles he wore black fringes of hair, and projecting from the upper portion of the calves, to which they were attached, were long spur like spikes, from which flowed down tufts of beautiful black and waving hair of the colobus monkey. Such was the elaborate array of the Masai Elmoran . . . only those who see it do not live to describe it.

(Haggard, 1931: 33–34)

If one of the effects of the passage is to credit the fear and negation of the cross-cultural encounter with the truth and measurement of science, the text also bears witness to the ritual particularity of its fright and its desires. The Masai as exotic other is 'beautifully' shaped, the narrator is particularly attentive to his physique and bodily attire. The Masai also carries a terrible spear, his shield is painted with 'strange heraldic-looking devices' while ostrich feathers frame a 'diabolical countenance'. These descriptions climax in the hysterical statement which abandons all pretence of objectivity in a singularly shocking phrase of disavowed desire: the Masai are 'bloodthirsty savages' (Haggard, 1931: 77).

A FANTASY OF WHITE BODIES AND BLACK BODIES

While the Orientalist discourse of science provides knowledge as stability, its essentialising vision is always under threat from history and narrative as 'the site of dreams, images, fantasies, myths, obsessions and requirements' (Bhabha, 1983: 24). Present in Haggard's detail of the Masai is an intense awareness of the *physicality* of his presence; the warrior is described as more 'ferocious or awe-inspiring' than any other figure seen in the past, 'enormously tall . . . and beautifully, though somewhat slightly shaped; but with the face of a devil.' This qualifying clause, quickly uttered after the pause of the semi-colon, breaks the hypnotic effect of the Masai's presence on Quatermain, just as the horror of blood later jolts Quatermain out of another prolonged bout of fascination with the native subject:

> Surely it was a nightmare! At the same instant a dim but devilish-looking face appeared to rise out of the water . . . and something warm spurted into my face. In an instant the spell was broken; I knew that it was no nightmare, but that we were attacked by swimming Masai.
>
> (Haggard, 1931: 38)

The description of the Masai attack contains all the tension of a sexually charged encounter.

Such a narrative moment is not isolated but belongs to the movement of the Orientalist gaze as both a disciplining and narcissistic eye/I. Its gaze which lingers on the physical surfaces of the black man's body is in this case also homoerotic. By returning the black man in the image of white men's desires, it panders to a male narcissism (Chapman and Rutherford, 1988; Mulvey, 1975). The discourse of primitivity sanctions the sexual fantasy by producing the black body as animal-like, sexually savage and regressive. The sublimated homoerotic desire exists in covert form by re-imagining the black body, within the conventions of romanticism and aestheticism, as noble savage (Dyer, 1987). Desire and its sublimation can be found in the writings of Haggard's contemporary, Baden-Powell, whose scouting movement was based partly on the contemporary cultural enthusiasm for what was portrayed as Zulu militarism. Baden-Powell here describes a Matabele warrior as if he was part of the exotic and beautiful wildlife of the land. The scopophilic pleasure of spying on the warrior is permitted because the discourse frames the Matabele as an indigenous wild animal drinking at the waterhole:

> Today, when out scouting by myself I lay for a quiet look-out among some rocks and grass overlooking a little stream . . . .. Presently there was a slight rattle of trinkets, and a swish of the tall yellow grass, followed by the sudden apparition of a naked Matabele warrior standing glistening among the rocks within 30 yards of me. His white war ornaments . . . contrasted strongly with his rich brown skin. His kilt of wild cat-skins and monkey's tails swayed round his loins. His left hand held his assegai beneath the great dappled ox-hide shield; and, in his right, a yellow walking-staff. He stood for almost a minute

perfectly motionless, like a statue cast in bronze, his head turned from me, listening for any suspicious sound. Then, with a swift and canny movement, he laid his arms noiselessly upon the rocks, and, dropping on all fours beside a pool, he dipped his muzzle down and drank just like an animal. I could hear the thirsty sucking of his lips from where I lay. . . . He pulled his weapons up, and then stood again to listen. Having heard nothing he turned and sharply moved away . . . I had been so taken with the spectacle that I felt no desire to shoot at him.

(Jeal, 1989: 189–190)

Baden-Powell fully clothed in riding breeches notices the kilt of animal skin which both conceals and draws attention to the Matabele's genitalia. The animal skin paradoxically inscribes the warrior as more – not less – naked through the metonymic association with wildness. The sexualised black body displays all the atavistic power of a beast. Yet both power and homosexual desire are muted and contained through a congruence with wildlife and sculptural form. The Matabele as animal becomes simply part of the landscape; his body framed by the conventions of high art. As Richard Dyer's study of Paul Robeson makes clear, this double articulation is needed to safeguard the heterosexual gaze – it is 'both a way of producing potentially erotic images while denying that this is what is being done, and also a way of constructing a mode of looking at the naked form . . . "dispassionately", without arousal' (Dyer, 1987: 121).

The visual and textual discourse that circulates around the black nude body can be read as the signifying negative to the semiotic of Otherness that accrues to cross-cultural dressing as empowerment. I will leave the analysis of that fantasy till later but will merely note that in this reading of cross-cultural dress, it is (more often than not) the white man who dresses up and the black man who reveals his body for consumption. If the black man presumes to the former, as with Kipling's Eurasians and Bengali babus, the narratives often work towards exposing him, revealing his blackness beneath the covering of clothes. The display of the black body, as indicated earlier, is caught up in the same movement of discrimination as the fetish of skin colour. The movement is linked to an atavistic trope of blackness, and marked against the white man's clothed and civilised body. Thus to claim his rightful inheritance as tribal Chief to the Kukuanas in *King Solomon's Mines*, Umbopa must take off his 'moocha' or girdle and stand naked before white men. John Laputa, the educated black missionary of John Buchan's African adventure, *Prester John*, sheds his clerical garments to practise 'some strange magic'. The act of shedding his clothes uncovers evil by exposing his anglicisation as merely a mask of whiteness. The white boy hero of the story exclaims, 'I had no doubt it was the black art, for there was that in the air and the scene which spelt the unlawful'. The homoeroticism of this secret encounter is repeated again on a wider political stage unearthed when the minister strips for his coronation. The effect on the hero is immense, 'I had a mad desire to be of Laputa's party. Or rather, I longed for a leader who should master me and make my soul his own' (Buchan, 1947: 18, 129), but desire is disavowed as 'the black arts'.

To return to Baden-Powell's text, despite being the subject of passive verbs, the narrator acts as the organising centre for the Matabele warrior's actions. His voyeurism, made all the more pleasurable by the warrior's seeming ignorance of him, transfixes him while the curiosity of his gaze obsessively explores the detail of the warrior's body. The isolation of the lone figure of the Matabele warrior is crucial to the sexual fantasy because its narcissistic staging of desire 'promotes the fantasy of an unmediated, unilateral, relation between seer and seen' (Chapman and Rutherford, 1988: 145). The passage's diegesis is predicated on his absence from the framed image. This means that as perspectival vanishing point, his presence can only be reconstituted through the black body of the warrior.

The heroic war illustration of the kind that was to be found in the illustrated presses during the Anglo-Zulu War exhibits a similar reconstitution. Epic encounters elevate single figures to an iconic level; they sublimate sexual desire by figuring the black/white encounter within a discourse of war and mutual sacrifice. But here more than anywhere else one finds the black man crucial to the heroic narrative of the white man writ large. In the battle of races, heroism on the side of the Zulu warriors only mirrors more heroism. To be defeated by such men was to be their equals, to defeat such an enemy was to be more than their equals. On Sept 6, the *Illustrated London News* carried such a front-page spread on Lord Beresford's 'hand to hand single combat' with a native warrior (Figure 3). The July 1879 *Illustrated London News* special supplement commemorating the death of the Prince Imperial is a case in point.

Figure 3 'Lord Beresford's encounter with a Zulu in the reconnaisance across the Umvolosi, July 3', *Illustrated London News*, Sept. 6, 1879.

Figure 4 'At Bay!: The battle of Isandula, Jan 22, 1879. The last order that we heard was "fix bayonets men and die like English soldiers do", and so they did – Extract from a letter by a survivor', *Graphic*, March 15, 1879.

Two illustrations show the European prince ambushed by Zulu impis, but both cannot possibly be true. In 'The Attack', the Prince holds the reins of a horse frightened by invading Zulu warriors emerging from the bush; he half turns to face these hostile warriors. In 'At Bay', Zulu warriors charge over a rocky plain; sword unsheathed, the Prince faces seven of his attackers squarely and is ready to defend his life. The image of the lone European Prince pitted against Zulu warriors dominates both illustrations. That the two sketches could not have been drawn from the actual attack (the Prince was ambushed from behind and the suddenness of the attack caught him unawares), or that both illustrations could logically be true does not seem to matter. What the Prince's death seems to offer illustrators is an opportunity for imaginative licence; his heroism is signed through the black men that surround him. To return to the Anglo-Zulu war, the spectacle of mounted (and uniformed) cavalry attempting to retain its colours or of foot-soldiers fighting for their country (Figure 4), presents the spectacle of the white man's courage in the face of native attack and certain death. Haggard's rewriting of the Isandhlwana battle (and the saving of the regimental colours), for Lang's children's book, narrates a breathless story of English heroism, which is only achieved through a portrayal of Zulu bravery and cruelty:

> desperate, lamed, and utterly outworn, the two friends [Lieutenants Coghill and Melvill of the 24th regiment] struggled up the bank and the hill beyond. But the Zulus had crossed that stream as well as the fugitive Englishmen. They staggered forward for a few hundred yards, then, unable to go further, the friends stood back to back and the foe closed in upon them. There they stood, and there, fighting desperately, the heroes died.
>
> (Lang, 1893: 145)

That these two Lieutenants were 'friends', standing back to back in order to face the Zulu warriors, heightens the drama of male courage. But if their deaths underscore the nobility of sacrifice, 'among men, immortal honour to their names!', such a narrative may only proceed by way of the black warriors who gave chase. Such mirrored symmetry can be seen in Captain Henry Parr's memoirs which were published in the aftermath of the Anglo-Zulu war (Parr, 1880). Parr, Sir Bartle Frere's military secretary in South Africa, wrote an apologetic account of the war, which relies on the praise each side offers to the other. Parr's narrative uses both Zulu warriors and British soldiers as focalisers in his accounts of battle. In *A Sketch of the Kaffir and Zulu Wars*, the Zulus, he writes, 'with keen and ready appreciation of gallantry, tell many tales of the way . . . [British] men struggle on, fighting to the last, and how they had struck before they could be subdued' (Parr, 1880: 221). Parr's account of Isandhlwana uses the Zulu warriors' verbal reports and also tells the battle from their view-point. Accounts of other battles give a version of Zulu 'bravery and recklessness . . . beyond belief' (Parr, 1880: 227–228). The narrative effect is symmetrical with exemplary modes of courage on both sides.

That this heroic cult of masculinity can only be formed through a reflection of blackness may also be seen in Haggard's texts. Umbopa seeking a position as carrier in Quatermain's expedition for the Solomon Mines, is asked to stand up for assessment. He does so, 'slipping off the long military great coat which he wore, and revealing himself naked except for the moocha round his centre and a necklace of lions' claws'. Sir Henry Curtis who walks up to inspect him is taken into the same frame of reference:

'They make a good pair don't they?' said Good; 'one as big as the other' 'I like your looks, Mr. Umbopa, and I will take you as my servant,' said Sir Henry in English. Umbopa evidently understood him, for he answered in Zulu, 'It is well'; and then added with a glance to the white man's great stature and breadth, 'We are men, thou and I.'

(Haggard, 1940: 48)

The text is coy in its references to Umbopa's sexuality; the black man is naked except for the moocha which hides his genitalia and the lion's claws which proclaim his sexual and military prowess. Henry Curtis's stature gains from association with Umbopa. But where one is naked the other is fully clothed. This visual difference is crucial to the doubling of Curtis/Umbopa. From this perspective, Good's remark is all the more revealing, 'they make a good pair . . . one as big as the other'. The Umbopa/Curtis doubling is repeated again later in the narrative when Curtis dresses himself as a native warrior. It leads Quatermain to observe,

The dress was, no doubt a savage one, but I am bound to say that I seldom saw a finer sight than Sir Henry Curtis presented in this guise. It showed off his magnificent physique to its greatest advantage, and when Ignosi arrived presently, arrayed in a similar costume, I thought to myself that I had never before seen two such splendid men.

(Haggard, 1940: 219)

But Umbopa cannot, of course, dress like Curtis. In this fantasy, cross-cultural dressing works in one direction only. Curtis is the white civilised hero with all the sexuality and physical power of a savage, but at best, Umbopa can only be the black noble savage.

It seems to me that these moments are of vital importance to the narrative which seeks to write the heroism of the white man in the discourse of empowered masculinity. The image of the black body becomes necessary precisely because it projects a simple physicality that may have been marginalised from the more conventional ideal of Victorian Christian manliness. The dream of the black body arises from the tensions in the changing ideal of manliness based loosely on the construction of masculinity around concepts such as 'character', and Christian values of honesty, earnestness, straightforwardness, chivalry, courage, fortitude and paternalism. On the one hand, the discourse of manliness privileges rationality, reason and the dominance of the spiritual over the physical and the emotional; Magan and Walvin remark, 'it represented a concern with the successful transition from Christian immaturity to maturity, demonstrated by earnestness, selflessness and integrity ...' (Magan and Walvin, 1988). On the other hand, the cult of muscular Christianity which emerged at mid century promoted the body as central to the values of self-control, discipline, physical perfection, achievement and patriotism. The athletic male body is disciplined, which as we shall see later, is crucial to a certain discourse of nationalism. The reflection of Umbopa is then vital to the characterisation of Curtis as hero; the dream of physical power masculinises his more benign and spiritual construction. Curtis's Berserkir forefathers, paradoxically (as with Baden-Powell's hunter), are only reconstituted through the wars of the Kukuanas. But the reflection is shot through with desire; and it is in this dream of (sexual/racial) power that the white man (mis)recognises his image in the physicality of the black body.

In Haggard's narratives, the spectacle of the masculine community based on narcissistic reflection has its own exclusionary rituals which enforce the separation of the sexes and bind white men to their black counterparts. Umbopa tells Henry Curtis in *King*

Solomon's Mines, 'We are men, thou and I'; and Umslopogaas, the black warrior in *Allan Quatermain* confesses:

> I am rough, I know it, and when my blood is warm I know not what to do, but yet wilt thou be sorry when the night swallows me and I am utterly lost in blackness, for in thy heart thou lovest me, my father, Macumazahn the fox . . . ay I love thee, Macumazahn, for we have grown grey together, and there is that between us that cannot be seen, and yet is too strong for breaking.
>
> (Haggard, 1931: 236)

Quatermain returns the affection, 'it was quite true, I was much attached to the bloodthirsty old ruffian. . . . [he had] fierce honesty and directness . . . almost superlative human skill and strength . . . he was absolutely unique'. Such bonds of affection which exist across racial and cultural groups are always singular relations between individual men. Because they are not communal they do not violate the *colonial* identity of the male subject predicated on cultural boundaries. Haggard, by narrating a relationship between individual black/white men, never has to negotiate the difficult problem of how these relationships translate between whole races or nations. These ties are also only temporary in that they terminate with the death or enforced absence of one of the pair near the novel's close.[3] Umslopogaas is the *last* black warrior of his generation; as Zulu warrior, he also represents the mythical last of the 'military' nation destroyed in the Anglo-Zulu war. From another angle, the bonding across the racial divide provides for a ritual sexual division and a homoeroticism that overcomes the accusation of homosexuality. In *Allan Quatermain*, Umslopogaas tells Quatermain:

> I [Umslopogaas] am weary of it, weary to death of eating and drinking, of sleeping and giving in marriage. I love not this soft life in stone houses that takes the heart out of a man, and turns his strength to water and his flesh to fat. I love not the white robes and the delicate women . . . .. When we fought the Masai at the kraal yonder, ah, then life was worth the living.
>
> (Haggard, 1931: 235)

The relation between Umslopogaas and Quatermain has the mythical overtones of the biblical story of David and a racially different Jonathan: it is a story of boyhood romance away from women and the responsibility of the 'domestic'. Its very transience authorises the expression of a powerful homosexual fantasy. The strong black man enables the white man to dream the 'boyish enterprise of adventure, lightly undertaken, which now would strike us as hazardous indeed.' He is necessary to a reproduction of the heroic male in contrast to his effeminised, civilised counterpart. By displacing women as the white man's object of affection, he narrates a culturally sanctioned romance of strong young men predicated on the enforced exclusion of women. In Kipling's words, this is the 'Ballad of East and West'.

CODA: PRIMITIVITY, GENDER AND THE NARRATIVE OF COLONIALISM

Primitivity, as reconstituted through the image of the noble savage and the imaginary bond between white adventurer and black man is central to the boy's story of heroic valour and moral fortitude. But what of the girl? Is the girl empowered through a similar metaphoric association? Concluding this chapter with such a question enables us to foreground the strategic overlap between gender and genre in the fantasy of 'savage' empowerment. To answer the question, I will refer briefly to *Allan's Wife* and *She*.

Allan's Wife is a short novel about the strange circumstances of Stella's life and the jealousy aroused in her companion, Hendrika, when Quatermain begins to court his future wife. The story of Stella is told after her death from complications associated with the birth of Allan's son. Stella was brought to Africa as a small girl by a father, Squire Carson, who was betrayed by his young wife. With the help of some natives, he created a self-sufficient village economy cut off from the rest of civilisation. Squire Carson, haunted by the memory of his betrayal, resolves to bring his daughter up as 'Nature's child' but on subsequent reflection decides that such an act would be tantamount to degrading her 'to the level of the savages'. Hendrika, Stella's companion, however, represents such a feral child. Hendrika was brought up by baboons in the mountains and has 'many of the ways of monkeys' (Haggard, 1915: 139). Unlike Edgar Rice Burroughs's hero Tarzan, whose inherent sense of civility distinguishes the nobility of man from that of the beast, Hendrika is the 'baboon-woman' whose physical appearance simply matches the beast within. Quatermain describes her as 'of white blood' but short, ' with bowed legs', 'enormous shoulders' and receding brow. Hendrika looks like 'a very handsome monkey'; she might have been, Quatermain remarks, 'the missing link' (Haggard, 1915: 122).

Hendrika has all the bodily attributes of the primates, despite clear evidence presented of her white ancestry. She grunts unintelligibly instead of speaking, and 'clicks like a bushman'. In contrast, Stella's is the 'sweetest voice . . . of winds whispering at night'. Where Stella is purity personified, Hendrika is all passion, rage and jealousy. Quatermain's scale of humanity is precise as to where the baboon woman belongs; for if 'women are more jealous than men, small-hearted men are more jealous than those of larger mind and wider sympathy, and animals are the most jealous of all' (Haggard, 1915: 172), then Hendrika must be more beast than human. But Stella's destiny is tied to the baboon woman. Caught and tamed by the mistress of the house, Hendrika is nurtured by Stella until she becomes inseparable from her mistress and forms her alter ego. The effect of the novel's polarisation of femininity is to link these two women. In the final scene of the novel, Quatermain encounters the baboon woman sitting by Stella's grave clothed in animal skins. Even in death, hers is the image that finally separates Quatermain from his more celestial wife.

As I have argued in chapter one, the link made between women and primitivity is not the exclusive property of Haggard. Sexual difference is an integral part of the hierarchy of evolution in Darwin's *Descent of Man* (1871); powers of intuition, imitation and rapid perception which characterise the female of the species are also some of the 'faculties . . . characteristic of the lower races, and therefore, of a past and lower state of civilisation' (Dijkstra, 1986: 172). Femininity and primitivity are linked; the woman is related to the primates and to the primitive savage. In Haggard's earlier adventure, *King Solomon's Mines*, Gagool the witch-doctor is described as 'a wizened monkey-like figure' creeping on all four limbs. Her body incarnates the fearful representation of sexual and racial difference. Gagool is literally primitive in her longevity; 'I knew your fathers, and your father's father's fathers [and] when the country was young I was here' she declares. But Gagool's monkey-like appearance represents a position several rungs down on the evolutionary ladder. From the furry covering she wears to her mummified appearance, her grotesque body is a sign of her primitive state of being. Ayesha in Haggard's infamous potboiler, *She*, turns into a wizened monkey when she is unmasked by the sacred pillar of fire. One of the onlookers screams, '*Look!–look!–look!* she's shrivelling up! she's turning into a monkey!' The 'loveliest, noblest, most splendid woman' is exposed as nothing better than a hideous ape. Her skin of perfect whiteness is revealed to be 'dirty brown and yellow' and the gauze coverings of her earlier beauty, nothing but the shroud of death and the wrappings of 'a badly preserved Egyptian mummy'.

The association of femininity and primitivity poses a problem for the narratives of the frontier which locate civility and development in the domesticity of settler communities. Domesticity is the mark of culture, and traditionally, women have borne the burden of representing domesticity. Men can be associated with primitivity in the guise of the noble savage, but women cannot – for not only are they nearer to beasts than men but they also represent the boundary between civilisation and savagery. Squire Carson's plan to bring Stella up as 'Nature's child' would have reduced her to the same level as Hendrika. Carson's edenic paradise necessarily includes the very civilisation he leaves behind. His pastoral habitation is not a state of nature, for it possesses all the 'luxuries of civilisation' including books, 'the crockery, and the knives and forks'. For without these, Stella would simply be savage and heathen, and there would be nothing to distinguish woman from beast. Flossie, the missionary's child in *Allan Quatermain,* who grows up in the wilderness, must also return to English civilisation, receiving 'some education and mix with girls of her own race, otherwise she will grow up wild, shunning her kind' (Haggard, 1931: 108).

This section can only end with a brief reference to *She*; for in *She* we have the moral behind the dominion of sons. *She* presents a social structure of matrilineal rule. Descent is traced through the mother's line with the result that individuals 'never pay attention to, or even acknowledge, any man as their father' even when true male parentage is known. Women select their male partners in marriage which is 'continued till one of them wearied of it'. Whilst there are titular male heads of households, women do as they please. As Billali, the male household head remarks, 'we worship them, and give them their way, because without them the world could not go on; they are the source of life' (Haggard, 1979: 96). Her rule, unlike Henry Curtis's gentlemanly reign in *Allan Quatermain* is 'unconstrained by human law' and 'unshackled by a moral sense of right and wrong'. Her power is based on terror and fear as the 'empire of the imagination' and on the fulfilment of her own ambitions. This is readily seen in her seduction of the sage Noot, in order to steal his knowledge of 'great invisible truths' of life. But such actions point to the fact that her knowledge is derivative rather originary; her superhuman state is the result of her deception of the old hermit, rather than to knowledge and skills acquired by her own efforts. Ayesha, as the negative image of Queen Victoria, is the uncivilised sovereign: her entry into England would be at 'a terrible sacrifice of life'; for her 'proud, ambitious spirit would be certain to break loose and avenge itself' (Haggard, 1979: 207).

She illustrates the moral that while woman might be the source of life, the evolution of society and politics is a narrative of sublimation, civilisation and patriarchal forms of responsible government. Squire Carson's transformation of the wilderness of Africa into a pastoral haven turns out to be nothing less than the establishment of patriarchy as a system of government. The founding of a new dynasty at the end of *Allan Quatermain* comes with the birth of a son from the marriage of Queen Nyleptha and Henry Curtis; their newborn is a 'regular curly-haired, blue-eyed young Englishman in looks'. This new political formation differs from the previous reign of the two sister queens in that it locates Henry Curtis at the very top of the state structure, as husband to Nyleptha and father of their young son. In *She*, only the two men return across the 'horrible gulf' of the abyss which separates the interior of Africa from the civilisation of the outside world. The body of the ancient queen remains behind in the cave.

3

MIMESIS OF SAVAGERY

One of the most important tropes in colonial fiction is that of the mirror. In these stories of Haggard's, the significance of the Other lies in the fact that he is symbolic of something that the Western mind must learn about itself. The journey across space is nothing less than a surreal journey into the self: the savage reveals the truth of the white man's self, if he only has eyes to see it. 'Civilisation is only savagery silvery-gilt', Haggard pronounces in the introduction to *Allan Quatermain*, 'we must look to the . . . savage portions of our nature if we would really understand ourselves' (Haggard, 1931: 14). We should beware of these rhetorical manoeuvres; for not only does this popular psychology of colonial fiction effect an insidious naturalisation of what are enforced dyadic relations, it also renders passive the 'savage' reflection of man.

The task of this chapter then is to read the historical context back into Haggard's African romances so as to disrupt the apparent ease by which such a reflecting surface is produced. We shall address Natalian settler politics, the creation and maintenance of Nguni reservations (sometimes referred to as the Shepstonian system), and the effects of the interpretation of 'customary law' as an act of temporal distancing and segregation immortalised in Haggard's *King Solomon's Mines* and its sequel, *Allan Quatermain*. We will also look briefly at the role that Haggard's mentor, Sir Theophilus Shepstone, plays as someone who has a privileged insight into the native mind. As Diplomatic Agent for the Native Tribes and later Secretary for Native Affairs, Shepstone was influential in the colonial administration for thirty years. His views were sought long after he relinquished those positions. Haggard's attitude towards Shepstone has been described as one of 'unabated idolization' (Dumins and Ballard, 1981: 71). Haggard in his autobiography,

Days of My Life, describes Shepstone as a man 'who had acquired many of the characteristics of the natives amongst whom he lived' and 'known and almost worshipped by every Kaffir in the land' he even appears as Haggard's muse in *Nada the Lily* as one who 'dwelt in the spirit of Chaka' and 'mastered . . . [the] people of the Zulu' (Haggard, 1933: 7). Shepstone is important in my account because his special status is contingent on a cultural and mythic transfer of Zulu authority onto himself. His view of himself was promoted and shared by the wider imperial culture. Shepstone emerges as a key player in accounts of the break-up of independent Zululand; the contravention of Shepstone's imperial decrees, read allegedly at Cetshwayo's coronation, formed the pretext for the invasion of Zululand. We will also look briefly at accounts of the Anglo-Zulu war as a frame for Haggard's famed elegiac romanticism of warfare.

REWRITING HISTORY

Natal was settled by English-speaking traders in the 1820s and later by Dutch trekkers and farmers in the 1830s. The British annexation of the republic of Natalia in 1843 led the majority of Boer farmers to trek further north, and a small number of British settlers replaced them. Natal was essentially an impoverished colony; its value for Britain was primarily strategic in so far as it controlled access to the coast, thwarted Boer aspirations for an independent homeland and prevented other European powers from claiming sovereignty (Kline, 1988: 2). Geographically isolated from important centres of South African commerce, it had neither the raw materials nor the favourable conditions that were needed to turn its economy around. The combination of a large resident African population and a shared border with the powerful kingdom of Zululand created enough insecurity in Natal to discourage large-scale settlement and investment (Guy, 1979: 41). Capital was invested in land and a significant proportion of Natal's 'best agricultural land' was in the hands of land speculating companies and out of the reach of small farmers and settlers (Guy, 1979: 39). By the mid 1870s, the colony had less than 40,000 white settlers, who cultivated 200,000 out of its 12 million acres in remote farm communities and were also outnumbered one to five by the native Nguni population (Schreuder, 1980: 36–37). Although Natal's black population increased steadily, large numbers were unwilling to enter into capitalist wage–labour contracts with white settlers;

others moved towards peasant agricultural production and became rivals (Guy, 1979: 40–41). Natal's segregationist policies, its creation of 'Locations' or 'Trust Reserves' to preserve traditional tribal groupings and customs, were then the most cost-effective way to contain confrontation between races within Natal and to manage its large African population (Kline, 1988: 2). But the establishment of reservations became a bone of contention among the white settlers who accused the colonial administration of constructing barriers to civilization and progress. More importantly, the settlers saw the Locations as denying them access to land and sources of labour; they also saw independent Zululand as a populous and fertile land that was easily within their reach (Guy, 1979: 43).

Security, land and labour shortages dominated white settler politics and lay behind Natal's expansionist policies for most of the nineteenth century. In a book which looks at colonial policy in Natal, Zululand and Transvaal, *Cetywayo and His White Neighbours*, Haggard addressed these problems (Haggard, 1882). He makes a careful distinction between the aboriginal of Natal and an increasing number of black 'immigrants'. The latter term is not applied to the white immigrants who are called *settlers*. 'Wholesale immigration from the surrounding territories' and neighbouring Zululand threaten to transform Natal from virgin territory into a black colony (Haggard, 1882: 49). Natal reservations under British protection had become a refuge for inhabitants of Zululand, Swaziland, the Transvaal and elsewhere in Southern Africa. Haggard explains that this is due to the fact that such an immigrant 'can rest secure in the protection of the Home and local Governments, and of enactments specially passed to protect him and his privileges'. Together with their polygamous customs, which has the undesirable 'effect of bringing about an abnormal growth of population', this steady 'stream of immigration' has led to the 'present enormous total'. To combat this accumulation of numbers, Haggard proposes two options. The first option involves integrating the native population into the culture and cash-economy of the white settlers. The second is a bold attempt at re-writing the history of colonialism by the enforced repatriation or the expulsion of natives to Zululand:

> Let Zululand be converted into a black colony under English control, and its present inhabitants be established in suitable locations; then let all the natives of Natal, *with the exception of those who chose to become monogamists and be subject to civilised law,*

be moved into Zululand, and also established in locations.
There would be plenty for them all.

(Haggard, 1882: 68–69) [my emphasis]

But as the historian Shula Marks remarks, 'that Natal was empty
of Africans was always an illusion, though one that died hard'
(Marks, 1970: 4). The white settlers' belief that Natal's black
population consisted not of indigenous tribes, but of refugees with
no claim to the land, was not borne out by contemporary re-
searchers (Welsh, 1971: 2–3). Shepstone, in a paper entitled 'The
Early History of the Zulu-Kafir Race of South-Eastern Africa', read
in 1875, acknowledged that Natal was 'thickly populated by numerous tribes under independent chiefs' that 'lived . . . close together'
before the *Mefcane* (Bird, 1965: 156). During the expansion of Zulu
militancy under Shaka, Natal was cleared as a buffer against hostile
enemies and tribesmen, and refugees hid and congregated around
the *Umzimkulu* and *Umzimvubu* rivers. The earliest settlers did find
scattered tribes, confusion and disorder due to a long period of
warfare. With the change of Zulu rulers (Dingane as successor to
Shaka) these tribes emerged from hiding and drifted back over the
country. 'Many of them', Marks writes, 'had found themselves on
the vast farms which the Voortrekkers had allocated themselves . . .
[and] for the privilege of returning to their original homes the
refugees were prepared to pay tribute in labour demanded by the
white farmers' (Marks, 1970: 4; Schreuder, 1980: 36–43). The
fertility of the land, coupled with 'the ease of conquering isolated
Nguni communities' and returning tribes, forged the myth, argues
the South African historian D. M. Schreuder, of 'Natal as an open
terrain for white settlement' (Schreuder, 1980: 38).

Thus, in Haggard's writings, the empty, wide and open landscapes 'where the traveller or settler could find good shooting,
cheap labour, and cheap living', inscribe a trope of settlers' rights
as opposed to those of black 'immigrants'. These black peoples, no
longer native to the soil/region, become *squatters* on private land.
Unlike the white agriculturalist, these Natal Nguni tribes are
foreigners whose cultural systems are destructive to the land they
dwell on:

their cultivation being of the most primitive order, and
consisting as it does of picking out the very richest patches of
land, and cropping them till they are exhausted, all ordinary
land being rejected as too much trouble to work, the posses-

sion, or the right of user, of several hundred acres is necessary to the support of a single family.

(Haggard, 1882: 58)

Haggard's critique was articulated as part of a colonial plan to bring traditional self-sufficient African communities into a wage–labour economy based on the development of Natal for white settlers. As a resident magistrate is quoted as saying, natives 'are in a very different position from the labouring population of Europe. So long as the natives are owners and breeders of stock, they will never . . . be a labouring population' (Schreuder, 1980: 37). Accusations of the natural indolence of the Zulu and Natal Nguni population, and the belief that such laziness was 'incompatible' with the ideals of civilised economy, can be traced directly to the demand for a supply of cheap black labour. Haggard's critique of native idleness is also invested with an anxiety about the easy fit between native and land which is evident in all his African romances, and which leaves no room for white presence. Paradoxically, this fit is made more snug by Natal's establishment of African reservations; Haggard complains, 'protected by a powerful Government, they do not [even] fear attack from without, or internal disorder'. In what seems to be an ironic trope of primitivity, the Natalian natives are seen as existing in a pre-lapsarian garden of plenty managed by the colonial administration. These inhabitants, unlike their white counterparts, are not bound by the consequences of the Fall:

> Their needs are few; a straw hut, corn for food, and the bright sun. They are not even troubled with the thought of a future life, but like the animals, live through their healthy, happy days, and at last, in the extreme old age, meet a death which for them has no terrors, because it simply means extinction. When compared to that of civilised races . . . their lot is a happy one.

(Haggard, 1882: 50)

Yet if this metaphor reads true, one might also be tempted to ask why this happy state of affairs has to be disrupted, and why they should not be held up as a model for emulation. The answer Haggard gives is startlingly revealing of the limits of the garden metaphor: these natives 'bear no share of the *curse* that comes to all other men as a birthright; they need not labour' [my italics]. Such an insight should make nonsense of the values and virtues of

Christianity for it reveals the birthright of the civilised Christian world to be alienation and hard labour. Yet this contradiction is fundamental to the Protestant exhortation of work and discipline as corrective of man's innate inclination towards sin. It also made perfect sense within the Victorian celebration of work as the making of man (Coetzee, 1988). It is a view actively endorsed by white settlers in Natal:

> the Natives must see that a continuance of this easy, happy, idle sort of life, without those stimulating elements of labour and hardship and danger, which go to make a man a man, and a man a nation, must only end in degeneration and demoralization; and if the Native is to profit by the blessings which a civilised Government gives to him, he must learn to share its lot of labour.
>
> (Schreuder, 1980: 40)

Locations

Natal's 'Native Policy', which differed from the Cape's single legal framework, arose out of the setting up of six African 'Locations' (totalling about two and a quarter million acres) between 1846 and 1864 by Theophilus Shepstone, then Secretary for Native Affairs. In principle, the Locations preserved traditional tribal groupings and customs as far as was possible. Under the Shepstonian system, African tribal law was recognised to apply to natives both inside and outside the Locations. What this meant for Natal's franchise, legal and administrative system was the existence and practice of a separate code of native law and a policy of segregation between the native and white populations.[1] Shepstone, defending the system remarked,

> Whilst humanity, and especially the injunctions of our religion compel us to recognise in the native the capability of being elevated to perfect equality, social and political, with the white man, yet it is as untrue as it would be unwise to say, that the native is now in this position, or that he is *in his present state* capable of enjoying or even understanding the civil and political rights of the white man. Her Majesty's government has most wisely recognised and acted upon this *principle* by providing a form of government for the natives of this district, *which while adapted to their present conditions*, is capable of being

71

modified as to advance their progress towards a higher and better civilization.

(Welsh, 1971: 51) [my emphasis]

From chapter two it should be clear that time and alterity are intertwined in colonial politics and discourse. The segregation of native reality from colonial reality is based on a temporal separation which ascribes to the former a primitivity beyond the pale of contemporary definitions of humanity. The denial of coevalness in the concept of (reservations of) primitive time flies in the face of the stated aims of trusteeship. Segregation and 'reservations' pretend to a pristine, frozen native time. Safely fossilised and petrified in the past, they make no serious attempt to address the issue of change and, contrary to what they pretend, they ignore the impact of colonialism on native cultures. To adopt a kindred metaphor from Johannes Fabian's critique of temporal politics in anthropological discourse, the 'propitiously angled mirrors' of segregationist policies 'have the miraculous power to make real objects disappear' (Fabian, 1983). At their worst, they knowingly engineer destruction of the very societies they claim to protect. Change came about with the interpretation (and later codification) of native law. The homesteads of tribal groupings were traditionally located in huts belonging to male magnates, wives and families, and arranged around a central cattle enclosure. The head of these enclosures was the senior male by descent; neighbouring homesteads contained clan members and uninhabited land separated different clan groupings. Several of these homesteads together formed a political unit, managed by chiefs who were male heirs in a senior lineage. Yet such a tribe or chiefdom, as Marks points out, was 'a political and territorial rather than purely kinship unit' (Marks, 1970: 28). The role of the chief involved performing judicial, administrative, legislative and quasi-religious duties; and in this he was helped by an *induna* (minister) and by a council of men. The power of the local Zulu chief was subordinate to the King, whose role and duties were similar to those of the local chief writ large. Yet as Marks points out, there were internal checks and balances in the system which prevented wholesale abuse of power; intrigues and hereditary disputes meant that the chief or ruler had to retain the loyalty of a number of political authorities (Marks, 1970: 27–32). Shepstone's knowledge of native culture and the political hierarchy enabled him to use it to his advantage, and

72

initiate a policy of divide and rule. Shepstone recruited dissenting chiefs (who traditionally left the group) to his scheme and deliberately sought a gradual breakdown of the political hierarchy:

> Instances constantly occurred of individuals, families and sections of tribes being dissatisfied with their hereditary chiefs and desiring to have them severed. I observed that these malcontents were not unwilling to be placed under headmen of no hereditary rank, all they cared for was that their new headman should enjoy the confidence of the government. . . . These 'unborn' chiefs being commoners, have no interest in supporting hereditary pretensions; all their importance depends on the government, and although their position is fully acknowledged, they are always looked upon as interlopers by the chiefs of ancient descent and weakeners of their power and influence. It is by the gradual and judicious extension of this system . . . that I think can be found the shortest and safest means of breaking down the power of hereditary chiefs, without losing the machinery as yet indispensable to us, of tribal organisation.
>
> (Marks, 1970: 34)

Destabilisation occurred in other ways. The enactment of native law was meant, by segregation and separation, to protect native society and custom from the white settlers. Yet the very interpretation and introduction of customary law inserted foreign elements within the political system, complicit with the broad aims and effects of colonialism. The historian David Welsh points to a 'distinction . . . between the law enforced in traditional, precolonial African states, and the version of that law recognised by colonial administrations'. Some of the former were either not recognised or were rejected as being 'immoral'; what was seen as tribal law was 'often mis-stated by European administrations, and changes instigated by the administration were grafted on to the body of tribal law' (Welsh, 1971: 5). Witchcraft, witch dances, the festival of first fruits and other rituals which underscored the chief's power in his domain were prohibited or regulated on political as well as moral grounds; in 1849 a proclamation to the chiefs and tribes read:

> it is necessary for [chiefs] to understand that in all things, the Government must be supreme; that smelling out of people

and punishments on account of witchcraft must cease, that no human life must be taken or stealing be practised whether from each other or from people beyond; that assembling in arms must cease, except on the order of the proper Government officer; the dance of the first fruits must not be celebrated by any chief except on special permission; in short that everything affecting life and property and the peace of the country which the chiefs had hitherto done on their own responsibility, must now be done on the authority of the Government appointed over them.

(Welsh, 1971: 21)

Early in 1847, the Locations Commission reported on the 'superstitious and warlike' nature of African life and came to the conclusion that tribes could only be ruled over by a 'strong arm of power' (Kline, 1988: 8). The commission concluded that steps should be taken to replace tribal authority with that of the British government. Shepstone, as Diplomatic Agent, constructed an 'autocratic system' of government that was effectively to place him in sole charge. He proposed that 'each location or mass of natives should be controlled from the seat of government by an officer representing the government to the natives generally' (Kline, 1988: 13). The Diplomatic Agent, standing in for the Lieutenant-Governor, would govern by adopting tribal law where appropriate, appoint chiefs, mediate between the colonial administration and the native tribes, and be able to command the obedience of a native army in an emergency. The Ordinance of 1849 sanctioned Shepstone's authority:

[the] officer hitherto denominated the Diplomatic Agent, acting under the authority and instructions of the Lieutenant Governor, whom the several native chiefs and tribes have hitherto regarded as their supreme chief, and to whom they have voluntarily yielded the same respect and obedience which they have been accustomed to yield to supreme chiefs of their own race.

(Kline, 1988: 14–15)

Thus, based on the Zulu political hierarchy, and on the colonist's concept of 'native despotism', the Governor of Natal became the Supreme Chief and had absolute authority over all the tribes. Yet this conception of 'native despotism', reflected in the 1852–1853

Natal Affairs Commission – 'the point upon which the whole of Kaffir Law hinges on are [*sic*] mutual responsibility and unquestioning obedience to the order of the chief . . . his word is law, his power absolute' (Marks, 1970: 38) – was a deliberate interpretation of events in accordance to colonial fantasies of dominance. The colonial image of absolute rule meant that the checks and balances integral to the functioning of the political hierarchy were taken away. Cetshwayo when questioned by the Cape Commission on Native Laws and Customs in 1883 regarding his powers of office, replied that no law could be abolished unless the whole nation agreed to it; even new appointments had to be ratified by ministers and councillors: 'No, the King has not the power of electing an officer as chief without the approval of other chiefs. They are the most important men. But the smaller chiefs he can elect at his own discretion.' In stark contrast, the Governor as Supreme Chief, and the Diplomatic Agent/Secretary for Native Affairs had all these powers. In the colonial mirror of production, the colonist's vision of native despotism became a mirror of his own political praxis.[2]

TEMPORAL POLITICS

The two important aspects of Natal's segregationist politics and her interpretation of tribal authority that I have emphasised – temporal distancing and the 'appropriation' of native authority – are imaginatively worked over in Haggard's writings. Temporal distancing operates both at the level of form and at the more specific level of content. In chapter one, we have seen that the boy's narrative of adventure in the new world is a version of the pastoral. But this pastoral idyll of the newly discovered world can only be invoked through the production of alterity based on the differential concepts of time. In the nineteenth century, the evolutionary paradigm produced a linearity of time which allowed colonial discourse to construct its geographical map within a gradation of time/development based on Western civilisation. This differential gradation of time and space is necessary to the colonial travel narrative, which reads the journey to Africa as a journey back in time. Temporal distancing is essential to Haggard's travel writing and to his adventure stories because his colonialist's arrival in the new land must be seen to be an arrival in a space without history. Haggard's journey into the up-country districts of Natal in 1876 'was like coming face to face with great primeval Nature, not Nature as we civilised people know her, smiling in corn fields, waving in well-ordered woods, but Nature as she was on the morrow of Creation'. Rather than produce an awareness of difference, travel presumes difference. The traveller through space was then also a traveller through time, and in the political praxis of colonialism, this difference was construed through primitivism. In 'A Zulu War Dance', the reader is invited 'to come to where he can still meet the barbarian face to face and witness that wild ceremony, half jest, half grim earnest' (Haggard, 1882: 282).

At the level of textual content, taking into account the contemporary segregationist politics of temporal distancing yields a reading of *King Solomon's Mines* different from the simple one of a treasure quest. The opening chapters of Haggard's text act as a frame for his narrative of adventure. Speeding past Natal in a steamboat, the hero Quatermain comes across a 'lovely coast all along from East London, with its red sand hills and wide sweeps of vivid green, dotted here and there with Kaffir kraals'. Quatermain remarks almost too casually that the landscape prior to Durban has a 'peculiar richness' which pleases:

> There are the sheer kloofs cut in the hills by the rushing rain of centuries, down which the rivers sparkle; there is the deepest green of the bush, growing as God planted it, and the other greens of the mealie gardens and the sugar patches, while now and again a white house, smiling out at the placid sea, puts a finish and gives an air of homeliness to the scene. For to my mind, however beautiful a view may be, it requires the presence of man to make it complete, but perhaps that is because I have lived so much in the wilderness, and therefore know the value of civilisation, though to be sure it drives away the game.
>
> (Haggard, 1940: 32–33)

Despite the praise of nature, colonial development and settlement are integral to the white man's feeling of security. As the place names suggest, civilisation and 'homes' inhere only with the absence of the African. Only when Quatermain sights a white house is a *man* recognised to be present. All the Kaffir kraals are merely part of the beautiful wilderness, and as such, are only visible as natural wildlife which require the presence of white man to render them human.

Yet the text also acknowledges that the white colonisation of

Southern Africa has not always been productive for its native inhabitants. The text's description of the landscape about Durban is preceded by a description of drunken natives. Furthermore, Quatermain's definition of a 'gentleman' ostensibly cuts across the racial divide:

> What is a gentleman? I don't quite know, and yet I have had to do with niggers – no I will scratch that word 'niggers' . . . I've known natives who *are*, and . . . I have known mean whites with lots of money and fresh out from home, too who *are not*.
>
> (Haggard, 1940: 4)

But the text's strongest critique of colonisation is given to the character of Gagool, the tribes' resident healer, shaman or 'witch-doctor'. While Gagool is a figure of evil and cunning, she is also marked as wise beyond the capabilities of ordinary men by virtue of her skill in divination, and her longevity and accumulation of knowledge across the centuries. Gagool taunts the white men with her memories of past exploitation of Africa from the time of Solomon to the present time. She warns of future subjugation under colonial rule if the Kukuana peoples decide to collaborate with the adventurers: 'I have seen the white man and know his desires. . . . It was a white people who were before ye are, who shall be when ye are not, who shall eat you up and destroy you. *Yea! yea! yea!*' (Haggard, 1940: 159–160). It is Gagool's critique of the treasure seekers which forces a crisis point in the story. For her later parody of the Englishmen's desires reads merely as an amplification of the nightmarish greed which fuels the contemporary diamond rush at Kimberley in the 1870s: 'there are the bright stones ye love, white men, as many as ye will; take them, run them through your fingers, *eat* of them, *hee! hee! drink* of them, *ha! ha!*' Later, Curtis, Quatermain and Good's initial reactions to the discovery of hidden treasure serves to confirm Gagool's divination:

> 'See!' he [Curtis] repeated *hoarsely*, holding the lamp over the open chest. We looked, and for a moment could make nothing out, on account of a silvery sheen which dazzled us. When our eyes grew used to it we saw that the chest was three-parts full of uncut diamonds . . . I fairly gasped as I dropped them. 'We are the richest men in the whole world,' I said. 'Monte Cristo was a fool to us.' 'We shall flood the market

with diamonds,' said Good. 'Got to get them there first,' suggested Sir Henry.

We stood still with pale faces and stared at each other, the lantern in the middle and the glimmering gems below, *as though we were conspirators about to commit a crime*, instead of being, as we thought, the most fortunate men on earth.

(Haggard, 1940: 308) [my emphasis]

Hitherto, the negative effects of colonial development have been countered in Haggard's story by the unfolding good that the Englishmen's effect on those they meet on their journey. But this passage indicates somewhat uneasily that Curtis, Quatermain and Good may not be the saviours of Kukuanaland that they are sometimes made out to be. The revelation of the adventurers' true inclinations forces the issue of exploitation to the surface of the imperial consciousness in a moment of narrative hysteria; but this hysteria is glossed over by the narrator as a moment of temporary insanity. Within *King Solomon's Mines* it is presented as a hiccup in the unravelling story. Avariciousness is here conceived literally as consumption. But the sheer absurdity of eating stones enables Haggard to gloss over the adventurer's greed and its implications:

At that moment there was something so ridiculous to my mind in the idea of eating and drinking diamonds, that I began to laugh outrageously, an example which the others followed, without knowing why. There we stood and shrieked with laughter over the gems that were ours, which had been found for *us* thousands of years ago by the patient delvers in the great hole yonder, and stored for *us* by Solomon's long-dead overseer . . . Solomon never got them, nor David, nor Da Silvestra, nor anybody else. *We* had got them: there before us were millions of pounds' worth of diamonds, and thousands of pounds' worth of gold and ivory only waiting to be taken away. Suddenly the fit passed off, and we stopped laughing. 'Open the other chests, white men,' croaked Gagool, 'there are surely more therein. Take your fill, white lords! Ha! ha! take your fill.'

(Haggard, 1940: 309)

Ironically, Gagool's intuition of the white men's aims can be reclaimed and integrated within a moral account of the treasure quest. The urging of the white men to take their fill of the diamonds when they have little food or hope of escape from the cave may be read as a form of black humour. But the imprisonment of the white men also allows the reclamation of their moral status. For by confronting the possibility of death in the cave, and through the exhibition of great courage and fortitude, Haggard's heroes can emerge from the treasure quest with their moral integrity intact. The incident enables a moral lesson to be learnt; as Quatermain acknowledges, 'truly wealth, which men spend their lives in acquiring, is a valueless thing at last'. The recognition of this moral truth allows Quatermain to have his cake and to eat it. His escape from the caves is achieved without having to give up the diamonds; he can now remark in all innocence, 'I may as well pocket some in case we ever should get out of this ghastly hole . . . I say fellows . . . won't you take some diamonds with you? I've filled my pockets and the basket' (Haggard, 1940: 324). But Gagool's critique accurately mirrors the real effects of the diamond-rush at Kimberley. The discovery and subsequent exploitation of mineral rights accelerated Lord Carnarvon's plan of a Southern African colonial federation of 'client assistants and collaborators' (Schreuder, 1980: 21) that would maintain British strategic, defensive and economic spheres of influence at the Cape. Diamonds were the single most important factor in transforming the sluggish Cape economy into a spectacularly prosperous one; given responsible government in 1872, the Cape became in one historian's words the 'vital Afro-centric agency of white expansion' (Schreuder, 1980: 26).

The diamond boom altered power relations both in the Cape region and in the outlying districts. Harbour, rail and public works, European immigration, the demand for black labour and the assault on African traditionalism produced by constant advance and encroachment, all helped further push the balance of power in favour of the white settler communities. With the combined pressure for labour and land for commercial and agricultural development, Southern Africa was remoulded as exclusively a white man's domain. Yet in the texts on Southern Africa, this state of affairs was represented as its reverse; the white land of Southern Africa was threatened by the savagery of *invading* black numbers. The independence hitherto of the indigenous chieftaincy was seen as a *conspiracy* against natural progress. In the words of the settler politicians, 'the long unsettled condition and warlike desires of the natives have seriously retarded the advancement' of the Cape:

The vast combination known to exist among all the tribes would have caused them to swoop down, first upon the white settlers in the Transvaal, and, extending their operations, mark their inroads by massacre, pillage and general destruction, and thus forcibly thrust back civilization in South Africa for many years, to the great loss of the agriculturalist, the capitalist, the merchant and the distress of the colonist generally.

(Schreuder, 1980: 30)

Such a text reconstructs African history as the natural development of 'the agriculturalist, the capitalist, the merchant' *against* tribal communities whose existence is conceived of as destructive, or at the very least, parasitic. The actions of raiding parties hark back to a classic trope of barbarism, and the listing of single individuals from the settler community as representative types against the 'vast combination' of African tribes highlights the paranoia of the colonist's mentality. From the Langibele rebellion, the Griqualand East revolt, the Gcaleka War, Gaika and Sotho uprising to the Zulu war, 'there was a deep laid plan entered into between all principal chiefs ... against the white man, whose civilising influences and justness' of cause were alienating the native folk from their chiefs. The attempt to destroy traditional groupings was deliberate; for until 'chieftainship is a thing of the past' as the resident of Pondoland remarked, 'our native subjects can never become peace-loving and industrious' (Schreuder, 1980: 69–70). Such a 'reality' generated unbearable tension which sought release in the enactment of the very brutality and destruction imputed to African tribes.

Boer republican ambitions and the Delagoa Bay railway scheme accentuated the need for imperial paramountcy and for the control of vital coastal areas as secure trade routes to India and the Far East (Robinson, Gallagher and Denny, 1981: 51–63). The 1877 annexation of Transvaal was meant to defuse all the threat of Boer expansionism and non-British colonialism. But with the British flag flying over Pretoria, colonial interests ran headlong into collision with the native trusteeship professed by the authorities of (according to Sir Henry Bulwer at the opening of the Legislative Council of Natal in 1875) 'a high mission of truth and civilization'. The year 1877 became 'the last year of political freedom outside the rule of white man' for the traditional African tribes (Schreuder, 1980: 17).

The years between 1877 and 1881 witnessed, in both the wars and peace-settlements which followed, the subjugation of the remaining major African political systems: the Gcaleka-Xhosa attacks in the Cape region (1877); the Griquas and Mpondos uprisings in 1878; the Badepi resistance led by Sekhukhune which begun as early as 1876, and the 1879 Anglo-Zulu War which saw the destruction of the Zulus as an independent military nation. Garnet Wolseley's settlement of Zululand was a strategy of divide and rule and led to bitter civil wars, as Rider Haggard himself records in *Cetywayo*:

> The Zulus were parcelled out among thirteen chiefs, in order that their mutual strength might be kept down by internecine war and mutual distrust and jealousy: and, as though it were intended to render this result more certain, territories were chucked out about in the careless way [*sic*] . . . whilst central authority was abolished, and the vacant throne is dangled before all eyes labelled 'the prize of the strongest'.
>
> (Haggard, 1882: 39)

It comes as no surprise that the character Umbopa/Ignosi's more solemn rebuke at the end of *King Solomon's Mines* re-stages the persistent problem of colonisation and development albeit in a minor key. It echoes the critique mounted by Gagool and exemplified in the treasure cave incident. If Ignosi's offer to share his kingdom reads like an invitation for British colonialism, it is also a plea for the recognition of a shared space and time,

> What have I done to you . . . that you should leave me desolate? Ye who stood by me in rebellion and in battle, will ye leave me in the day of peace and victory? What will ye – wives? . . . A place to live in? Behold, the land is yours as far as ye can see.
>
> (Haggard, 1940: 358)

The chief's invitation is refused by Quatermain who answers, 'we would seek our own place'. Ignosi's bitter accusation that 'ye love the bright stones more than me' rings true in the face of Quatermain's dreams of living like a millionaire: 'Ye have the stones; now ye would go to Natal and across the moving black water and sell them, and be rich, as it is the desire of a white man's heart'

81

(Haggard, 1940: 339). That the white man 'loves not to live on the level of the black or to house among his kraals', argues for the separation of black and white worlds. Such an enforced division, it may be argued, avoids the pitfalls of white colonisation as expressed by the black chief of Kukuanaland:

> No other white man shall cross the mountains, even if any man live to come so far. I will see no traders with their guns and gin. My people shall fight with the spear, and drink water, like their forefathers before them. I will have no praying-men to put a fear of death into men's hearts, to stir them against the law of the king, and make a path for the white folk who follow to run on. If a white man comes to my gates I will send him back; if a hundred come I will push them back; if armies come I will make war on them with all my strength, and they shall not prevail against me. None shall ever seek for the shining stones.
>
> (Haggard, 1940: 340)

The fictional chief's accusation is not far from the comments of the Mpondomise chief, Mhlontlo, on the increased white settlement in African frontiers in 1880:

> We are harshly treated . . . . Faith has been broken with us over and over again. We could however, have put up with all this; but what is coming has led the black races to combine against the white man. Our cattle are to be branded; our arms are to be taken away; and after that our children are to be seized and carried across the sea [as labour apprentices].
>
> (Schreuder, 1980: 64)

In *Allan Quatermain*, the character of the newly crowned king draws up a similar policy of exclusion of foreigners that would help protect Zu-Vendi country from the unwelcome change brought about by speculators and capitalists. The text's earlier praise of Englishmen as 'adventurers to the backbone' with their 'magnificent muster-roll of colonies' are disavowed in Henry Curtis's conservative charter:

> I am convinced of the sacred duty that rests upon me of preserving this, on the whole, upright and generous hearted people the blessings of comparative barbarism. Where would all my brave army be if some enterprising rascal were to attack

us with field-guns and Martini-Henrys . . . I [will not] endow
it with the greed and drunkenness, new diseases, gunpowder,
and general demoralisation which chiefly mark the progress
of civilisation amongst unsophisticated peoples.

(Haggard, 1931: 310–311)

In the contemporary historical world of segregationist politics and
African locations, the 'separation' that Ignosi seems to be advo-
cating only leads to a denial of the effects of the white presence,
not to their diminishing. In a sense, the separate times of Southern
Africa are also a way of textually resolving the problem of guilt and
the repercussions of the diamond discovery. What Haggard creates
in *King Solomon's Mines* and in its sequel, *Allan Quatermain*, is a
mythic 'interior' African space which allows the acquisition of
treasure without also having to explain the contemporary history of
the diamond boom. Both romances begin in a contemporary Africa
which is carefully marked by the references to place-names and the
material culture of the region. The location of Solomon's mines
and Zu-Vendi country in relatively unexplored regions permits an
important gap in the geography of time to be made. By placing the
treasure in the mythical realm of Kukuanaland, or by situating the
kingdom of Zu-Vendi in a time warp which operates within its own
strict parameters, the narrative allows Haggard to mystify the
treasure quest and limit the impact of the white men's discoveries.

But the colonial demarcation of 'native' and 'settler' space and
time which ends *King Solomon's Mines* and *Allan Quatermain* is not
strictly observed even within the bounds of the text. In *King
Solomon's Mines*, the colonial presence may be seen to demand
changes in traditional culture that are comparable with the changes
brought about by the formations of Locations in contemporary
Southern Africa. Like Shepstone's reforming list of prohibitions for
the management of Locations, Henry Curtis demands a promise of
change if ever Umbopa/Ignosi is installed as chief of Kukuanaland.
The two demands that Curtis makes – that of doing away with the
'witch' dances, and that of a fair trial for anyone accused of a crime
– fall under the Locations' definition of 'laws, customs, and usages
. . . abhorrent from and opposed to the general principles of
humanity and decency' (Kline, 1988: 10). Quatermain's parting
words to Ignosi detail once more the promises made as favours to
the white travellers. Ignosi is bound by Quatermain to keep these
promises because of the white men's help in installing him as chief;

as Quatermain reminds him, 'Behold, Ignosi, thou camest with us a servant, and now we leave thee a mighty king'. The proposed changes to Kukuana custom and law mirror the alleged four 'decrees' read out by Shepstone at Cetshwayo's coronation as successor to the deceased Zulu chief in 1873:

1st. That the indiscriminate shedding of blood shall cease in the land.

2nd. That no Zulu shall be condemned without open trial and public examination of witnesses for and against . . .

3rd. That no Zulu's life shall be taken without the previous knowledge and consent of the King, after such trial has taken place . . .

4th. That for minor crimes the loss of property, all, or a portion shall be substitute for the punishment of death. [3]

The carving up of Southern Africa into different temporal zones becomes yet another way of differentiating black from white in a way which denies the viability and existence of the former, while deferring the responsibility for the imposition by the latter. 'Native' history, however, records a deliberate subversion of chieftain authority; as a chief complained to Shepstone:

> in these days, I am no longer their chief, you have put my people over my head, they are greater than I; if any of them do wrong and I attempt to punish them by force or any other means they acknowledge the justice of it, but as it is impossible to please two parties in a case, the losing one runs off to the Magistrate, and I am told that I have no right to punish or to fine, and that I must restore the fine. When you want labourers for the harbour works or the public roads, then I am chief, then I have people . . . . You pay me nothing and you allow me to get nothing from my people, one day you object to my ruling and then again you threaten to punish me if I do not make my power felt by the people enough to make them go to work.

(Welsh, 1971: 124)

NATIVE AUTHORITY

On reading *Nada the Lily*, Andrew Lang commented in a letter to his friend Haggard, 'I like "Eric" [Brighteyes] better, but this is perhaps more singular. How any white man can have such a natural gift of savagery, I don't know. The wolves are astonishing.' Charles Longman, his publisher, on May 14, 1890 wrote:

> 'Nada' strikes me with wonder and awe. It is in some ways the greatest feat you have performed: I mean because you have constructed a story in which the dramatis personae are all savages and yet you have kept the interest going throughout. . . . I never read such a book. It is frightful, and the only justification for it is the fact that it is history, not the imagination. . . . The wolves are delightful; I wish you could have given us more of them. I was very glad to meet our old friend Umpslopogaas as a boy.
>
> (Haggard, 1926: 17, 19)

The book was first serialised in the *Illustrated London News* from January to May, 1892, and published soon after by Longman Green. *Nada the Lily* presents most clearly a vision of savagery, and a mythopoetics of masculinity. Lang begins with his admiration for Haggard's unique ability as a white man to evoke the savage world of the Zulus. In the craft and performance of story-telling, Haggard is described as possessing the singular *natural* gift of savagery. Longman's praise is written along very similar lines. Haggard's construction of this savage tale inspires both wonder and awe; its frightful content is justifiable because of 'the fact that it is history not the imagination'.

It should be clear by now that this stitching together of history and the imagination, fact and fiction, black and white turns on narration. In Haggard's African fiction, the 'natural' artifice of story-telling attempts to reappropriate the mythic space ascribed to the very civilisation imputed as savage. *Nada the Lily* is a fantasy of Zulu life under their legendary king, Shaka. It aims to chronicle, with poetic licence, the epic of Zulu history before the coming of white men through a number of characters: Chaka, Mopo (his shaman/witch doctor), Umpslopogaas (Mopo's adopted son and Chaka's real one), Nada (daughter to Mopo and Umpslopogaas' second wife), Zinita (his first wife) and Galazi (Umpslopogaas' wolf-brother). The tale is narrated by Mopo to a white man and follows the events leading to Shaka's assassination, and the political intrigues surrounding the Zulu throne and the chieftaincy of the People of the Axe.

Haggard's colonial fabula resurrects the mythic dimensions of the story-teller by framing his novel as if it were a story told by one character to another. The story of Zulu history is told by a Zulu witch doctor to a white hunter. But the Zulu witch doctor dies at the end of his tale and therefore is not present at the start of the story narrated by the white hunter. Haggard's novel is predicated on figures who gain authority and stature through metonymic association with other 'absent' figures. For not only does the hunter gain his authority from the now dead Zulu shaman/witch doctor, Haggard's preface invokes both Zulu border agents and ex-colonial officials as sources for his imaginative reworking of Zulu history. Furthermore, Haggard begins *Nada* with a dedication to his former chief, Sir Theophilus Shepstone. Addressing him in the style of Zulu rituals of praise, and using his native name 'Sompseu', Haggard attempts to suture British and Zulu customs. Shepstone becomes part of the Zulu inheritance and mythology through his reincarnation as Shaka: 'their nobles did you homage, and they gave you the Bayete, the royal salute, declaring by the mouth of their Council that in you dwelt the spirit of Chaka'.

The actual ceremony which invested Shepstone with the spirit of Shaka is one which results from a famous incident at Mpande's royal kraal at Nodwengu and is the subject of quite different accounts. The laudatory account immortalised in the dedication to *Nada* is not borne out by other accounts, including those written by people who were sympathetic to the Secretary for Native Affairs.[4] Shepstone's journey to the royal house to proclaim Cetshwayo's inheritance before the death of the incumbent king was undertaken to prevent the Boers from securing cooperation and territory from the Zulu nation (Etherington, 1981: 45). While Cetshwayo did not specifically request Shepstone's presence, he did accept the visit as part of his own political manoeuvring to settle the problem of succession, and to demand the return of Mpande's other son, Mkungu. But as Donald Morris points out, Cetshwayo's ministers regarded Shepstone's proposal as an intrusion into domestic affairs; he did not possess any power to confer the rights of inheritance onto the heir-apparent (Morris, 1969: 203). Furthermore, one of Shepstone's party had upset the Zulus by wandering through the royal kraal and going to see the sisters of Mkungu; the visit to the sisters was read as 'political' and put the whole British party in a dangerous position.

The situation was finally resolved by investing Shepstone with the spirit of Shaka and by Shepstone's own force of persuasion. In

Haggard's account, Shepstone's presence of mind averted cata-
strophe through what was seen as a maverick trick of speech and
theatre. Haggard's retelling of the story of Shepstone's encounter
with the Zulus is by no means due entirely to his personal desire
to embellish the colonial tale of bravery, but is also regurgitated
in other accounts of imperial myth-making. It enters Haggard's
fictional writing as a prophetic moment in history. Haggard
recording the bluff of Shepstone's bravado which out-did the
natives, also records a white man who is more than equal to native
power:

> he was surrounded by a mob of shouting savages, whose
> evident objective was to put an end to him and those with him.
> For two hours he remained sitting there . . . but not showing
> the slightest emotion, till at length he got an opportunity of
> speaking, when he rose and said, 'I know that you mean to
> kill me; it is an easy thing to do; but I tell you Zulus, that for
> every drop of my blood that falls to the ground, a hundred
> men will come out of the sea yonder . . . and bitterly avenge
> me.' As he spoke he turned and pointed towards the
> ocean, and so intense was the excitement that animated it,
> that the whole great multitude turned with him and stared
> towards the horizon, as though they expected to see the long
> lines of avengers creeping across the plains.
>
> (Haggard, 1933: 7–8)

Shepstone's 'imperturbability and well-timed address' had not only
saved the party but, Haggard adds, made his name a power in the
land. The ceremony conferring the spirit of the great Zulu king on
the white man is constructed as a legitimation of his mastery of the
natives. It was read both as an enhancement of his personal status
and a manifestation of power inherent in the position of Secretary
of Native Affairs. This latter reconstruction of customary law as
native despotism, only serves to sanction the fantasy of absolute
colonial power. Thus Haggard records of the so-called coronation
of Cetshwayo,

> Who was so fit to proclaim the successor to the throne as the
> great predecessor of the prince proclaimed? To us this seems
> a strange, not to say ludicrous, way of settling a difficulty, but
> there was nothing in it repugnant to Zulu ideas. Odd as it was,
> it invested Mr Shepstone with all the attributes of a Zulu king,

such as the power to make laws, order executions, &c., and those attributes in the eyes of the Zulu he still retains.

(Haggard, 1933: 9)

The alleged Zulu mythology that surrounds Shepstone's status confers on him the role of patriarch, law-giver and life-provider; the English text naturalises Shepstone's power. In the name of the Father, and with the august authority of an Old Testament king, Shepstone may now claim to have mastered a whole tribe of warriors. In 1878, the *London Quarterly Review* recounts the effects of the scene of the morning after the night of Shepstone's performance:

> Next morning Cetywayo humbly begged an interview, which was not granted but on terms of unqualified submission. From that day Cetywayo submitted to British control in the measure in which it has been exercised, and has been profuse in his expressions of respect and submission to Sir T. Shepstone.
>
> (Haggard, 1933: 8)

But there are conflicting accounts of Shepstone's meeting with Cetshwayo; Bishop Colenso refers to the MacKenzie sisters' alternative version of events. In MacKenzie's account of the incident, it was the Zulus' demand for the return of Mkungu that prompted Shepstone's reference to Queen Victoria and her powerful army. Shepstone had refused to return Mpande's young son, arguing that he would be in danger of his life. His refusal, framed within a speech about British imperial power, is much less dramatic:

> But we care nothing about your assegais. We could make an end of you if we pleased, but we have no wish to do so. You must not think of Natal only. We are the subjects of the Queen of England who lives far away in that direction, and if we could ourselves consent to such a disgraceful thing as giving him up, we should have to answer for it at home. The Queen would send [*sic*] and blow us to pieces. We are nothing but a cattlefeeding kraal to the great nation to which we belong . . . at home they care nothing for you and your assegais, or for us either, only they care about this, not to do a dishonourable thing.[5]

Shepstone's speech as MacKenzie tells it is a more diplomatic and less heroic account of personal importance than Haggard's. In MacKenzie's account, Shepstone's importance lies in his capacity as a functionary in her imperial majesty's colonial administration.

She emphasises Shepstone's good sense rather than his personal heroism. MacKenzie commends his firm refusal to let his servant enter into the verbal fray as an act which forestalled bloodshed: 'Mr Shepstone saw if he allowed Ngoza to speak, some of these wild young fellows would insult him, and then his blood would be up, and that of his friends, and in the row, mischief was sure to be done.' The historian and critic Norman Etherington dismisses Shepstone's claims to have been officially hailed with a royal salute proper to one who inhabited Shaka's persona as 'mostly nonsense' (Etherington, 1981: 19). The royal salute is important because it was later given as the reason for Shepstone's invitation back to Cetshwayo's coronation on Mpande's death. In Shepstone's report to the British Parliament, he presents himself as above contemporary sources of Zulu authority:

> In theory the Zulu knew nothing of Cetywayo, except that he was *the* child. It had been arranged that I should . . . take possession of him, and present him to the assembled nation, and then proceed to install him as King. . . . I came as Chaka. . . . I was commissioned by the Zulus and by the Government that was superior to the Zulus, and I had my own special rank besides; no one could contest that right with me, and no one ventured to contest it.[6]

Present historians take a dim view of Shepstone's authoritarian persona. Schreuder remarks of Shepstone's strategic manoeuvres in South Africa, 'he saw himself on a large scale, standing well above the various contending elements within the framework of local empire and the plural communities of Southern Africa' (Schreuder, 1980: 45). Guy remarked that after thirty years of 'personal' and 'authoritarian rule in Natal', Shepstone believed that his influence over Africans was not based on his office of state but on his 'status as the representative of a superior civilisation together with his insight into the native mind' (Guy, 1979: 46). Guy records an incident where Shepstone, furious not to be addressed by what he saw as his proper title is supposed to have said, 'who is calling me by my name and not addressing me as "Inkosi" (Chief, King)?'. Accused by the Zulus of siding with the Boers after being made Administrator of the annexed Transvaal, and angry at their questioning of his honesty and integrity, Shepstone's attitudes towards the Zulus deteriorated (Guy, 1979: 47). Shepstone was instrumental in propagating the idea of the Zulus as a 'military organisation' and Cetshwayo as a 'despot'.

In Haggard's depiction of Shepstone as 'master . . . over this peoples of the Zulus' through his sheer force of will and story-telling, the seams between a white mythology and a black history are hidden. Yet if Shepstone's paternalist authority may be seen in his segregationist policies and his enactment of native law in Natal it is also included in his planned liberation of Zululand from its 'arbitrary and barbarous' government. Haggard's mastery of Zulu life and representation parallels Shepstone's bid for colonial authority. As the colonial author of the text, Haggard presumes to 'think with the mind, and speak with the voice of a Zulu of the old regime'; the appropriation of the mythic space of this 'wild tale of savage life', achieved through the convention of the confessional tale told by the black witch doctor on his death bed, [7] is presented as an act (merely) of translation. Where the continuity between the white mythology and black history is achieved, Haggard's task of narrating Zulu history becomes not merely an anthropological task of cultural translation and interpretation but of transparency and appropriation: 'the author's aim, moreover, has been to convey in narrative form, some idea of the remarkable spirit which animated these kings and their subjects, and to make accessible, in popular shape, incidents of African history' (Haggard, 1933: 12). As Eric Cheyfitz writes of Fenimore Cooper's *Pioneers*, the 'activity of colonization as translation' is 'precisely not to understand the other that is the original inhabitants . . . [but is] to understand that other all too easily, that is, as if there were no question of translation'; such an act marks the point 'where the other becomes usable fiction' (Clark, 1985: 74).

THE BODY POLITIC: THE GLAMOUR AND TRAGEDY OF THE ANGLO-ZULU WAR

I want now briefly to address the reporting of the Zulu war in two popular metropolitan family weeklies, the *Graphic* and the *Illustrated London News*, as a frame for Haggard's romanticisation of warfare and his retelling of native history in *Nada the Lily*. These weeklies are important because their engravings and news reports represent the nineteenth-century version of news footage of the war. Their visual and textual accounts of the Anglo-Zulu War provided a mirror for British individual and national heroism and the specular image of warfare in which Haggard's texts find their inspiration.

The Zulu War was started amidst paranoia about a black conspiracy in Southern Africa; as Schreuder remarks, the Zulu state 'stood as the symbol of African independency and challenge'. Described by Sir Bartle Frere (who was influenced by Shepstone) as a 'man-slaying human military machine', it needed to be destroyed before the plan of confederation could be effected. Ironically, in the aftermath of the war, it was also held up to be the sort of model disciplined army which the British military establishment desired to be. The war started on January 11, 1879. The *Graphic* begins its recording of the war on February 1, with ambivalent feelings towards the Zulu ruler. They describe Cetshwayo as a 'military despot, who has been for years training his Zulu warriors for the express purpose of trying conclusions with the English'. The paper also stresses the costly burden to tax-payers of far afield colonial wars and admits that the Zulu king's grievances are not totally unfounded. After February 15, following news of the battle at Rourke's Drift and the defeat of Chelmsford at Isandhlwana, the *Graphic* takes matters more seriously and ventures information on Zulu militarism:

> The Zulu may be savages, but they are not as savages usually are – a loose congregation of isolated bands provided with miserable weapons; these men possess enough of the civilised instinct to submit to a stern military despotism, they are, after a primitive fashion, well-drilled and (as our loss has proved) well led, and, thanks to the unpatriotic enterprise of the white traders, they are excellently armed.
>
> (Feb 15, *Graphic*)

This war, the weekly paper is not afraid of admitting, provides thousands with 'a pleasurable excitement' from war reports and illustrations. Its editorial declares 'in spite of that thin film of civilisation with which we are coated, we are still fighting animals, and where we cannot ourselves fight, we like to fight by proxy and so we stare with all our eyes at soldiers "bound" on active service' (Feb 22). In the same issue, the *Graphic* carries a special illustrated supplement on Zululand, and provides ethnographic detail on the culture and lives of its peoples.

February 22 of the *Illustrated London News* carries a full-page picture of the naked half-body of the Zulu king on its front cover (Figure 5). The paper uses Cetshwayo's body to make concrete the description, circulating at home and abroad, of the Zulu king as a 'black Napoleon'. Drawn for English audiences, it locates in

Figure 5 'The Zulu War in South Africa: Cetewayo, the Zulu King', *Illustrated London News*, Feb 22, 1879.

Cetshwayo's body all the power and savagery of the black beast. The Zulu nation is described as 'not, indeed, a very large kingdom, but its absolute despotic constitution and singular military organisation' which renders to its peoples 'an innate love of fighting'. The *Illustrated London News* includes remarks from Captain Lucas' new book on Zululand – 'he speaks most favourably of the Zulus as a race; describing them as the finest of all the Kaffir nations, tall of stature, good-looking and rather "European in feature", sober and temperate, cleanly and decent' – and concludes that while this despotic nation ought to be destroyed and 'their tyrant deposed', it would be unworthy of 'English manliness' to practise 'indiscriminate slaughter of that brave peoples in the way of "revenge"'.

With images of the noble savage in mind, the Zulu methods of fighting, which were useless against the superior firepower of the British, came in for much praise in the aftermath of the war. Their charging armies (impis) made spectacular pictures (Figure 6) which again located valour not only as belonging to singular individuals but also as belonging to the national/collective body. Zulu (male) courage exhibited in this form of battle became a stereotype against which other African cultures were measured:

> The remarkable valour, and also the semi-discipline of the Zulu troops, have tended in some respects to shorten the war. If the Zulus had resembled most of the other South African tribes, they would have kept in the bush, and rarely showed themselves in the open. In this way they would have avoided the terrible slaughter which has on several occasions been inflicted on them by a superiority of armament when brought to close quarters. Instead of this, the valiant savages, with the most utter disregard of their personal safety, boldly charge solid squares of British troops armed with weapons of precision.
>
> (Aug 2, *Graphic*)

Garnet Wolseley held up the Zulu army as a model of excellence as part of the political rights's attempts to seize British identity from what they saw as liberal emasculation and effeminacy. His remarks show how compelling the fantasy of masculine heroism imputed to the Zulu nation becomes. Wolseley reminds his readers to beware lest the loss of the 'craving for constant practice and employment [of muscular activity] in [British] blood' results in a similar fall from grace:

> the difference ... between the Zulu and several of his neighbours in South-eastern Africa [is]. . . cowardice. Over-cultivation [kills] all virile energy, and when that dies, not only the greatness of the nation but its independent existence are buried in the same grave.
>
> (Wolseley, 1888: 692)

93

Figure 6 'An Attack of Zulu Warriors', *Graphic*, May 3, 1879.

Figure 7 'The Zulu War: Embarkation of the 91st Highlanders at Southampton', *Illustrated London News*, March 1, 1879.

That the Zulu military strategy would have been suicidal for the
British troops to emulate did not register in these portrayals of
heroism; they became necessary to the glamour and the tragedy of
war. But as Bishop Colenso was tirelessly to argue, the Zulus were
an *armed* people, not a standing army. Guy's account of the Anglo-

Zulu war confirms this. He asserts that the Zulu 'mobilization of the able bodied males' did have disruptive effects on the society: 'with men on active service, the Zulu women and children, together with vulnerable herds of cattle, were in danger from British troops, and even from sections of the Zulu army as well, if they were traversing the area' (Guy, 1971: 503). A 'standing army', in contrast, is able to operate without 'seriously affecting the continuity of the essential functions in the society to which it belongs'. But Guy's historical critique, while absolutely correct, also misses the point; the issue here is not one of knowledge but of desire. Conventional accounts of the Anglo-Zulu war focus on the 'pitched battles' of Isandlwana, Rourke's Drift, the defeat of the Zulus at Kambula and Ulundi. As Guy himself observes, these stories 'together with accounts of the disciplined Zulu regiments, armed primarily with shields and assegais, charging into the ranked volley-firing of the British coats' (Guy, 1971: 563) not only excited the British imagination at the time, but created the spectacle of the Zulu war machine. The image of the Zulu peoples was invested with the unconscious desire of colonial subjectivity; the nation's demise assuaged anxiety about Britain's declining status among the nations of the world, and spawned a whole series of illustrations. The image of the individual Zulu warrior doing battle with the British soldier became an iconic dream of masculinity and heroism. The pathos of soldiers killed in the war as illustrated in both the *Graphic* and the *Illustrated London News* is integral to the cultural and epic theatre of war. Soldiers leaving home present an exciting and colourful spectacle which links the familial domesticity of the metropolitan culture with the might of a larger nation (Figure 7). They remain part of an imperial fantasy of power in black and white.

Haggard's representations of Zulu battles in *Nada the Lily, King Solomon's Mines* and to a lesser extent *Allan Quatermain*, draw on and rework codes of masculinity and warfare centred on the self-contained world of men, and the glamour, grandeur and theatre of battle. The muscular contortions of the pictures (Figure 8), drawn by Richard Woodville (a well-known illustrator of imperial warefare) for Haggard's serialisation of the novel, offer the spectacle of masculinity as power and as narrative.[8] This is extended to epic proportions by Haggard's 'The Last Stand of the Greys' in *King Solomon's Mines*. Martin Green argues that Haggard's 'most impressive passages are those describing battle, or meditating on it. Their stychomythic dialogues and ritual and rhythmic formulas are not

Figure 8 'Umslopogaas smote as he rushed, and the great blade of the great spear that was lifted to pierce him fell to the ground hewn from its haft', *Illustrated London News*, Feb. 27, 1892.

original, but they have power' (Green, 1980: 232). This is evident in the Zulu past under Shakan rule in *Nada the Lily*:

Ah! the battle! – the battle! In those days we knew how to fight, my father! In those days the vultures would follow our impis by thousands . . . and none went away empty. . . . All night our fires shone out across the valley; all night the songs echoed down the hills. Then the grey dawning came . . . the regiments arose from their bed of spears – yes! they arose! the glad to die! the impi assumed its array regiment by regiment. . . . The morning breeze came up and fanned them, their plumes bent in the breeze; like a plain of seedling grass they bent, the plumes of the soldiers ripe for the assegai. . . . They knew it; they saw the omen of death, and, ah! they laughed in the joy of the waking of battle. What was death? Was it not well to die on the spear . . . . Was it not well to die for the king? Death was the arms of victory. Victory should be their bride that night, and oh! her breast is fair.

(Haggard, 1933: 52–53)

Green calls this emphasis on the pride and glory of regimental training and organisation, a 'lyrical or threnodic militarism'. Yet what remains occluded in Green's commentary is the sexual politics of warfare.

To return to Haggard's passage, what is apparent in the glorification of battle is the spectacle of supreme male power and bonding in death. The victory that is imaged as 'bride' to these warriors is death. The very act of battle is sexualized; the battleground is, in effect, a metaphor for the marriage bed. The laughter that the warriors fling in the face of violence and certain doom becomes, perversely, a sign of their power and their orgastic ecstasy. Such orgastic killing is punctuated by the Zulu war song, 'the music of which has power to drive men mad':

> We the king's kine, bred to be butchered,
> You, too are one of us!
> We are the Zulu, children of the Lion,
> What! did you tremble?
>
> (Haggard, 1933: 53)

The slaughter was truly awful . . . and from among the shouts of warriors and the groans of the dying, set to the music of clashing spears, came a continuous hissing undertone of 'S'gee, s'gee', the note of triumph of each victor as he passed his assegai through and through the body of his fallen foe.

(Haggard, 1940: 244)

Haggard's battle scenes produce a seductive image of war and death; they attempt to give expression to a fantasy of ultimate masculine and authoritarian power. The text takes an unsettling pleasure in the subordination of civil life to military ends and in the spectacle of the native army's response to command, as *one total male body*:

I looked down the long lines of waving black plumes and stern faces beneath them. . . . Never before had I seen such an absolute devotion to the idea of duty, and such a complete indifference to its bitter fruits. . . . 'Behold your King!' . . . there was a moment's pause, then suddenly a murmur arose from the serried phalanxes before us, a sound like the distant whisper of the sea, caused by the gentle tapping of the handles of six thousand spears against their holders' shields. Slowly it swelled, till its growing volume deepened and widened into a roar of rolling noise, that echoed like the thunder against the mountains, filled the air with heavy waves of sound. Then it decreased, and by faint degrees died away into nothing, and suddenly out crashed the royal salute.

(Haggard, 1940: 238–240)

In a piece published in *Macmillan's Magazine*, 'A Zulu War-dance' he writes of another thrilling moment when the chief is hailed: 'The next moment five hundred shields are tossed aloft, five hundred spears flash in the sunshine, and with a sudden roar, forth springs the royal salute, "Bayete".' Shaka's order (Figure 9) to the disciplined, glistening and erect bodies of the Zulu warriors 'there is the foe. Go and return no more!', prompts instant obedience: 'We hear you, father! they answered with one voice, and moved down the slope like countless herd of game with horns of steel.' This is a grand illusion of power; bio-power becomes a fantasy where representations of body as state are inscribed. The figure of Lord Chelmsford receiving a salute from the native army in the *Illustrated London News* positions him at the head of the native army (Figure 10). Shepstone's roles as Diplomatic Agent and Secretary for Native Affairs, in principle, place him in the position of absolute authority over all the tribes. 'Native despotism' is invested with colonial fantasies of dominance.

In the pulsing rhythms of the battle ground in *Nada the Lily*, the Zulus are made to seem as if they have a pre-colonial tradition of military victory, and do not accept failure in the battleground. Deaths inflicted by the British army can be read as part of the Zulu way of things (Figure 11). In the portrayal of the Zulus as cattle, 'bred to be butchered', the guilt of British expropriation of territory is assuaged. Haggard's metaphor had visual precedence in the 1879 *Illustrated London News*' image of Zulus crossing a river as part of a fatal charge (Figure 12). Guilt is also displaced in

Figure 9 'Then again Chaka speaks: "Charge! Children of the Zulu!"',
Illustrated London News, Jan. 16, 1892; serialisation of *Nada the Lily.*

Nada by narrating the break-up of the Zulu nation as if it were
the natural consequence of internal politics and familial feuds. The
colonial fabula stitches together white mythology and black history;
but this act of dispossession mirrors the dispossession of colonialism and the ease with which it colonises the space of African
significations with its own fantasies.[9]

Figure 10 'The Zulu War: General Lord Chelmsford reviewing the native contingent on the banks of the Tugela', *Illustrated London News*, May 10, 1879.

Figure 11 'The Zulu War: The Gallant Defence of Rorke's Drift by Lieutenants Chard and Bromhead and one hundred and thirty-seven men', *Graphic*, March 15, 1879.

Figure 12 'The Zulu War: Zulus Crossing a River', *Illustrated London News*, April 12, 1879.

TRANSITIONS

The occupation of India was unlike that of Africa because it was enacted on a society and state which had 'recognisable' and 'significant' cultural, political, imperial and military traditions of its own. The reinterpretation of Mughal customs and authority reflected a grafting of alien experience onto the Indian tradition. British trade in India ensured a certain familiarity with the Mughal empire even before her rule over the sub-continent; the development, evolution and domination of India was made easier by the exploitation of previous knowledge of native government. While the nineteenth century saw a gradual cognizance of the Zulu, not simply as a 'Kaffir' race but as a distinct political and social group, Zulu culture and history did not figure prominently in popular or scholarly work until the middle of the nineteenth century. The Anglo-Zulu war changed this; the war resulted in a flood of literature not only detailing the war effort but also also ethnographic and historical accounts of Zululand.[1] Thereafter, the name 'Zulu' entered the popular European imagination and was 'widely identified with an idea of African savagery, bravery and a barbarous nobility' (Guy, 1979: xx). Haggard's novels did much to popularise this romanticised account of the Zulu noble savage for an established readership interested in romance and adventure fiction. His work provides readers at home with a narcissistic and symmetrical fantasmatic reflection of empowered manhood, detailing a clean, taut, heroic and militarised masculinity in an African land 'whereof none know the history'.

In contrast, India was the object of long and sustained British scholarship dating back at least to William Hastings' governorship in the eighteenth century. The East India Company's history of rule has traditonally been divided into an 'Orientalist' and

'Anglicist' phase. During his 'Orientalist' phase of government, Hastings promoted knowledge of Indian languages, law, culture and tradition as a strategy for more effective government, arguing that 'every accumulation of knowledge, and especially such as is obtained by social communication with people over whom we exercise a dominion founded on the right of conquest, is useful to the state'. As Svati Joshi argues, the British drive towards a knowledge of India 'was impelled by the mercantile political economy which required knowledge, negotiation and partial preservation of the intricate, often baffling indigenous systems of landed property' (Joshi, 1991: 14). But scholarship and archives independent of immediate colonial utility also flourished and Orientalists such as William Jones and Charles Wilkins sought to introduce the West to the literary treasures of the East and to 'reintroduce the natives to their own cultural heritage' (Joshi, 1991: 14–15; Viswanathan, 1990: 28). The Anglicist phase instituted by Lord Cornwallis, who succeeded Hastings, represented a reaction to the policy of promoting 'native' learning. Cornwallis sought to evolve a method of government which rested on what was seen as the strengths of constitutional, rather than personal, authority and for this he turned to English principles of government and jurisprudence (Viswanathan, 1990: 29–31). Utilitarian and evangelical movements in England added momentum to the movement to reform and reconstruct Indian society. The abolition of the Company's monopoly in 1813, the opening of India to missionary activity and the agitation for specific reforms in Hindu custom did much to further Anglicist goals in the first decades of the nineteenth century (Wolpert, 1965: 90–91). But while the Anglicist phase is commonly held to have triumphed by the 1830s, the clash between tradition and reform was far from over when company rule passed into British rule. The Queen's proclamation of 1858, as Bernard Cohn notes, contained not only modernist–reformist but also traditional–feudal vindications of British rule (Hobsbawm and Ranger, 1983: 165–167).

Cohn points out that the location of Britain's 'position as a national power *within* the Indian state system of the eighteenth-century' was derived from 'their appointment as Diwan (chief civil officer) in Bengal' in 1765 and their installation as 'protectors' of the Mughal throne after the capture of Delhi (Hobsbawm and Ranger, 1983: 170). The 1858 proclamation did not dispense with the feudal structures of power. It relocated the hereditary rights of the Indian princes in the British Queen (Hobsbawm and Ranger, 1983: 168–169). The proclamation pledged to respect 'the rights, dignity and honour of native Princes' and to honour 'the feelings of attachment with which the natives of India regard the lands inherited by them from their ancestors'. It also promised 'to protect them in all rights' and to pay 'due regard' 'in framing and administering the law . . . to the ancient rights, usages and customs of India' (Phillips, Singh and Pandey, 1962: 10–11). This deliberate decision to maintain the indigenous status quo was not neutral; it was seen as an important strategy for dividing opposition to British rule in India. The Mutiny, after all, had taken the form of an effort by rebels to restore the old feudal rule. The proclamation was, in part, a calculated policy of goodwill towards the upper classes of India – the rajahs, the zamindars and the Indian officials – in order to minimise their opposition (Gopal, 1965: 7). As Lord Canning, the first Viceroy of India put it, 'Saxon domination' required the cooperation of sections of the Indian public in order to ensure its uninterrupted rule. Challenges posed by other imperial European nations would also be limited by ties of loyalty:

> I believe there is but one way of meeting this danger, and that is to bring the influential classes – the native states first and afterwards our own chief subjects – into that condition and temper in which, when the moment comes, we may as completely as possible throw the reins on their necks and entrust to them the keeping of internal peace and order.
>
> (Gopal, 1965: 11)

Loyal Princes who kept the peace would be rewarded in a durbar, by the confirmation of titles, ranks and additional decorations. Disloyal Princes were threatened with deposition or even annexation (Gopal, 1965: 113–114). Various Viceroys implemented this policy to a greater or lesser extent, reflecting their own political persuasion. Lord Dufferin, in Kipling's time, began his term of office believing in a policy of placating native Princes (with a few exceptions) and establishing personal contact (Gopal, 1965: 156). If in the later period of his term of office Dufferin showed a more conciliatory atitude to the National Congress (whom he called 'a microscopic minority'), his early Viceroyalty exhibited what Gopal has termed 'the mind of a landlord' (Gopal, 1965: 162). Dufferin's opposition to the Bengal Tenancy Bill, drafted to protect the raiyats against ruthless zamindars, resulted in heavy concessions for the latter. Peasant uprisings subsequent to this ruling would have the not unwelcome effect of bringing landed interest closer to the government.

British administration and rule during most of the nineteenth century produced an ambiguous relationship with Indian customs and traditions, through active manipulation of India's historical past and traditions. The durbars Lord Canning undertook in his tours of North India after the proclamation, for example, were appropriated from the court rituals of the Mughal Empire and 'adapted ... with English officials acting as Indian rulers' (Hobsbawm and Ranger, 1983: 168). The need to exploit an alliance with native rulers contributed to a recognition of the legitimacy of their rule and their traditions. The feudal character of the Mughal Empire also made India more accessible to British rulers from aristocratic or upper class backgrounds. The British legitimation and codification of India's cultural heritage which started during the Company period continued well after it had ceased. Cohn argues that the archaeological survey of great monuments in India in the 1860s was part of a concerted expansion of European scholarship on India which matched political dominance with cultural control. 'Census operations' and the 'establishment of an ethnographic survey' were part of a systematic and scientific codification of India's 'cultures and peoples' in the 'laboratory of mankind' (Hobsbawm and Ranger, 1983: 183). Indian arts and crafts were collected, studied, exhibited and preserved in museums and art schools such as Lockwood Kipling's Mayo School, which taught and interpreted Punjabi arts and crafts to native craftsmen. What they in fact attempted was a definition of Indian-ness from an official and 'objective' sense; they presented, in Cohn's words, a 'reified and objectified vision of India['s] ... life, thought, sociology and history' which celebrated the 'completion of the political constitution of India' through the establishment of British India (Hobsbawm and Ranger, 1983: 183).

The Charter Act of 1833 paved the way for unrestricted migration, and the cessation of Company rule opened up greater career opportunities in administration, trade, the military and the railways. But despite a long history of government, unlike that of the Dominions or the Cape colonies, India was never the focus of a settlement policy that sought to produce a civil society modelled on British lines. The survival of the colonial government depended on a steady supply of British people willing to live and work in India but immigration and settlement were discouraged during the Raj. India was never 'home'. Children were sent back to England for their education; and when colonial administrators and civil servants retired, they also returned home. The small community of Anglo-Indians kept its connection to the mother country through its ritual gatherings at Simla and the Club; newspapers like the *Pioneer* and the *Civil and Military Gazette* were filled not only with government reports, local and national news from within India but also with news from Europe and England. Accounts of fashion, leisure and cultural activities from Europe contributed to a sense of living in exile: Pinney observes that 'those who were there did not look upon the country as home but as a place of labour in exile' (Pinney, 1986: 2) while Michael Edwardes records that the 'word "Home" . . . always meant England; nobody calls India home – not even those who . . . are never likely to return to Europe' (Edwardes, 1969: 42).

Benedict Anderson makes the observation that print technology is essential to the representation of a 'kind of imagined community that is the nation'. He argues that the predominantly realist mode of narration that developed in novels and newspapers is integral to the development of an imagined sociological solidity which is taken as the community of the nation. The realist mode relies on a presentation of 'homogeneous empty' calendrical time which allows characters to coexist simultaneously with other characters within a bounded space of the novel's created world; solitary reading experience can be made to signify a communality because one could imagine that others were also reading at the same time. Newspapers bind a community together in their 'presentation of simultaneity' because while a reader 'will never meet, or even know the names of more than a handful of his 240,000,000-odd [fellow citizens] . . . he has complete confidence in their steady, anonymous, simultaneous activity' (Anderson, 1983: 30–31). But if newspapers create an imaginary community in Anglo-India, that community is predicated on alienation and estrangement; Anglo-Indian newspapers fostered a dual sense of unity and exile that was crucial to the formation of a cultural ambivalence towards both India and Britain.[2] Anthony King describes Anglo-Indian society as a culture permeated by a fundamental 'dualistic orientation' (King, 1976: 74).

Bart Moore-Gilbert's assertion that the Anglo-Indian community were not simply the British abroad is also well worth remembering. While close political and cultural links were sustained with the metropolitan centre, there also existed a distinct corporate identity which separated Anglo-Indians from their contemporaries at home (Moore-Gilbert, 1986: 6–7). In post-Mutiny British India for example, the conviction that the metropolitan community neither perceived nor understood the pressures and vulnerabilities of Anglo-Indian life contributed to tensions between the centre and the periphery. In particular, the extremely vocal and hostile reception which greeted Lord Ripon's liberal programme stemmed from the view that political directives from Britain sometimes put Anglo-Indian communities at risk. The language and experience of long service in India was also felt to have set them apart from fellow Englishmen and women at home not only in their own eyes but in the eyes of their compatriots at home (Moore-Gilbert, 1986: 6). From the 1830s, the Anglo-Indian literary market grew with the increased distribution and production of newspapers, reviews, books and journals to form what Moore-Gilbert calls 'the development of a local, autonomous culture' (Moore-Gilbert, 1986: 5–9). Yet while there was neither integration nor settlement in India on a significant scale, there was – to appropriate Francis Hutchins' phrase – an 'illusion of permanence'. The creation of the civil society which followed the conversion of trading and commercial aspirations into administrative and territorial rights is marked by an uncertainty towards colonial subjectivity and state power. This shows up in what James Manor has called the 'split personality of the raj' which finds itself caught between its own discourse of liberalism and the civilising mission, and its 'concern with the maintenance of the imperial enterprise', which by necessity must preclude the cessation of Empire (Jeffrey, 1978: 307). The Anglo-Indian community existed in a peculiar state of limbo; in Maud Diver's words, 'English men and women in India are, as it were, members of one great family, aliens under one sky' (Allen, 1975: 51).

Haggard began writing fiction after he had ceased to consider making a home in Southern Africa, whereas Kipling's first volume of short stories, *Plain Tales From the Hills*, was collected mainly from the work he published in the Anglo-Indian, Lahore-based newspaper, the *Civil and Military Gazette*. Moore-Gilbert's discussion of Kipling's intended audience points to a division of allegiance between India and Britain, for by Kipling's time, important publishers such as Thacker and Spink, Charles Wheeler, Newman and Higginbotham made it possible to publish in India before

London (Moore-Gilbert, 1986: 9–10). Unlike Haggard's easy appropriation of Zulu history, the Englishman in Kipling's India is an alienated figure who searches constantly for the meaning of his existence in a land hostile to his presence.

Part II

4

THE COLONIAL UNCANNY

Adrian Poole describes the classic Victorian narrative as characterised by optimism regarding the possibility of reconciling individuals and society. Fiction at the turn of the century, however, is dominated by a crisis of faith over the possibility of ever healing the schism between the public and the private world. Literary, social and political fragmentation present authors with the difficulties of identity; late Victorian writers exhibit an 'unprecedented intransigence in terms of the opposition between the inner, personal and subjective, and the outer, public and objective' (Poole, 1975: 8–9). For Poole, Kipling represents a throwback, a modern writer who in a gesture of bad faith indulges in the pleasures of demarcation. Kipling 'essay[s] a Dickensian confidence about naming', thriving on his 'ability to define "us" and "them"'. Unlike George Gissing, Thomas Hardy, Henry James and Joseph Conrad who are all 'examining the disastrous consequences of man's propensity for naming the living and moving into fixity', Kipling exalts in the fiction of absolute control that finds political justification in the ideas of imperialism (Poole, 1975: 22–23).

In sketching the concerns of an incipient modernist aesthetic, Poole is perhaps wilfully missing the uncertain voices which come from a more dialogic reading of the impact of colonialism on the culture and literature of writers of Empire. Poole cites Conrad's texts with approval, but argues that Kipling's writing merely exhibits a 'magical correspondence between names and things'. In this chapter, I hope to show that the 'Dickensian confidence' alluded to in Kipling's early work is tenuous and fragile, and by no means established with ease. Robert Miles, in his survey of gothic fiction, argues that the gothic is best understood as a 'coherent code for the representation of fragmented subjectivity', a subject 'dispossessed of its own house [and] in a condition of rupture, disjunction, fragmentation' (Miles, 1993: 2). Patrick Brantlinger locates a relatively recent variant – imperial gothic – within the late Victorian preoccupation with the occult: the transformation of gothic into imperial romances. The imaginary and exotic worlds of imperial romances take on a darker hue with invasion fantasies, narratives of atavism, decline and regression – all despite the 'seemingly scientific progressive, often Darwinian ideology' of the age (Brantlinger, 1988: 227). Brantlinger's isolation of the 'imperial gothic' is valuable in highlighting the anxieties apparent in the imperial centre but less helpful on the reverberations at the colonial periphery. Because it is the latter that I wish to foreground in my examination of a selection of Kipling's early gothic texts, I propose to use the term 'the colonial uncanny'.

The term signals the tensions manifesting itself in Kipling's use of gothic form in his prose works. The word 'uncanny' seems appropriate for my purposes because it catches the particular dilemma of Anglo-Indian identity in two important ways: from within and without. Both relate to Freud's play on *heimlich/ unheimlich*. Freud's division between 'what is familiar and agreeable' and 'what is concealed and kept out of sight' leads to the definition of the uncanny as 'the class of the frightening which leads back to what is known of old and long familiar' (Freud, 1955: 224–225; 220). The uncanny in this sense is that which reflects back to the colonial identity another image of itself based on the inversion of its normal structure: a home that turns out not to be a home and a self that turns out to be some other being. Freud sited the uncanny within such an ambivalence: 'Thus *heimlich* is a word the meaning of which develops in the direction of ambivalence, until it finally coincides with its opposite, *unheimlich*. *Unheimlich* is in some way or other a sub-species of *heimlich*' (Freud, 1955: 226). In this respect, cultivation of the gothic form provides us with the clearest examples of what Bhabha describes as an ambivalent vacillation in colonial discourse between pleasure/unpleasure and mastery.

This alienating 'doubling' – of a subject possessed of an Other and divested of its own house – is readily apparent in the Anglo-Indian community whose sustained presence in a foreign land created particular pressures on the maintenance of an 'Anglo' cultural identity. I would argue that paranoia about the physical and psychical threat posed by the native community to Anglo-Indian safety and well being is expressed in uneasy narratives of unexpected malevolence such as 'The Strange Ride of Morrowbie Jukes' and 'The Return of Imray'. The hallucinatory quality of Trejago's double life in 'Beyond the Pale' and the violence that erupts in 'The Mark of the Beast' also suggest a disquieting look at what constitutes normality or the real. Miles's reminder that the gothic is 'not fantasy in need of psychoanalysis' but a 'code for the representation of fragmented subjectivity' indicates the need to address both form and content in analysis. Accordingly, I shall attempt close readings of Kipling's early narratives – both for the insights they yield about the relationship between narrator and reader, and the tensions that inflect the drive towards narrative authority – its successes and failures. In particular, my focus on Kipling's travels in Rajasthan, 'Letters of Marque', is meant to isolate what I see as an anxiety of cultural authority that is inflected narratively. 'Letters' present a troubled meditation on the nature and function of Anglo-Indian presence in India that is handled generically through the (de)stabilising features of the travelogue. Mixing reportage with romance, Kipling's excursion into Rajasthan oscillates between the stable spaces of progress and modernity contingent with the British rule in India and a dark and terrifying gothic alterity associated with India's past. 'Letters' can be read literally as a struggle over the competing histories and legacies of colonial history.

THE STRANGE RIDE OF MORROWBIE JUKES

'The Strange Ride' is one of Kipling's earliest Indian stories. Published in *Quartette*, a family magazine printed in India for the Christmas of 1885, it is a tale of Anglo-Indian insecurity offered as the hallucinatory experience of a young Anglo-Indian who has a touch of fever. The central protagonist, Morrowbie Jukes, is an ordinary English engineer who stumbles accidentally on an Indian village located in a huge sand crater, during a midnight ride in the desert. The inhabitants of this village – literally the living dead – form a grotesque caricature of the subjects that people the Englishman's 'real' Anglo-Indian world. Enforced exiles from the world of health and sanity, none of the villagers are allowed to escape from the crater once they are deposited within. These inhabitants are cut off from the real world of the Raj and consequently care nothing for the niceties of the 'outside' colonial world. Instead a crude Darwinian logic applies: the most powerful and cunning of the species survives the longest. Terrorised by hostile natives and denied the special status of a Sahib of the British Raj, Jukes resorts to violence in order to maintain his position. His downward spiral of degeneration, despair and gradual impotence gives the story much of its emotional force. The 'strange ride' opens up a different reality from the familiar security of the Anglo-Indian world. Yet in many ways, the ride is not a strange one at all for it simply intensifies the terror and hostility which are already present in colonial relations.

The gothic narrative of the engineer's tale is triggered by something out of joint. The intrusion of the unknown and the irrational on the normally calm and sensible world of the civil engineer is signposted by conventional means. There is a full moon and Jukes has a 'slight attack of fever' (Kipling, 1914: 169). Finding himself in a state of nervous excitement brought on by the sound of baying hounds, he chases a stray dog over the desert sands in order to kill it. Reckless riding causes him to stumble and fall into 'a horseshoe-shaped crater . . . with steeply graded sand walls' opening out to a river. Rushing its steep banks is unproductive for the crater turns out to be 'a trap exactly on the same model as that which the ant-lion sets for its prey' (Kipling, 1914: 172). Furthermore, a small native vessel patrolling the river opening prevents escape from the other end. It fires at the unfortunate Jukes with a 'regulation Martini-Henry picket'. Bewildered and trapped, Jukes can only rail at his circumstances:

> Was ever a respectable gentleman in such an *impasse?* The treacherous sand-slope allowed no escape . . . and a promenade on the river frontage was the signal for a bombardment from some insane native in a boat. I'm afraid that I lost my temper very much indeed.
>
> (Kipling, 1914: 173)

Armed with colonial artillery expertise, the native boat which shoots at the Sahib is only one of a series of rude shocks which take place within the dream landscape of the tale. In this grotesque and inverted world of the living dead, life is a mockery of colonial relations. The belief in the white man's superiority cannot be relied upon; no 'civility from . . . inferiors' nor 'recognition of [Jukes's] presence' is accorded the respectable member of the British Raj.

Instead, the Sahib is greeted by the laughter of 'superior[s] or at least of . . . equal[s]':

> the ragged crew actually laughed at me – such laughter I hope I may never hear again. They cackled, yelled, whistled, and howled as I walked into their midst; some of them literally throwing themselves down on the ground in convulsions of unholy mirth.

> (Kipling, 1914: 174)

Daily contact with unclean natives is unavoidable; even his den has 'sides . . . worn smooth and greasy by the contact of innumerable naked bodies'. Hygiene and sanitation which are part and parcel of normal life are non-existent. Food comes in the shape of unclean crows, caught by impaling wounded birds as bait. Jukes loses all privileged status in this environment. 'Representative of the dominant race', he is here rendered 'helpless as a child and completely at the mercy of his native neighbours'. In this village of underground tunnels, all seem to take pride in parading their filth and repulsiveness to mock the white Sahib. In particular, a former subordinate, Gunga Dass, delights in 'malicious pleasure'. Jukes recalls indignantly,

> In a deliberate lazy way he set himself to torture me as a schoolboy would devote a rapturous half-hour to watching the agonies of an impaled beetle, or as a ferret in a blind burrow might glue himself comfortably to the neck of a rabbit.

> (Kipling, 1914: 182)

Jukes's behaviour alters accordingly. Arguing that fellow inmates are kept servile only through 'calmly threaten[ing] violence and murder', he resorts to brute force in order to gain some standing in the community. He clubs those nearest to him till 'the laughter gave place to wails for mercy'. The formerly respectable and unruffled 'average Englishman' is in a short space of time effortlessly transformed into the voice of the murderous and violent Sahib of the village.

By imaginatively detaching the support systems created to cushion the impact of India on Anglo-Indian consciousness, the story amplifies the cultural shock of the encounter. Jukes's experiences in the crater present a magnification of his phobia. Negative emotions are intensified. With no hope of returning to the safe haven of camp, surrounded by servants and subordinates, Jukes

117

testifies to an overwhelming and 'inexplicable terror'. Despite claiming the unimaginative temperament of an engineer, Jukes is nevertheless completely given to 'nervous terror' and paranoia which rehearses the trauma of colonial insecurities in the face of the Other. But much of these feelings simply reflect the ordinary experiences between Anglo and Indian. Anxiety, claustrophobia and alienation render the writing close to the recorded real life experiences of many Anglo-Indians stationed in India. As Bart Moore-Gilbert notes, 'motifs of imprisonment in the tale' and the 'image of India as a cemetery' recall the 'claustrophobia and sense of exile so prominent in Anglo-Indian literature' (Moore-Gilbert, 1983: 108).

But Jukes's smooth transition from civility to brutality is a little worrying to his readers because it shows a different side of the respectable Anglo-Indian from the one normally advanced. If the tale is subtlely corrosive of the positive image of imperial duty and service, it is also an uncanny reflection of the representative of the dominant race as alternately violent, helpless, paranoiac and sui-cidal. Jukes's emotional investment in the construction of the village as a leviathan governed by the laws of the strongest takes the moral brakes off his capacity for brutality. His behaviour is argued to be that needed to cope with the norms of the village in which 'there was no law save that of the strongest' (Kipling, 1914: 186). But the ease with which he inhabits another personality hints at the equatability of the forms of behaviour. If the figure of Gunga Dass paves the way for Jukes's transgression by indicating what kind of opposition he is up against, Dass also presents Jukes with a mirror image of himself as malevolent patron. The figure of Dass functions as a licence for deplorable behaviour; but this could only emerge if there was something else behind the image of the respectable man. Dass enables the figure of Jukes to play out his unconscious desires. This is borne out by the fact that Jukes sets out to imitate Dass's behaviour. The brutalised version of government offers an ambivalent double: 'at the time it did not strike me at all strange that I, a Civil Engineer, and a man of thirteen year's standing in the Service, and, I trust, an average Englishman, should thus calmly threaten murder and violence' (Kipling, 1914: 186).

Despite his use of violence, Jukes's ascendancy in the community is never guaranteed. The Dass character shares all his outer-world stereotype's propensity for deceit. Dass tricks Jukes into sharing information about the secret escape route left behind by a previous

Sahib and departs without Jukes. The somewhat lame and abrupt ending of Jukes's tale comes as an anti-climax after the unspeakable horrors of his imagined experience. In the moment of deepest despondency and 'unreasoning fury', Jukes's faithful servant Dunoo appears with a rope to rescue his master. This substitution of Dunoo for Dass reinstates one of the cornerstones of the imperial myth, that of the good and faithful servant. The good native is upheld as a fetish against the nightmarish conflictual relations of empire and allows the narrative to attain a degree of equilibrium. Dunoo returns Jukes to a semblance of normality. Yet by suggesting an all too powerful alternative, Kipling's gothic tale interrogates the finished quality of the mythic-text of colonial normality.

The 'double-take' of the benevolent image of imperial rule is reinforced by the structural ambivalence concerning the veracity of the tale. Jukes's story of his experiences in the village is balanced between fantasy (his nightmare) and the 'the real', and draws its narrative power from the ironic juxtaposition of the two spheres. On a simple level, the authenticity of Jukes's tale is uncertain because we do not know if it is the result of his fevered imagination or real experience. Framed by another narrator, Jukes's first person monologue, is told in such a way as to highlight the character's limitations. He is depicted as a respectable and somewhat pompous Anglo-Indian with a limited imagination and a penchant for facts and figures. Jukes's ride and his experiences consequently seem too bizarre for him to have invented (which renders the text's vision of anxiety, claustrophobia and paranoia all the more acute). But the frame-narration is not altogether straightforward; the shrewdness of its staging of Jukes's tale teases the reader with the implications of an all too easy willingness to believe. The frame-narrator's ironic commentary on the plausibility of Jukes's tale and by extension, colonial fears, is a clever trap.

The frame-narrator states in the very first sentence of the short story that 'there is no invention about this tale'; Jukes only 'by accident stumbled upon a village that is well known to exist'. The clause 'well known to exist', of course raises the question 'well known to whom?' It is not answered directly but met with the frame-narrator's knowledge of Indian customs and local myths:

> A somewhat similar institution used to flourish on the out-skirts of Calcutta, and there is a story that if you go into the heart of Bikanir, which is in the heart of the Great Indian

Desert, you shall come across, not a village, but a town where
the Dead who do not die, but may not live, have established
their headquarters.

(Kipling, 1914: 168)

This introductory framing of Jukes's monologue is done slyly
and ironically, for the narrator declares in the same breath that
'it is perfectly true' that the self-same Desert holding the village
also holds a wild and wonderful Oriental city, rich beyond the
imaginations of ordinary people. This supplementary statement
is a transferential trap. For if a city of rich money-lenders who
'drive sumptuous C-spring barouches, and buy beautiful girls,
and decorate their palaces with the gold and ivory and Minton
tiles and mother-o'-pearl' exists, then, concludes the frame-
narrator craftily, 'I do not see why Jukes's tale should not be true'
(Kipling, 1914: 168).

Tim Bascom points out that the use of a narrative frame within
the short story usually provides a point of contact between the
frame-narrator of the tale and the readers of the story which aids
the story's credibility. The narrator, by being like us (or one of us)
mediates between reader and the tale. This overlap, Bascom argues,
is necessary to produce the suspension of disbelief vital to the
progress of the tale (Bascom, 1987: 162). We believe him because
he is one of us. But Kipling's narration adds another dimension to
the problem even as it provides the reader with a sense of a kindred
spirit. The declarative statements presented by the frame-narrator
of the 'Strange Ride' about the character of the civil engineer are
undercut by a series of enigmatic, short and often ironic supplementary sentences. Jukes is described as the *only* Englishman to
have visited the village 'well known to exist'. Common-sensical and
stolid Jukes 'never varies the tale in the telling', writing the story of
his experiences 'quite straightforwardly'; yet we are later informed
that 'he has touched it up in places and introduced Moral Reflections'. In addition, the narrator announces that Jukes, a civil
engineer by trade, is unlikely to 'take the trouble to invent
imaginary traps' because 'he could earn more by doing his legitim-
ate work'. Does this mean that the narrator in reconstructing Jukes's
strange tale undertakes illegitimate work?

What Valerie Shaw has called 'casually-dropped "studied remark" and the pause' in Kipling's anecdotal narration (Shaw, 1983:
88), contributes to the teasing quality of the framed introduction,

120

which taunts Anglo-Indian readers with the supposed security and certainties of some of their cherished beliefs. They disrupt the conventional normality of the Anglo-Indian world by taking in all seriousness some of its Orientalist mythologising – as if to say, quite mockingly, that the story of Jukes's experiences in the village exists on the same imaginative plain as that of the sumptuous Oriental palace in the Desert, managed by refugee millionaires. Also, while the frame-narrator's position seems to be detached, his challenge is issued from *within* the colonial community. Significantly, as if to highlight his contradictory position between invention and documentation, the frame-narrator is rendered metaphorically impotent and contributes nothing to the ending of this short story. 'Strange Ride' terminates abruptly with a final one and a half paragraph detailing Jukes's rescue. This brevity and the alteration of tone sit in contrast with the sustained passions and turmoil of Jukes's experiences in the crater and call attention to their awkward staginess. Is this the illegitimate and fictional work alluded to by the narrator?

THE RETURN OF IMRAY

'The Return' can be grouped with 'The Strange Ride'. Both locate paranoia and native malevolence at their emotional core. At its most primary level, 'Return' reworks the fear of a recurrence of the Indian Mutiny, by telling the story of Imray's haunting and the subsequent discovery of his murder and his appeasement. Unlike 'Strange Ride', it locates colonial vulnerability squarely within the familiar and domestic. All the action occurs within the confines of the colonial residence. Through an unfortunate cultural misunderstanding, Imray's servant murders his sleeping master and conceals the body in the loft. After much spectral haunting, Strickland, who takes over both servant and home, discovers the decaying body. Within the context of the narrative, the confession he forces seems at best trivial and at worst simply a product of bizarre superstition. The story gains its force in the suggestion that attack, which may be sudden and unexpected, may also be seemingly random and unwarranted – at least in accordance to the rules of rational conduct of the European world. Edmund Gosse's contemporary review, for example, refers to 'the hopeless impenetrability of the native conscience'. Not only does the indecipherability of the native mind make anticipation of violence nearly impossible, but the story builds on the paranoia that all subservient behaviour may simply be a dissembling ruse. To employ psychoanalytic language, the essentially narcissistic desire of the master that his servant recognise the fullness of his authority and conform to his image will always be in excess of the demand. That a native subordinate might throw off his servitude and slay his master by catching him unawares, links Imray to Strickland to the journalist narrator; 'I shuddered', Kipling's narrator remarks, 'My own servant had been with me for exactly that length of time'.

As with many of Kipling's early tales, 'Return' begins with the tragic and sometimes wasted life of the ordinary Anglo-Indian in the civil service. These men are reduced to cogs in a vast machine that neither recognises their humanity nor rewards their loyalty and service. Imray's absence is attended to by the Anglo-Indian community only because 'he was hampering, in a "microscopical degree", the administration of the Indian Empire'. Furthermore, it is noticed only for a 'microscopical moment'. The wheels of the Empire roll remorselessly forward and Imray becomes 'such a thing as men talk over at their tables in the Club for a month, and then forget utterly'. Alienation, the condition of Anglo-Indian life, is further symbolised by the mis-match of man and environment. The journalist narrator–character tells of his physical discomfort and mental depression spent in a climate of hot summers and rains which fall 'like ramrods on the earth'. Low in spirits and covered with prickly-heat, his estrangement is felt more keenly given the harmony of the natural world outside his bungalow: 'The bamboos, and the custard-apples, the poinsettias, and the mango-trees in the garden stood still while the warm water lashed through them, and the frogs began to sing among the aloe hedges' (Kipling, 1897: 228). In this Indian world of interlocking and mutually supportive segments, the narrator has no place. Engulfed by the darkness he tries continually to dispel by artificial means, he, like Strickland, is haunted by a shadowy figure: a 'voice . . . no more than a whisper' – 'a fluttering, whispering, bolt-fumbling, lumbering, loitering Someone'. The ghostly figure has no material substance and the narrator never confronts him as such. Yet one 'could see the curtains between the rooms quivering where he had just passed through . . . [and] hear the chair creaking as the bamboos sprung under the weight that had just quitted them' (Kipling, 1897: 230, 231). In these darkened and silent rooms, the ghostly figure of Imray is the uncanny counterpart of the solidity and substance of the white man's presence.

Strickland, the Sherlock Holmes of Kipling's tales, stands as the ultimate defence against the emptying-out of authority. His actions are aimed at appeasing the ghostly presence by uncovering his murderer. His interpretation of past events acts to wrench the spectral tale back into the normality. Everything is not what it seems. Strickland inherits Imray's residence, but the 'desirable' residence with a 'ceiling-cloth which looked as neat as a white-washed ceiling' is not the English house it appears to be. The white ceiling-cloth is described as hiding 'the dark three-cornered cavern of the roof ... the beams and the underside of the thatch harboured all manner of rats, bats, ants, and foul things'. Chancing upon a pair of brown snakes behind the ceiling-cloth, Strickland pursues them and stumbles on the half decaying body of Imray, whose throat has been slit from ear to ear. Like Holmes, Strickland discovers Imray's murderer through a process of deductive mental logic and hands down a sentence of death by hanging. The discovery of the culprit restores to the colonial text the control it obviously lacks. Strickland asserts, as sure as 'the sun shines or the water runs', Bahadur Khan, Imray's servant, will hang for his crime. Yet the native servant does not hang at the story's close but dies by his own hand. However, the ceasing of Imray's haunting indicates the triumph of Strickland in the cause of justice. But does it?

Kipling's gothic tale presents a dark vision of colonial occupation. Imray's death is one of partial decapitation. His throat is slit from ear to ear, rendering him *voiceless*; the narrator comments, 'That's why he whispered about the house'. The voiceless ghostly figure only symbolises the de-materialisation that can overtake the members of the Raj. Native insurrection is matched by a disruption of colonial meaning. The captured Bahadur Khan's confession and contrition is an example of this ambivalence of meaning which slips beyond the pale. Within a nineteenth-century English sensibility, Khan's motives for Imray's murder are incomprehensible. He kills Imray for having patted his son on the head and pronounced him 'a handsome child'. Khan's specific stand on religious and cultural beliefs points to the limits and estrangement of Western models of explanation. In doing so, the universal applicability of rationality which supports Strickland's authority is disturbed and suddenly, there seems to be a disruption in the signs required for the recognition of colonial authority. In 'Return', Khan's combination of subservience and agreement sits oddly with his wilful manifestation of different beliefs and codes of conduct:

'I have seen [the body]. I am clay in the white man's hands. What does the Presence do?'

'Hang thee within the month. What else?'

'For killing him? Nay, Sahib, consider. Walking among us, his servants, he cast his eyes upon my child .... Him he bewitched, and in ten days he died of the fever – my child. Wherefore I killed Imray Sahib in the twilight, when he had come back from the office, and was sleeping. Wherefore I dragged him up into the roof-beams and made all fast behind him. The Heaven-born knows all things. I am the servant of the Heaven-born.'

(Kipling, 1897: 237)

Khan's presentation of positions of subservience looks suspiciously like a mere mimicry of what his master desires and presents a source of tension in Kipling's dialogues between master and servant. In this manner, 'The Return of Imray' attests to what Bhabha has called a characteristic 'splitting' in the colonising discourse which renders authority ambivalent. The narcissistic desire for 'a re-formed, recognizable Other', twined with a necessary 'slippage' and an 'excess', in turn disavowed, produces an uncanny scene of menace and resemblance (Bhabha, 1984: 126–127). Khan's earlier statement in reply to Strickland's verbal trap, 'What do I know of the ways of the white man, Heaven-born?', can only be effectively answered with Strickland's lame reply, 'Very little, truly':

'What time was that [i.e. when Khan first entered Strickland's service]?'

'Hast the Heaven-born forgotten? It was when Imray Sahib went secretly to Europe without warning given; and I – even I – came into the honoured service of the protector of the poor.'

[. . .] 'And thou wilt take service with him when he returns?'

'Assuredly, Sahib. He was a good master, and he cherished his dependants.'

'And Imray Sahib has gone to Europe secretly! That is very strange, Bahadur Khan, is it not?'

'What do I know of the ways of the white man Heaven-born?'

'Very little, truly.'

(Kipling, 1897: 236)

An underlying impotence lurks behind Strickland's insistent demand that Khan acknowledge the full nature of his crime and punishment. By taking his own life, Khan's last act resists Strickland's attempt to position him. The snake which Khan uses to kill himself highlights impotence because 'if you look into the eyes of any snake you will see that it knows all and more of the mystery of man's fall, and that it feels all the contempt that the Devil felt when Adam was evicted from Eden' (Kipling, 1897: 232). The presence of the narrator's servant at the end of the story mirrors Bahadur Khan's; his length of service in the employ of the journalist narrator matches Khan's with Imray exactly. His attitude to the narrator discloses no visible insurrection; in fact he actively encourages the Sahib's faith in him. 'Gently, Sahib', the narrator's nameless servant reassures, 'Let me pull off those boots'. Yet his servant is not left in the dark; his knowledge of the circumstances of Khan's death is as complete as his master's. The uncanny similarity of their situations is reflected in the final encounter between master and servant, which veils rather than reveals, unsettles rather than soothes: '"What has befallen Bahadur Khan?" said I. "He was bitten by a snake and died. The rest the Sahib knows."' The reference to the authority and status of the interrogator can be read alternatively as sly (on the part of the servant) or paranoid (on the part of the master); but both are mirror images of one another. 'The Return of Imray' ends not with Strickland's confident shout but with the 'idle, empty, ceiling-cloth' left trailing on the table in the next room. The narrator's exchanges with his servant and his reminder of the ceiling-cloth all convey a paranoiac knowledge that moves beyond Strickland's belief that Imray's ghost may finally rest in peace.

(IN)HABITING THE BEAST

If both 'Return' and 'Strange Ride' locate the rupture of colonial subjectivity as the danger stemming without, stories such as 'The Mark of the Beast' and 'Beyond the Pale' look at the threat from within. Both 'The Mark of the Beast' and 'Beyond the Pale' deal with the transgressive desire for the Other. They show the dispossession of the self through the inhabitation of the Other. But more importantly, both stories convey a terrible and unwanted secret. Andrew Lang remarked of 'The Mark of the Beast' that the story was 'poisonous stuff' and had 'left an extremely disagreeable impression on [his] . . . mind' (Green, 1971: 14). Knowledge and experience gained outside the pale dispels naivety and corrodes innocence; Trejago's illicit alliances make him a different kind of man in 'Beyond the Pale' while Strickland and the journalist–narrator's joint decision to torture the leper 'had disgraced . . . [them] as Englishmen for ever'. Both stories also show how the generation of imperial authority is tied up with the projection and protection of masculinity.

Like 'Strange Ride', 'The Mark of the Beast' was initially published in magazine form in India. The story concerns an alleged. native curse put on a white planter, Fleete, who in a state of drunken stupor vandalises an important Hindu temple. As a direct result of his thoughtless action, he is punished by the agents of the temple's god by being made to regress to the state of a beast. Strickland is saddled with the task of reversing this curse. He captures the native magician and tortures him into revoking the curse. But in doing so, a strategic line is crossed; the legal and moral boundaries separating the civilisation of the colonising culture from the barbarity of the colonised one is transgressed. Kipling's story matches evil for evil, native and colonial diabolism. But all these events are of course contained within the gothic form. Like 'Strange Ride', 'The Mark of the Beast' is balanced between hallucination and actual event. Fleete recovers from the spell, but when Strickland calls on the temple authorities the next morning to offer redress for Fleete's actions, he is 'solemnly assured' that nothing happened. Yet despite the containment afforded by labelling the event a dream, the aberrant 'experience' or fantasy produces contaminating knowledge. Put 'before the public' to clear the mystery, the transfer of this 'rather unpleasant story' – seeing 'what Strickland and I saw' – must also implicate the reader. The story's title refers not only to Fleete's condition but to Strickland, the narrator and the reader.

Kipling's story begins with a framing series of casual declarative statements polarising East and West. The West is firmly placed under 'the direct control of Providence' and the Church of England. 'East of Suez', however, these benevolent influences cease; they only exercise 'an occasional and modified supervision in the case of Englishmen'. Despite its overt Orientalist division, the opening paragraph throws open the question of colonial authority in its suggestion that a state exists outside Western explanatory structures of rationality and salvation. The native proverb which prefaces the narrative proper teases readers with a riddle, 'Ye Gods and my Gods – do you or I know which are the stronger?' (Kipling, 1897: 208). But even to pose this question is contrary to a Western system of interpretation whose status depends on the universality of its application. Sandra Kemp remarks that Kipling's gothic narratives 'are characteristically duplicitous and equivocal'; they 'relativize the European colonial discourse which frames them ... and work to expose the continency and relativity of Western valuations of "masculinity" and "rationality"' (Kemp, 1988: 18). Kemp is right to argue that Kipling's writings often interrogate official culture from the standpoint of the margin, but his version of the margin sometimes advocates a brutality that is hard to swallow. For Strickland's role in the text presents the interface between the totalising symbolic mode of the colonial civil state and a competing gothic mode that vindicates the encounter of force with force. In doing so, the story throws open questions of reading, identity and narration as it attempts to persuade us of its version of the truth.

It begins with the festivities of New Year's Eve, when celebrations run 'riotous', and Anglo-Indians forsake propriety in their merrymaking. In a particularly masculine atmosphere of horseplay and drink, Fleete bursts into the native temple of Hanuman and grinds the ashes of his cigarette in the forehead of its icon. Fleete's callousness is underscored by his Biblical joke: 'Shee that?' he tells Strickland, 'Mark of the B–beasht! *I* made it. Ishn't it fine?' His action, the narrative would have us believe, results in Fleete's own marking. Fleete's world is turned inside out as he progressively becomes more beast-like. The animal nature previously imputed to the native other in contemporary racist discourses applies literally in the case of white colonial planter. Fleete's new personality is part of a series of inversions. The temple's priest, the Silver Man, who effects the alleged curse is himself part of this inverted world. He is a native stricken with leprosy, a disease which is accompanied by Biblical reverberations of sin, pollution and uncleanliness. Yet the Silver Man does not hide himself but appears 'perfectly naked in that bitter, bitter cold'. His body is described as shining like 'frosted silver', a precious commodity; he is described as a 'leper as white as snow'. But this phrase turns out to be an inversion of the original biblical metaphor – that of washing away one's sins to attain a state of purity. In effect, the Silver Man presents a travesty of man. He has no face and 'mews' like an otter. More importantly, his

127

behaviour is depicted as strangely effeminate. The Silver Man's disease gives him a spectral semblance of whiteness but his theatrical and grotesque courting of Fleete hints at a sexual aberrance:

the Silver Man ran in under our arms, making a noise exactly like the mewing of an otter, caught Fleete round the body and dropped his head on Fleete's breast before we could wrench him way. Then he retired to a corner and sat mewing . . . .

In the silence of the watching we heard something without [the bungalow] mewing like a she-otter. We both rose to our feet, and . . . actually and physically felt sick. . . . In the moonlight we could see the leper coming round the corner of the house. He was perfectly naked, and from time to time he mewed and stopped to dance with his shadow. It was an unattractive sight.

(Kipling, 1897: 211, 218, 220)

The inversion holds true for other members of Hanuman's temple. The other priest at the incident speaks perfect English and contrary to Strickland's expectations does not harm the English intruders. The priest's promise of retribution materialises in the sanctity of the house compound. Fleete's eating habits deteriorate and he is fascinated by the over-powering smells of blood and slaughter-houses in the air. Soon Fleete is described as 'unpleasant to look at'; he speaks 'quickly and thickly'; he rolls in the garden dirt. His eyes had a 'green light behind them . . . his lower lip hung down'. 'Fleete could not speak, he could only snarl, and his snarls were those of a wolf, not of a man.' The narrator concludes 'We were dealing with a beast that had once been Fleete' (Kipling, 1897: 217).

At this point, the Silver Man appears in the vicinity of the bungalow. According to Strickland, the Silver Man's return signals his attempt to lay claim on Fleete's soul. Strickland's unorthodox methods are required to return Fleete's proper manhood. The narrator hesitates before assenting to Strickland's version of events, 'so wildly improbable' to 'every right-minded man', but agrees to help with the torture of the native priest. The violence that follows is justified as necessary to a situation which requires white men to 'overmatch . . . [natives] with their own weapons' (Kipling, 1897: 212). In choosing to credit Strickland's interpretation of the events with the truth, and agreeing to the savage torture of the Silver Man, the narrator (like Strickland) is turning his back on his own civilised identity. In his own words, 'I put away all my doubts and resolved to help Strickland from the heated gun-barrels to the loop of twine – from the loins to the head and back again – with all tortures that might be needful' (Kipling, 1897: 220).

The tortures inflicted on the Silver Man have the effect of mocking the ideals of Empire by interrogating the so-called civilising process which marks the white colonialist as superior. Both Anglo-Indians choose to cross the threshold of civility. They bind the Silver Man with ropes and place heated gun-barrels on his flesh. The narrator confesses to a sadistic pleasure in Strickland's lynching of the Silver Man:

> I understood then how men and women and children can see a witch burnt alive; for the beast was moaning on the floor, and though the Silver Man had no face, you could see horrible feelings passing through the slab that took its place, exactly as waves of heat play across red-hot iron – gun-barrels for instance.
>
> (Kipling, 1897: 221)

Just as the doctor's diagnosis of Fleete's affliction was previously rejected as incorrect, both Strickland and the narrator decide that the Silver Man's pathetic 'mewings [under torture] had not been satisfactory'. He must be made to talk. Made an adjunct to Strickland's narrative, the leper is told 'to take away the evil spirit'. The violence of Strickland's torture is terminated only with the submission of the Silver Man to his interpretative code.

The torturers' hysteria at the end of the tale expresses a violence and sadism which is literally censored from the text. It remains the blind-spot in the demarcation of colonial identity; as the narrator freely admits, 'then it struck me that we had . . . disgraced ourselves as Englishmen for ever, and I laughed and gasped and gurgled just as shamefully as Strickland' (Kipling, 1897: 223). The scene censored from the text – 'this part is not to be printed' – is presented in retrospect as a Manichean struggle, a will to power for both sides of the cultural divide; the narrator reports, 'it struck me that we had fought for Fleete's soul'. The Silver Man is portrayed as the only person who knows the solution to the mystery and the only one able to reverse the curse of Hanuman's temple. Yet readers are told nothing of the Silver Man's purpose in his apparent pursuit of Fleete; there is no vantage point from which we may judge the validity of Strickland's accusations.

The aesthetic symmetry of Kipling's narrative covers a multitude of sins and makes it easier for readers to sanction the immoral steps taken to reverse Hanuman's curse. Two Anglo-Indians' quest for Fleete's soul may proceed through devious means because its was lost through devious and perverse means. But like Haggard's, this symmetry is the effect of projection and reappropriation: the colonial mirroring of Otherness which reflects and yearns for barbarity as part of its authoritarian fantasies. Yet if the concept and application of native magic *sanctions* Strickland's transgression of the law, surely the reinstatement of colonial normality must be a sham. This is a problem which Kipling's narrator never resolves because he is party to the act of violence. The telling of a 'rather unpleasant story' can only be brought to a close by an ironic invocation of 'common' sense: 'it is well known to every right-minded man that the gods of the heathen are stone and brass, and any attempt to deal with them otherwise is justly condemned'. What haunts 'The Mark of the Beast' is whether the Beast in question is really the two disgraced Englishmen.

CASTRATING MORALS

'Beyond the Pale' pushes our theme of identity, narration and reading even further. This story can be contrasted with 'The Beast' as a tale of a man whose affinity for native disguise and custom matches that of Strickland. The narrative tells the tale of a forbidden liaison between a white man and a native girl which results in tragedy. Trejago, on one of his nightly excursions, meets a young widow Bisesa and forms an attachment with her. Her uncle finds out about the relationship and punishes his niece. Trejago returning to Bisesa's room in the native city after a time of absence is greeted by the startling sight of Bisesa, with her 'hands . . . cut off at the wrists . . . the stumps . . . nearly healed'. On entering the room, Trejago is knifed:

> someone in the room grunted like a wild beast and something sharp – knife, sword, or spear, – thrust at Trejago in his *boorka*. The stroke missed his body, but cuts into one of the muscles of the groin, and he limped slightly from the wound for the rest of his days.

> (Kipling, 1897: 165)

'Beyond the Pale' is framed as a moral fable; readers take away a story about the consequences of inter-racial romance in order not to make the same mistake as Trejago. Yet the narrative itself is so riddled with ambivalences that the tale creates more problems than it solves. As a cautionary exercise, the story fails to make good its promise, as a host of different critical interpretations attest. For example, in a particularly fine reading of 'Beyond the Pale' Robert MacDonald argues that this short story highlights contradictions in the dominant ideology, through its manipulation of conflicting discourses offering information on this particular 'tragedy' of transgression (MacDonald, 1986: 413–418). Like Holden in 'Without Benefit of Clergy', Trejago's nightly excursions open up a world of passion and delight that renders his day-time world an unreal and 'unlovely one' (Kipling, 1897: 132). MacDonald argues that the moral of the tale is one of knowledge – the 'Knowledge of the Other . . . [which] subverts the imperial myth' – and understanding which must be cultivated because it brings sympathy. He asserts, 'with knowledge comes sympathy, with sympathy comes a question. Who is responsible for the "tragedy"? The final enigma rests on the title: beyond whose pale?'.

The very title of the short story draws up boundaries between 'us' and 'them'. It relies on the reader's implicit agreement: beyond *our* pale – beyond the line which divides civility, and the white colonial residences from the wild and black native quarters.[1] Yet this necessary division is immediately qualified by an epigraph, a native proverb acknowledging the potency of love and romance: 'Love heeds not caste nor sleep a broken bed. I went in search of love and lost myself.' The knowledge offered by the Hindu proverb sets up an alternative vision to the necessary observation of cultural and racial boundaries. But rather than setting them aside, these confines are again invoked in the opening two paragraphs of the text: 'A man should, whatever happens, keep to his own caste, race and breed. . . . This is the story of a man who wilfully stepped beyond the safe limits of decent everyday society, and paid for it heavily' (Kipling, 1897: 159).

What these two paragraphs offer is a warning to observe correct behavioural codes. A (white) man should keep to his side of the divide; otherwise trouble will ensue. The penalty will be a heavy one; but even here, the discourse seems troubled by the hesitant delivery of its metaphoric flaming sword. Trejago's transgressive behaviour as a man who *wilfully* steps beyond *safe* cultural and racial limits will be met by trouble, 'sudden' and '*alien*'. Warnings are

often supported by hard information about the possible consequences of misconduct. The imperative tone produces such
expectations. Yet the narrative refuses to divulge actual information
about the punishment. Later in the story, the punishment itself
seems not to fit the crime of miscegenation. Why or how Trejago's
'slight stiffness' constitutes 'heavy' punishment is not clear. What
incident is sudden, alien and unexpected? No real information is
forthcoming. Instead what is offered is a teasing series of allusions
and puzzles which are not resolved.

Like that in another tale of inter-racial romance, 'Without
Benefit of Clergy', the relationship between Trejago and Bisesa is
that of a father–protector and lover. Bisesa is only fifteen years of
age; she is continually referred to as 'little Bisesa' or 'the child'. Her
childlike nature is reinforced by her ignorance of the wider world,
her halting attempts at speaking English and her childish tantrums.
Bisesa's attraction lies in Trejago's perception of her as both child
and woman: 'Trejago laughed and Bisesa stamped her little feet –
little feet, light as marigold flowers, that could lie in the palm of a
man's hands' (Kipling, 1897: 164). In this regard, Trejago's position is the structural equivalent of her uncle's; the girl-child
functions as the object of contestation by rival figures of male
authority. This paternal and sexual triangle replicates the Oedipal
triangle; the Oedipal narrative is, of course, signalled by Trejago's
limp. To return to MacDonald's sympathetic reading and the stark
warning of the opening paragraphs, the key question must be:
'Does this "man" define man, does his act qualify the masculinity
of Empire?' Having posed the question, MacDonald himself does
not press the issue but quickly glosses over the enigma by passing
onto the horror of Bisesa's severed hands. MacDonald argues that
the 'tragedy' of the story is Bisesa's far greater punishment. His
reading concurs with the story's conclusion: 'Trejago pays his calls
regularly, and is reckoned a very decent sort of man. There is
nothing peculiar about him, except a slight stiffness, caused by a
riding strain, in the right leg' (Kipling, 1897: 166). But close
attention to a sentence which links 'peculiar' with 'riding strain' in
relation to the central protagonist begs the question of why readers'
attention should be drawn to such a connection in the first place.
Trejago is 'reckoned a very decent sort of man'; but surely this
statement prompts another, namely, what kind of *man*? What is the
relation between Trejago's masculinity and the 'slight stiffness'?

In his night-time visits to Bisesa, Trejago wears a native cloak – a *boorka* – which enables him free passage into alien and forbidden (Hindu) territory. But this is an article of dress belonging properly to a woman's wardrobe. John Forbes Watson, the director of the Indian Museum, in his detailed contemporary survey of Indian costume and textile manufacture, classifies the *boorka* as a 'voluminous' 'sheet veil' used by North Indian Muslim women (Watson, 1867: 39). The narrator seems himself to have this information when he seeks to dispel the incongruity: a *boorka* 'cloaks a man as well as a woman'. But one cannot be certain if the reference to sexual ambivalence is proleptic – the narrative tripping over itself by offering dreaded information ahead of time[2] – or is meant to cast doubt on Trejago's masculinity. In either case, the sexual identity of Trejago is deliberately put into question.

Yet the early stages of the inter-racial romance point to the character's control of the situation and would seem to suggest an affirmation of Trejago's authority. Like the colonial policeman, Strickland, he seems to be a figure whose power is heightened by a mastery of racial and sexual disguise. Trejago penetrates the native world both metaphorically and literally. As father and lover to Bisesa, he occupies the two most important positions in patriarchal exchange. In order to effect a cautionary tale against inter-racial sexual liaisons, the narrative must counter sexual fantasy with the horror of castration. Is the reference then to Trejago's sexual indeterminacy proleptic? In resolutely refusing to speak directly about it, the narrator's coyness contrasts with the repeated references to the projected outcome of the warning.

The uncle's revenge centres around a castration that is not fully revealed. In keeping with the theme of sexual ambivalence, the uncle's power is placed, on the one hand, within the realms of a feminised bodyscape: a cul-de-sac with windowless walls on its two sides and a 'dead-wall pierced by one grated window'. On the other, Durga Charan's power is associated with paternal law and the power of castration.[3] He or his substitute waits for Trejago in Bisesa's room and thrusts a 'knife, sword, or spear' at Trejago in his *boorka*. We are not told the extent of physical damage only that the stroke 'cut into one of the muscles of the groin' causing him to limp from the wound for the rest of his days. If the narrator is not as forthcoming about Charan's action and Trejago's wound as he can be, the reverse is true for Bisesa's mutilation. Detailing her injury in the sentence preceding allows one to associate Bisesa's stumps with Trejago's injury; because the story is mostly narrated using Trejago as focaliser, the association is an easy one to make. But could the severing of Bisesa's hands not be a displacement of the horror and unmentionable act of Trejago's castration? Indeed, within the context of the story, the severing of Bisesa's hands is suspicious because the narrative offers no reasons as to why Bisesa's uncle should enact this particular form of punishment: it simply presents the horror of her mutilation as a *fait accompli*. Instead, the sight of Bisesa's stumps is immediately followed by the thrust at Trejago. Like Freud's tale of the fetish object, can the sight of Bisesa's stumps act as a disavowal and projection of Trejago's castration? Trejago is himself associated with bewilderment, speechlessness and lack: he 'cannot tell', 'does not know', 'cannot get', 'he has lost'. He suffers from repetition compulsion: 'something horrible had happened, and the thought of what must have been, comes upon Trejago in the night now and again' (Kipling, 1897: 166). The narrative invites a reading of castration yet it also seeks to displace such a reading by drawing attention away from Trejago to Bisesa, and by suggesting that such a knowledge is not public.

In many ways, 'Beyond the Pale', is different from other tales in *Plain Tales* because it focuses on the inter-social rather than the intra-social relations of Anglo-Indian society that seem to preoccupy the stories that precede or succeed it. The story's use of deictics ('One day', 'Then he saw', 'Next Morning', 'That night'), the introductory frame and direct authorial intrusions impart a discursive and oral impression to the story. 'Beyond the Pale' is preoccupied with the creation and termination of exclusive communities; both in imagining the intense and private fantasy of Trejago and Bisesa's romance and in binding readers together in the act of listening. But the bonds of this community 'within the pale' could be based on castration anxieties and the horrible and hidden secret of Trejago's injury. The narrative transfer of information and experience between narrator and reader involves the inscription of castration. Peter Brooks's comment on Maupassant's 'Une Ruse' is pertinent; he argues that the narrative contract in Maupassant's story leads to 'contamination, the acquisition of unwanted, sullying wisdom' (Brooks, 1984: 218). By luring the colonial reader into hearing a mildly sensational story about a man who pays heavily for his misdeeds, the narrator in Kipling's story has managed to pass on something that his narratees may not want to hear.[4] Certainly, total helplessness and lack characterises Trejago after his experiences with Bisesa and Charan. Yet there are suggestions that Trejago's previous life among the members of the Anglo-Indian community was also identified with lack. His double life with Bisesa is described as an 'endless delight', a 'dearer, out-of-the-way life' and so pleasurably 'wild' that it possessed the quality of a dream. In contrast, Trejago is described as driving through his 'routine of office-work' or putting on his ritual 'calling-clothes' when 'compelled' to enter the Anglo-Indian round of social activities. Desire for the Other is overlaid on the impoverishment in the Anglo-Indian identity. The succession of adjectives hints at the lack within the pale: safe limits/ordinary/decent everyday society without real excitement or pleasure (Holden and Ameera's inter-racial liaison is described, furthermore, as 'absolute happiness . . . happiness withdrawn from the world, shut behind the wooden gate'). The moral lesson is then both melancholic and empty, and we may ask, following MacDonald: does this 'man' define man, does his lack qualify the masculinity of Empire?[5]

NARRATIVE AUTHORITY AND CULTURAL IDENTITY

To help answer this question, some attention to Kipling's travel writing would be productive. For travel, as James Clifford argues, implies 'displacement, interference, and interaction' that call into question the security of culture as unproblematic, bounded and organically whole (Lawrence and Grossberg, 1992: 101). Travel necessitates the interrogation of the cultural travelling self even if only to reinstate a more powerful version of self-identity at the journey's end. Travel writing as a distinct genre developed with the Enlightenment and the gradual secularisation of time and space. Travel was no longer tied to pilgrimages for edification and sanctification, but one travelled from sites of learning and power. Travel was linked to the self-realisation of man; it became the 'temporal/spatial "completion" of human history' and philo-sophical knowledge (Fabian, 1983). Mary Pratt locates two domin-ant forms of travel writing in the nineteenth century which were based on differing modes of narrative authority. The information-orientated branch is supported by interlocking disciplinary modes of inquiry such as botany, geography, ethnography, and the corres-ponding sentimental branch is anchored in the authenticity of someone's (often the narrator's) felt experiences (Pratt, 1985; Pratt, 1992: 76). Both strands are predicated on a cultural kinship with its implied readers which may or may not be foregrounded. But because travel presumes physical, geographical, temporal, cultural and textual displacements, the overlap between narrative and cultural authority is often one that has to be negotiated rather than assumed.[6] Trejago's excursions into the native city pose problems for the solidity and substance of his cultural identity; his encounter with Bisesa opens up a pleasurable world that is not available to him within Anglo-Indian society. Kipling's story cannot but be read as an ideological and narrative struggle over the significance of Trejago's lack. Even if Kipling's story is read as a straightforward cautionary tale, and the narrator's task that of a forceable reinscription of those boundaries, the act of narration necessitates disequilibrium before order is restored and cultural identity reinforced. Hence, in order to understand the interrogation and reinstatement of Anglo-Indian identity, I shall be turning to Kipling's travels in Rajasthan.

'Letters of Marque' is a series of travel sketches published initially in the all-India newspaper, the *Pioneer*, and subsequently reissued in Britain. 'Letters' concerns Kipling's travels to the Native Princely States of Jaipur, Amber, Udaipur, Chitor, Jodhpur and Boondi, which were not formally incorporated into the British Empire; it also offers his reflections on the architectural and historical achievements of modern and ancient Rajput culture. The narrative is organised loosely around the perceptions, observations and adventures of an 'Englishman' on the road, and records conversations with Residents, political agents, Maharajahs, stable-boys, carriage drivers, salesmen, tourists and 'loafers' met along the way. In effect, Kipling's travels trace a journey which is mapped as temporally proportional to the geographical distance travelled from the borders of British jurisdiction. Jaipur is the nearest city of the Rajput kingdoms to British India; its proximity to civilisation is heralded by a modern museum, a hospital, a school of art, gas and water works – 'all the things in fact which are necessary to Western municipal welfare and comfort' (Kipling, 1919a: 11). Boondi, on the other hand, represents the 'utter untouchedness' of native life and a stepping back into distant Indian history.

But 'Letters of Marque' does not follow the path of a simple regression into atavism the further the narrator travels from the Anglo-Indian border. If that were the case, the traveller's cultural identity would not be put under the sustained pressure it finds in the narrative. Kipling's text, falling more within the orbit of the sentimental narrative form, is dialogic by virtue of its representation of the speaking subject in dialogue with the voices of self and Other. Split between the self that sees, the self that sees itself seeing and that which sees itself being seen (Pratt, 1985: 132), the parodic and mock-heroic potential is exploited in Kipling's self-conscious adoption of different voices and personas. Yet ultimately his travels in Rajasthan are relevant to the present context because they posit the issue of narrative authority and cultural identity in more or less direct relation to questions concerning the nature and function of the British presence in India. Because Kipling's writing is concerned specifically with the Native Princely States, the answers it formulates or avoids cast light on the poetics and politics of Anglo-Indian identity.

'Letters of Marque' presents a troubled meditation on the historical and cultural difficulties of Anglo-Indian identity. Despite the easy bravado or the avowed indolence of the Englishman–narrator on holiday, this text – relentlessly self-conscious and ironic – is traumatised by an anxiety about the nature or purpose of the colonial enterprise. The narrative's oscillation between respect, veneration and fear inspired by Rajput history, and its admiration for the reforms generated by British Residents, can be in part understood in relation to political ambivalence with a solid historical base in conflict between an Orientalist and Anglicist mode of government. But mixing reportage with romance, the narrative's vacillation between the progressive spaces of modernity and that of exotic antiquity is reflected as a vacillation between narrative modes which never entirely settles. Positioned between two radically different cultures, the travelogue veers between two narrative strains: gothic and realist. The latter belongs to the domain of mimetic stability but up against the perceived alterity of India's 'cruel' and 'dark places', colonial discourse is shot through with desire and turns into a form of paranoia. This other knowledge exhibited by the text is fantasmatic and uncanny, and located in shadowy spaces where things exceed their naming and slip away from authoritative pinning down. The text's gothic mode can be most clearly discerned in the narrator's fear of native bodily contact, imagined as an invasion of private space and a deracination of self. Framed within the struggle for cultural and territorial advantage, and surrounded on all sides with architectural reminders of Indian history, the Englishman–narrator's phobia of native bodies can be read as an uncanny metaphor of the sudden collapse of discursive authority.

Travels in another land

Written for the resident Anglo-Indians, 'Letters of Marque' begins with a desire for the freer lifestyle of the traveller on the road motivated only by 'personal inclination'. The journey is rationalised as an escape from a 'old and well-known life' which has turned stale and claustrophobic (Kipling, 1919a: 1); British India is the place where 'Commissioners and Deputy-Commissioners, Governors and Lieutenant-Governors, Aides-de-Camp, Colonels and their wives, Majors, Captains and Subalterns after their kind move and rule and govern and squabble and fight and sell each other's horses and tell wicked stories of their neighbours' (Kipling, 1919a: 3). The long list of functionaries indicates the minute hierarchical divisions of departmental politics and the sometimes parochial character of the community's obsessions. The text's recurring article ('and') robs these personages of their significance, and satire serves to deflate any importance attached to their function in the colonial government. 'Rule' becomes coterminous with 'squabble', and 'government' with the comic bathos of gossip and horse trade. But the desire to remove oneself from an all too familiar world for the mystique of the Orient is also self-consciously ironised. To become a tourist is hardly an improvement; it is to become a 'globe-trotter', 'a man who "does" kingdoms in days and writes books upon them in weeks' (Kipling, 1919a: 1).

The globe-trotter is not the only persona Kipling's narrator adopts. He is also a pioneer, whose encounter with India is imagined as the mythic harmony of man's kinship with his environment. The pastoral form legitimises the Englishman's presence in India. Unlike his globe-trotter counterpart, who is an outsider touring the native land, the pioneer–settler's claim to territory is lent all the naturalism of Adam's exertions in a land free of history. The narrator's engagement with Boondi begins on the road to the city; 'nature's great morning song' inspires the hearer to 'go forward and possess that land'. The daybreak over Boondi recalls the 'First Day' and the Genesis story. Yet even this persona is ironised when it turns out that his tasks are purely imaginative:

> It is good, good beyond expression, to see the sun rise upon a strange land and to know that you have only to go forward

and possess that land – that it will dower you before the day is ended with a hundred new impressions and, perhaps, one idea.

(Kipling, 1919a: 136)

But the unmasking of the narrator's frontiersman persona as 'only a loafer in a flannel suit bound for Boondi' is part a narrative strategy for revealing the true pioneering heroes.

As opposed to the narrator's fraudulent pioneer, the text suggests that the real heroes of 'independent' India are the Residents and Engineers of the Princely States. Kipling's inhabitation of different masks is directed at making certain contrasts more effective. The real frontiersmen are a 'large-minded breed'; their work constitutes the real toil of Empire, in contrast to the merely bureaucratic. They embody the epic ideals of Empire in a prosaic age through their selfless devotion which 'bring ... good to thousands', and through the 'consecrat[ion of] their lives to that state in all single-heartedness and purity'. In the outskirts of Empire, away from state control, these men fulfil their true potential and become 'veritable tiger men':

tough, bronzed men, with wrinkles at the corners of their eyes, gotten by looking across much sun-glare. . . . and this to the [Anglo-]Indian Cockney, who is accustomed to the bleached or office man, is curious, there are to be found many veritable 'tiger-men' – not story-spinners but such as have, in their wanderings from Bikaneer to Indore dropped their tiger in the way of business. They are enthusiastic over princelings of little known fiefs, lords of austere estates perched on the tops of unthrifty hills, hard riders, and good sportsmen.

(Kipling, 1919a: 62–63)

Deliberately distinguished from their effeminate counterparts and the imitation men of the Presidencies, these men are real towers of strength. Kipling's text naturalises their place in India. They and not the Native Princes, are the 'real feudal princelings' of little known fiefs; they are the 'hat-marked' caste or 'men who bear the hat-mark on their brow as plainly as the well-born native carries the trisul of Shiva' (Kipling, 1919a: 62). But here, in an effort to glamorise their representation, the narrator mixes metaphors. Because the text presents them as feudal lords, they cannot be represented in terms of their routine labour and function but only in terms of their leisured lifestyles. Furthermore, their epic and romantic discourse of excess contradicts the technological and democratic revolution they bring to these backward states. Less loquacious than the bleached office man, these tiger-men are the silent totemic emblems of masculinity. Portrayed as not wanting to sing their own praises, their place in the roll call of imperial excellence must be invoked by others; by their deeds ye shall know them. And such a requirement, as we shall later see, creates problems.

Anglo (In)dian

Paradoxically, given the nature and effects of their modernising tasks, the land which bears least trace of the 'hat-marked caste' is presented as the most desirable. Because travel writing relies on the difference between the home one journeys from and the place one travels to, the pleasure of the Orient is inversely proportional to the penetration of colonial civilisation. The romance of exotic locales is best located in states which discourage English visitors. The utter 'untouchedness' of Boondi is its very attraction; it boasts a rare harmony of man and nature that renders the modern hybrid British territories out of joint. The city shows a real interlocking of lives and livelihoods that contrasts positively with the urban metropolis of the Presidencies, or of London in the mother country:

> The newer shops are built into, on to, over, under time-blackened ruins of an older day, and the little children skip about tottering arcades and grass-grown walls, while their parents chatter below in the crowded bazaar. . . . They do not hurry themselves. They sit in the sun and think, or put on all the arms in the family, and, hung with ironmongery, parade before their admiring friends. Others, lean, dark men, with bound jaws and only a tulwar for weapon, dive in and out of the alleys on errands of the State. It is a beautifully lazy city, doing everything in the real, true, original native way, and is kept in very good order by the Durbar.
>
> (Kipling, 1919a: 160–161)

The 'real, original native' lifestyle is differentiated from the hurly burly of a modern 'nickel-plated civilisation'. The original Durbar represents a cosy domestic and familial history of face-to-face contact under a paternalist state government. The narrator wanders with envy through the plenitude of 'sunlit, sleepy courts, gay with painted frescoes' reaching an 'inner square, where smiling grey-bearded men squat at ease and play *chaupur*' (Kipling, 1919a: 37). These shared public spaces of the old native city shelter an older and more cohesive culture than the dissonant one that the colonial imposition of modernity brings.

Like Boondi, the state of Udaipur is 'as backward as Jeypore is advanced' and does not approve of the intrusions of Englishmen. Yet she is hospitable and promises the 'soft splendours' of a cushioned house-boat on the Pichola Sagar. Udaipur is a romantic dream-landscape of peace and tranquillity. She is an Orientalist land of pleasure and luxury; the hills 'glow like opals' and the journey of the boat on the lake is like 'the noise of silk'. The journey to Udaipur from Chitor draws on the *Arabian Nights*:

> At sunset the low hills turned to opal and wine-red and the brown dust flew up pure gold; for the tonga was running straight into the sinking sun. Now and again would pass a traveller on camel, or a gang of *Bunjarras* with their pack-bullocks and their women; and the sun touched the brasses of their swords and guns till the poor wretches seemed rich merchants come back from travelling with Sindbad.
>
> (Kipling, 1919a: 46)

Yet the very extravagance of this myth forces a recognition of its status as fantasy. The narrative parodies its own desire and there are distinct moments of unease when the gold-tipped peasants turn back into 'poor wretches' and the generous slaughter of ducks for the Englishman's feast is little else save a 'double-barrelled murder perpetrated in the silence of the marsh'. Unsettling questions do not go away: does the hospitality of the Princely States smooth over the Englishman's status as foreigner to allow the illusion of harmony and belonging? Is the traveller–narrator merely an alien tourist in an Oriental land?

The traveller is, of course, a foreigner in Rajasthan; he is a resident of British India and not of the Native Princely States. But the traveller–narrator is also a foreigner in the Indian land in which he resides as a member of the British Raj; in Maud Diver's famous words, 'English men and women in India are, as it were, members of one great family, aliens under one sky' (Allen, 1975: 51). The implied reader of 'Letters of Marque' is the Anglo-Indian resident; the text inscribes this cultural kinship in its address, reinforcing feelings of community and thus mitigates feelings of alienation. Told specifically from the viewpoint of a *resident*, the narrative contrasts familiarity with the Indian landscape with a *foreign* traveller's naivety. The globe-trotter character Kipling's narrator meets on a train is a fresh-faced 'pink-cheeked, whiskered, and superbly self-confident' young man from Manchester, who 'conceived the modest idea of "doing India" in ten days' (Kipling, 1919a: 7, 5). With an Indian Bradshaw in hand, this tourist 'does kingdoms in days' and is 'much pleased' with Agra and Delhi; to the disgust of his fellow traveller, he can only describe the Taj Mahal as 'nice'. He is 'pleased as a child with his Delhi atrocities'; his souvenirs consist of 'silver filigree work modelled on Palais Royal patterns', shawls and jewellery deemed 'really Eastern'. Despite his familiarity with the railway timetable, the tourist's hasty assimilation of the country does not represent a real engagement with India. Unlike the Anglo-Indian resident, his mastery of information and images has no real depth.

The inclusion of this youthful figure in the text is ingenious because it displaces the resident Englishman's status as foreigner onto the figure of the tourist, who is now seen as the naive and innocent outsider. In comparison to the young man from Manchester, the Anglo-Indian is the 'old resident' of India whose long habituation with the native sub-continent leads him not to 'wear his *pagri* tail-fashion down his back', nor to say 'cabman' to the driver of the *'ticca-ghari'*. His knowledge of native craft would certainly prevent him from falling foul of the Delhi boxwallah swindlers. The introduction of the figure of the British tourist gives the narrator more of a residental status than he is perhaps due. Kipling's globe-trotter tourist is a young man from an industrial city on vacation while his narrator is an Anglo-Indian on a working holiday. The use of the tourist enables the narrative to reclaim the title of 'Englishman' without the negative connotations of being a foreigner. But the oscillation between narrative personas reveals an underlying anxiety; the globe-trotter, for all his faults, does not claim a place in India. The tourist is 'going home for Christmas' to a 'genial, cheery British household'. The Anglo-Indian's place in the land of his adopted home is, in contrast, conditioned by the degree of devotion he expresses towards it. There will be no friendly household to welcome him. Even the men who bear the caste-mark of the hat on their brow and take a 'poor impoverished State as a man takes a wife' appear to do it more for the worse than for the better. Despite the cynicism of the knowing insider, the Anglo-Indian cannot help envying the globe-trotter: his own *home* for the time was not in England but in a 'dark bungaloathsome hotel'.

'Letters' exhibits a double alienation. On the one hand, there is the alienation of an exile from the 'real' home of England. This is made evident when a bout of homesickness brought on by a cuckoo causes the narrator to dream of English gardens and apple-orchards. On the other, there is the – perhaps more insidious – alienation of one who must continually assert India as a kind of home. It is the latter who must discover enough reasons to justify his presence in a foreign land when all around him works towards denying him that justification. The difficulty of the Anglo-Indian's position lies precisely in his occupation of these two states of estrangement. Kipling's globe-trotter has no need to defend his cultural identity; the Anglo-Indian, with one eye on the metro-politan culture and one eye on India does. Not to do so would leave the Anglo-Indian figure with nowhere to call home.

BATTLELINES: HISTORIES PAST AND PRESENT

As indicated in the previous chapter, British administration and rule in India in the nineteenth century produced an ambiguous relationship with Indian customs and traditions through its manip-ulation of Indian history. 'Letters of Marque' can be located within a debate regarding the nature and function of British rule in India, emphasised by its direct reference to the Native Princely States. The need for exploiting an alliance with native rulers contributed to a recognition of the legitimacy of their rule; their traditions and the feudal character of the old empire made India more accessible to British rulers with aristocratic or upper-class sympathies. The relations with the Rajput states fall within such a domain. Colonel James Tod whose name was associated with Rajasthan in the nineteenth century, and whose publications and surveys of central India literally put Rajasthan on the map, was appointed political agent to the Western Rajput states in 1818. Tod, whom Kipling quotes with approval in 'Letters', was taken by the romantic feudal past of Mewar (Udaipur) and worked to restore it. His role, as he saw it, was 'to bring back matters to a correspondence with an era of their history' (Jeffrey, 1978: 212). Even when Mayo College was set up in 1875 to train and form young princes into proper state leaders, the colonial administration supported existing clan chiefs and centralised control.

The history of Rajasthan in 'Letters of Marque' does not depart from the conventional view of Rajput history as romance: stories of 'heroic fighting' are equivalent in form and content to the chivalric and courtly romances of medieval times. 'Letters' frames Rajput history as the epic and nostalgic story of great individuals such as Jey Singh, Pudmini (an Indian 'Helen of Troy'), Bappa Rawul, Ala-ud-din, Rana Lakhsman Singh and Udai Singh Jey Singh – a 'tangled tale of force, fraud, cunning, desperate love and more desperate revenge, [and] crime worthy of demons and virtues fit for Gods' (Kipling, 1919a: 8). Jey Singh, for example, stands out as the 'Solomon of Rajputana' whose military might matched his intellectual prowess. He studied astronomy, engineered the grid-like system of Jaipur's roads, 'reformed the Mahometan calendar', established a 'superb library' and built numerous palaces, gardens and temples. Jeemal of Bedmore and Kalla, both Rajput warriors were famous for battles and had 'two stone *chhatris*, each carrying a red daubed stone' erected in their honour. Rajasthan's past is depicted as full of vigour and life. The desolation of the ghost city, Amber, is a 'small measure' of the 'riotous, sumptuous, murderous life' of an India before British rule. In Amber, there was beauty and 'more than enough strength' in the palaces of Kings 'royal and superb'. Despite the overt Orientalism of the 'intrigue of unruly princes and princelings [who] fought Asiatically', this feudal history brooks no comparison with the British era of the monogrammed coronet-crowned lamp-post, and heavy machinery. In Kipling's words, the nineteenth-century artifacts of engines, hydraulic presses and neat corrugated iron roofs, 'somehow did not taste well' after Amber's sumptuous architecture and her historic past.

The cultural legacy of the Indian Empire offers a comparative case of ambivalence. The period between 1860 and 1877 saw what Cohn terms as the 'rapid expansion' of knowledge with regard to Indian civilisation; the 'definition and expropriation' of this history and culture far exceeded the initial narrow scope in relation to law and revenue collection (Hobsbawm and Ranger, 1983: 182). The study of Indian languages and classical texts, the survey and conservation of architecture, the setting up of schools for arts, craft and design was part and parcel of a definition and reification of India's history. One example was the archaeological survey of India which determined for the indigenous people the very buildings considered vital for their cultural heritage. It was initiated with the founding of the Archaeological Department in 1862 and Sir Alexander Cunningham's appointment as Director of Archaeology. His brief was to 'make an accurate description of such remains as most deserve notice, with the history of them so far as it is traceable and a record of the traditions that are retained regarding them' (Cumming, 1939: 1). In 'Letters of Marque' architecture appears as the measure of India's cultural legacy. The text acknowledges that the legacy more than matches what Europe has to offer. For the narrator of 'Letters', Jaipur is the 'Versailles of India', Jodhpur's House of Strife is the 'work of giants', and the Taj Mahal an awesome aesthetic achievement. The Taj is 'sign made stone', 'the embodiment of all things pure, all things holy' and all things tragic. The Taj 'wrapped in the mists of the morning' stands as a shifting 'splendour' 'floating free of the earth', 'taking a hundred new shapes, each perfect and each beyond description'. This 'unearthly pavilion' strikes the Englishman dumb with the weight of its majesty and its history: 'it is certain that no man can in cold blood and colder ink set down his impressions if he has been in the least moved. . . . It is well on the threshold of a journey to be taught reverence and awe' (Kipling, 1919a: 5). The validation of such knowledge has some repercussions. If the setting up of museums and schools teaching indigenous crafts, census taking and ethnographic surveys describing 'the peoples and cultures of India'[7] were defining what was Indian in an official and 'objective' sense, it was also legitimising and rendering valuable what was preeminently non-British.

In a land eloquent of a non-British past, the contemporary present became a battleground for cultural and territorial advantage. In 'Letters', architecture is literally monumental history; in this competition of signs, architecture is construed as 'leaving one's marks' on both Indian geography and history. New buildings initiated and built by resident engineers of the Princely States are imagined as *marking one's own territory*; 'in truth, to men of action few things could be more delightful than having a State of fifteen thousand square miles placed at their disposal, as it were to leave their mark on' (Kipling, 1919a: 29). The 'riotous, sumptuous, murderous life' of the Native States had 'been put [to] an end' when Colonel Jacob as successor to Jey Singh (and not the present Maharajah), provides a programme of gas works, schools and museums which are 'necessary to Western Municipal welfare and comfort'. Administrative efficiency, social and health reforms are an integral part of the British stamp on these backward parts. Their semiotic value lies in their indication of British rule and progress.

Despite his praise of the programme of reform, the narrator of 'Letters' is careful to insist on the distinction between the modernity symbolised by the British Resident and that accruing to the Rajput states. Signs of European civility and 'progress' among Indians are disavowed and denigrated as comic-ironic, grotesque or even bizarre. 'Letters' tells the readers that deprived of a meaningful existence as a warrior the Maharajah of Jaipur has no real function. He shops imperially; his palace is 'overwhelmingly rich in candelabra, painted ceilings, gilt mirrors, and other evidences of a too hastily assimilated civilisation' (Kipling, 1919a: 37). Jaipur city is satirised for its incongruous juxtaposition of old and new: the sacred bull 'trips over the rails of a steel tramway which brings out the city rubbish' while the painted cart 'catches its primitive wheels in the cast iron gas-lamp post' (Kipling, 1919a: 11). For all the signs of modernity, from museum and hospital to water and gas works, 'the [same] old, old game of intrigue goes on as merrily as of yore' (Kipling, 1919a: 37). Education is merely a 'mask' for the true horrors connected with the House of Amet. The Mayo College English-educated Rawat of Amet reverts to his more primitive side whenever the opportunity presents itself. Staking its authority on the logic of the civilising mission, colonial discourse must decry all imitations of progress in order to legitimise its own continually deferring trusteeship. The text's colonial gaze denies the Princely State its modernising impulse by calling attention to the comic grotesqueness of its half-baked attempts at imitation. But these statements also show a fundamental indeterminacy within the very structure of a colonial discourse. If the discourse confers instead a sense that the Native State may *never* be like the English one, the representation of these reformed colonised subjects begins to reevaluate the colonising culture's claim to be a model of excellence. An ambivalence of meaning attaches to Kipling's indictment of Jaipur: the 'lamps of British Progress . . . converted the city of Jey Singh into a surprise – a big, bewildering practical joke' (Kipling, 1919a: 11).

The text is also permeated with contradictory desires. Often, the preservation of power achieved by the discourse of discrimination comes into conflict with narcissistic and mimetic demands. To use a psychoanalytic phrase coined by Bhabha, it is 'the ambivalent space where the rite of power is enacted on the site of desire' (Bhabha, 1985: 154). That hesitancy begins with the text's delineation of native reaction. For while it is one thing to build more gas works and hospitals, it is another to obtain the loyalty and love from subjects that will be necessary to affirm one's place in a strange land. When the narrator's attempts to persuade the strong and silent English engineer of Jaipur to talk about his achievements fail, he turns towards the native residents of Jaipur city. The engineer's plan of beautifying the city and making it 'clean and wholesome' must have earned him the people's praise.[8] There one may find 'how well their pleasure [i.e. that of the British Residents] has suited the pleasure of the people' (Kipling, 1919a: 29). But the narcissistic desire for a reflection that returns the exact requirement of love will always be unfulfilled: 'When, in love I solicit a look, what is profoundly unsatisfying and always missing is that – you never look at me from the place from which I see you' (Lacan, 1977: 103). Reading psychoanalytically, the text's natives function to reflect the colonial image as undivided, unalienated and miraculously whole. Their role is to affirm and secure the Englishman's identity. The character of the native visitor to Jaipur provides the opportunity for just such a faithful and unbiased reflection. Kipling's native 'was evidently a stranger to the place . . . he knew nothing of Jeypore, except the names of certain Englishmen in it, the men who, he said, had made the Waterworks and built the Hospital for his brother's son's comfort' (Kipling, 1919a: 28). The text implies that the Resident's presence must be highly valued if even a stranger to Jaipur knows the names of Englishmen who had built the waterworks and the hospital. Yet this man also makes the absurd and naive assertion that hospitals and waterworks were built solely to nurse his sick nephew. The inclusion of the stranger's silly view of the public-spirited good of the Englishman's building programme indicates an innocence that is necessary for the text's designation of his differential status. After all, the stranger must be a genuine native Indian gentleman in order to return authentically the look of love. But by creating such a differential textual frame, the narrative leaves a stain on the surface of the image that ushers in division and loss. While the portrait presents the mirror image of love and pleasure – of looking at what I wish to see – the narrator's differential comic undercutting of the native gentlemen's belief disturbs his narcissistic demands. The reply may be ironic or simply dismissed as the response of some simple-minded fool. The narrator may never return the fullness of the Englishman's authority and presence in India because his authority and presence are based on differential signs. Even the natives not of the political high road seem genuinely crafty. In attempting to play the role of Greek chorus to his modest and silent 'Englishmen who made the State their fatherland, and identified themselves with its progress as only Englishmen can', the narrator is made more insecure. He chronicles his attempts to persuade others to play their part in his fantasy and seems to find some who are willing: 'the men at the stand-pipes explain that the Maharajah Sahib's father gave the order for the Waterworks and that Yakub (Jacob) Sahib made them – not only in the city, but out away in the district' (Kipling, 1919a: 29). To his eager question, 'Did the people grow more crops thereby?', comes the non-committal and clever reply, 'Of course they did. Were canals made only to wash in?' Another attempt to draw a favourable report of these Englishmen – 'How much more crops?' – is greeted with an artful brush-off: 'Who knows? The Sahib had better go and ask some official.' Kipling's narrator can only fill in answers to these queries about modernisation and progress with an official re-sponse: 'Increased irrigation means increase of revenue for the State' (Kipling, 1919a: 29).

THE COLONIAL UNCANNY

If ambivalence is the product of colonialism's split and fractured discourse of authority, the uncanny is also put into motion with Kipling's use of the gothic in describing the essential experience of the Native States. The establishment of the colonial civil society in India which follows the dissolution of the East India company is articulated within a narrative of realism, knowledge and power. Michel Foucault's thesis that power functions as knowledge to 'create a space of exact legibility' applies here (Foucault, 1980: 154). Foucault locates the origin of the modern disciplinary regime in the period following the French Revolution. The latter estab-lished a new regime of 'opinion' which sought to implement justice through subjecting and 'immersing people in a field of total visibility where the opinion, observation and discourse of others would restrain them from harmful acts'. The corresponding excess of signification produced from the new civil regime's paranoia of things unknown, and of things which 'seem' to escape classification, is a result of psychic and political overdetermination:

> A fear haunted the latter half of the eighteenth century: the fear of darkened spaces, of the pall of gloom which prevents the full visibility of things, men and truths. It sought to break up the patches of darkness that blocked the light, eliminate the shadowy areas of society, demolish the unlit chambers where arbitrary political acts, monarchical caprice, religious superstitions, tyrannical and priestly plots, epidemics and the illusions of ignorance fermented. The chateaux, lazarets, bastilles and convents inspired even in the pre-Revolutionary period a suspicion and hatred exacerbated by a certain political overdetermination.
>
> (Foucault, 1980: 153)

Foucault's invocation of the landscape of gothic novels with their 'ruined castles, terrifying and silent convents', as the 'imaginary spaces' that are the 'negative . . . transparency and visibility' of the modern civil state (Foucault, 1980: 154), is particulary relevant to the manner in which 'Letters of Marque' constructs the gothic alterity of the Native States. India's romantic past and her traditional forms are imagined as 'dark places of the earth, full of unimaginable cruelty'. In Kipling, the colonial gothic is located in the realm of shadowy spaces of ruined empires or in the *zenanas*, symbol of intrigues and native *realpolitik*. Foucault's description of the obsessions of the post-revolutionary civil regime correspond to my reading of the colonial gothic. The *zenanas* escape the panoptic surveillance of the male colonial eye as dark, inaccessible, feminised and veiled places of darkness. Control and surveillance in 'Letters' are reversed, as paranoia fills palaces with hidden eyes. They are magical and terrifying sites which turn the colonial gaze back onto itself and reduce the subject to a state of helplessness:

> All Palaces in India excepting dead ones, such as that of Amber, are full of eyes. In some, as had been said, the idea of being watched is stronger than in others. In Boondi Palace it was overpowering . . . . There were trap doors on the tops of terraces, and windows veiled in foliage and bull's eyes set low in unexpected walls and many other peep-holes and places of vantage. In the end, the Englishman looked devoutly at the

floor, but when the voice of the woman came out from under
his feet, he felt that there was nothing left for him but to go.
Yet, excepting only this voice, there was deep silence everywhere, and nothing could be seen.

(Kipling, 1919a: 182)

Like Boondi, Chitor generates paranoia. It is a deserted and
ruined Rajput city with an ancient epic history of strife 'by riot and
the sword'. Chitor is a place of human death; its decaying and
inanimate objects seem to have a macabre life of their own. Chitor
possesses ghostly winds singing of past gatherings in a Hall of
Audience and 'marauding trees' invading the very stone structure
of the palace. Its wind-sown peepuls 'had wrenched a thick slab
clear of the wall' and hold the stone 'as a man holds down a fallen
enemy under his elbow and forearm' (Kipling, 1919a: 96). Into
this scene wanders the solitary English figure who may not even
make an innocent joke without hostile forces seeming to take
offence:

> The Englishman wandered so far in one palace that he came
> to an almost black-dark room, high up in a wall, and said
> *proudly* to himself: 'I must be the first man who has been here';
> meaning no harm or insult to any one. But he tripped and
> fell, and as he put out his hands, he felt that the stairs had
> been worn hollow and smooth by the tread of innumerable
> naked feet. Then he was afraid, and came away very quickly,
> stepping delicately over fallen friezes and bits of sculptured
> men, so as not to offend the Dead.
>
> (Kipling, 1919a: 96–97) [my emphasis]

The 'black-dark' room narrates the scene of pride before a fall. The
Englishman pretends to the status of the pioneer – but 'first man'
as compared with whom or what? His presumption is soon followed
by his tripping in the same room. This uncanny coincidence causes
him to attribute his fall to the evil forces in the palace taking
exception to his innocent jest. He apologises hurriedly, 'meaning
no harm or insult to any one'. His earlier boast is corrected by the
touch of his hands on the hollow and smooth stairs. There *had* been
people previous to his entrance – invisible and innumerable
natives, the tread of whose naked feet even now threaten to trample
this lone white man. Smooth stones and 'innumerable' naked
bodies become a recurring motif in the rest of the narrative.

INNUMERABLE BODIES

In addition to Chitor, there are two other places in which this phobia surfaces in 'Letters': Kumbha Rana's Tower of Victory with its accompanying descent into the spring below and the interiors of the palace of Boondi as mentioned above. Both record feelings of disorientation, repulsion and a phobia of physical contact. Seen from afar, the Tower of Victory is 'nine storeys high, crowned atop . . . with a purely Mahometan dome' and is a structure commemorating victory in battle. Seen from within however, this Jain edifice could never be the place of triumph. The narrator offers none of the measured responses of aesthetic and historical information he offers earlier in the travelogue. The tower within invokes intense repugnance; it is 'not a soothing place to visit'. The walls are wreathed in a 'confusing intricacy of . . . figures' characteristic of Hindu art, and the 'lavishness of decoration . . . worked toward the instillment of fear and aversion'. Earlier in Udaipur, the narrator had complained of the repulsive character of Hindu art whose 'clustered figures of man and brute who seem always on the point of bursting into unclean wriggling life' (Kipling, 1919a: 58). Here, the confusion and profusion of figures in the tower is presented in terms of an actual tactile threat to the English individual. In the tower, he warns, 'while you are ascending, you are wrapping yourself deeper and deeper in the tangle of . . . thronging armies of sculptured figures [and] the mad profusion of design splashed impartially'. Disorientation soon gives way to a much more specific fear of physical contact; 'and, most abhorrent of all, the slippery sliminess of the walls always worn smooth by naked men' (Kipling, 1919a: 98). The touch of these indistinguishable and invisible native bodies is presented as a primal trauma and repeatedly alluded to in the narrative. The fear registers three distinct aspects: innumerable numbers, the physical touch of naked black bodies and faces, and the imagined effect of such contact which wears stones smooth.

The climb to the top of this phallic tower with its aura of aberrant and perverse sexuality would have repeated the act of triumph that was granted the Jains. But the Englishman's desire to recreate this feeling only results in its opposite. The descent into the Gau Mukh or cow-mouth spring is a continuation of the nightmare. It takes the form of a mythic descent into a world of death. The phobia of native bodily contact takes on new proportions in the Gau Mukh as myriad naked black feet are imagined to cross even the protective barriers of time and civilisation. His modern shoes offer no protection; stepping on the 'smooth, worn rocks and he felt their sliminess through his bootsoles'. The feeling of horror and terror which accompanies the journey condenses into a single startling image: 'it was as though he were treading on the soft, oiled skin of a Hindu' (Kipling, 1919a: 101). Furthermore, the descent into the claustrophobic womb-like shrine of obscene phallic worship (the Lingam) is followed by a reminder of the subterranean tomb of the princess Pudmini and her followers, slain on a burning pyre. The descent presents a mythic journey and a 'time warp' in which the colonial present is obliterated by the ancient primeval and feudal past:

> It seemed as though the descent had led the Englishman firstly, two thousand years away from his own century, and secondly, into a trap, and that he would fall off the polished stones into the stinking tank, or that the Gau-Mukh would continue to pour water until the tank rose up and swamped him, or that some of the stone slabs would fall forward and crush him flat.
>
> (Kipling, 1919a: 100)

The polished stones are formed by the sheer numbers moving over them. This symbolises the overwhelming weight and pressure of two thousand years of ancient Indian history and civilisation on the seemingly fragile present of the British presence in India. This place of the past is subversive of colonial intent; it 'made the Englishman feel that he had done a great wrong in trespassing into the very heart and soul of all Chitor'. This place of 'years and blood' also destroys notions of colonial superiority in its dialogue with mortality: 'above all, he did not care to look behind him, where stood the reminder that he was no better than the beasts that perish' (Kipling, 1919a: 100). Yet the desire to restage such an encounter is strong; the 'Genius of the Place' lures the writer back into the 'unspeakable Gau Mukh' in the dead of the night to reenact the earlier dream sequence. But the subsequent scene 'lovely, wild, and unmatchable as any that mortal eyes have been privileged to rest upon' is an encounter that the narrator's readers will never know because he will keep it as a private and secret sexual fantasy; he is to keep it as a 'love letter, a thing for one pair of eyes only'.

The palace of Boondi echoes the terror of Chitor by emphasising the element of physical decay. In this journey, the Rajput body is depicted as the diseased and maggot-ridden corrupt body of India's overripe civilisation. The crowded steps of the palace become a metaphor of contamination and repulsion: 'the sunlight was very vivid without and the shadows were heavy within, so that little could be seen except this clinging mass of humanity wriggling like maggots in a carcass' (Kipling, 1919a: 174). Rajput history and culture is transformed metaphorically into the unclean body of death and degeneration; it threatens to infect the white clean English body with its taint of death. Boondi palace is that 'palace of uneasy dreams – more the work of goblins than of men', a labyrinth of corridors, courtyards, surface and subterranean passages with no beginning and no end. The architecture of the Rajput palace defies the Englishman's 'archaeological researches' and 'careful notes'; it 'defied pinning down before the public'. Built in and out of the hillside, it gives the impression of an 'avalanche of masonry'. Kipling's text resurrects the same signs of anxiety; footworn stones 'follow the contours of the ground' and everything in the Palace 'shone from constant contact of bare feet and hurrying bare shoulders'. The grim history of palace intrigue inspires a meditation on these foot-worn stones: 'at the best of times men slip on these smooth stones; and when the place was swimming in blood, foothold must have been treacherous indeed' (Kipling, 1919a: 173). The narrator, bewildered and confused by the constant stream of native traffic sees 'the rush of people' as rounding and softening every corner 'as a river grinds down boulders' (Kipling, 1919a: 177). The predominantly realistic and nominalistic mode of colonial discourse is transformed into paranoia in the encounter with Boondi. The narrator feels an overpowering sense of being watched; he is terrorised by a palace full of eyes and disembodied voices. 'In an unknown Palace in an unknown land', in this state of magical terror, language is slippery and epitomises the difficulty of knowledge: 'it is the catching of a shadow of a meaning here and there' (Kipling, 1919a: 174). Boondi has made the Anglo-Indian narrator–traveller feel his insignificance in India's roll-call of history; he confesses, 'what made him blush hotly, all alone among the tombs on the hillside, was the idea that he with his ridiculous demands . . . should have clattered and clattered through any part of it at all' (Kipling, 1919a: 182–183). Boondi, the

most fearful and untouched of Rajput states, is also the Indian state
with little or no room for the Englishman.

AT THE END OF THE PASSAGE

In this collision of different civilisations and different times, the
imperial encounter does not necessarily privilege the telling of the
British story. Or more correctly, it does so only under a series of
complex manoeuvres. The ideology of British rule cannot simply
be framed as the progress of history and modernity. The discourse
of evolution has its own ruthless logic; in the survival of the fittest,
new civilisations are always under threat of usurpation by even
newer ones. The rise of civilisation is always shadowed by its fall;
the Englishman looking at the images of Rajput decay abroad will
be reminded of the image of the Roman Empire's decline which
haunts the 'Condition of England' question at home. Kipling's
narrative of the desolation and destruction of cities contains
Biblical intonations which reverberate beyond its simple salutary
lessons for the contemporary imperial regime. *All* earthly civilisation must pass away; everywhere there are signs to remind the
Englishman of his own mortality. Stumbling upon a sun-dial in the
palace gardens, he retreats, chastened by a shadow on the dial. He
moves away

> struck by the fact that the shadow of the Prince of Dials moved
> over its vast plate so quickly that it seemed as though Time,
> wroth at the insolence of Jey Singh, had loosed the Horses of
> the Sun and were sweeping everything . . . into the darkness
> of eternal night.
>
> (Kipling, 1919a: 40)

Corruption and death envelope the unsuspecting Englishman–
tourist as he surveys the ruins of ancient Rajput cities. His anxiety
takes more concrete form in the fear that the 'marks' he leaves on
the landscape will vanish. The natural successor to Jey Singh of
ancient times is Colonel Jacob Sahib, and it is he who fashions the
new Jaipur. But the dead cities of Amber and Chitor are a reminder
that nothing will stand the test of time. Furthermore, the natural
environment which overruns dead cities is also one which threatens
present British monuments. Portrayed as an anarchic wilderness
ever present on the margins of civility, it 'inspires an Anglo-Indian
Cockney, with unreasoning fear'. Just as the harsh Indian climate

wears down the Anglo-Indian potental for health and happiness, the desert landscape of Rajasthan eats away at the outposts of progress:

> The red-grey hills seem to laugh at it, and the ever-shifting sand-dunes under the hills take no account of it, for they advance upon the bases of the monogrammed, coronet-crowned lamp-posts, and fill up the points of the natty tramway near the Waterworks. . . . Pass between a tramway and a trough for wayfaring camels till your foot sinks ankle-deep in soft sand, and you come upon what seems to be the fringe of illimitable desert.
>
> (Kipling, 1919a: 26–27)

Monuments – or their remains – provide those traces vital to the continuity of cultural life; but entropy characterises all. The question of whether the British will leave their mark on the land is answered by the rapidity with which tracks melt away into sand and the shifting sand-dunes advance on lamp-posts. At Chitor, the narrator narrowly escapes from the 'place of blood and years', not caring to look behind 'where stood the reminder that he was no better than the beasts that perish'. The travelogue's fear also sheds light on another of Kipling's obscure gothic allegories. In the story 'At the End of the Passage', the preservation of any semblance of cultural and social identity in the outback of the Civil Service is near impossible and the story's protagonist, Hummil, and his coterie of friends were 'lonely folk who understood the dread meaning of loneliness' (Kipling, 1897: 161). In this outpost of civilisation, India is the place where the Anglo-Indian civil servant encounters a spectral likeness of himself that terrifies. At Hummil's death, his native servant is asked for his version of the story; he remarks, 'Heaven-born, in my poor opinion, this that was my master has descended into the Dark Places, and there has been caught because he was not able to escape with sufficient speed'. Hummil's doctor friend and his fellow service men suppress the story and the evidence associated with it.

5

THE CITY OF DREADFUL NIGHT

The settler's town is a well-fed town, an easy-going town;
its belly is always full of good things. The settler's town
is a town of white people, of foreigners. The town
belonging to the colonized people, or at least the native
town, the Negro village, the medina, the reservation, is
a place of ill fame, peopled by men of ill repute. . . . It
is a world without spaciousness; men live there on top
of each other, and their huts are built one on top of the
other. . . . It is a town of niggers and dirty arabs. The
look that the native turns on the settler's town is a look
of lust, a look of envy . . . . The colonized man is an
envious man. And this the settler knows very well; when
their glances meet he ascertains bitterly, always on the
defensive 'They want to take our place'.

(Fanon, 1983: 30)

If 'Letters of Marque' delineates a troubled meditation on narrative
and cultural authority, Kipling's exploration of British India's
urban spaces, notably the city of Calcutta, produces a companion
travelogue of cultural coherence under threat. Kipling's 'City of
Dreadful Night' (Kipling, 1919b) is structured around the metaphor of the distorted mirror. The narrative offers Calcutta as a poor
mimesis of the imperial city of London and satirises the cultured
and civilised life that it seems to offer. Englishmen wear black frock-
coats and top hats in the intense heat of the Indian sunshine; they
keep palatial residences on 'Chowringhi' road and employ 'natives'
as concierges. In addition, Bengalis, attired in formal English
clothes, engage in parliamentary debates over the Calcutta Municipal Bill and turn democracy into linguistic farce. All the while,
the real Calcutta that is associated with disease, pollution, gambling

156

dens and native brothels, carries on as of old. Producing Calcutta as a bastardised version of her imperial and metropolitan counterpart allows the narrator to undermine the status of the Anglo-Indian city: despite all the effort and care taken, Calcutta simply appears as a surreal and absurd imitation of London.

Yet compared with the gothic mode of his short fiction or travel writing, Kipling's 'City of Dreadful Night' moves into a new key in its unconscious foregrounding of the hybrid interlocutory spaces between metropolitan imperial subject and colonial identities. In this and in Kipling's other 'urban' writings, we have an unwilling recognition of cultural difference *in the same time and place* as the production of a secure and culturally uncontaminated British colonial identity. Despite the geo-politics of the colonial city, the assertion of an Anglo cultural identity – and its corresponding myths of cultural origination – takes place as a struggle against all things Indian. Despite nostalgia, the dual ancestry of the Anglo-Indian city makes it impossible for the colonial text to return to an original moment of Englishness. The city as both textual and cultural space is produced in a founding moment of instability and ambivalence. Its ambivalence, as Bhabha has pointed out, is part of the structure of its representative mould.

In this chapter I will argue for a thorough-going exploration of the concept of ambivalence. I will examine both the development of the colonial city as a geographical and cultural space in nineteenth-century India, and the development of the colonial city as a rhetorical space that draws on the language and vocabulary of nineteenth-century London. In the overlap between the two sites, I will argue that the 'City of Dreadful Night' constitutes a split and hybrid text of paranoiac misanthropy. Anglo-cultural and psychic boundaries are continually breached by shadowy figures evading surveillance while the present time of the Anglo-Indian port city is always haunted by the 'memory' of an ideal prior English state. More importantly, Kipling's satirical language of disavowal directed at Calcutta hollows out her original ideal. For while the text ends self-consciously with the image of the pure angel in the house – Lucia, 'virtuous maid and faithful wife' – even this image of the 'fair Kentish maiden' is sullied by the figures of 'Dainty Iniquity' and 'Fat Vice' in Calcutta's version of the St John's Wood prostitutes. In this blatant manipulation of woman as representative national symbol, two possibilities are posed: was she bought and sold 'following the custom of the country' or was she a maiden who 'wed the man of her choice'? The narrator, of course, opts for the latter. Yet having chosen to read Lucia's story as one of love and tragedy, his account of her life ends with her husband's callous and quick remarriage; what remains is a 'battered tomb' and a husband who 'took comfort' in the next batch of maidens that sailed up the river into Calcutta.

THE COLONIAL CITY

The Anglo-Indian sector of the colonial city was composed of two geo-political halves: the civil station, responsible for the political, administrative and bureaucratic functions of Empire, and the cantonment, which housed the military personnel that enabled the enforcement of those functions. The indigenous city was separated from the colonial settlement and was also known as the native city, native quarter, or referred to by the anglicised version of its usual name (King, 1976: 88). The native city, with its different set of cultural, ideological and architectural values was marked as a potential source of danger to the Anglo-Indian inhabitants. The native city was associated with infection and disease (MacLeod and Lewis, 1988: 40); segregation operated as the means for safeguarding the welfare and identity of the colonial settlement. Where contact was necessary, a set of rules regulated the terms of the encounter. The semantic violence meted out on the word 'native' parallels the social and political. Far from being defined as 'autochthonous' or indigenous to the region, the word 'native' was taken to refer to something unnatural or foreign.

Nineteenth-century Anglo-Indian society orientated itself towards Britain and Europe and cultivated a deliberate distance from local and indigenous cultures. As Anthony King has pointed out, nowhere is this seen more clearly than in the terrain of colonial health, where hygiene functioned both as preventative medicine and cultural identity-formation. Western medical knowledge structured concern about the nature of 'zymotic' infections and reinforced cultural prejudices through notions of purity and pollution. Material and social space within and without the Anglo-Indian settlement were governed in relation to prevailing European systems of health and sanitary science (King, 1976: 103; MacLeod and Lewis, 1988: 40). Cantonments, in particular, were established within a strict disciplinary regime. Elaborate rules and regulations attended the creation and maintenance of army residences. Air, water, soil and elevation became the main criteria governing the choice of sites (MacLeod and Lewis, 1988: 40). The rules called for the provision of adequate ventilation, efficient systems of drainage and waste disposal, clean water supplies and made elevation a necessity. In accordance with theories of miasmic contagion, careful attention was paid to prevailing winds; a site was ideally placed where there was 'plenty of cool and dry air' and where vegetation was not dense. Avoidance of excessive contact with native life was deemed desirable; as a manual puts it, 'ravines full of dead animals and the ordure of many thousands of natives' were clearly unsuitable (King, 1976: 108). If the chosen site did not have these natural advantages, or was located in a previously populated area, the new settlement had to be protected by high walls and wide spaces. Anglo-Indian civilians kept to the windward side of the offending area, erected barriers, and lived in fear of their lives.

Contact with the Indian population became an inevitable source of anxiety and the pattern of segregation, coercion and regulation repeated itself even here. The easy spread of venereal disease among the British troops stationed in India spurred the introduction of the more punitive Indian version of the British Contagious Diseases Acts. For example, The Cantonment Act of 1864 made a provision for the regulation of all Bazaars (regimental brothels) and lock hospitals, all of which could extend beyond cantonment boundaries when required (Ballhatchet, 1980: 42). Under the rules of the Cantonment Act, women 'frequented by Europeans' would have to register with local authorities. They would be issued with a ticket outlining cantonment rules and be subjected to a monthly medical examination. They were also required to record medical results on these tickets. In addition, if a woman was believed to be infected, she could be locked up until certified cured of it. In 1868, the Indian Contagious Diseases Act was passed which allowed local authorities (with the approval of the Governor General) to take any necessary provision to combat the spread of disease. Measures included mandatory registration, medical examinations, the enforced treatment of women and the prevention of known prostitutes from living in specified areas (Ballhatchet, 1980: 43–44).

Cantonment Acts were, of course, not only aimed at managing the contact between the military and the civilian population but also directed at managing the encampment within. The Acts decreed, 'whenever it shall appear necessary for the protection of troops . . . it shall be lawful for the Governor General in India to extend the limits of any military cantonment . . . and to define the limits around such within which such rules . . . shall be in force'. Behaviour seen as breaking established codes of conduct met with severe punishment. Such Acts did not restrict themselves to the category of preventive medicine but were also directed at any behaviour which contravened the carefully managed culture within. Examples of behaviour prohibited within military grounds included carrying 'exposed meat', letting fall 'nightsoil', carrying an 'indecently covered corpse', failing to bury a corpse within twenty-four hours, torturing or abusing animals (King, 1976: 119–120). Indigenous cultural practices permitted outside the area of the cantonment were prohibited within. In this way, King argues, 'a total cultural area was established where the environment was modified not only according to culture-specific theories of "medicine" but also, to accord with equally culture-specific olfactory, aural and visual preferences' (King, 1976: 120).

Paranoia about unhealthy sanitary practices of the native city and bazaar led to an obsession with possible health hazards. Such nervousness is shared by both investigator and respondent in a Royal Commission interview of 1863 despite measures enforcing the separation between cultural groups:

Did you not state that the neighbourhood was crowded by low native houses? – At a short distance it is so, in the Colinga, Durumotollah, and the Bow Bazaar neighbourhoods for example. The influence in certain winds of these places is quite perceptible . . . although there is a very good esplanade between the fort and these bazaars. Is there not considerable space of open ground surrounding the fort? – Yes, it may be called considerable space; but on ascending to a height, Ouchterlony's monument, for example, a person at once perceives how trifling this space is when compared with the vast densely covered area by which it is immediately surrounded.

(Parliamentary Papers, 1863: 2146)

As the interview makes explicit, 'there is no doubt there would be much more mortality among the troops were they not to some extent separated from those [native] influences by the open space surrounding the fort'. The first 1859 Royal Commission into the sanitary state of the army in India was initiated by concern over high mortality rates; but by the time of the 1863 Royal Commission, Radhika Ramasubban argues, a colonial mode of health based on the legislation of social and physical separation had come into being that had far reaching consequences. From the time of the 1863 Royal Commission, even the 'location and layout' of military and civilian lines were decided by the 'criteria of health' defined by 'medical scientific theories of miasma and environmental control rather than political or strategic criteria' (MacLeod and Lewis, 1988: 41).

Residential space for the European civilian community reflected a corresponding disciplinary regime geared towards not only the production of health but also the control of cultural communities. Travel and family health manuals offered advice, from the specific mode of dress suitable for the Indian climate to the detailed management of residential spaces. William Moore's much praised and government-sponsored *Manual of Family Medicine For India* details some of the many steps needed to ensure a safe and culturally secure environment. The position of the house should be determined not only by the direction of prevailing winds but also by the diurnal sun line. Elevation, soil, air and water should receive equal attention:

> As regards site, the first thing to look for is good drainage, and therefore a slight elevation of the ground will be the preferable locality. . . . [where in parts of the country] this desideratum cannot . . . be served . . . the elevation of the dwelling house above ground is the more requisite. The facility of procuring water for garden purposes, the proximity of trees not overhanging the house . . . the windward position to any marsh, stagnant pond, or Native village, a gravelly soil in preference to black or clay soils . . . the absence of rocks . . . which would radiate heat on the house are all desiderata.

Servants' quarters should be separated from the main bungalow complex. Indian dwellings located within the compound had to be specially separated and set away from the main building. Kate Platt's guide, *The Home and Health in India and the Tropical Colonies* argued that 'for hygienic reasons, especially in malarious and unhealthy districts, close proximity is not desirable' (Platt, 1923: 21). T. Firminger's gardening manual, *A Manual of Gardening for Bengal and Upper India,* argued that they ought to be kept at the rear of the house and away from prevailing winds, preventing even 'the noise and smell of cooking and servants' chatter from [reaching] the house' (King, 1976: 141).

Purity

Given the significantly shortened life-expectancy of the civilian or soldier in India, I am not denying the general motivation behind hygiene as a strategy for survival. What I am asserting is that European sanitary science – and the plethora of travel and family health manuals that advised its application – was also instrumental in producing European cultural identity abroad. The anxiety surrounding the possible breach of cultural boundaries between settler and native populations was expressed through the language of contagion. My argument regarding social patterns of order is based on the one Mary Douglas makes in her book, *Purity and Danger* (Douglas, 1984). In the conception of the native environment as inherently polluting and in need of expulsion from the settler communities, ideas of dirt and contagion cannot be seen in isolation but must be interpreted as part of the way a society creates, expresses and regulates its social, political and cultural space. The argument that (Western) ritual practices of cleanness are solely based on hygiene, and that 'dirt' comes solely from the 'context of pathogenicity' is disingenuous. Such practices also carry a 'symbolic load' and are part of an expressive and systematic ordering of society. Douglas invokes the old definition of dirt 'as matter out of place' in her examination of the way symbolic systems operate:

> This [old definition] is a very suggestive approach. It implies two conditions: a set of ordered relations and a contravention of that order. Dirt then, is never a unique, isolated event. Where there is dirt there is a system. Dirt is the by-product of a systematic ordering and classification of matter, in so far as ordering involves rejecting inappropriate elements. This idea of dirt takes us straight into the field of symbolism and promises a link-up with more obvious symbolic systems of purity.
>
> (Douglas, 1984: 35)

Symbolic systems provide us with a way of regulating and making sense of impressions and images in the 'real' world, by constructing a stable set of references which provide the substantiality and solidity necessary for cultural continuity. They render a 'stable world in which objects have recognisable shapes, are located in depth, and have permanence'. Notions of purity and pollution provide a culture with a way of thinking about itself; 'pollution behaviour is the reaction which condemns any object or idea likely to confuse or contradict cherished classifications' (Douglas, 1984: 36). Douglas' version of national culture (as continuity and as change) is one governed by patterns of order and classifications. Ambiguous or discordant impressions must either be slotted into the social *schema* or rejected as dirty, polluting or repulsive (Douglas, 1984: 36–39); this much is evident in much of Anglo-Indian advice on how to guard against contamination from native habitation and behaviour.

Unsurprisingly, the Anglo-Indian city is figured within a topos of linearity and geometry. Platt's guide characterises the civil and military lines as being 'well laid out with wide shady roads' (Platt, 1923: 26). G. W. Steevens, writing in 1899, describes the stations as composed of 'broad straight roads' 'arcaded with trees', broad houses with 'pillared fronts', 'large, walled or hedged enclosure[s], part garden, part mews, part village' (King, 1976: 125). W. H. Russell, special correspondent to *The Times*, uses the same terms. In *My Diary in the Years 1858–9*, stations are depicted as 'laid out in large rectangles, formed by wide roads'. Each house is separated from others by walls 'enclosing large gardens, lawns and out-offices' (Russell, 1860: 180). These geometric lines are not only literal descriptions of the physical settlement patterns of the European community, but are also vivid testimonies to the culture's persistent interest in demarcation, naming and segregation. The obsession with walls, detachment and spaces-in-between signals a fear, an imagined pressure from the native quarters, whose bodily secretions and metaphorical productivity threaten to run riot and spill over established boundaries. Lines of demarcation were also lines of defence. Compounds and walls in Anglo-Indian residences function both as a picturesque frame and as a visual bulwark against undesirable outsiders. Dress, language, behaviour, the collection of objects in the house and the cultivation of a garden offer the occupants a comforting set of references which help secure the community's links with their cultural origins. English gardens, for example, were a sustained attempt to inscribe a leisured pastoral ideal of Englishness in a foreign land; as an Englishwoman admitted, 'great efforts were made to grow English flowers, which generally looked rather sickly in the Indian climate. We could have had the most marvellous gardens with orchids and all sorts of things, but no, they must be English flowers' (Allen, 1978: 125).

Gardens were valued for their ability to counter the polluting influences of what was reinscribed as foreign:

> The early mornings especially are as pleasant as anything I can imagine: they have all the sweetness and freshness of an English summer. The air smells of hay and flowers, instead of ditches, dust, fried oil, curry and onions, which are the best of Madras smells. . . . I saw a real staring full-blown hollyhock, which was like meeting an old friend from England, instead of tuberoses, pomegranates . . . we have apples, pears and peaches . . . [which] look like English fruit.
>
> (King, 1976: 143)

Surrounded by familiar objects and smells, the bungalow-complex struggled to manage its residential space and attain a high degree of self-sufficiency. Vere Birdwood, describing the mem-sahib's life, gives the impression that the Anglo-Indian community managed a perfect and natural reflection of its metropolitan ideal:

> We were in India, we were looked after by Indian servants and we met a great deal of Indians, and some of us undoubtedly made a very close study of India and Indian customs, but once you stepped inside the home you were back in Cheltenham or Bath. We brought with us in our homes almost exact replicas of the sort of life that upper middle class people lived in England at that time. . . . You went from bungalow to bungalow and you found the same sort of furniture, the same sort of dinner table set, the same kind of conversation. We read the same books, mostly imported by post from England, and I can't really say that we took an awful lot from India.
>
> (Allen, 1978: 72–73)

In this recollection, the Anglo-India woman mirrors her middle and upper-class English sister's iconic status as responsible moral, spiritual and cultural guardian. Her environment seems to reproduce effortlessly the leisured life and Austen landscapes of Bath and Cheltenham, away from India and a 'great many Indians'. But as I have tried to indicate, the expatriate Anglo-Indian community was produced through a complex process of interaction between two very different notions of cultural environment. Rewriting India in terms of the social and cultural boundaries of one's own man-made environment was a process of intense material and ideological struggle. This struggle is signalled in Birdwood's rhetoric by the way her Englishness is constructed against her incessant repetition of Indian things, customs and people.

Danger

Douglas argues that pollution characterises anything that defiles the cultural as sacred space. Polluted objects must be expelled; but these objects may gain symbolic power in their expulsion as signifiers hostile to (the generation of) patterns of order. Such symbolic power is isolated in Frantz Fanon's representation of colonial city as a divided world of settler culture and native discontent (Fanon, 1983: 29–33). The native quarter in Fanon's analysis of colonial representation is 'the depository of maleficent powers, the unconscious and irretrievable instrument of blind forces' (Fanon, 1983: 32). In much Anglo-Indian literature, a manichean allegory operates in the polarisation of the vile native city versus the good, clean Anglo-Indian one.[1] The language of the disciplinary and regulatory discourses produces an Other city which is always sinister, mysterious, and dark, and whose shadow always falls on the city of light. This Other, expressed through the nineteenth-century privilege of the body as transcoder of difference, always threatens to spill over the geometric divisions of the civilised body, oozing its contaminated bodily wastes, disgusting odours and noxious smells. It thrives under the sign of the ubiquitous body of the native which is forever invading hallowed ground. Even the liberal journalist, Russell, is not exempt from such a collective cultural nightmare. His binary vision of the European versus the Indian city sets linearity and detachment against a contrasting 'aggregate of houses perforated by tortuous paths ... resembling a section of worm-eaten wood'. The east 'grumbles, propagates, squabbles, sits in its decaying temples, haunts its rotting shrines ... drinks its semi-putrid water' (Russell, 1860: 180). The Indian city of graveyards and ancient civilisations, of newly sprung-up bazaars and tenements, is also the out-of-bounds city where the living and the dead intermingle. This fantasy is the hybrid and carnivalesque world of the bazaar city where nothing is delineated but everything exists in a chaotic state of intermingling: a carnival of night and a dream landscape of darkness, noise and offensive smells and obscenities.

Pollution and disintegration are important structuring metaphors in Kipling's journalistic writing on the colonial city. For example, in an early piece written for the *Civil and Military Gazette* in 1885 entitled 'Typhoid at Home' (Pinney, 1986) Kipling's inquiry into the milk supply of the European community leads to an exposé of the unsanitary conditions of milk production. But 'Typhoid at Home' is also a narrative about inspecting the environment located in the native division of the Lahore city nearest the Delhi Gate. The narrator, guided by a policeman away from the main street into the narrow and tortuous side streets of the native quarter, is immediately confronted with how the other half lives and works. Sanitation is non-existent and sewage overflows onto roads from neighbouring houses; a 'stream of bluish ooze, gay atop with the rain-bow hues of putrescence' flows down the worn brick pavement, cow dung is everywhere. That the native inhabitants of Lahore city can have no 'feelings higher than those of swine' (Pinney, 1986: 76) is the conclusion reached from Kipling's literal reading of the environment he encounters. The unclean passages and gullies through which the reporter makes his way are narrow, high-walled and claustrophobic and threaten to cave in on the hurrying figures. The investigator–journalist tropes his anxiety. He rushes

> past closed and shuttered windows; past small doors in blank walls, giving access to dark courtyards even more uncleanly than the region through which he was making his way; beyond the reach of sunlight, into high clefts (it is impossible to call them lanes) where it seemed that last summer's sultry breath still lingered; and eventually halted in a *cul-de-sac*.
>
> (Pinney, 1986: 70)

Closed doors, blank walls, *culs-de-sac* and feigned ignorance on the part of its inhabitants deny the reporter's quest for documentary evidence for his newspaper exposé. Kipling's native quarter is positioned as the grotesque body that disrupts boundary-formation. Located under the sign of pollution, body-scape of the native city with its 'milky mothers' (Pinney, 1986: 72) is also en-gendered as feminine against the clean and institutional masculine of policeman and investigative journalist. This feminised body oozes with disgusting bodily fluids and 'unutterable aroma[s]' which spill into public spaces. Her pitiless dead walls, 'barred and grated windows' 'were throbbing and humming with human voices' – all of which are hidden from the disciplinary gaze, as the scene turns on the vulnerability of the colonial identity:

Voices of children singing their lessons at school; sounds of feet on stone steps, or wooden balconies overhead; voices raised in argument, or conversation, sounded dead and muffled as though they came through wool; and it seemed as if at any moment, the tide of unclean humanity might burst through its dam of rotten brickwork and filth-smeared wood, blockading the passages below.

(Pinney, 1986: 73)

Private and public spaces are not delineated; *charpoys* (beds) are laid in streets and courtyards; men and women sit openly on beds and children crawl beneath them. And always, there is the ubiquitous Indian, ready to touch and to pollute, 'by unclean corners of walls; on each step of ruinous staircases; on roofs of low out-houses; by window, housetop, or stretched amid garbage unutterable'. The text strains under its own paranoia of contamination, and by its inability to control the terms of the encounter.

The narrative, weighed down by its manichean rhetoric, teeters on the edge of instability. Kipling's reporter finds the grotesque body of Lahore city 'inconceivably foul' and filled with 'nameless abominations'. Milk sold to the *sahibs* is subject to the most filthy contamination; cows are accommodated in 'stall, stable, or cess-pit'. Brass *lotahs* (vessels) bear traces of 'greasy fingers and daubs of cow-dung', and milkmen are scarred with small pox. Metonymic associations and metaphoric identifications of an underworld's excesses threaten not only the structure of the piece but also its narrative authority. Impartial distance, measure and control are thrown away as the narrator's anxieties and desires are alternately rehearsed in the narrative. A very particular inversion is also made possible through the text's metaphoric patterns. The inquiry into milk-supply yields a feminised Indian body producing milk and points towards the Anglo-Indian community's dependency on its host nation. However, the usual parent–child relation of colonial rhetoric is subverted by the subtle child–mother relation which also inhabits this text. The feminine native body produces life-giving milk for the alien community. The Anglo-Indian ideal of purity, separation and independence disintegrates as the ambivalence of the prose is also reflected in the title, 'Typhoid at Home'. As metropolitan alter-ego, Anglo-Indian Lahore looks towards England as home. But Lahore is where the Anglo-Indian community resides. If the title reads typhoid 'at *home*', then home must refer to India. Such contradictions exist at the very heart of Anglo-Indian identity. Despite all efforts to the contrary, British military and civil establishments are still located in and dependent on their host nation. Acts of negation and exclusion are constitutive of and not external to their cultural identity. Here, the colonising culture comes face to face with an indication of its own hybridity as Anglo-Indian. In the uncanny logic of the gowalla's [cowherd's] innocent declaration in Kipling's investigative piece, the Anglo and Indian communities are intimately linked. If the government represented health, reform and the elimination of dirt and disease, then the milkyard would be shut down. But it has not been closed, and hence the cows here give good milk which goes . . . to the *sahib logue*.

THE DECADENT CITY

In the late nineteenth-century texts on the city, the symbolic potential of pollution comes not only from the power that accrues to it by virtue of horror and repulsion, but by a more consciously literary source. The urban carnival of night is already available in early sociological texts such as Frederick Engels' *The Condition of the Working Class in England* in 1844, Henry Mayhew's 1861 *London Labour and the London Poor* and later Condition of England tradition as displayed by Andrew Mearns, *The Bitter Cry of Outcast London*, George Sims's *How the Poor Live*, William Booth's *In Darkest England*. The literary tradition of urban description, which encompasses figures like Charles Dickens, Elizabeth Gaskell, Honoré de Balzac, Emile Zola, George Gissing, Edward Thomson situates the city between the familiar and the phantasmagoric.[2] I will leave Kipling's direct echo of Dickens until later but here simply wish to point out that Kipling's urban pieces draw on the vocabulary and rhetoric of nineteenth-century writing on the city. Kipling's colonial city is not only about the dynamics of 'purity and danger' in colonial relations but also belongs to a mixed bag of romantic and decadent writing.

The title of Kipling's two prose pieces on Lahore and Calcutta, 'The City of Dreadful Night' is taken from James Thomson's poem of the same name.[3] The short descriptive essay on Lahore draws on Thomson's imagery of London as the city of death, and his wakeful poem as a narrative agency for its series of images of alienation. The controlling perspective is that of a night-walker, a lonely insomniac roaming the streets of a sleeping city. Thomson's writing, as Adrian Poole has pointed out, is built on a series of differences; a set of contrasts between the 'isolated, stigmatised consciousness of the wakeful poet and the secure, frozen fixity both of the "real" city and its inhabitants' (Poole, 1975: 42). The figure of an isolated poetic consciousness has its literary roots in the tradition of the romantic poet in exile where the poet–philosopher–artist is set against the security of the slumbering mass of the rest of humanity. Raymond Williams points out that the structure of the poem brings together the 'real' urban spaces of the nineteenth century and a new 'anguished consciousness' where the poetic vision becomes both a warning and a testament to a 'London of isolated units, struggle, social indifference, loss of purpose, loss of meaning' (Williams, 1985: 236). The poet as seer does not suffer 'sleep's easy dreams':

> For me, accurst, whom terror and the pain
> Of baffled longings and starved misery . . .
> Drove forth as one possest.
>
> (Williams, 1985: 236)

But Thomson's images also belong to a generation of writing which emphasises despair, gloom and decadence. Richard Shannon argues that this 'extreme sensibility' became a characteristic voice of the period: *nostalgie de la boue*, 'a craving for the gutter, for debasement, a deliberate adoption of the role of the outcast, a kind of living damnation of narcotics and alcohol' (Shannon, 1984: 273). The Thomson connection brings to light a 'Kipling that nobody reads'. Kipling's family connections with the Burne-Joneses (his aunt married Sir Edward), and his holidays at the Grange, gave him contact with artists such as Morris, Browning, Swinburne, Hardy and Wilde in his childhood years.[4] This would certainly have given him a chance to read the literature written by such figures; Carrington in his biography of Kipling refers to this early period as 'decadent' in influence:

> No one then regarded Kipling 'Gigger' as a writer of 'patriotic' verse. He was a rebel and a progressive which is to say, in 1882 – paradoxically – that he was a decadent. His friends, his teachers, were liberals, his tastes were 'aesthetic', the writers he most admired were the fashionable pessimists.
>
> (Carrington, 1970: 74)[5]

Kipling's novel *The Light That Failed* dates from these decadent years. By setting his protagonist, Dick Heldar, in the artistic bohemia of London before the turn of the century, he could write about the continental influence – impressionism – on the art world in England. *The Light* shows an interesting split between the different sides of Kipling's heritage. Its portrayal of the Oriental cities through which the hero travels shows a contemporary fascination with low-life and the delights that such a world has to offer. Heldar's Port Said is the quintessential Oriental city of vice with 'gaming tables', 'saloons', sexual perversity and 'dancing-hells'. As an artist, Dick is a voyeur *par excellence*, parasitic on the energy of his subjects' music-hall stereotyped celebration of iniquity and vice:

> 'All things are for sale in Port Said,' said Madame. 'If my husband comes it will be so much more. Eh, 'ow you call – 'alf a sovereign.' The money was paid, and the mad dance was held at night in a walled courtyard at the back of Madame Binat's house. . . . the naked Zanzibari girls danced furiously by the light of the kerosene lamps. Binat sat upon a chair and stared with eyes that saw nothing, till the whirl of the dance and the clang of the rattling piano stole into the drink that took the place of blood in his veins, and his face glistened. Dick took him by the chin brutally and turned that face to the light.
>
> (Kipling, 1907: 33)

Heldar's descent into the inferno is reminiscent of the voyeuristic fascination of artists like Henri de Toulouse-Lautrec and Edgar Degas with the world of prostitution and dance-halls. His most moving portrait, of a 'Negroid-Jewess-Cuban with morals to match' draws inspiration from this underground world of forbidden gratifications. But on the other hand, this feminised decadent world of death, pain, hedonism, sensual pleasure and sexual revelry is rejected for the alternative, healthier and cleaner, military world of male camaraderie. Heldar paints both worlds with feeling and absorption and can perhaps been seen as a character-surrogate for Kipling's dual heritage. The masterpiece Heldar paints is entitled *Melancholia*, inspired by James Thomson's *City*, itself inspired by Dürer. Yet when Dick chooses to abandon these influences by journeying back to the Sudan to his male friends, the novel charts – in some small measure – the kinds of choices Kipling would take in his later writing career and foreshadows the 'official' version of Kipling with which we are more familiar.

Kipling's *The Light That Failed* points us towards a less familiar Kipling by tracing the correspondences between his romantic imaging of India and Empire, and the representations of the decadent city in the late Victorian and Edwardian period. His short stories, 'Beyond the Pale', 'In the House of Suddhoo', 'The Gate of the Hundred Sorrows' and 'To Be Filed for Reference' all concern adventures or experiences gained from living in or traversing parts of the native city out of bounds to Englishmen. The cities described in all these narratives open up a world of underground gratifications; they are associated with prostitution, murder, opium dens, occult influences, sexual excesses and forbidden knowledges. This fantastic and nightmarish city is hidden and out-of-sight to those who people the normal day-time world, as the character–narrator asserts of the secret door to the opium den in 'The Gate of Hundred Sorrows', 'I defy [any person] . . . to find the Gate, however well he may think he knows the City. You might even go through the very gully it stands in a hundred times, and be none the wiser' (Kipling, 1898: 255). It is the city of the damned and is only available to those who, like McIntosh Jellaludin in 'To Be Filed for Reference', are 'past redemption' and can sample the delights of sin and debauchery. Dick Heldar's Port Said holds 'the concentrated essence of all the iniquities and all the vices in all the continents'; 'Cairo, Alexandria, Ismailia and Port Said' are all Orientalist cities of hell to the European city of light. But if the Oriental city becomes an imaginary negative of London and allows for the contemporary evocation of London's underworld as an Orientalist fantasy, Kipling's writing also envisaged Lahore and Calcutta as London.

The borrowing of rhetorical clothes is a two-way affair. Kipling's 1885 prose piece on Lahore, 'The City of Dreadful Night' echoes Doré's illustrated pilgrimage to London. Doré's gothic romanticism may be identified from what an art critic has called his extravagant and 'dramatic use of light and dark, tunnelling perspectives, dwarfed images [and] massed crowds'. Kipling's piece exhibits similar *chiaroscuro* and grotesque body-imagery; in 'the witchery of the moonlight' men and women are 'horribly changed' to 'silvery white and ashen grey' lepers. Slumbering masses metamorphose into lifeless corpses stifled by the oppressive heat:

More corpses; more stretches of moonlit, white road.. . .
Wherever a grain cart atilt, a tree trunk, a sawn log, a couple

of bamboos and a few handful of thatch cast a shadow, the ground is covered with them. They lie – some face downwards, arms folded, in the dust; some curled up dog-wise; some thrown like limp gunny-bags over the side of grain carts; and some bowed with their brows on their knees in the full glare of the Moon. It would be a comfort if they were only given to snoring; but they are not, and the likeness to corpses is unbroken in all respects save one. The lean dogs snuff at them and turn away.

(Kipling, 1897: 323)

The narrator's gaze shares the moon's deforming illuminations while the 'high-house walls' radiate heat, and poisonous 'fetid breezes eddy' in 'obscure side gullies'. Lahore, framed within a familiar and similar rhetoric of the sight, sound and smell of Unknown England, is London's double. Surveying the city from the 'minar' of Lahore's central mosque, he turns to the native quarters to ask, 'How do they live down there? What do they think of? When will they wake?' His observations conform not so much to the disciplining and policing gaze of power/knowledge in the Foucauldian sense, but to a visual feast of surfaces. In the heat of the night and among the 'spectacle of sleeping thousands', Kipling's narrator imagines a carnival of night as his waking dream.

Susan Buck-Morss's analysis of Benjamin on Baudelaire, suggests that 'the combination of distracted observation and dream-like reverie . . . is characteristic of the flaneur' (Buck-Morss, 1986: 103). But if, as she argues, the flaneur 'inhabits the streets as [his] living room' in a narrative act of possession and familiarity (Buck-Morss, 1986: 118), what does this do for the positioning of the colonial artist as flaneur? He is, after all, a white colonist in a foreign land and city to which he belongs neither by race nor by creed. This observation is crucial because the structural correspondences of these two descriptive narratives of Thomson and Kipling lead one to assume a natural bonding between the narrator and his city. The narrator's role as alienated visionary–poet depends on a prior primary link. For Kipling to position himself in this way with regard to the Indian quarters would suggest an intimate bond between Lahore and his narrator-persona. But the geo-politics of colonial cities based on separation and segregation would suggest a negation of such an association. Even if one argues that the romantic literary ancestry eases the way for a cross-cultural trespass through its tradition of low-life writing, the physical and imaginative crossing of cultural boundaries still constitutes a breaking of the cultural taboos. The point is worth emphasising because ambivalence characterises not only Anglo-Indian cultural identity but Kipling's recourse to 'Anglo' traditions of writing.

THE OTHER NATION

Kipling's 'City of Dreadful Night', written in 1888, is an exemplary text of the kind of structural and metaphoric ambivalences that I have been addressing. Kipling's tour of the city-scape of Calcutta is meant to signal a similarity with and difference from London's city-scape. This text on Calcutta works towards disowning the connection between the colonies and the metropolitan culture, through a disjunctive mimicry between Calcutta and London, the anglicised Bengalis and 'real' Englishmen. The text's portrayal of the anglicised Bengali as almost-the-same-but-not-quite-English is an attempt at illegitimation but one based paradoxically on the very desire for colonial similitude. The narrative of 'City' begins with the narrator's entry into the British Indian Presidency from the Provinces. He walks down the main thoroughfare, takes in its hotels and government buildings, and describes the activities that take place within these public places. He then proceeds to the 'Writers' Buildings' and observes a session of the Bengal Legislative Council. Leaving the Council debate, the narrator strolls down the dock-lands of the Hughli river and is taken for a tour of the Calcutta Police headquarters. He is given a police escort and guide for his night-time excursion of the native division of Calcutta city. At the end of his trip, Kipling's narrator visits the Old Park Street cemetery and imagines early imperial Calcutta.

On entering the city of Calcutta, and the state of Bengal, the narrator describes a feeling of uncanny familiarity despite having never visited the city in the past. Entering Calcutta is described as leaving the darkness of India for the familiarity of London:

> We are all backwoodsmen and barbarians together – we others dwelling beyond the Ditch, in the outer darkness of the Mofussil. . . . We have left India behind us at Howrah Station, and now we enter foreign parts. *No, not wholly foreign. Say rather too familiar.*
>
> (Kipling, 1919b: 201) [my emphasis]

Calcutta is a city made in the image of London:

> Fancy finding any place outside the Levee-room where
> Englishmen are crowded together to this extent! Fancy sitting
> down seventy strong to *table d'hote* and with a deafening clatter
> of knives and forks! Fancy finding a real bar where drinks
> may be obtained! and joy of joys, fancy stepping out of the
> hotel into the arms of a lone, white, helmeted, buttoned,
> truncheoned Bobby!

(Kipling, 1919b: 208)

British India's premier city with its 'oceans of roofs', fog, 'deep, full throated boom of life and motion and humanity' conjures up the 'lost heritage of London'. It possesses shopping malls, shops with glass fronts, pretty ladies, a steady roar of traffic and has 'crowded and hurrying life, business, money-making, carriages, gentlemen with top hats, gardens and even sumptuous parliamentary establishments'. Anyone might be forgiven for thinking that this city *is* London. Any expatriate Englishman would feel that he were returning home and exclaim in excitement, 'why, this is London! This is the docks. This is Imperial. This is worth coming across India to see!' (Kipling, 1919b: 203).

The text's undertow of irony forges a constitutive difference between Calcutta and the real article at the same time as it lists their similarities. Tension generated by the personal pronoun 'we' of the Mofussil, identified those 'dwelling beyond the Ditch' that have 'been deprived of . . . [their] inheritance' and the privileged 'them' of this special Presidency city. Similarity is deliberately undercut as illusion and difference not long after the utterance is completed. The desire for home makes one hallucinate; the narrator tells us 'Calcutta [only] holds out false hopes of some return'. The likeness that causes the narrator's double take is always only partial. 'We have [not really] left India behind us at Howrah Station [at all]'. The narrator's encounter with the Calcutta *durwan* is one of the many instances revealing the great Calcutta hoax. As native concierge, the *durwan* keeps guard over Anglo-Indian establishments but is 'more *insolent* than any of the French variety'. He chews *pan* or sugar cane, not taking 'the trouble to get rid of his quid'. He is an animal that has to be taught deference by the English narrator. His [ab]use of the English language is the ultimate 'head and front of his offence'; he is put right only through the narrator's severe and correct speech.

Parliamentary democracy and the Native State

Kipling's strident attack on municipal government as a poor imitation of English parliamentary democracy forms the next subject of the text's tour of Calcutta. While Kipling's critique may be located within the discourse of mimicry outlined above, it should also be understood in the context of the contemporary politics of Bengal in general, and the politics of Calcutta in particular. The economic, political and strategic interest in Calcutta shares in what one historian has called the 'split personality in British rule' (Jeffrey 1978: 307). From the Mutiny to the period just before the First World War, the British stake in India grew at a phenomenal rate. As Rajat Kanta Ray notes, the bulk of British overseas trade was focused on India. She paid approximately two fifths of British trade deficits with the rest of the world while home charges of civil and military expenditure, railway debts, shipping, insurance and other services contributed towards an annual return estimated at between thirty and thirty-five million pounds (Kanta Ray, 1984). This economic burden was not evenly distributed over all of India; it was concentrated in a large measure on Calcutta and its hinterland. Calcutta was at the centre of the economies of tea, jute and coal produced in Assam, Bengal and Chota Nagpur; Bengal also provided the most significant market for English cloth in India. Kanta Ray argues that Calcutta was vital to movement of British trade in South Asia and also 'enjoyed the largest concentration of British capital in Asia'.

The dual economy of Calcutta and its hinterland involved an urban export–import sector based in the metropolis which exerted a monopsonistic control over the peasant subsistence economy, engaged in agricultural production for this, its only market (Kanta Ray, 1984: 13). Foreign monopoly capital ensured exclusive European domination of the economy even as it spawned Indian professional and service groups to administer the bureaucratic needs of the system. Local assistance by the colonial administration, as the historian Kanta Ray puts it, was crucial to the imperial structure as a whole and fostered the 'sub-imperialism' of Bengalis who were found at all levels of the colonial administration (Kanta Ray, 1984: 2). This intermediate class was therefore 'an essential collaborating elite' within the state apparatus even while the top rungs of the imperial ladder were firmly denied to native aspirants. As further rise would only result in a clash of interests, the attempt by native professional classes to enter into the higher positions of power in the bureaucracy in the late nineteenth century was blocked. Impediments to this movement fostered a nascent nationalism rooted in the metropolitan community.

The quest for control of the Calcutta Corporation and the Legislative Council, which Kipling disparages, forms part of the struggle for power. The system of administration in Calcutta had roots in the old Mughal system of taxation and tribute (Ray, 1979: 12–13). In 1793, *zamindar* rights were granted by the Mughal emperors to the East India Company and an English *zamindar* appointed to look after municipal affairs and the collection of rent. Indian *zamindars* were also appointed under English control to aid the process of collecting ground rents in the towns. Because of widespread corruption among both blacks and whites, Cornwallis abolished the *zamindari* system in Calcutta. A system of corporate control was installed and Justices of the Peace were appointed to administer municipal affairs. Real control however, lay in the hands of the Chief Magistrate of Calcutta who was also the Commissioner of Police (Ray, 1979). In 1863, a more representative element was introduced into the constitution. Justices were given general control of municipal expenditure and were to be selected from official as well as non-official Europeans and natives. Under the Act of 1863, landed magnates and men from the upper ranks of native society were appointed to be Indian justices. Excepting the few under aristocratic patronage, there were virtually no middle-level tax payers among these ranks. And while these native Justices had some influence on the municipal deals of the Calcutta Corporation, significant power still lay in the hands of the official Chair of the Corporation and the Commissioner of Police.

In the 1870s there was agitation for change within municipal politics. Although Europeans always enjoyed a majority on the council, many non-officials wanted more influence and efficiency within the executive. The Government was not opposed to the move for greater representation because a more representative Council could better implement the proposed increase in taxation. Debates on the Legislative Council finally resulted in the Calcutta Municipal Bill of 1876, providing for a Corporation of seventy-two members, of which only a quarter would be elected by the Government. Forty-eight commissioners were to be elected by rate-payers and overall direction invested in the Chair drawn from Indian Civil Service officials. It was calculated that the European majority could be maintained on the basis that the twenty-four commissioners nominated by central government would be expected to be joined by another fourteen white elected members. Opposition to the Bill, which came from both European and native (mainly aristocratic) quarters, resulted in an unexpected majority of professional Bengalis. A European boycott of the elections and lack of support from notables coupled with Bengali political agitation achieved an 'electoral mobilization of an unexpected scale' (Kanta Ray, 1984: 88). Racial tension generated by Calcutta politics proved that native electoral support could not be taken for granted. This reform signalled a turning point in the politics of the city; these new professional politicians were independent figures – not bound to either native magnate patronage or European merchants – and therefore exercised influence in quite different directions from the former and the latter (Ray, 1979: 22–23). Britain's economic and ideological needs had spawned a new generation of English-speaking Bengalis whose power sprang from the very ties of dependence which initially bound them. This new mood was reflected in English complaints about the growing 'cheek' and 'insolence' of the native population; the *Englishman* in 1893 reported, 'Europeans are insulted, abused and jeered at by the lowest type of natives and if they retaliate, they are set upon by a mob' (Kanta Ray, 1984: 28).

In Kipling's text, the narrator works hard to undermine the imitation parliamentary proceedings of the Legislative Council sessions of Calcutta. The sumptuous octagonal room in which debates are held is full of 'first-class furniture, the inkpots, the carpet, and the resplendent ceilings'. 'Beautifully polished desks' lead up to a 'black wooden throne, comfortably cushioned in green leather' which forms the Speaker's Chair. In this atmosphere of 'chastened gloom', one may find all the great men gathered in debate. But the Council Chamber of Calcutta which 'might be a London Board-room' is not the London Parliament; 'English office fittings [may be] responsible for the warp' but repetition of familiar signs do not add up to a whole. Quoting from Rabelais' *Pantagruel* to mock this council of false gods, Kipling's savaging of Calcutta self-government finds its inspiration in the nineteenth-century English satirical tradition of attacks on urban bureaucracy in London. For example, J.S. Mill terms the Corporation of the City of London 'that union of modern jobbing and antiquated foppery'. Dickens's attack on parish government depicts it as debating 'the question of

whether water could be regarded in the light of a necessary of life'
(Welsh, 1971: 37–38). The pompous dignity of vestrymen 'tran-
scendently quarrelsome' in 'playing at Parliament' is mocked in a
piece in *Household Words*:

> This was a great occasion. But, our Vestry shines habitually.
> In asserting its own preeminence, for instance, it is very
> strong. On the least provocation, or on none, it will be
> clamorous to know whether it is to be 'dictated to', or
> 'trampled on', or 'ridden over rough shod'. Its great watch-
> word is Self-government. . . . It was our Vestry – pink of
> Vestries as it is – that in support of its favourite principle took
> the celebrated ground of denying the existence of the last
> pestilence that raged in England, when the pestilence was
> raging at the Vestry doors. Doginson said it was plums; Mr
> Wigsby (of Chumbledon Square) said it was oysters; Mr Magg
> (of Little Winkling Street) said, amid great cheering, it was
> newspapers.
>
> (Dickens, 1899: 247)

But perhaps because much more is at stake in the preservation
of colonial boundaries, Kipling's satire is more hysterical and less
controlled in its critique of the Calcutta local government proceedings. This 'council of the gods' meets to discuss vote allocations and
wards in the Municipal Bill in the midst of what the narrator terms
the Calcutta Stink. There are 'rubbish heaps in Chitpore Road',
'dirty little tanks at the back of Belvedere', 'street[s] full of small-
pox', 'reeking ghari-stands' and an intolerable 'stench that runs up
and down Writers' Buildings staircases'. Whilst the country outside
these 'uncommonly well-upholstered' chambers is prey to the fever,
these Bengali councillors debate the 'plurality of votes' in a manner
that renders the English language absurd:

> Is section 10 to be omitted, and is one man to be allowed one
> vote and no more? How many votes does three hundred
> rupees' worth of landed property carry? Is it better to kiss a
> post or throw it into the fire? Not a word about carbolic acid
> and gangs of sweepers, the little man in the black dressing-
> gown revels in his subject. He is great on principles and
> precedents, and the necessity of 'popularising our system'. . . .
> For a practical answer to this, there steals across the council

chamber just one faint whiff of the Stink. It is as though some one laughed low and bitterly.

(Kipling, 1919b: 219)

What is left when meaning departs is a proliferation of empty signs. Signifiers refer neither to their familiar signifieds, which may only be granted meaning within the context of European humanism, nor to the social and political 'real', confronted by the olfactory reality of the Stink. The eloquence and fluency of the Bengali 'babu' (or English-educated clerk) betray his distinct lack of sense. Each phrase appropriated from the mother language serves only to underscore an absence of logic and his undeniable difference from the mother culture:

He quotes from one John Stuart Mill to prove it. There steals over the listener a numbing sense of nightmare. He has heard all this before somewhere – yea; even down to JS Mill and the references to the 'true interest of ratepayers'. He sees what is coming next. Yes, there is the old Sabha, Anjuman journalistic formula – 'Western education is an exotic plant of recent importation'. . . . He is haunted by the ghost of all the political platforms of Great Britain. He hears all the old, old vestry phrases, and once more he smells the Smell. *That* is no dream. Western education is an exotic plant. . . . We made that florid sentence.

(Kipling, 1919b: 220)

The narrator's emotional investment in this critique crystallises in the simple statement, 'they want shovels not sentiments *in this part of the world*'. The narrator's image of the educated Bengali undergoes progressive regression and hostility. The educated Bengali spouts a 'torrent of verbiage', concealing the real filth that lurks behind the nice words. Western education for the Bengali is a perversion of humanist ideals. It is an horrific attribute – as 'monstrous as a banian' – choking all *real* civilisation by virtue of 'thickly spreading' roots in the 'fat soil of Bengal'. These hyperbolic metaphors form part of the colonial rhetoric of unnatural excesses; native men, including educated ones, are 'born and raised of . . . surfeited muck-heap', their land is that of a 'damp, drainage-soaked soil . . . sick with the teeming life of a hundred years'. It is this primeval muck-heap which finally defines their racial difference and their destiny of perpetual subjection:

179

why, asks a savage, let them vote at all? They can put up with
this filthiness. They cannot have any feelings worth caring a
rush for. Let them live quietly .... Surely they might be
content with all those things without entering into matters
which they cannot, *by nature of their birth*, understand.

> (Kipling, 1919b: 206) [my emphasis]

Here, the educated native is disavowed as a mutation or bastard;
education, fluency and intellectual dexterity which mark the civilised man are marks of the fraudulent native as mimic man. Early
in Kipling's career as journalist, the Ilbert Bill was being put
forward to remove the Anglo-Indian privilege of trial by European
judges in special courts. Native judges would be allowed to try
Europeans. In the inaugural meeting of the European and Anglo-
Indian Defence Association formed to pressure the government
against the Ilbert Bill, race emerges as the crucial issue. J. Keswick,
argues that colonial education made no difference:

do you think the Native Judges will by three or four years'
residence in England become so Europeanised in nature and
character, that they will be able to judge as well in charges
against Europeans as if they themselves were Europeans and
born? Can the Ethiopian change his skin or the leopard
his spots?

> (Ray, 1979: 32)

Keswick's Bengali babu is an 'unbecoming' malcontent because he
uses the gift of 'Education which the government has given' him
against the spirit of the giving, by 'flaunt[ing] it in a discontented
spirit'. In a parody of the civilising mission, Keswick asks the
question, 'what would they have been today if the British had not
taken the country?', answers it with the assertion that they would
be exactly where they are today:

The Education which the Government has given them, and
which they use chiefly to flaunt it in a discontented spirit,
would not put courage into their hearts to defend their own
hearths and homes and these men, for a description of whose
nature, and for the chief characteristics of whose crimes, I
would refer you to Dr Chever's book on Medical Jurisprudence, now cry out for power to sit in judgement on and
condemn the lion-hearted race whose bravery and whose

blood have made their city what it is, and raised them to what they are.

(Ray, 1979: 32)

Colonial discourse as a civil discourse within a tradition of European humanism authorises a universalist narrative of English liberty; yet it continually encounters those signs of mimicry which have to be disavowed, if it is to achieve legitimation. But if these signs of civility have their meaning emptied out in the articulation of colonial authority, these self-same signs of racial and cultural prestige are stripped of their ideological value. What the discourse of mimicry inadvertently produces is an ironised portrait of colonial ideology by mocking and parodying its very model of civility. As Bhabha puts it, 'at the intersection of European learning and colonial power', 'the great tradition of European humanism seems capable only of ironizing itself' (Bhabha, 1984: 128). A colonial text of this type produces an awareness of the real rules of the game; the disjunction between England and Calcutta forces a recognition of inequality achieved only through a repressive exercise of power. As Kipling fantasises,

> Then a distinctly wicked idea takes possession of the mind: 'What a divine – What a heavenly place to *loot!*' This gives place to a much worse devil – that of conservatism. It seems not only a wrong but criminal thing to allow natives to have any voice in the control of such a city – adorned, docked, wharfed, fronted and reclaimed by Englishmen, existing only because England lives, and dependent for its life on England.
>
> (Kipling, 1919b: 203)

On duty with Superintendent Lamb

Calcutta's difference lies primarily in the native city's visual, aural and olfactory assault on the white middle-class journalist's senses. The native quarters form the text's grotesque body. Its urban landscape is both contaminating as well as deeply polluted; the darker portions of Calcutta are described as a journey into a 'wilderness' of 'long-neglected abominations'. These are the places where no Europeans ought to tread and where the miasmic air threatens to overwhelm the healthy colonial body. The text's journey from the parliamentary 'council of gods' to the more exotic and seedy parts of the native quarters in the dead of night is entirely

181

in keeping with its project of disavowal. For there, within the 'City of Dreadful Night', we shall encounter the Bengali babu again.

In this section of the narrative, the narrator is accompanied by the Calcutta police, whose warning 'that there were places and places where a white man, unsupported by the arm of Law, would be robbed and mobbed . . .' is heeded. Kipling's text here reflects the conflicting demands of power and representation in its image of the policeman as law-enforcer and law-provider: the former seeks to implement the systems of justice set up by the constitutional and legal framework of the state, while the latter, as guarantor of the colonial state, is the sole arbiter of law and order. Superintendent Lamb, the narrator's escort, fulfils both roles; he shores up the insecurity of the narrator through his role as the all-powerful and all-knowing figure of authority. The confusing 'human jungle' of the native city with its 'wilderness' of 'mysterious' and 'conspiring tenements' is all brought under Superintendent Lamb's inspecting gaze. Power located in the disciplinary gaze is diffused through all the native quarters; the voice of authority – at once predatory and reassuring – will be able to account for each creature in this god-forsaken terrain.

The police headquarters at No 22 provides the organising centre for such a massive task. It sits at the very heart of a 'great web' of telecommunication, organisation and information: 'the centre . . . where Justice sits all day and night looking after one million people and a floating population of one hundred thousand' (Kipling, 1919b: 236). The fire look-out is an observation 'sentry-box' on the top of police offices; from this 'eyrie'-like look-out, one may hear 'the heart of Calcutta beating'. This gaze, as Kipling's narrator concedes, has 'very little to do' with where the white 'respectables live'; this tower only surveys the enclosed landscape of the native city, as a sort of social 'quarantine' (Foucault, 1979: 216). Such an eye enforces the strict divisions in the racial geography of Calcutta. South and west of a line drawn from the Howrah Bridge to the east end of Park Street were the wealthy and spacious suburbs of Anglo-Indian residences, leading hotels, official and commercial establishments. On the north and east of the city, there were crowded Indian sections. E. P. Richard remarks:

> All that lay north and east of the line was of intense density, a slum-like city mass that contained the best and worse of Indian residential quarters and housed the bulk of the

population of Calcutta. These 2,500 acres of almost streetless property, arranged anyhow, were severed by an abnormally sparse set of right-angle, narrow main roads that bound some 19 huge blocks of property.

Richard's task for the Calcutta Improvement Trust in 1914 was to improve upon these racial and economic lines in a plan to rebuild Calcutta; but the distinction and division of spaces were already clearly visible at the time which Kipling was writing:

> And now, 'let us see the handsome houses where the wealthy nobles dwell'. Northerly lies the great human jungle of the native city, stretching from Burra Bazaar to Chitpore. That can keep. Southerly is the *maidan* and Chowringhi. 'If you get out into the centre of the maidan you will understand why Calcutta is called the City of Palaces.'
>
> (Kipling, 1919b: 211)

Foucault argues that the disciplinary dream, organised around the inquiring gaze, is one where an economy of power may be exercised on all surfaces through the accretion of a body of knowledge which 'insidiously objectifies those on whom it is applied' (Foucault, 1979: 216). The police fulfil such a dream by opening up the maze of the native city to the production of knowledge:

> 'How long does it take to know it then?' 'About a lifetime and even then some of the streets puzzle you.' 'How much has the head of the ward to know?' 'Every house in his ward if he can, who owns it, what sort of character the inhabitants are, who are their friends, who go out and in, who loaf about the place at night, and so on and so on.' 'And he knows all; this by night as well as by day?' 'Of course. Why shouldn't he.'
>
> (Kipling, 1919b: 251)

The Calcutta bobby is 'a white man, and has to deal with some of the "toughest" folk that ever set out of malice aforethought to paint Job Charnock's city vermilion' (Kipling, 1919b: 209). But he is also the best guide into non-white territory. The narrator's childlike dependence and admiration of this omnipotent figure recalls Dickens's slumming narrative, 'On Duty with Inspector Field'. Sections five, six and seven of 'The City of Dreadful Night' are similar both in narrative lay-out and imagery to Dickens's expedition to Ratcliff Highway and St Giles in London. Kipling's acknowledgement of Dickens is explicit: the 'great wilderness of packed houses' are 'just such mysterious, conspiring tenements as Dickens would have loved' (Kipling, 1919b: 244). The world holds no terrors for the Anglo-Indian or the middle-class Londoner because protection is offered by a knowledgeable and more-than-human policeman:

> Inspector Field's eye is the roving eye that searches every corner of the cellar as he talks. Inspector Field's hand is the well-known hand that has collared half the people here, and motioned their brothers, sisters, fathers, mothers, male and female friends, inexorably to New South Wales. Yet Inspector Field stands in this den, the Sultan of the place. Every thief here cowers before him, like a schoolboy before his schoolmaster. All watch him, all answer when addressed, all laugh at his jokes, all seek to propitiate him.
>
> (Dickens, 1899: 178)

In a colonial turn of phrase, Dickens's police inspector is described as 'the Sultan' or lord of this familiar den of thieves and vagrants because he is better than any of them in what they do. If such a metaphor betrays a sneaky kinship between policeman and thief, the inspector can claim the weight of institutional power behind him. It is the ends and not the means that matter; the policeman simply betters the thief at his game. In Kipling's text, the predatory nature of the policeman is part of his attraction and the security that he provides. The licensed coffee-house is a den of vice. In 'The City' the Superintendent's entrance is likened to a ferret's appearance in a rabbit warren: 'the Police laugh, and those nearest in the crowd laugh applausively, as in duty bound. Perhaps the rabbit grins uneasily when the ferret lands at the bottom of the burrow and begins to clear the warren' (Kipling, 1919b: 249). The reassuring figure of the superintendent shields the narrator from all danger; as the source of all reliable information, he also enables the preservation of the narrator's clean, pure colonial identity and his vicarious pleasures:

> 'Remember, if you are here alone, the chances are that you'll be clubbed, or struck, or, anyhow mobbed. You'll understand that this part of the world is shut to Europeans – absolutely. Mind the steps and follow on'. . . . out in the smells and gross

184

darkness of the night, in evil, time-rotten brickwork, and another wilderness of shut-up houses.

(Kipling, 1919b: 247)

The psychic energy invested in this authoritative figure is directly proportional to the degree of insecurity felt by the middle-class voyeur–tourist, purposefully straying from the domestic privacies of the Victorian/colonial drawing-room to experience first-hand the excitements and dangers of another culture and class. As the art historian Griselda Pollock remarks of *Gustave Doré's London: A Pilgrimage*, the 'question of who is looking at whom with what effects . . . structures [the] range of disparate texts and heterogeneous practices which emerge in the nineteenth-century city – tourism, exploration/discovery, social investigation, social policy' (Pollock, 1988: 26). Superintendent Lamb reveals yet more 'horrors' as the narrator wanders deeper and deeper into the City of Dreadful Night, '"Where are we now?" "Somewhere off the Chitpore Road, but you wouldn't understand if you were told. Follow now, and step pretty much where we step – there's a good deal of filth hereabouts"' (Kipling, 1919b: 243). There is no real danger to personal safety from the horrors of unknown London or Calcutta. Sheila Smith describes Dickens's narrative as that of a 'small boy' 'going to the Zoo where the lions were safely behind bars' (Smith, 1980: 56). The vicarious thrills which result from the narrator's journey are those of a child treated to the visual spectacle of performing circus animals or the changing scenes of a colonial 'magic lantern . . . each more squalid than its predecessor' (Kipling, 1919b: 247). This tour of misery meets with the narrator's approval, 'Who's complaining? Bring on your atrocities'. Like its metropolitan counterpart, this version of the illustrated slum journey depicts opium dens, gambling houses and streets of prostitutes. The textual complicity between reader and narrator allows the former his/her vicarious thrills where danger can be viewed from comparative safety.

Racial hybridity

'The City of Dreadful Night' returns to its obsessive unveiling of the fraudulent native by taking a tour of Calcutta's 'St John's Wood'. Off Chitpore Road, the Bengali babu is found with prostitutes in native dens of iniquity and sexual licentiousness. He functions here as an emblem of hyperbolic excesses and forbidden sexual pleasure disguised in the *form* of Englishness. His mimicry of Englishness unsettles because it portrays English identity as Other. The surreal effect of this reflection prompts a torrent of abuse on the narrator's part:

> English furniture of a gorgeous and gimcrack kind, unlimited chandeliers, and a collection of atrocities. Continental prints are scattered about the house, and on every landing squats a Bengali who can talk English with unholy fluency. The recurrence suggests – only suggests, mind – a grim possibility of the affectation of excessive virtue by day, tempered with the sort of unwholesome enjoyment after dusk – this loafing and lobbying and chattering and smoking, and unless the bottles lie, tippling, among the foul-tongued handmaidens of Dainty Iniquity.
>
> (Kipling, 1919b: 246)

Off Chitpore road one may find not only babus revealing their true selves but prostitutes soliciting. Kipling's 'City' draws on the nineteenth-century discourse on prostitution as an urban phenom-enon, but with a difference. Prostitution breaks the cultural, physical and social boundaries carefully set up between settler and native and is therefore the most feared source of contagion. In 'Coolootollah', sailors are to be found among the prostitutes. The text describes one of these dens of iniquity in a typically melo-dramatic fashion; a 'pure-blooded white' with the 'flush of inno-cent sleep on his cheeks' is asleep in a cot in a witch's coven. Prostitution also leads to miscegenation. Mrs D is a mixed-blood Eurasian prostitute with 'whatever shame she may have owned . . . long since cast behind her'. She is accompanied by a 'shapeless Burmo native', 'with high cheek bones and a mouth like a shark', who calls her Mem-Sahib. Kipling, shocked by the 'common foulness' of the Eurasian woman objects to this titular distinction. Boundaries are meant to be preserved: 'the word jars unspeakably'. 'Her life is a matter between herself and her Maker, but that she – the widow of a soldier of the Queen – has stooped to this common foulness in the face of the city, offends against the white race' (Kipling, 1919b: 256). Native blood must be differentiated from white blood in order that the hierarchy of power and privilege may remain intact.[6] As Kipling's narrator openly admits,

Then the secret of the insolence of Calcutta is made plain. Small wonder the natives fail to respect the Sahib, seeing what they see and knowing what they know. In the good old days, the Honourable directors deported him or her who mis-behaved grossly, and the white man preserved his face. He may have been a ruffian. . . . He did not sink in the presence of the people. The natives are quite right to take the wall of the Sahib who has been at great pains to prove that he is of the same flesh and blood.

(Kipling, 1919b: 256)

Kipling's text strains under the paranoia of its own manufacture, continual vigilance against pollution is difficult, if not impossible, to maintain. The ambivalence produced by the hybrid construction of Calcutta – made hysterically in the image of London – rends colonial subjectivity asunder. The result is a text of paranoiac misanthropy where all human subjects in Calcutta are in some way implicated in the process of entropy and contamination. Calcutta as Anglo and Indian city threatens the geo-political colonial hier-archy because its filth and misery are not restricted to the native quarters. There is 'no escape from it'; the Calcutta stink 'blows across the maidan', and brings disease in its wake. The miasmic smell of spreading filth is found even among sanitised Anglo-Indian residences of drawn shutters:

Chowringhee is a stately place full of sumptuous houses, but it is best to look at it hastily. Stop to consider for a moment what the cramp compounds, the black soaked soil, the netted intricacies of service-staircases, the packed stables, the seeth-ment of human life round the *durwans*' lodges and the curious arrangement of little open drains mean, and you will call it a whited sepulchre.

(Kipling, 1919b: 213)

Disease is rife within the luxury of these spacious surroundings. It is ever present on the margins of civilisation: 'it can lodge comfort-ably on roofs, climb along from the gutter-pipe to piazza, or rise from sink to verandah and thence to the upmost story' (Kipling, 1919b: 213–214). As a result, white men are not immune to it, even 'healthy [white] cut flesh will not readily heal'.

Hybrid contamination even infects the English in Calcutta. Even Anglo-Indians exhibit the typical symptoms of doubling reserved for anglicised Bengalis. Resident Calcuttans express their English-ness in a foreign community by riding 'natty little pillbox' broughams, wearing black frock coats and top-hats. Yet these clothes suffer from the same ambivalence fate as the babus, because they wrench act from context and enact identity – not as an immutable given – but as a performance:

> But top-hats are not intended to be worn in India. They are as sacred as home letters and old rose-buds. The friend cannot see this . . . and cannot see why a barbarian is moved to inextinguishable laughter at the sight. . . . The effect is curious, and at the same time fills the beholder with surprise.
>
> (Kipling, 1919b: 210–211)

Eminent gentlemen riding 'fretful horses on diabolically severe curbs' cannot reproduce the home culture. They only reinforce feelings of alienation by calling such cultures into question. They become part of Calcutta's inverted culture. Black cab drivers are given votes; black men adorn both the corridors of Parliament and the streets of prostitution, speaking 'English with an uncanny fluency'. Wild black orderlies block the entrances to government offices giving instructions to white men on how to behave. The grey Englishman in the Chamber is part of this inversion and will do nothing to set the picture right:

> He looks a strong man, and a worldly. Surely he will say, 'yes, Lala Sahib, all this may be true talk, but there's a vile smell in this place, and everything must be cleared in a week, or the Deputy Commissioner will not take away any notice of you in the *durbar*.' He says nothing of that kind. This is a Legislative Council, where they call each other 'Honourable So-and-So'. . . . Is he then like the rest[?] Perhaps after long years among the pens and papers its occupants grew to think that it really is, and in this belief give *résumés* of the history of Local Self-Government in England.
>
> (Kipling, 1919b: 221)

In Kipling's text, the constitution and institutions forming the basis of British democracy and rule become a farce, a 'hopeless, hopeless fog' of words, where 'orators plunge *in media res*' and only throw an occasional 'sir' to the Speaker of the House.

Against this hybrid contamination, Kipling places the rugged frontiersman of the Henry Lawrence variety[7] – the up-country savage, 'backwoodsmen and barbarians' whose very lack of civility qualifies them for the name of civilisation. They are the 'we' invoked by the narrative against the 'they' of the 'civilised' Presidencies, the masculine vigour of frontier states against the effeminate bureaucracy of the Anglo-Indian metropolis. Paradoxically, such a model is the reverse of the colonial situation where occupation narrates the creation and sustenance of a civil society. Hybridisation as a discourse of difference and disavowal creates tension and contradictions through its powerful rhetoric of contagion, and it is this threat which pushes the text into its suspicion of any human construction. Difference constantly infringes on the sanctity of the pure, original English identity. Tagore's assessment of Kipling's writings in 1894 is helpful in this respect:

He is trying to get the Englishman in England to understand that the government of India is like a circus company. They are skilfully directing a dance of strange and wonderful animals of diverse species staged before the civilised world. A moment's turning away of the steady watchful eyes kept on them would inevitably result in all these animals springing at one's neck from behind.

(Kanta Ray, 1984: 24)

Applied to 'The City', this is a lucid comment on both the spectacle of the hybrid world and the stress that these 'steady, watchful eyes' have to endure out of fear. Kipling's colonial text is extremely unstable. Fear turns Calcutta on its head – the Anglo-Indian hierarchy is robbed of authority and is implicated in its own demise. Civility is at some Other place. In the promotion of terror as a means of constructing boundaries, the white colonial master sees fear in every object and is ultimately left only with the ghost of Lucia, the womanly symbol of Victorian and Edwardian purity.

The question of where such an unsulled identity may be found – or how far one is to go back to ensure the purity of colonial identity – occupies the last chapter of Kipling's narrative. The journey into the past is an attempt to right the wrongs of the present. It is a devastating disavowal of contemporary Anglo-Indian society. The narrator's visit to the Park Street Cemetery in Calcutta leads to his discovery of a 'big and stately tomb' dedicated to Lucia (1776 AD). Verse on the gravestone which 'goes well, even after all these years' lead Kipling to speculate on the type of community living in those early years of British conquest. Lucia's husband, 'knew Clive well, had had dealings with Omichand, and talked to the men who had lived through the terrible night in the Black Hole'. He was rich from trade and could promise (and fulfil) her heart's desire. Lucia, on the other hand, was a frail, fair Kentish maiden who lived in a romantic age where young writers composed poetry and duelled for her honour. She danced with the greatest of men and was a 'toast far up river'. But the dream which partakes in the romantic myth of a rural England and the angelic domesticity of the woman in the house is difficult to sustain in a foreign land. Such an ideal cannot survive inhospitable climes, and Lucia falls ill with putrid fever. The faithful wife and maid that symbolises all the virginal purity of England becomes contaminated with this 'teeming life of a hundred years'. But was the dream rotten from the very start? Was Lucia no better than the prostitutes who ply their wares in the native city, selling sex for money? In the arrival of marriageable women in India, the sanctity of this most holy of contracts is altered:

> What pot-bellied East Indiaman brought the 'virtuous maid' up river, and did Lucia 'make her bargain' as the cant of those times went, on the first, second or third day after her arrival? Or did she, with the others of the batch, give a spinster's ball as a last trial – following the custom of the country.
>
> (Kipling, 1919b: 267)

Lucia's husband was in no doubt as to which version of history he was party to; on her death, his grief was spent on a sumptuous grave. Yet, as the narrator continues, it is only 'a little later on [that] he took comfort . . . [in] the next batch' out from England. The purity of English colonial identity cannot be sustained in the face of the nightmare of the writer's own construction. All that remain are gravestones, a gloomy testimony to the 'failure to comply with the contract' of honoured remembrance: 'the slab is out of his tomb, and leans foolishly against it; the railings are rotted, and there are no more lasting ornaments than blisters and stains, which are the work of the weather, and not the result of the 'warm yet unavailing tear' (Kipling, 1919b: 266). The writer ends in ironic frustration, 'let us go about and moralise cheaply on the tombstones, trailing the role of pious reflection up and down the pathways of the grave'.

6

THE COLONIAL MIRROR

In the two preceding chapters, I have been concerned with a dialogic reading of the impact of colonialism on the culture and literature of Empire that is able to register the ambivalences of Kipling's gothic and urban texts. Kipling has a certain affinity for the gothic form because it allows him to address powerful feelings of fear and loathing. Gothic narratives cultivate uncertainty and offer a 'double-take' on a realist and mimetic enumeration of names and things. These stories generate a dream-like atmosphere of terror and paranoia through their presentation of a self that is possessed of an Other, or a self that is divested of its own house. In a similar manner, Kipling's colonial city can be approached as a place of uneven structural and narrative ambivalence. Calcutta is a historical and geographical location that is inscribed by the politics of segregation. But Kipling's city is more than this, it is also a hybrid discursive space produced through the rhetoric of contagion and the ironic re-staging of Calcutta within the language and literature of nineteenth-century London.

In this chapter I will ground the discussion thus far within a more formally psychoanalytic sketch of mimesis and self-formation. Recent work in racial stereotyping will provide the terms for this debate; Fanon, Bhabha and Lloyd, among others, have used psychoanalysis to interrogate the racial politics of identification within the colonial arena. Their work details the predominantly visual basis of this formation of colonial identity; the obsession with the racial body analysed in their writings will underpin this chapter's analysis of the fantasy of cross-cultural disguise in Kipling's stories and its narrative analogue. Kipling's stories rehearse the anxiety, alienation and horror of the Anglo-Indian imagination; these emotions form the nub of a psychic trauma that results from the encounter between two very different cultures. Despite the substantive power available to the colonising culture, these emotions surface again and again in the contemporary writing of the period. In such a climate of terror and uncertainty, the figure of the all-knowing colonial policeman–anthropologist provides a comforting fantasy. The figure of the white man in native costume is an imaginary fantasy of the white man *as* native; in psychoanalytic terms, his racial and cultural disguise is both an assertion and a denial of difference.

The fascination with costume can be situated within a historical preoccupation with theatre and Oriental fashion in the nineteenth century; yet I shall contend that the transformative energy that accrues to costume in these narratives must also be understood within the dynamics of a racial fantasy which centres on body-images. Dress and role-playing are part of theatrical performance. Yet from chapter one, we have seen that popular medical accounts at the time assumed that the environment influenced human health, and that human diversity could be mapped according to climatic zones. Acclimatisation produced different types of bodies over time and clothes were an integral part of the process of adaptation. Consequently, the fantasy of disguise spills over into that of different bodies. The fantasy of transformation moves beyond simple theatrical performance; it can be understood both in literal and in symbolic or metaphoric terms. My purpose in reading Kipling's stories within the psychoanalytic framework of fetishism is motivated by bodily transformation; in particular, it will be directed at understanding precisely how different biological bodies, indicated by their different body-images, are caught up in a fantasy of assigned roles. I shall look specifically at Strickland and Kim, characters in Kipling's fiction who dress in native costume in order to fulfil their occupations as policeman and spy more effectively. They are Anglo-Indians whose talents for disguise enable them to pass without detection, and to penetrate the deepest recesses of the native underworld without fear. Strickland is the colonial counterpart of Conan Doyle's maverick detective Sherlock Holmes; his efficacy as a policeman is a direct consequence of his skill at disguise. Strickland and Kim, the boy-spy of Kipling's 1901 novel, both present a fantasy that treads a fine line between transgressive adventuring and law enforcement. While it is undoubtedly the case that these stories offer an exciting and theatrical fantasy of a world beyond the pale, by locating cultural transgression within the generic frame of the spy/police story, the enjoyment of breaking cultural taboos is harnessed to the re-establishment of cultural and political boundaries.

THE MIRRORED BODY

Psychoanalysis and anti-imperial politics have proved strange but fruitful bed-fellows in some recent work in colonial discourse theory. Despite individual differences between theorists, this psy-choanalytic theory of colonial discourse is centred on how identity is formed through the self–Other trajectory, and pays close atten-tion to a visual coding of difference. Homi Bhabha's extremely productive re-reading of Fanon's early text, *Black Skin/White Masks*, is perhaps the best example of this work, though separate articles published by David Lloyd, Victor Burgin, Kaja Silverman and Slavoj Žižek have also contributed to a specific understanding of how racial differences have impacted on a range of activities. Their work extends collectively from the unpacking of imperial fantasy to a critique of the Enlightenment project and its conception of citizen-ship. In this section, I want to focus on the body and body-image in psychoanalysis. This will enable me to prepare the ground for a notion of the racial body in colonial discourse, and to comment on its analytic value for my exploration of costume in Kipling's stories of cross-cultural disguise.

The visual coding of alterity, the dynamics of identification and identity formation, relies on the psychoanalytic theory of the body's function in self-formation. In psychoanalysis, the body acts as a model for investigating the psyche. Body-image, and the bound-aries that it produces, are integral to the formation of self. Freud asserts that the ego 'can be regarded as a mental projection on the surface of the body'; Jacques Lacan provides a theory of spatialised identifications in the 'mirror stage' of the infant's development where the body functions as the base and precondition of subject-ivity.[1] Lacan asserts that the imaginary unity of the self is obtained via the introjection of a specular image of the corporal body in the 'mirror stage'. The 'mirror stage' outlines the 'captation' of human form by providing the first 'visual *gestalt*' of the body – 'an ideal unity, a salutary imago' – on which to hang the 'self'. Prior to the mirror stage, the infant's experience of the body is composed of an uncoordinated and fragmented bundle of sensations and motions (Lacan, 1977: 18–19). The infant is governed exclusively by an unformed mass of libidinal impulses and draws no distinction between its own body and the world. In the drama of the mirror stage, Lacan describes a child's fascination with its supposed reflected image; the infant identifies with this reflected image and introjects it as its own. This 'jubilant assumption' of the specular image by the infant child, still awkward and lacking in motor coordination, forms the basis of the symbolic matrix that will later form the subject of signification (Lacan, 1977: 2). But if the mirror stage ushers in a narcissistic moment of idealisation, it also brings with it a 'correlative tendency' of 'agressivity'. The mirrored body presents a body of agency and control; the child's libidinal over-investment in the figure results in frustration and jealousy: 'it is invested with all the original distress resulting from the child's intra-organic and relational discordance during . . . physiological natal prematuration' (Lacan, 1977: 19). Also, if the image in the mirror provides a pleasurable and erotic process of self-affirmation, it also produces a unpleasurable process of alienation and retroactive nostalgia for wholeness. The reflected image, after all, is not the self but an image of the self as Other; identification is hence both recognition and misrecognition. The erection of bodily boundaries signals a differentiation and separation of self from Other, of inside from the outside and of child from the maternal body. Identification, Lacan argues, is the relation 'in which the human individual fixes upon himself an image that alienates him from himself'; thus 'this *Gestalt* . . . by these two aspects of its appearance, symbolizes the mental permanence of the *I*, at the same time as it prefigures its alienating destination' (Lacan, 1977: 19, 2).

It is well worth emphasising that what we 'see' is as much social as 'natural'. Elizabeth Grosz points out that the fundamental importance of the body's significance in the Lacanian mirror stage comes from his insistence that the ego results from the circum-scription of libidinal energies effected through the 'tracing of the subject's perceived corporeality'. Yet this body should not be taken as a self-evident, generic, natural or complete category; seeing the body, as Grosz puts it, is not simply a matter of vision but also a matter of learning to 'see and understand according to prevailing systems of meaning and value'. This means that the mirrored body is not the real 'body of anatomy and physiology' but 'an internalised image' of culturally shared and individualised bodily significance; the body, as such, functions as the 'hinge' between the individual and the social (Wright, 1992: 35–40). Grosz's concept of the 'imaginary anatomy' is drawn partially from work by Paul Schilder who replaces the view of the body as a static naturalised structure with the body-image as a constructive process of cultural structuration. Schilder's work extends beyond Lacan's infant mirror-stage by highlighting the continuing process of self-formation and body-imaging. He argues that our body-image is always relational; we change the way we see, think about and experience our bodies in relation to others around us:

> there is from the beginning a very close connection between the body-image of ourselves and the body-image of others. We take parts of the body-images of others into others, and push parts of our body-images into others. We may push our own body-images completely into others, or in some way there may be continuous interplay between the body-images of ourselves and the persons around us. This interplay may be an interplay of parts or wholes. . . . the social relation of the body-images is not a fixed 'gestalt.' But we have a process of forming a 'gestalt' or 'gestaltung,' or creative construction in the social image.
>
> (Schilder, 1970: 235, 241)

IDENTIFICATION AND THE RACIAL BODY

Edward Said's critique of the Orient in Western cultural texts, and his location of forms of knowledge within a geo-political East–West global economic and historical division, has been enormously productive in gaining an understanding of the knowledge/power interface. Said argues that the European culture 'gained in strength and identity' by virtue of defining itself against an Orient which functioned as 'a surrogate and even underground self' (Said, 1978: 3). The re-discovery of Fanon and the various re-readings of early Fanon have added to an awareness of this political dialectic by actively including a specific racial dimension to this negating trajectory of self-definition. In the chapter 'The Fact of Blackness', Fanon recounts a pivotal moment comparable with the Freudian primal scene, when the black man is transfixed by the racist gaze of the white man and impelled to position himself within that reflecting surface: 'Look, a Negro! . . . Mama, see the Negro! I'm frightened' (Fanon, 1986: 112). This encounter carries the same symbolic weight as Lacan's mirror stage. The interpellation of the black man as racial body is a 'captation' and describes the coming together of fantasy and reality in a mixture of violation and fear that will provide the narrative matrix for subsequent racist confrontations. In the exchange of looks, the black man is alienated from himself. Made to signify the racialised body, the black man's sense of bodily composition and dimensional solidity crumbles into an 'epidermal schema' of colour. Captation is effected through the obviousness of colour which secures and shores up white identity within the projected racist narrative history of a fragmented black objecthood: 'I was responsible at the same time for my body, for my race, for my ancestors. . . . I discovered my blackness, my ethnic characteristics; and I was battered down by tom-toms, cannibalism, intellectual deficiency, fetishism, racial defects, slave ships . . .' (Fanon, 1986: 112). Yet the process of Othering is not a symmetrical one; 'Only for the white man the Other is perceived on the level of the body-image, absolutely as the not-self – that is, the unidentifiable, the unassimilable' (Fanon, 1986: 161).

White operates as an invisible norm in racist cultures and exnominates itself as a colour by positioning itself outside the self/Other dialectic. Victor Burgin, Diana Fuss and David Lloyd have all recently analysed how whiteness exempts itself from this dialectical logic. Burgin argues that whiteness opposes 'colour' or 'blackness' with a disembodied entity, 'To speak of the colour of skin is to speak of a body. "People of colour" are embodied people. To have no colour is to have no body' (Burgin, 1990: 68). Lloyd's critique is directed at the interlocking mechanisms of racism from the level of individual subject formation to the 'metaphoric structure of culture' at the level of social institutions. In this scenario, white occupies the position of ideal universal man – the 'subject without properties' – in the narrative transformation from 'absolute specificity' to 'the pure formality of representative man' (Lloyd, 1990: 84, 81). Finally, Fuss critiques the 'considerable cultural capital' accumulated by the 'colonisation of subjectivity' that claims for whiteness the status of transcendental signifier: 'As a self-identical, self-producing term, white draws its ideological power from its proclaimed transparency, from its self-elevation over the very category of "race"' (Fuss, 1994: 22).

Bhabha's re-reading of Fanon is a calculated intervention against an all too easy acceptance of the stability of colonial identity. His early work has sought to fracture the reification of identity as it is presented in the colonial mirror of representation; as such, his work avoids the re-mystification of colonial power as absolute and without resistance. Bhabha reads the project of colonial self-formation 'against the grain' to foreground Fanon's 'Manichean delirium' in the interlocutory spaces between self and Other. Insisting that the process of identification is ambivalent, and that positions in fantasy are always open to the possibility of inversion, Bhabha reminds us that Lacan's representational mirror works by virtue of a spatial splitting. Subjectivity is premised on being 'called into being in relation to an Otherness, its look or locus':

> the question of identification is never the affirmation of a pre-given identity, never a self-fulfilling prophecy – it is always the production of an 'image' of identity and the transforma-tion of the subject in assuming that image. The demand of identification – that is, to be *for* an Other – entails the representation of the subject in the differentiating order of Otherness. Identification . . . is always the return of an image of identity which bears the mark of splitting in that 'Other' place from which it comes.
>
> (Bhabha, 1986: xvi)

Drawing on Freud's paper, 'Splitting of the Ego', Bhabha argues that what is expelled from within threatens from without. More importantly, the contradiction between the subject's narcissistic demand for imaginary wholeness and its avowal of difference results in a splitting of the site of enunciation – preventing the completion of self-identity. Bhabha calls the new colonial split subject a 'hybrid'. Hybridity points to the emergence of identity '*after* the traumatic scenario of colonial difference . . . returns the eye of power to some prior, archaic image or identity' (Bhabha, 1985: 150). Hybridity is a discourse of partiality which works against the colonial reproduction of (unitary) meaning; it 'reverses the effects of colonialist disavowal' (Bhabha, 1985: 157). Consequently, neither the desire for racial and historical originality nor the demand for absolute obedience – based on this origination – will be met. The formal strategies of disavowal are also inherently unstable because the Other in the colonial mirror is both a point of identity and a product of a discriminatory gaze. In the colonial gaze, the image bears the traces of its production. Depicting the gap between image and image-maker, the perspectival stain on the surface of the colonial image betrays the process of its production (the colonial gaze) and hence prevents closure. For the very frame of the gaze/address necessarily includes the point of issue; such a perspectival vanishing point marks an irrevocable splitting of subjectivity, preventing the completion of self-identity. Slavoj Žižek puts it somewhat more lucidly:

> The gaze marks the point in the object (the picture) from which the viewing subject is *already gazed at*: it is the object which is gazing at me. Thus, far from guaranteeing the self-presence of the subject and his/her vision, the gaze functions as a spot or stain in/on the picture disturbing its transparent visibility and introducing an irreducible split in my relation to it. I can never see the picture at the point from which it is gazing at me: the view and the gaze are constitutively dissymmetrical. The gaze as object is a blemish that prevents me from looking at the picture from a safe, 'objective' distance, framing it as something which is at the disposal of my grasping view. It is, as we might say, the point at which the very frame (of my view) is already inscribed in the 'content' of the picture.
>
> (Žižek, 1989b: 8)

It is this marking which allows Bhabha to turn the Freudian reading of disavowal inside out and make the transition between the fetish and the hybrid object, from mere reproduction to mimicry. The marking of the subject as split and contradictory alters the terms of relation even while the defensive mechanisms of disavowal remain.

Colonial discourse will always reflect an ambivalence that emerges from its split subjectivity; its very language will inscribe absence, loss and lack within its assumption of agency. Bhabha's critique points to the limits of the Enlightenment assumptions of humanism and universal reason on which the discourse of the civilising mission is founded. In this schema, collectivity is read as uniform culture and citizenship as a unity of identity. History, furthermore, plays handmaid to the teleological dream of total knowledge and identity – 'the indispensable correlative of the founding function of the subject . . . the guarantee that everything that has eluded him may be restored to him; the certainty that time will dispense nothing without restoring it in a reconstituted unity' (Gloversmith, 1984: 98). As Bhabha points out, a cultural identity based on the metropolitan ideal of civility – which is rearticulated in a colonial context – is unstable precisely because its universalist narrative and representational locus will always come up against difference and disavowal. Caught between narcissism and aggressivity, the colonial Other is subject to a double demand: 'be mimetically identical, be totally other' (Fuss, 1994: 23). In the language of the civilising mission, the reformation of the 'native' subject is the object of colonial enterprise; but this reformation must also be continually denied in order to enforce the separation between the coloniser and the colonised. Consequently, education, fluency and intellectual dexterity which mark the civilised man within the colonial space must also be disavowed in order to secure the continuation of colonial occupation. The 'educated' natives are only mimic men, mutations, bastards; they can never be the genuine article. But the same movement which produces the native as mimic man also produces a 'double-take' on the civilising mission. If in the assertion of colonial authority these signs of civility have their meaning emptied out, then these self-same signs of racial and cultural prestige must be stripped of their applicability to the colonial context. It is this uncanny re-configuration that produces a disturbing rendering of colonial representation.[2]

What the discourse of mimicry inadvertently produces is an ironised portrait of the civilising mission; one that mocks its own model of civility:

> Mimicry is also the sign of the inappropriate . . . a difference or recalcitrance which coheres the dominant strategic function of colonial power, intensifies surveillance, and poses an imminent threat to both 'normalized' knowledges and disciplinary powers. The effect of mimicry on the authority of colonial discourse is profound and disturbing. For in 'normalizing' the colonial state or subject, the dream of post-Enlightenment civility alienates its own language of liberty and produces another knowledge of its norms.
>
> (Bhabha, 1985: 126)

The effect of this discursive 'limitation or prohibition *within* the authoritative discourse itself' is that mimicry 'is at once resemblance and menace' (Bhabha, 1984: 127). Hybridity's alteration in the field of relations unsettles colonial discourse's 'mimetic or narcissistic demands'; deformation and difference undermine this base of agreement on which authority is generated. For the language of difference which enables the colonial authority both to survey and discriminate against its subjects also renders them elusive: 'if discriminatory effects enable the authorities to keep an eye on them, their proliferating difference evades that eye, escapes that surveillance' (Bhabha, 1985: 154). The result is a magical and terrifying evasion of the disciplinary eye and the realist security of representation. In Bhabha's words, 'hybridity represents that ambivalent "turn" of the discriminated subject into the terrifying, exorbitant object of paranoid classification – a disturbing questioning of the images and presences of authority' (Bhabha, 1985: 155).

BLACK MASKS

How does the fantasy of cross-cultural costume operate in Kipling? How does the racial body function in the fantasy of cross-cultural disguise? What are its narrative forms? How do the theories of identification and hybridity help us to understand the fantasy of cross-cultural costume? These are some of the questions that will structure my attempt to come to terms with what I see as an exemplary case of the politics of colonial mirroring and representation. To begin, I shall focus on the two best known cases of cross-cultural disguise in Kipling's stories, Kim and Strickland. *Kim* is the story of a young boy who grows up amongst Indians and whose knowledge of native culture and affinity for disguise earns him a place in the imperial spy network (Kipling, 1912). One day he meets a Tibetan lama and agrees to accompany him on a pilgrimage to Buddhist holy places. The first section of the novel details the adventures of these two companions in an episodic and loosely picaresque fashion, describing both scenery and people met on the road. This first section abruptly comes to a halt with Kim's discovery of his father's Irish regiment. Father Bennett, the regiment's priest, discovers the boy's white ancestry and prevents him from completing his journey with the lama. Instead, the young orphan is sent to a school for 'sahibs', paid for and also approved of by the lama. In the meantime, Kim is recruited as a secret agent by friends and contacts from his past who know his craving for adventure and his talent for disguise. Initiated gradually into the demands of the secret service, he is taught firstly by the spy-master, Lurgan-Sahib, in Simla and then 'supervised' by his friend and mentor, Mahbub-Ali, the horse-trader spy. Kim returns to complete his pilgrimage with the lama after his graduation from these two 'schools'. But Kim's career in imperial espionage is not forgotten as the second phase of his pilgrimage presents him with opportunities to prove this worth.

Of all Kipling's fiction, *Kim* is the most critically acclaimed. Philip Mason has called *Kim* 'a series of clearly sketched figures moving against brilliant scenes from the India that Kipling remembered' (Mason, 1975: 180) while Edward Shanks praises it as a novel about 'the infinite and joyous variety of India for him who has eyes to see it and the heart to rejoice in it' (Shanks, 1940). In addition, J M S Tompkins asserts that *Kim* is a testimony to Kipling's masterful 'appeal to the aural imagination', 'the charm of the pictures', the presentation of 'contrasts' reflecting 'the depth of memory and delight from which it was drawn' (Tompkins, 1959: 26). *Kim* bears testimony to a varied literary heritage; the conventions of romance, adventure tales, the picaresque and the spy-thriller all inform its narrative structure. Its panoramic view of the Indian landscape, cultures and peoples leads many critics to place this novel above all others as generous in 'wisdom and humanity'; many confirm that the novel presents a 'living contradiction of nine-tenths of the charges levelled against its author' (Rutherford, 1965: 197). My discussion of *Kim* will be limited strictly to the novel's handling of native disguise; but it is here that my disagreement with conventional Kipling criticism is most evident. In my reading of *Kim*, the novel's empathetic vision is produced alongside its anxious reinforcement of the racial divide.

The first part of *Kim* sets the tone for the novel's ostensibly sympathetic handling of India by its concern with local lives and a culture that is hidden from those who inhabit the official world of Anglo-India. Kim's adventures all occur within the 'dearer, out-of-the-way life'; as a young street-wise orphan, Kim keeps company with natives of the lowest kind. He avoids white men of 'serious aspect' and lives 'hand in glove with men who led lives stranger than anything Haroun al Raschid dreamed of; and he lived in a life wild as that of the Arabian Nights' (Kipling, 1912: 3). The association of Kim's lifestyle with exotic tales of the East opens up a colonialist fantasy which, as Benita Parry has pointed out, 'transfigures India as the provider of libidinal excitation' (Parry, 1987: 56). Kim, nicknamed 'Little Friend of all the World', is comfortable with all aspects of native life and custom and is looked on fondly by all around him. He eats from the same dish as the 'ash-smeared *faquirs*', quotes native proverbs and even knows how to banter with local people with familiarity and ease.

Narrative pleasure in *Kim* inheres in the fictional recovery/ discovery of a world that colonial and metropolitan readers are excluded from; costumes have a special place in this text by offering an imaginative access to this other world. At its most basic level, dress functions as a visual prop to Kim's skill in mimicking native mannerisms; costume enables the young white boy to pass as a low or high caste native. But costumes are also imbued with a symbolic significance that goes beyond their visual appearance; costumes in *Kim* are endowed with powers that enable the wearer to undergo a whole cultural and bodily metamorphosis. Clothes function as the privileged sites of racial and cultural difference. Kim put on 'a complete suit of Hindu kit, the costume of a low-caste street boy' whenever 'there was business or frolic afoot'. Disguises enable not only his unchallenged 'prowl through dark gullies' but also provide him access to the hidden 'sights and sounds of the women's world'. The magic of costume lies in its ability to substitute a part for the whole; wearing the dress of a low caste Hindu boy enables Kim to function effectively as a low caste Hindu boy. A 'little dye-stuff and three yards of cloth', an oriental courtesan 'dabbing a twist of cloth into a saucer of brown dye' and twisting a turban around Kim's head, transforms him into a 'low-caste Hindu boy, perfect in every detail' (Kipling, 1912: 179–180). Attired in Hindu or Muslim apparel, Kim's passage from one religious culture to another is conducted with the supreme ease of changing clothes.

Kim is contrasted with other boys he meets in school; Anglo-Indian boys like the plodding De Castro whose body is covered in prickly heat, and the ignorant drummer boy who is continually misled by his servants' deferential attitude. Kim's affinity for disguise is, on the contrary, marked as a joyous inhabitation of another culture. British army trousers and jacket are described as crippling to Kim's quickness (Kipling, 1912: 150); consequently, Kim's transformation into a native boy is depicted as an epiphany, 'a demon in Kim woke up and sang with joy as he put on the changing dresses and changed speech and gesture therewith' (Kipling, 1912: 226). Characterised by a release of libidinal energy, the change effected by native costume leaves Kim with a freedom far beyond the narrow worlds of his white peers. The sense of being totally familiar, totally at ease in an alien world produces intense pleasure; the awareness of not only 'being' but consuming the other's life and culture:

Kim sat up and yawned, shook himself, and thrilled with delight. This was seeing the world in real truth; this was life as he would have it – bustling and shouting, the buckling of belts, and beating of bullocks and creaking of wheels, lighting of fires and cooking of food, and new sights at every turn of the approving eye. . . . India was awake and Kim was in the middle of it . . . for he borrowed right-and left-handedly from all the customs of the country he knew and loved.

(Kipling, 1912: 103)

Kim's fascination with native clothes must be read within the wider cultural fascination with the theatre of Empire. Exotic costume formed part of Victorian indulgence, and a wealth of detailed material, from the illustrated press to the encyclopedias on world costume, was produced on the subject. F. M. Coleman's *Typical Pictures of Indian Natives* includes special reproductions of vivid hand-coloured photographs of native castes to help readers realise the 'charm' of the 'Gorgeous East'. Coleman's 'Mohamedan' (Figure 13) wears a

turban . . . twisted into a peculiar shape, full at each side and falling below the ears, [with] trousers . . . almost close fitting to the leg below the knee, and . . . fastened by buttons from the calf downwards. [His] boots are of patent leather, adorned with silver buckles. The undress costume consists of a small oblong skull cap, and while no coat is worn, a waistcoat, generally of a gorgeous colour, plentifully sprinkled with gold or silver spangles in front and rear, is exposed to view.

(Coleman, 1897: 28)

Albert Racinet's *History of Costume* published between 1876 and 1888 catalogues Indian costumes under '19th century antique civilisations'; his Rajput warrior's costume is minutely detailed (Figure 14). He wears an 'unusual turban . . . made of fine silk' and held in place by 'a golden ribbon with pearls and an emerald in the centre':

At its top is a golden jewel, representing the sun, set with large rubies; this fastens a spray of fine feathers that bend down under the weight of two diamonds. A band of pearls and fine stones is attached at the base of the feathers and hangs down on either side of the turban like a necklace. An under-jerkin

Figure 13 'A Mohamedan' (from Coleman, 1899).

Figure 14 'The Rajputs of Telingana, India' (from Racinet, 1988).

covers all the upper body, and is fastened by a belt at the waist. . . . Wide silk trousers taper down beneath the narrow fit at the ankle. Then come velvet slippers, slightly turned up at the toes and leaving the heels exposed.

(Racinet, 1988: 96)

In Aileen Ribeiro's introduction to a re-issue of Racinet's book, she argues that there was a 'veritable flood of costume books' as part of a romantic rebellion against what was felt to be an increasingly industrialised and drab civilisation. The 'glamour of far-away' times and places was to be seen in the paintings ('glorious and senti-mental episodes in history'), novels and plays with historical themes. Ribeiro adds that historical accuracy of costume design was 'expected by a sophisticated and visually aware audience' (Racinet, 1988: 96). Whether or not one agrees with all of Ribeiro's com-ments, the drama of Empire thrived on Oriental display and actively encouraged spectacular theatre. Military spectacles such as *The Indian Mutiny, The Storming of Delhi, The Battle of Waterloo, The War in Zululand* and *The Kaffir War,* were often staged at Astley's theatre.[3] Victorian spectacles like the *Forty Thieves* indulged in an ostentatious parade of dress. Contemporary reviews also reflect an extraordinary interest in costume detail and design. In the pro-duction of the *Forty Thieves,* Michael Booth notes, lavish designs of the costumed pantomime attracted so much attention that two special articles on costume were published in addition to the *Era*'s usual review of the play (Booth, 1981). These give a detailed account of the appearance, fabric and texture of Oriental dress; the opening dancers are described as clad in

small Indian or Persian bodice, and trousers to correspond in satin, sleeves, loose bodice, and closely pleated skirts to the feet in gold-striped gauze, confined at the waist by silken sashes of a contrasting colour which tint is repeated in the head-dress accessories, jewelled crescents and gold coins. . . . white silk gossamer draperies, with diamond tiaras and orna-ments, and fringes of prismatic beads.

(Booth, 1981: 161–162)

Everywhere, 'richness' is displayed;

Captain Abdullah (Miss Blande) is clad entirely in heliotrope silk, embroidered in gold and gemmed with rubies; a drape

of heliotrope plush, lined with apricot colour and orna-
mented with revers, richly embroidered in gold and rubies in
a series of graduated crescents and stars.

(Booth, 1981: 161–162)

But if the accumulation of the adjectival in these passages is meant
to recreate the luxury of the Oriental spectacle in its 'semi-barbaric
picturesqueness', the listing of the English actress's ordinary name
anchors the theatrical illusion to a more homely reality.

Kim presents the Oriental world for visual and material consumption. His Afghan outfit also conveys Oriental excesses; the
gold fringed and embroidered cap conveys the promise of Oriental
riches, rich and loose robes gesture towards a culture that is 'ample
and flowing' and full of sensuousness. The touch of silk and the
heavenly smells of Russia-leather slippers 'with arrogantly curled
tips', the ornamental design on the turban-cap and cloth point to
alien artistry and mystique. This is borne out by the photographs
of John Lockwood Kipling's terracotta plates which functioned as
illustrations to his son's text in the Macmillan edition of *Kim*.
Created to simulate temple reliefs, these plates act as framed
postcards to the exotic array of figures in the book, from the Teshoo
Lama attired in the costume of a Tibetan monk (Figure 15) to the
Punjabi farmer (the Jat) and his sick child. The plates complement
the narrative's moving diorama of Indian life and customs; as Parry
remarks, Kipling's India appears as a 'frieze or a pageant, and [is]
romanticised as an object of sensuous and voluptuous pleasure to
be enjoyed by Europe' (Parry, 1987: 55).

Lurgan Sahib, the spy-master and antiques dealer who initiates
the boy into the arts of disguise, is also drama-master extra-
ordinaire; Lurgan refines Kim's gift for theatre and the theatrical
illusion. Lurgan had a 'hawk's eye to detect the least flaw in the
make-up' and 'would explain by the half-hour together how such
and such a caste talked, or walked, or coughed, or spat, or sneezed,
and, since "hows" matter little in this world, the "why" of
everything':

He [Lurgan Sahib] could paint faces to a marvel; with a brush-
dab here and a line there changing them past recognition.
The shop was full of all manner of dresses and turbans, and
Kim was apparelled variously as a young Mohammedan of
good family, an oilman, and once – which was a joyous

Figure 15 'The Lama' (from Kipling, 1912).

evening – as the son of an Oudh landholder in the fullest of full dress.

(Kipling, 1912: 226)

Lurgan Sahib's curiosity shop in Simla is presented as the entertaining and eroticised counterpart of the Lahore museum. Described as being filled with more precious and mysterious items than the Museum's 'house of Wonders', the shop is filled with 'ghost-daggers and prayer wheels from Tibet; turquoise and raw amber necklaces', 'gilt figures of Buddha, and little lacquer altars', 'dull copper incense-burners neither Chinese nor Persian, with friezes of fantastic devils running round them . . . and a thousand other oddments . . . cased, or piled, or merely thrown into the room'. The narrator's long and lovingly rendered list of exotic items presents not only an India that is exotic and novel for its colonial and metropolitan readers, but renders India as an extravagant spectacle much in the same manner as costumed pantomimes like the *Forty Thieves*. What emerges from a reading of *Kim* is a celebration of the novelty of the Oriental opulence that India presents to contemporary readers.[4]

In Lurgan's lessons, Kim's youthful fascination with costume and disguise is harnessed to the more adult discipline of espionage. Lurgan anchors theatre to undercover work. A comparison with Sir Richard Burton's spy memoirs in India is useful here because it unearths a similar movement. In Burton's cross-cultural transformation, we find the same attention to Oriental detail, the same playful appreciation of costume and a kindred libidinal excitement which comes with theatrical illusion:

> With hair falling upon his shoulders, a long beard, face and hands, arms and feet, stained with a thin coat of henna, Mirza Abdullah of Bushire – your humble servant – set out upon many and many trip. He was a Bazzaz, a vendor of fine linen, calicoes, and muslins; – such chapmen are sometimes admitted to display their wares, even in the sacred harem, by 'fast' and fashionable dames – and he had a little pack of *bijouterie* and *virtu* reserved for emergencies. . . . What scenes he saw! What adventures he went through! But who would believe, even if he ventured to detail them?

(Burton, 1924)

Burton's *Pilgrimage to Al-Madinah and Meccah* is a spectacular record

Figure 16 'Richard Burton as "The Pilgrim"' (from Burton, 1893).

of his adventures in the disguise of a Muslim pilgrim from Afghanistan (Figure 16). Like Kim, who adopts different disguises to suit
different contexts, Burton's ability to take on the role of an Afghan
is part of his protean ability to switch identities at will. In the early
chapters of *Pilgrimage* he is variously disguised as a 'Pathan', a
'wandering Darwaysh' and an Indian doctor. As a medical man,
Burton 'revels in the utmost freedom of [his non-European] life
and manners'. The account of his 'face to face' encounters with
native men and women is suffused with the almost child-like delight
in his hoax:

> there was something infinitely seducing in the character of a
> magician, doctor, and fakir . . . even respectable natives, after
> witnessing a performance of 'Madal' and the Magic mirror
> opined that the stranger was a holy man, gifted with super-
> natural powers, and knowing everything. One old person sent
> to offer me his daughter in marriage; he said nothing about
> the dowry, – but I thought proper to decline the honour.
>
> (Burton, 1893: 12–13)

Burton's texts are as much about knowledge/power as they are
about pleasure. Whatever his subjective and emotional experiences,
Burton trades on his awareness of his position as a European in the
Orient. Burton's footnotes to his travel account address a European
audience, and provide anthropological and geographical information. Edward Said remarks that 'what is never far from the surface
of Burton's prose is another sense it radiates, a sense of assertion
and domination over all the complexities of Oriental life' (Said,
1987: 196).

WHITE SKINS

Said's comments on the ambivalence of address in Burton's narratives also applies to Kipling's *Kim*. Although it is a novel that
attempts to create an empathetic experience of Indian culture and
lifestyle, *Kim* obsessively returns to a fundamental racial and
cultural fault-line. The Hindu boy who is Kim's companion in Simla
finds disguise beyond his ability and 'played this game clumsily';
the narrator informs readers, 'that little mind, keen as an icicle
where tally of jewels was concerned, could not temper itself to enter
another's soul'. Mahbub Ali and Hurree Babu do not work in
disguise; E.23 the spy is helped by Kim to maintain the semblance

of a Saddhu. Not only is the novel careful in its selection of the few who have the ability to 'enter another's soul', but the novel is also careful to insist on Kim's white identity when detailing his disguise as native Indian. What is particularly striking about *Kim* is a series of joking references to his white colonial identity which seem to be unmotivated by actual events in the narrative.

The opening sequence of the book is instructive. Kim, consorting with all the small bazaar boys in 'perfect equality' plays a game with a young Hindu and a Muslim boy. He sits astride the cannon outside the Lahore Museum, playing a 'king-of-the-castle-game' with his native friends. But this scene, purportedly innocent of adult politics, relies on knowledge of British rule in India to activate another level of signification. There is more than meets the eye to the text's seemingly artless remark, 'who holds the Zam Zammah . . . holds the Punjab . . . for it was the first of the conqueror's loot'. The Zam-Zammah cannon features in the historical struggles for dominion over the north of India. Used initially by the Afghans in 1701 to defeat the Hindu Mahratta army, the cannon was again used by the Afghans when Lahore was taken over by the Sikhs. When the Punjab was annexed in 1849, and the Sikhs defeated, the cannon passed into British hands. The novel's presentation of Kim's game as innocent is contradicted by the narrator's joking reference to the historical realities of Empire: 'there was some justification for Kim . . . since the English held the Punjab and Kim was English' (Kipling, 1912: 1). The joke is made at the expense of Chota Lal or Abdullah. For while the children's reactions may be 'read' intra-textually as innocent horseplay, extra-textual readers of the text can activate its second level of signification. The narrator links the child's action with that of his historical and imperial counterparts. The joke is that Kim's ancestors did kick his friends' ancestors off the trunnion and it is the historical significance of such an action that the boy Kim must learn as he moves from being a street-wise urchin to an imperial spy. It is only when Kim understands the symbolic dimensions of the cannon that he inherits a weapon of his own.

White colonial identity is precisely what is at stake in passages like this. Without it, neither Kim's seemingly unorthodox childhood nor his later occupation as a spy can be understood. For example, the second paragraph reads, 'though he was "burned black"', though he spoke Urdu and English only as a second language, though he 'consorted on equal terms' with his native peers, 'Kim was white – a poor white of the very poorest'. In this sequence, the colour 'white' functions as a residual 'truth' which cannot be erased despite Kim's appearance and behaviour. The narrator insists on the truth of Kim's racial ancestry behind all native masks that the young bazaar spy may choose to adopt. Authorial intervention with regard to the question of racial ancestry is deliberate and sustained throughout the text. In the opening paragraphs, intervention takes the form of a set of clauses which mark Kim as different from his native friends. Later in the novel, there are repetitive references to Kim's 'white blood', a 'white man's horror of snakes' and a 'European lust for meat' even when, to all intents and purposes, the character would know very little of such European fears and customs. Narrative intervention also accounts for the humour of mistaken identities as Kim's restlessness in the heat of the afternoon prompts him to take a stroll. In this sequence, a native escort's disgust at Kim's foolish behaviour prompts him to remark 'Only the devils, and the English walk to and fro without reason'. The joke arising from the reader's privileged information is that Kim is, of course, English.

Many other scenes maintain this contradiction in Kim's characterisation but I will only detail two more incidents. The first incident is found at the point of the narrative where Kim says farewell to the Lama outside the school gates of St Xavier. Here the narrator informs us that Kim wailed, 'all forgetful that he was a Sahib'. But this remark cannot be motivated by the events in the narrative, for Kim at this juncture has not learnt the behaviour proper for his race. The narrator's reference to Kim's status as Sahib must be based on his racial and cultural identity. The second incident is early in the narrative. On Kim's seeing his father's former regiment, the narrator suggests that Kim would have thought in English if he could:

> lastly, – and firstly as the undercurrent of all his quick thoughts, – this adventure, *though he did not know the English word*, was a stupendous lark – a delightful continuation of his old flights across the housetops, as well as the fulfilment of a sublime prophecy.
>
> (Kipling, 1912: 118) [my emphasis]

But references to a grammar school vocabulary are all the more out of place because Kim's own English is, as we are told on the very next page, the 'tinny, saw-cut English of the native bred' (Kipling,

1912: 119). Insistence on Kim's whiteness betrays a certain anxiety about Kim's talent for masks. By virtue of Kim's birthright and his later socialisation at St Xavier, the text constantly reassures readers of Kim's 'Sahibness'. The question 'who is Kim?' is purportedly the crisis of identity at the heart of the novel: is Kim a Sahib by nature or do the authorities (such as St Xavier and the imperial spy bureau) have to 'make a Sahib' out of Kim? The narrator's insistence on Kim's racial identity short circuits all such problems; for the text's question is met by a safety net which renders a certain circularity in formulation. Sahibness is the (residual) truth of race that is above all other properties; one must be white in order that one may acquire the cultural behaviour of a Sahib.

The novel's racial fault-line is exhibited uneasily in Kim's encounter with the Chaplains of the Mavericks. Father Bennett mistakes Kim for a native thief but reconsiders when Kim is found to speak English. But the significance of Kim's possession of English is not literal but metaphorical, that is to say it signifies something above the mere possession of language. Kim's English is significant only because he is white. The parchments that Bennett finds on Kim are at first mistaken for fetishes, 'some sort of heathen charm' or 'scapular', but are later discovered to be documents that prove Kim's white ancestry beyond doubt. But Father Bennett's initial assessment is actually not far from the truth; Kim's baptismal and birth certificates are charms and fetishes because they are the only objects able to reconstitute Kim's racial and cultural identity, given his childhood in the back streets of Lahore. They are objects which confirm his status as a white man and indicate that he, unlike other brown boys, is worthy of the priests' attention. As soon as Kim's ancestry is accepted, colour is invoked by Father Victor as the reality behind his appearance. Kim is revealed as truly white: 'You see, Bennett, he's not very black' (Kipling, 1912: 121). Bennett who had formerly dismissed him with 'little boys who steal are beaten', now alters his tone: 'It is possible I have done the boy an injustice. He is certainly white. . . . I am sure I must have bruised him' (Kipling, 1912: 122). A racial truth determines all other truths of language, power and culture. Kipling's *Kim* constitutes an anxious reading lesson: 'though he was burned black as any native; though he spoke the vernacular by preference, and his mother tongue in a clipped uncertain sing-song; though he consorted on terms of perfect equality with the small boys of the bazaar; Kim was white' (Kipling, 1992: 1).[5]

What the narrator offers anxiously is a guide to good reading practices. Clothes form one of the ways in which cultural and racial differences are signed. Father Bennett thinks Kim a native because of his Indian clothes and treats him like a young native boy. Father Victor, a better reader of signs, acts differently. He unmasks Kim's colour by taking off the outer garment to expose the whiteness under the native costume. The lesson is that while on the one level visible difference constitutes racial difference, on another level, that difference must be disavowed. Kim is white on the inside; colour, clothes, dirt are merely empty signifiers. It is important to hold this observation in mind because it is only through a fetishism of Kim's whiteness that the colonial text is secured and the reader enabled to participate in the pleasurable fantasy of cultural/racial metamorphosis. Whatever the joys or traumas of cross-cultural costume, the narrative must simultaneously proclaim Kim's English identity alongside his protean ability to change identities at will. The character of Kim is never allowed to forget who he is. The lesson Kim remembers, for all his 'negative capability' is that he *is* white: 'One must never forget that one is a Sahib, and that some day, when the examinations are passed, one will command natives.' And Kim, we are explicitly told, took note of this, 'for he began to understand where the examinations led' (Kipling, 1912: 177).

GOING NATIVE: STRICKLAND AS SHERLOCK HOLMES

Before we tackle the fetishistic psycho-dynamics of the cross-cultural fantasy, I want to draw attention to another instance of disguise that functions within a narrative of surveillance. The character of Strickland, like Kim, has a special place in Kipling's canon. Strickland appears as a character in five different stories and is given a small cameo in *Kim*. Strickland predates Kim and is a character that lives in more fearful times. In many ways the distance between the policeman–detective and the joyful figure of the boy-spy is an indication of how much the anxiety and cultural shock of India have receded and given way to a nostalgic vision. But tracing their connection is also an important part of showing how little Kipling has travelled between the two characters. We have already come across Strickland in chapter five's discussion of 'The Return of Imray' and 'The Mark of the Beast'. In this section, I shall simply discuss Strickland's similarity to Sherlock Holmes and the resonances the character picks up from other exploratory and urban 'slum' writings of the period.

In Kipling's stories, Strickland is a maverick policeman–detective who has intimate knowledge of the native world and its criminal underclasses. Strickland's unorthodox methods, Kipling's narrator tells us, are sometimes frowned upon by the colonial elite. Yet story after story sanctions his familiarity with native life for the rewards it reaps in the task of law-enforcement. Strickland's knowledge of Indian culture and custom is the basis of his control over them: 'Strickland hates being mystified by natives, because his business in life is to overmatch them with their own weapons.' His exposure of native crime and falsehood is relentless; 'Strickland on Native Progress as he had seen it was worth hearing. Natives hated Strickland; but they were afraid of him. He knew too much' (Kipling, 1898: 27). Possessing the same elevated status as Holmes in the Conan Doyle stories, Strickland inspires fear among the native criminal classes; his mere presence in the district courtroom is enough to compel the lying Muslim into withdrawing his fraudulent testimony in 'The Bronckhorst Divorce-Case' (Kipling, 1898).

Strickland is 'extraordinary' in the Kipling canon in the sense that he is given a quasi-magical status as the subject who is supposed to know as much about native culture, customs and dress as it is possible for a white man to know. His innate curiosity and affinity for disguise lead to his intimate acquaintance with all aspects of native life. The single most remarkable thing about Strickland is his talent for undercover work; his knowledge of Indian subculture is directly related to his clandestine wanderings among 'the native riff-raff' of British India. In 'Miss Youghal's Sais', we are told that his affinity for 'native patter' and talent for disguises were responsible for the solving of the Nasiban Murder Case (Kipling, 1898: 26). In the same short story, he is also described as having been 'initiated into the *Sat Bhai* at Allahabad . . . the Lizard-Song of the Sansis, and the *Halli-Hukk dance*', all of which prove that 'he has gone deeper than the skin' (Kipling, 1898: 26). Aspiring to the status of a Haroun al Raschid, the powerful Persian caliph of the *Arabian Nights* who wanders in disguise, Strickland aims 'to have the gift of invisibility and executive control over many Devils'.

'Miss Youghal's Sais' is a story purportedly about Strickland's extraordinary courtship of Miss Youghal in the face of family disapproval. The story details Strickland's disguise as a native groom and his devotion which finally wins over both the father and

a rival lover. But the story also seems to be about something else –
notably Strickland's love affair with Indian life. The narrator's
introductory paragraph turns on the key word 'romance': 'Some
people say that there is no romance in India. Those people are
wrong. Our lives hold quite as much romance as is good for us.
Sometimes more.' Romance must in these sentences refer to
Strickland's courtship of Miss Youghal. Yet the next two and a half
page description of Strickland's adventures in the native underworld puts a different gloss on the word. Romance is linked not to
the Youghal affair but to Strickland's adventures in native disguise;
it is Strickland's disguise which seems to open up an exciting and
romantic parallel universe to the official 'Departmental' world
available to Anglo-Indians. Just as Strickland's romance refers to
two separate things, the object of Strickland's desire also relates to
two separate women. On the one hand, Miss Youghal is Strickland's
heart's desire; she is the reason behind the elaborate disguise, and
his devotion through the difficult period of her parents' disapproval is the real test of his affection. On the other hand, native
culture is also positioned as an object of Strickland's desire; his
seven-year education under the man who 'can pass for Hindu or
Mahommedan, hide-dresser or priest' is testament to his seriousness of intent. Indian culture is here positioned as the rival source
of Strickland's affection; she is the woman who calls 'to him to come
back and take up his wanderings and discoveries' even after his
marriage. Feminised and sexualised, Indian culture is positioned
as an illegitimate mistress who must vie with Miss Youghal for
Strickland's sexual favours. In 'The Bronckhorst Divorce-Case',
Strickland's need to return to his old detective work is describe as
a 'lust' which exists alongside his more respectable love for his wife.
The choice implicit in 'Miss Youghal's Sais' is between two sorts of
women, and this turns out not be any kind of choice at all.

Kipling closes the chapter on the transgressive adventures of
Strickland in the only way that he can; the narrator tells his readers
that 'Strickland and Miss Youghal were married, on the strict
understanding that Strickland should drop his old ways, and stick
to Departmental routine'. This short story which introduces the
character of Strickland turns out to be one of the last in his line of
adventures (Strickland returns briefly in 'The Bronckhorst Divorce-
Case'). Stories such as 'The Return of Imray' and 'The Mark of the
Beast', which appear later in *Life's Handicap* are retrospective
narratives of Strickland's case-histories. This manipulation of

narrative time, allows Kipling to create a potentially 'transgressive' figure whilst limiting the potential complications of the fantasy. In addition to securing cross-cultural transgression to surveillance, Kipling also secures Strickland's narrative firmly to the side of the imperial elites. Women, marriage and domesticity will stop the tempting sounds of the streets and bazaars of the old life, for 'these were full of meaning to Strickland, and these called to him to come back and take up his wanderings and his discoveries' (Kipling, 1898: 32). Marriage, however, will enable Strickland to fill in 'his Departmental returns beautifully' and resolve the problem of what one is to do with the proliferating narrative of the male misfit-adventurer.

Stories like 'Miss Youghal's Sais', 'The Bronckhorst Divorce-Case', and to a lesser extent 'The Mark of the Beast' and 'The Return of Imray', gesture towards the need for a powerful figure whose basic function is that of reassurance. The fantasy of cross-cultural dressing in these narratives of detection is a fantasy that is able to counter the potential dangers of the Other world. The function of the Strickland character in Kipling's stories is comparable with that of Sherlock Holmes. Both revel in the cut and thrust of surveillance. Just as Strickland's territory in Kipling's early stories includes the native city, Holmes's domain stretches over the urban underworld. From seedy visitors 'looking like . . . Jew pedlar[s]' to 'slip-shod' elderly women to 'shallow, rat-faced dark eyed' fellows, Holmes's street urchins 'can go anywhere, see everything, overhear everyone' (Conan Doyle, 1986: 17).[6] Holmes's disguises encompass various classes and are often invaluable in the solving of his cases. In one particular instance, dressed as an old man with wig, whiskers, eyebrows, weak legs and a 'proper workhouse cough', Holmes confides to Watson, 'You see, a good many of the criminal classes begin to know me – especially since our friend here took to publishing some of my cases: so I can only go on the warpath under some simple disguise like this' (Conan Doyle, 1986: 79).

In the late nineteenth century, 'slumming' expeditions with police protection were not uncommon. Sociological and philanthropic literature with titles such as Henry Mayhew's *London Life and London Labour*, Andrew Mearns's *The Bitter Cry of Outcast London*, William Booth's *Into Darkest England* (echoing Stanley's journey in Africa) and Charles Booth's multi-volumed, *Life and Labour* made visible the underside of London life. The 'Into Unknown England' tradition of writing produced a literature of documentary, discovery, exploration and adventure. George Godwin, writing in 1854, makes explicit connections: 'to brave the risks of fever and other injustices to health, and the contact of men and women as lawless as the Arab or Kaffir' (Keating, 1971b). While cross-class costuming cannot be taken to be identical to its cross-cultural counterpart, the similarities in the dynamics of these two fantasies may help clarify our present concerns.

James Greenwood is credited with having started the vogue for slumming (Keating, 1976: 16); his 'A Night in the Workhouse' serialised in the *Pall Mall Gazette* sees him disguised as a casual bound for a London workhouse 'to learn by actual experience' what being a casual is like. Greenwood's disguise is exhaustively described and brings to the documentation of destitution and poverty, a touch of the dramatic. But it is to Jack London's exploration of urban poverty in the city of London that we must turn in order to have a clear indication of how costume participates in physical and cultural metamorphosis (London, 1903). More than Greenwood, London's use of disguise in *The People of the Abyss* emphasises the theatrical. London's quest to see the East-End culture from an insider's viewpoint may be read as the adventurous counterpart of the anthropologist's quest as participant–observer. Both present forms of knowledge and power, but London's account – as with Burton's and Kipling's – is suffused with the pleasure of his hoax. To adopt a Kiplingesque phrase London, like Kim, is a player of the Game. London compares himself with Conan Doyle's detective, 'Shades of Old Sleuth and Sherlock Holmes!' Dressed in a pair of 'well-worn trousers, a frayed jacket with one remaining button, a pair of brogans which had plainly seen service where coal was shovelled', London magics an *instant* transformation. He is now able to meet the lower classes 'face to face, and [know] them for what they [are]':

> No sooner was I out on the streets than I was impressed by the difference in status effected by my clothes. All servility vanished from the demeanour of the common people with whom I came into contact. Presto! in the twinkling of an eye, so to say, I had become one of them. My frayed and out-at-elbows jacket was the badge and advertisement of my class, which was their class.
>
> (London, 1903: 13–14)

Paradoxically, London's adoption of a poor working man's disguise enables his narrative to convey both a sense of active mastery and a release from the strictures of respectability. London's narrative parallels Kipling's and Burton's for the importance he attaches to the magical power of his costume to turn him into one of 'their class' or their race. For all three writers, the fantasy of cross-cultural dressing centres on their identification of clothes as 'badge and advertisement' of their ability to cross the class and cultural gap.

In the depiction of this drama of race and class, the superficial aspect of apparel is emphasised alongside its transformative potential. According to this textual (dis)play of difference, one can put clothes on or take them off at will. At the end of their escapades, both London and Kim are able to cast off their costumes and return to their original identities. Some object guarantees the integrity of their identities during the metamorphosis. Kim's identity as a white boy is marked initially by the leather amulet-case, containing his birth certificate, strung round his neck; later, his identity as British spy is marked by a silver amulet containing one small turquoise. London's descent into the abyss is cushioned by nothing less than a gold coin sewn into his outfit. His lodgings in the East End provide a refuge from the gross humanity that populates the city of London: 'not too far distant, into which I could run now and again to assure myself that good clothes and cleanliness still existed' (London: 1903: 13). In sane surroundings, London could compile his anthropological notes or 'sail forth occasionally in changed garb to civilization'.

In Strickland and in Kim, we have an ambivalent fantasy based on appearances and the intimate connection between knowledge and vision – a knowledge which is manifested through costume and a knowledge which is gained by disguise. This coupling of knowledge with costume is in keeping with a racial vision that is based on truth gained from appearance and simple physiognomic analysis. A knowledge based on racial appearance can be very reassuring. In John Forbes Watson and John Kaye's contemporary ethnographic mapping of Indian caste groupings, *The People of India*, knowledge is tied to the way people look. Forbes Watson and John Kaye's illustrated Indian Museum publication of 1868 is an early encyclopedic catalogue of Indian castes and tribes. 'Prepared under the authority of the Government of India', 'each 'photographic illustration' is accompanied by a 'descriptive letterpress' detailing caste, race (physical description), language, caste/tribal history, geographical location, religion, dietary habits, typical occupation, and the vices and virtues of each grouping (Watson and

Kaye, 1868). As an attempt to produce a definite map of castes, the eight volumes might be said to constitute a spectacular failure. The entries are not standardised. In some, very little information is recorded and in others, movement between groups and geographical areas taxes the documenter's comprehension and ability to process information. Occasionally, frustration at the lack of cooperation from 'native informants' is written into individual entries that accompany the emblematic caste photograph. But what forms a more or less stable core in all the entries is dress: descriptions of the traditional costume, or alternatively, descriptions of what the photographic subjects are wearing. The 'Khantis', for example, are described as a wild frontier tribe in Assam, 'of whom very little is known'. What is offered confidently to the reader is a series of impressions based on their physical appearance and their apparel. 'Khantis' wear 'consists of a single dhotee or sheet, folded around the waist, and falling below the knee; this, with a dyed blue cotton jacket, extending below the waist, and well fitted to the body'. They resemble the Chinese and have a countenance 'which leaves anything but a favourable impression of their benevolence of their dispositions' (Watson and Kaye, 1868: vol.1, 27). The use of photographic reproductions does not hinder a full description of what the subject is wearing; for example, a photograph of Rae Doona Chund (Figure 17), identified as 'a native gentleman' of the Jain sect is accompanied by a detailed depiction of his costume: 'the Photograph represents him in the honourary dress conferred, which is of rich cloth of gold, with a valuable Cashmere shawl disposed over the lower part of his figure. In his turban he wears the "sirpech", or jewel of gold set with precious stones' (Watson and Kaye, 1869: vol. 2, 208). Appearance offers a sense of security when all else fails; through appearance a certain stability may be reached despite the fluidity of local caste groups. Sara Suleri remarks of Watson and Kaye's project that 'where the physiognomy of racial difference can evoke only a colonial fear of the greater cultural alternatives it symbolically represents, costume provides . . . a sartorial aesthetic that somehow suggests that the colonised can be completely known' (Suleri, 1992: 108).

RACIAL FETISHISM

We have in the fantasy of disguise (read in the light of Holmes, and Watson and Kaye) two separate but interrelated moments. The first

RAE DOONA CHUND.
BANKER.
JAIN SURONGIE.
SIMLA.
(208)

Figure 17 'Rae Doona Chund' (from Watson and Kaye, 1968–75).

is associated with voyeurism and surveillance and is part of the fantasy of invisibility that gives Strickland, Holmes and Kim the aura of omnipotence and omniscience. Unlike the carefully cultivated objective distance of the disciplinary and scientific gaze, this dream of cross-cultural dressing has more to do with the pleasures of an active and theatrical *display*. Strickland's, Kim's and Holmes's elaborate disguises allow them to pry into native affairs, just as Kipling's narratives reveal a voyeuristic glimpse of exotic spectacles. Edmund Gosse, in a revealing turn of phrase, talks of Kipling as a 'master of a new kind of terrible and enchanting peepshow' who plays on his readers' heightened state of excitement; Kipling 'tantalises' his readers and confirms their utter dependency on his story-telling so that they 'crowd around him begging, for "just one more look"' (Green, 1971: 108). But more important for my purposes, the second aspect of the fantasy of disguise is related to the desire for psychological reassurance. If there were a figure who truly knew all about the native world it is possible to know, then such a person would be a source of comfort in troubled times. Indian culture in its different guises and shapes would not seem the bewildering and unreadable text that it can some times be. There would always be someone to interpret, someone who would be one step ahead of trouble. The ever-present fear and anxiety of Anglo-Indian life and its daily cultural shocks, arguably, creates such a fantasy. Yet such a psychological account leaves untouched the distinctiveness of the fantasy of cross-cultural costume. Why should Strickland's and Kim's power be based on their ability to be native – on their (to use Kinkead-Weekes's phrase) 'negative capability'? George Stocking observes that polygenist beliefs in the separate origins of man lasted well into post-Darwinian anthropology and is apparent in acclimatisation and miscegenation debates that took place well into the early twentieth century.[7] If Stocking is correct then surely Kim's and Strickland's transformations do not represent simple costume changes but must be situated within a more general understanding of bodily transformations. How are we to understand alleged bodily differences in these stories?

The psychoanalytic account of racial fetishism, the politics of colonial identification and its contradictory mimetic impulses provide the first steps in shaping an answer. In psychoanalysis, a fetish is an object of substitution. Endowed with more power than it actually has, it accrues metaphorical energy in its function; in one psychoanalyst's words, 'fetishism is a story masquerading as an object'. In the classic Freudian account of fetishism, a fetish stands in for the woman's lack of a penis and allows the male fetishist to acknowledge and deny castration simultaneously. The male child, refusing on one level to recognise the threat of the woman's lack, accepts it on another; the fetish-as-substitute contains castrating difference even as it disseminates its discriminatory effects. This 'double-take' allows the male subject to maintain sexual difference while repressing the anxieties of difference. But as indicated at the start of this chapter, the revisionist readings of fetishism do not equate lack with lack of a penis. They argue that whilst Freudian and Lacanian accounts of human subjectivity are premised on lack, understood as the irreversible division and separation that under-writes the process of self-formation, such accounts do not have to be understood within strict anatomical correlations.[8]

Bhabha's work locates colonial discourse between the twin modes of narcissism and aggressivity in the Lacanian model of Imaginary identification. He reads lack through the myth of historical and racial origination ('all men have the same skin/race/culture') as difference ('some men do not have the same skin/race/culture'). Bhabha's early re-reading of Freud via Fanon focuses on the psycho-dynamics of disavowal and repetition, and reads racism as a fetishistic defence (Bhabha, 1983). Racial stereotyping is marked by discursive splitting; in its production of the colonised as a 'fixed reality which is at once an "other" and [yet] entirely knowable', racial stereotyping invokes both racial difference and its disavowal (Bhabha, 1983: 23). Racist discourse discriminates through the production of difference; its characteristic feature is the repetition of a fixed set of traits (which are said to be the properties of the racial or cultural group in question) across differing histories, cultures and geographies. Bhabha argues that such simplification is an 'arrested, fixated form of representation'. Constant repetition signals a psychic trauma that is returned to anxiously again and again. In Bhabha's reading of the racial stereotype as fetish, the 'structural' problem of lack is covered up by the defensive *and* masterful use of certain bodily differences that masks division. A fetish is an object which allows the fetishist to mask lack; in Bhabha's words, 'the fixation on an object [the fetish]' allows the masking of difference and 'restores an original presence' (Bhabha, 1983: 27). But by its very nature, fixation is always going to be caught between security and threat; for every time the fetish is used, lack is both signalled and disavowed. The use of the fetish object to mask difference ('all men have the same skins/race/culture') contains the trace of the anxiety associated with difference ('some do not have the same skin/race/culture'):

> The process by which the metaphoric 'masking' is inscribed on a lack which must then be concealed gives the stereotype both its fixity and its phantasmatic quality – the *same old* stories of the Negro's animality, the Coolie's inscrutability or the stupidity of the Irish *must* be told (compulsively) again and afresh, and are differently gratifying and terrifying each time.
>
> (Bhabha, 1983: 29)

Bhabha's reading of racial fetishism has been enormously productive even while his own account acknowledges two major problems in using a theory of sexual fetishism for the analysis of racism. I suggest, however, that both difficulties can be met. The first relates to Freud's implicit if ambivalent equation of female anatomical difference with lack. Freud's theory of sexual fetishism is derived from a theory of castration which posits the male body as the norm. Bhabha is not unaware of the problems inherent in the perception of the female body as that of a castrated male. In a footnote he acknowledges that the Freudian reading of fetishism as the fear of bodily 'castration' ties it firmly to men. Hence 'the body in this text is male' (Bhabha, 1983: 18). But as Laplanche and Pontalis have indicated, the discovery of anatomical differences as a *perception of reality* is a central paradox in the classic Freudian theory of fetishism. If the disavowal of castration is the basis for other types of disavowal, 'then it becomes difficult to talk in terms of perception or of reality' for absence is only perceived and made real when it is related to presence. If it is the absence of the penis that is being disavowed, then fetishism is not perception *per se* but a 'sexual theory of children' (Laplanche and Pontalis, 1983: 120). Some psychoanalytic theorists have taken lack to refer to earlier divisions, for example the division between mother and child. Kaja Silverman, for example, by arguing that lack is not equivalent to lack of a penis, [9] re-reads the fear of lack as a projection of male anxiety that retroactively inscribes castration onto the female body.[10] Fetishism as projection overcomes some theoretical difficulties in Bhabha's essay; for through projection, bodily differences *in themselves* lead neither to a theory of racial/sexual difference nor the visible structuration of discrimination.

Bhabha's further distinction between the sexual and the racial fetish on grounds of concealment presents a second problem. Bhabha argues that sexual fetishism is secret and racial fetishism is played out openly; 'skin, as the key signifier of cultural and racial difference in the stereotype, is the most visible of fetishes'. Yet this distinction belies a powerful dependence on vision to secure both sexual and racial difference. Sexual cross-dressing provokes extreme hostility because the visual divide between assigned gender identities is transgressed. That sexual difference must be fetishised to the point of visibility is evident in the not untypical response that greets sexual cross-dressing: we want to know the 'real' or core sexual identity of the transvestite cross-dresser. Ambivalence is unsettling and definitive categorisation brings relief. In this respect, fetishism as a defensive projection relies on visual 'evidence'. Marjorie Garber's discussion of the politics of transvestite cross-dressing makes the point that the simple equation of transvestism with homosexual identity isolates a moment of defensive projection in mainstream heterosexual and homophobic culture. Her reaction is worth quoting in full:

> It is as though the hegemonic cultural imaginary is saying to itself: if there is a difference (between gay and straight), we want to be able to *see* it, and if we see a difference (a man in woman's clothes), we want to be able to interpret it. In both cases, the conflation is fuelled by a desire to *tell the difference*, to guard against a difference that might otherwise put the identity of one's own position in question. (If people who dress like me might be gay, then someone might think I'm gay, or I might get too close to someone I don't recognize as gay; if someone who is heterosexual like me dresses in women's clothes, what is heterosexuality?)
>
> (Garber, 1992: 130)

The colour of one's skin, while allegedly the most *obvious* of signifiers is based on this differential projection. Projection represents a casting-off of the unwanted aspect of self onto another where it attains visibility; racial discrimination depends on visible difference. The minute racial classification of apartheid policy testifies to the desire to draw a *cordon sanitaire* around all categories of non-whites and prevent crossover. 'Skin as a signifier of discrimination', as Bhabha puts it forcefully, 'must be produced or processed as visible' (Bhabha, 1983: 31).

PSYCHIC VESTMENTS

Grosz and Schilder's insistence on reading the body in psycho-analysis as the internalised image of culturally shared and individualised bodily significance is helpful in considering how clothes might affect the body schema. Schilder's theory of the body of signification, in particular, exceeds the literal physical body and consider clothes as part of the body schema: 'Whatever article of clothing we put on immediately becomes part of the body-image and is filled with narcissistic libido' (Schilder, 1970: 203). Changes of costume may bring changes of behaviour and attitudes; replacing our work day suits with evening wear may effect an alteration in conduct 'partly because the body-image as such is in the closest relation to our libidinous strivings and tendencies'. Re-writing the body in this way allows us to connect cross-cultural costume with the body in fantasy, notably the production of the fantasmatic body in the dynamics of identification and fetishism. Laplanche and Pontalis define fantasy as the playing out of desire; their definition emphasises theatre and vision: 'phantasies are still scripts (*scenarios*) of organised scenes which are capable of dramatisation – usually in visual form . . . the primary function of phantasy . . . [is] the *mise-en-scène* of desire' (Laplanche and Pontalis, 1983: 318). Laplanche and Pontalis' use of the theatrical metaphor helps our analysis because the fantasy of cross-cultural costume, I would suggest, is the 'role-playing' of desire which treats costume as an extension of the body-image. Garber's study of sexual cross-dressing highlights the fundamentally theatrical nature of the fantasy of sexual identity and body-image: 'the transvestite keeps the fantasy in play, though often in a ritualised way by deploying a rhetoric of *clothing, naming* and *performance* or *acting out*' (Garber, 1992: 134). Cross-dressing is literally the play and display of sexual difference. While it is beyond the scope of the present work to address the phenomenon of sexual cross-dressing, or actual case studies of sexual/racial cross-dressers, I want to suggest that theatre, fantasy, body-image and race all intersect in cross-cultural disguise.

Colonial cross-cultural costume shares cross-dressing's fascination with boundaries and theatricality. Metamorphosis in this respect is accomplished by clothing the self in the guise of cultural others. But what of the politics of 'clothes' in this scenario? Does the crossing of cultural boundaries divest the cross-cultural dresser of colonial power? Fanon, in *Black Skin/White Masks* argues that because white operates as the invisible norm in racist culture, the ontological relation between black and white is not symmetrical. Fanon's cautionary remarks point to the asymmetrical nature of a colonial fantasy which treats the Other as usable fiction: 'for not only must the black man be black; he must be black in relation to the white man. Some critics will . . . remind us that this proposition has a converse. I say this is false. The black man has no ontological resistance in the eyes of the white man' (Fanon, 1967: 110). Yet if painstaking efforts were taken to draw up cultural boundaries why was 'transgression' deliberately cultivated?

Some theorists have ventured analyses of real cases of cultural cross-dressers. Garber's chapter on 'The Chic of Araby' does not offer a general theory of cultural cross-dressing but looks at a variety of different (male and female) cases and explores their implications for a theory of transvestism as disruptive of gender binarisms. Her study is directed at how the Middle East provides the West with models and metaphors that allow it to explore contradictions and fantasies that are both derivative and disruptive of an Orientalist imperialism. Silverman's essay on Lawrence of Arabia traces the quite different positions Lawrence occupies in his fantasy of masculinity and masochism. She argues that T. E. Lawrence's homosexuality enables his narcissistic identification with the figures of Arab nationalism. Lawrence's transformation in costume represents a corresponding psychic transformation. But if his imitation of Arab dress and conduct is based on an identification with the Arab, it also is based on a matching 'self-aggrandisement' and introjection of the image and symbol of the movements' leaders. There are two different kinds of Arab identification in Lawrence's 'theatrically inflected' emphasis on 'pose and *mise-en-scène*': 'one predicated upon a perception of himself as a member of the Bedouin group, and hence subject to its norms, and one predicated upon a perception of himself as the *leader* of that group, and hence *a model to be imitated*' (Silverman 1992: 313). The spirit of self-aggrandisement was not, in principle, incompatible with the image and symbol of Arab nationalism because it involved bettering the Arabs at their own game. Silverman reads Lawrence's fantasy as based on the interlocking forces of 'reflexive masochism' (identifying with the active partner in the masochistic ritual) and (sublimated) homosexuality. But Silverman also locates a contrary movement of desublimation and passive masochism which can be traced in Lawrence's subsequent repudiation of power and his identification with Royal Air Force men. She concludes that 'Lawrence's cultural masquerade is ultimately less successful in eliciting Arab conformity to his image than in rewriting his own subjectivity'.

In contrast, Robert Stoller's analysis only addresses transvestism but is perhaps useful in signalling the complex of pleasure and power that lie behind the fantasy of cross-cultural costume (Stoller, 1975). In Stoller's terms, fetishistic cross-dressing is characterised by sexual excitement in the donning of garments of the opposite sex. Stoller's theory of transvestism applies only to heterosexual men who, when not cross-dressing, identify strongly with what may conventionally be labelled as 'masculine' forms of behaviour. Thus maleness and masculinity are an integral part of the disguise: 'The fetishistic cross-dresser believes his [phallus], his maleness, and his masculinity to be valuable, endangered and preservable only by means of his [cross-dressing] (more or less)'. His 'double-take' is frozen in a single moment; he is the woman with the phallus (the phallic woman). According to Stoller these men not only derive their greatest erotic pleasure from their genitals; their sexual excitement is also expressed through the active possession of the penis. More importantly, its hidden 'presence sensed beneath the women's garments' gives an added excitement: 'They never quite forget the trick: the hidden penis. The thought that they are fooling the world is surpassed in enjoyment only by the moment when they can reveal the secret' (Stoller, 1975: 144, 154). But if Stoller's analysis of transvestism is helpful in pointing out that sexual excitement arises not from being a woman but seeming to be a woman, his theory is problematic in that it relies on a notion of core identities. Stoller grants validity to only one specific form of cross-dressing. And even this is perhaps better understood as occurring in fantasy than in 'reality', for male to female cross-dressing provokes extreme hostility in the wider culture.

In both Stoller and Silverman, we encounter the paradoxical situation of how identification with a subordinated culture/sex – to the point of appearing to be like them – is understood not as a simple wish to divest oneself of power. In the example of Stoller's fetishistic cross-dresser, where female attire is used to signify lack, the penis is integral to the costume because its presence disavows lack. Silverman's reading of T. E. Lawrence is more nuanced and sensitive to the shifting and contradictory positions available in the fantasy of cross-cultural dress. But she also acknowledges that

Lawrence's identification with the figures of Arab nationalism – his desire to be the icon of Arab nationalism – is also based on a narcissistic self-aggrandisement which involves beating the Arabs at their own game.

Kipling's creations such as Strickland and Kim are also based on a narcissistic self-aggrandisement in so far as more, rather than less, symbolic power accrues to the figure who crosses boundaries. As discussed earlier, Kim's costumed transformations are depicted as epiphanies, 'a demon in Kim woke up and sang with joy as he put on the changing dresses and changed speech and gesture there-with' (Kipling, 1912: 226). The change effected by native costume leaves Kim with a sense of adventure and freedom far beyond the narrow worlds of his white peers. But the narrative thrust in *Kim* is also to remind the reader of the real body underneath his clothes; the story harnesses the real purpose of cross-cultural dress to espionage. Yet if *Kim* works to emphasise rather than to erase the racial fault-line, there is also an unmistakable sense that Sahibness/ whiteness is reconstituted through native culture. As a woman remarks of the cameo appearance by Strickland in *Kim*, 'these be the sort to oversee justice. They know the land and the customs of the land' (Kipling, 1912: 107). At St Xavier, Kim learns that 'one must never forget that one is a Sahib, and that some day, when the examinations are passed, one will command natives' (Kipling, 1912: 177).

Strickland's propensity for 'going Fantee' among natives is not depicted in as sustained and extravagant a fashion as Kim's but proceeds more elliptically. But like Kim who invariably knows the right thing to say or do, Strickland's knowledge and authority throughout the different stories he appears in are unquestioned. In 'The Bronckhorst Divorce-Case', Strickland is invoked as the genius who will find a way through Bronckhorst's trumped-up charges of adultery. His undercover work reveals that the evidence given by a native witness is essentially manufactured. In 'To Be Filed for Reference', Strickland is invoked as a source of authority as to whether a manuscript left behind by a dissolute loafer is of any significance. In the 'Mark of the Beast', it is Strickland's interpreta-tion of events which the narrator validates and his plan of action that the narrator supports without question; even the telling of the tale is done at Strickland's instigation. In 'Miss Youghal's Sais' he is presented as an object of fascination for the narrator. Strickland stands out from the herd and catches the narrator–character's attention as a person who is ostracised by the official 'Depart-mental' crowd. Strickland is unusual in that he goes against conventional wisdom by holding the 'extraordinary theory that a Policeman in India should try to know as much about the natives as the natives themselves' (Kipling, 1898: 25). His knowledge leads directly to his ability to solve crime; nothing is a mystery for this man. The narrator, like Dr Watson, records Strickland's adventures and his different case histories. The narrator of Kipling's stories hangs onto Strickland's every word. In 'Miss Youghal's Sais', Strickland tells the narrator the story of his experiences as a *sais*, to which the narrator adds, in an aside to the reader, 'one of these days, Strickland is going to write a little book on his experiences. That book will be worth buying; and even more worth suppressing' (Kipling, 1898: 29).

What the Strickland example points to is the existence of a transferential structure at work between the narrator and Strickland and by implication also between reader and narrator/Strickland. Transferential structures also exist in *Kim*, particularly in the manner in which major and minor characters channel our atten-tion to the special status of the boy-spy. Laplanche and Pontalis define transference as 'a process of actualisation of unconscious wishes' in the clinical situation where 'infantile prototypes re-emerge and are experienced with a strong sense of emergency' (Laplanche and Pontalis, 1983: 455). Lacan defines transference as applying when trust and dialogue are confirmed between analysand and analyst. The status invested in each subject by the other establishes the terrain of transference: 'as soon as the subject who is supposed to know exists somewhere . . . there is transference . . . the question is first, for each subject, where he takes his bearings from when applying to the subject who is presumed to know' (Lacan, 1977: 232–233). Peter Brooks finds in transference an allegory of narrative interaction or transaction; psychoanalysis is 'narrative discipline', 'the relation of teller to listener [is] inherently . . . part of the structure and the meaning of any narrative text . . . And if the story told has been effective, if it has "taken hold", the act of transmission resembles the psychoanalytic transference' (Brooks, 1994: 50). The Kipling stories differ from Brooks's ideal of mutual production and active participation that problematizes the privileged position of the analyst. Instead, Kipling's creation of Kim and Strickland petrifies them within the initial investment; they form the subject who catches the narrator (and implied

(British) reader) in a transferential relationship, by embodying in their adventures, the narrator–reader's desire of perfect identity: total knowledge and total power.

It should be clear by now that my purpose in examining the significations of cross-cultural costume has lain less in offering a theory of cross-cultural dress than in providing an understanding of how dress operates in fantasy and narrative. Attempts at providing a psychoanalysis of Kim and Strickland to match those undertaken by Silverman, Stoller or Garber would not only be foolhardy, as my two case studies are not real case histories of cross-cultural disguise, but also misguided, as the differing contexts in which real case histories occur may alter the actual meanings assigned to the transformation. What I have been concerned with is narrative, and the particular scripted roles and positions made available in the fantasmatic playing out of these narratives. In particular, I am interested in the narratorial investment in figures who cross-culturally dress – particularly in the way narrators and characters promote their interest in these figures – and what such investments might signify for the culture at large. Hence, I separate the analysis of the actual cross-cultural dressing from the analysis of its psychic and narratorial investment for the narrator/readers at large.

Drawing together the earlier discussion of racial fetishism, the denial of lack conceived as a myth of racial and cultural origination and the frozen transferential investment in the subject who is presumed to know, it appears that cross-cultural dress is invested with a magical fantasy of wholeness that can make good colonial alienation and lack. Cultural and racial difference can perhaps be disavowed and circumvented by a figure who appears to be Indian but who is really white. That special figure could also better control Indian subjects for he would know them inside out. Furthermore, figures like Strickland also provide fascinating stories of exotic and strange terrains, for they have first-hand experience of them. Cross-cultural dressing in the Kipling stories provides just such a contradictory fantasy. Strickland's special attribute lies in his marginality to mainstream colonial culture; he was, the narrator tells us, 'a doubtful sort of man and passed by on the other side' (Kipling, 1898: 33). Paradoxically, his transgressions and unorthodox behaviour are absolutely necessary for the policing of the colonial state. His power over natives is produced not by adhering to the ideals and values of colonial civility but because he plays the native game 'one better' than they. The exercise of power and surveillance exists alongside the fascination and desire for alterity.

More importantly, *Kim* and the Strickland stories position both characters as the subject of knowledge; they know as much about Indian culture as it is possible to know. In both narratives, knowledge is linked to power; their status as spy/policeman overlaps with their status as (amateur) anthropologist. Both observe, participate and seek to translate Indian culture in a way that promises to be accessible and useful for the imperial state; if Indian culture is not made transparent for readers of these stories, mystery and alterity only enhance their larger-than-life status. For the narrator (and sometimes the character) of the Strickland stories, then, the policeman/spy is presented as the subject whose knowledge can fulfil the demand for an imaginary plenitude before the onslaught of cultural difference. The Strickland stories and *Kim* offer a translation of Indian culture that paradoxically relinquishes none of its projected alterity; consequently, more status accrues to their heroes by virtue of their intimate knowledge of the translated object. More, rather than less, symbolic power accrues to the figure who crosses boundaries (literal or metaphorical); these transgressive figures are depicted as caught between their marginality to the colonial civil state and their absolute necessity to its functioning or completion. The characters are thus liminal symbolic figures who embody cultural contradictions in a way that effectively exploits and channels them. Their distinctive mythic status resides in the offer of a figure who makes good the lack of colonial subjectivity, a lack which can be made good only through metonymic 'leakage' from originary 'native' (as opposed to colonial) cultures. In psychoanalytic terms, the fantasy promotes an 'Orientalised' or 'primitivised' figure of the white man as the subject who presumes to know – the subject beyond lack.

WRITING AS OTHER

Kipling's own fascination with the native underlife puts him in the same position as the characters he creates. His letter to Margaret Burne-Jones shows a corresponding will to discover a world outside Anglo-Indian society:

> Underneath our excellent administrative system; under the piles of reports and statistics; the thousands of troops; the

doctors; and the civilian runs wholly untouched and unaffected the life of the peoples of the land – a life full of
impossibilities and wonders as the Arabian Nights. I don't
want to gush over it but I do want you to understand Wop
dear that immediately outside of our English life is the dark
and crooked and fantastic; and wicked: and awe-inspiring life
of the 'native' . . . I have done my best to penetrate into it.[11]

Native life is contrasted with the arid bureaucratic 'piles of reports
and statistics' of Anglo-Indian life. Native life is also topologically
'underneath', a subterranean world below English civil and military
life. Kipling's other world is demonic ('dark, crooked and fantastic') but it forms the source and inspiration of his stories; it is a
life which *seduces*, an 'Arabian Nights' and magical world promising
'impossibilities and wonders'. This alien world invites the coloniser's penetration. Kipling's letter goes on to allude to the 'queer
jumble of opium dens, night houses, night strolls with natives' and
the 'long yarns that my native friends spin me'. The contact, if not
taboo, is certainly illicit. Significantly, his contact/seduction is also
textual (the stories he hears) and it is out of these associations that
Kipling's authority emerges.

Yet Kipling also speaks of how 'little an Englishman can hope to
understand [these natives]': 'I would that you see some of the
chapters in Mother Maturin [his unfinished lost novel] and you will
follow more closely what I mean.' Here, then, is the contradictory
movement in Kipling's project. His task is to make people 'see'; to
become the authoritative voice on native affairs, the interpreter
that would seek to translate native terms into English ones. The
myth of the authorial voice which is all-knowing of native life is one
which clings onto a culturally sanctioned metropolitan view of
Kipling's status. Kay Robinson, a contemporary journalist and
editor of the *Civil and Military Gazette*, writes of Kipling precisely
within this construct. Robinson speaks of Kipling's wonderful
insight into the 'strangely mixed manners of life and thought of
the natives in India' in the following way:

He knew them all through their horizontal divisions of rank
and their vertical sections of caste; their ramifications of race
and blood; their antagonisms and blendings of creed; and
their hereditary streaks of calling or handicraft. Show him a
native, and he would tell you his rank, caste, race, origin,
habitat, creed and calling. He would speak to the man in his

own fashion, using familiar, homely figures which brighten
the other's surprised eyes with the recognition of brother-
hood and opened a straight way into his confidence.

(Orel, 1983: 82)

The diversity of India's peoples, castes and customs may be bewildering but the mind that informs Kim's masterful grasp of India
is not bewildered. In the community of the train's carriage-
compartment which throws all sorts of peoples and castes together,
Kim is able to place them all: the burly Sikh artisan, the turbaned
Hindu Jat from 'the rich Jullundur district', the Amritzar courtesan
or the young Dogra (Rajput Hindu) soldier. The culturally sanctioned (Western) myth of Kipling's mastery echoes Kim's anthropological knowledge.

In an earlier article in *McClure's Magazine*, 1896, Robinson writes,
'No half-note in the wide gamut of native ideas and custom was
unfamiliar to him: just as he had left no phase of white life in India
unexplained' (Orel, 1983: 82, 72). In *Kim*, the young Anglo-Indian
boy adopts the correct rituals of begging from the 'open shop of a
kunjri, a low-caste vegetable seller', to the wealthy Sahiba. Kim
addresses one woman in tones of easy familiarity, 'O my mother'
and flatters the other through flirtation: '"Ahai! I am only a
beggar's brat, as the Eye of Beauty has said," he wailed in
extravagant terror' (Kipling, 1912: 97). Native words are also
handled dextrously; Kim's witty pun on yogi/yagi raises a smile on
the old vegetable seller's face. The plan of Lahore city, with its 'belt-
tramway line down the Motee Bazar' opposite the vegetable-seller's
shop, is sketched for all to see. To adopt a metaphor in keeping
with the theme of cross-cultural dress, the very words of Kipling's
text take on native clothes and by active appropriation, also become
signifiers of his authority.

Stephen Arata in a recent article suggests that Kipling's India was
made deliberately opaque for domestic audiences; untranslated
Anglo-Indian phrases and 'unglossed allusion, the unapologetic
gesture towards structures of feeling and experience which had no
counterpart outside the enclosed world of Anglo-India' divided
'those who already knew and those who would never know such
stories' (Arata, 1993: 12). I think that this paradoxically enhanced
his authority and reputation in those early years. Andrew Lang,
taken more with Kipling's portrayal of Indian culture than of Anglo-
Indian, for example, is impressed by Kipling's

knowledge of things little known – the dreams of opium smokers, the ideas of private soldiers, the passions of Pathans and wild Border tribes, the magic which is yet a living force in India ... nothing but these qualities keeps the English reader awake and excited.

(Green, 1971: 48)

Thomas Ward, writing in *The Times* in 1890, tells his readers that Kipling's prose 'appear to lift the veil from a state of society so immeasurably distant from [their] ... own and to offer [them] ... glimpses of unknown depth and gulfs'. Ward also adds that Kipling 'has given evidence of a knowledge of Indian life which would be extraordinary in any writer and is phenomenal in one so young' (Green, 1971: 51, 53). Edmund Gosse's assessment of Kipling's reputation in 1891 captures the transferential mechanics of story-telling and the narrative authority given over to this 'new star out of the East'. Gosse argues that at times it seems futile to take Kipling to task for his stylistic crudities when as a reader all he wants to do is to learn more of the fates of the characters that people his fiction, 'what became of Kehni Singh, and whether the seal-cutter did really die in the House of Suddhoo ... who it is who dances the *Halli Hukk*, and how, and why, and where' (Green, 1971: 107–108). Gosse also mentions Kipling's approval of Strickland and in a short space of time, makes his own endorsement of Kipling's 'wisdom and experience' in the very same terms that Kipling establishes for his fictional character:

Mr. Kipling is perfectly willing to take us below the surface, and to show us glimpses of the secret life of India. In doing so he puts forth his powers to their fullest extent, and I think it cannot be doubted that the tales which deal with native manners are not merely the most curious and interesting ... but are also the most fortunately constructed.

(Green, 1971: 116)

In Kipling, more than in Haggard, we find instances of a character who is likened to an anthropologist in so far as he is depicted as having knowledge of the 'native' world which far exceeds that of ordinary people. Within my textual trajectory suggested by Holmes–Greenwood–London and Strickland–Kim—Burton–Kipling, cross-class/cultural disguise is not only pleasur-able but also instrumental to the production of their powerful status. Their elaborate disguises give them the magical power of invisibility, which in turn renders them a figure of omnipotence and omniscience. But what is really fascinating about Strickland and Kim is the amount of narrative energy invested in their fictional personas. Figures like Strickland and Kim move in and out of the Indian world as easily as changing clothes; they are the figures on which such narratives are built. In the transferential spaces of story-telling, the narrator's fascination with these figures secures our interest; his interest becomes an expression of our desire to know more about their transgressive life-stories. The transferential relationship is first and foremost founded on the axis of desire. But the subject does not really possess knowledge; he is perceived to have knowledge simply by virtue of being a subject of desire, or where desire is focused. Kipling's contemporary status as imperial story-teller and knowledgeable anthropologist/writer suggests that an authoritative status accrues to him precisely for his alleged crossing of cultural borderlines. The special status accorded to anthropologists who cross cultural boundaries in the disciplinary pursuit of information has traditionally been that of the authoritative subject who presumes to know, the subject outside the circuit of desire. What Kipling's writing captures so accurately is the ambivalent cultural, political and psychic investment in such an authoritative figure. Unmasking the figure of knowledge and power is perhaps a task that must be attempted from both sides of the cultural borderline.

7

LOAFERS AND
STORY-TELLERS

In chapter two, we saw how the ideological figure of the 'boy' is invested with unconscious desire. The privileging of boyhood functions in Haggard's adventure narratives as a mythic-text of Empire by enabling an easy transition from the innocence and youth of the boyish adventurer to an inheritance of the newly discovered world. Representing a world unsullied by the decadent corruption of age and civilisation, the boy-child is necessarily the only figure capable of returning to or founding a brave new (colonial/pastoral) world. At the end of the last chapter, we located another figure invested with desire, that of the policeman/spy whose crossing of cultural boundaries promises a colonial identity without lack – a subject of knowledge in the face of difference and alienation. In this chapter, I shall end my exploration of Kipling with yet another such figure, the loafer.

The loafer presents a perennial source of fascination in Kipling's early stories; on the one hand, the loafer represents the complete opposite of sanctioned figures of authority such as colonial policemen or district officers, and on the other, he represents the logical extension of the very modes of cultural transgression that give figures like Strickland and Kim their special status. The loafer is different from the boy in Haggard's fiction because he is characterised as cynical and machiavellian rather than as innocent; he is different from the boy-spy in Kipling because his energies are not harnessed by the state for law-enforcement. He is a character who appears repeatedly in Kipling's narratives as one who rejects fair play and advocates colonial exploitation. In contrast to the district officers who uphold selflessly the ideals of the imperial cause, loafers are vagrants and confidence tricksters who live by their wits and their ability to exploit the situations and the people they come across. They have an uncanny knowledge of Indian life and custom and may, when inclined to do so, pass as native. Their presence in Kipling's texts is yet another indication of ambivalence and contradiction. Loafers voice populist irritation with the rhetorical trappings of Anglo-Indian statecraft and its civilising mission; they preach a simple politics of opportunism, and promote a brutalised version of native society. If their marginality and distance from the centres of imperial power permits the articulation of such desires, those very qualities are recuperated for the centres of imperial power.

My interest in the loafer is also motivated by another agenda. The previous chapter concludes with the remark that figures like Strickland and Kim are liminal symbolic figures who embody cultural contradictions in a way that effectively exploits and channels their energies. By virtue of the narrative energy invested in them, they are positioned in Kipling's narratives as 'subjects who presume to know'; their distinctive mythic status resides in their being subjects outside the circuit of desire. A similar status accrues to Kipling who is celebrated as having (anthropological) knowledge of the 'native' world that exceeds the reach of most. What I want to make clear in this chapter is that the 'subject who is presumed to know' – 'the very place where meaning, and *knowledge* of meaning, reside' (Brooks, 1994: 58) – is produced through narrative. In particular, my analysis of 'The Man Who Would Be King' aims to explore the transferential mechanics of story-telling. Kipling's short story has a number of different story-tellers and different listeners; each story told to each listener catches him/her in a position of transference. The dynamics of the transferential experience activated by the frame narrator of the tale are similar to the dynamics of seduction in story-telling. The framed narrator's fascination with the two loafers secures our interest; his interest becomes an expression of our desire to know more about their transgressive life-stories. The framed story of the loafers' rise and subsequent fall in 'The Man Who Would Be King' provides readers with a clear-sighted exploration of a colonial grammar and syntax of desire; but it also presents the colonial text as a hoax – a 'scam' -pulled off by enterprising vagabond story-tellers. In this respect, Kipling's fascination with the figure of the loafer represents the shadowy side to his persona as imperial story-teller; loaferdom presents an alternative portrait of the artist as journalist always in search of a good story and the artist as petty thief and trader of lies and lives. It is perhaps not the conventional portrait of Kipling but one necessary to do justice to the complexity of his writing.

In the last section of this book, the argument will return to the general questions that motivate the writing of this book. How does narrative mediate and channel desire? What is the relation between fantasy and ideology? Does the metaphor of the mirror provide a productive approach to colonial fictions of alterity? Concluding the book with these questions will also enable us to assess the similarities and differences in Kipling and Haggard's approaches to the predicament of Empire.

THE POLITICS OF LOAFERDOM

'The Man Who Would Be King', like many of Kipling's other short stories, seems to be a parable but one whose moral instructions are either ironised or rendered ambivalent. It invites conflicting interpretations; it tells the tale of two enterprising drifters, Peachey Carnehan and Daniel Dravot, who manage to stage the biggest confidence trick of all time by convincing the inhabitants of some far-flung territory of their divine right to rule. The story presents fraud and cynical opportunism as the founding legend of Empire. Carnehan and Dravot run out of places and people to dupe in British India; bemoaning the lack of entrepreneurial initiative in governmental circles, Carnehan tells the narrator,

> you can't lift a spade, nor chip a rock, nor look for oil, nor anything like that without all the Government saying – 'Leave it alone and let us govern'. Therefore [we will] . . . go away to some other place where a man isn't crowded and can come into his own.
>
> (Kipling, 1914: 212)

Disguised first as a native priest and his servant and later as 'heathens' armed with rifles and ammunition, they journey to Kafiristan to create nothing less than an alternative Pax Britannica. Their kingdom is established through superior firepower and through a cynical manipulation of Freemason symbolism, after a chance discovery uncovers Kafiristan's similar religious and ritual ancestry. Their downfall is caused by Dravot, who commits the fatal error of believing his own propaganda and desires a queen to rule by his side. When his bride-to-be unmasks his humanity, the natives of Kafiristan shout, 'neither God nor Devil but a man!'. Dravot is killed on a bridge of his own construction, and Carnehan is crucified. Much later, Carnehan returns in a state of delirium and madness to tell his story to his friend, the journalist. It is Carnehan's tale, and the story of their meeting, that the journalist frame-narrator imparts to us.

Carnehan and Dravot are first and foremost 'loafers'. A definition of the term would perhaps be useful. The etymology of the word in the *Oxford English Dictionary* begins with its American meaning, 'to loaf', 'to thieve'. In its later usages, the word is also taken to refer to someone who spends his life in idleness – as contrasted with those who do purposeful work. Leland in *The English Gypsies and their Language* has this to say of 'loafers':

> When the term first began to be popular in 1834 or 1835, I can distinctly remember that it meant to pilfer. Such, at least, is my earliest recollection, of school boys asking one another in jest, of their acquisitions or gifts, 'Where did you loaf that from?' A petty pilferer was a loafer, but in a very short time all of the tribe of loungers in the sun, and the disreputable pickers up of unconsidered trifles . . . were called loafers.
>
> (*Oxford English Dictionary*, 1961)

David Arnold's study of European orphans and vagrants in nineteenth-century India is also useful for the specific context which we have to deal with; Arnold's work is a reminder of the harsh attitudes towards loafers prevalent among Anglo-Indians who were concerned with racial respectability. Loafers' vices such as drunkenness, debt, liaisons with native and Eurasian women were listed as factors bringing the white race into disrepute. The Commissioner of Patna writing to the Judicial Secretary of Bengal in 1867 asserted that 'the sight of Europeans in the lowest depths of degradation brought on by drinking and profligacy must . . . degrade [the white] race in the eyes of all who see them'. Fellow Anglo-Indians noted the wearing of Indianised costume with displeasure and were quick to condemn costume which made these European vagrants seem 'more like a Native than a European'. Lord Canning declared that a 'floating population of Indianised English loosely brought up, and exhibiting the worse qualities of both races' was a 'glaring reproach' (Arnold 1979: 114, 110).

The perception of loafing as a disreputable activity, linked with thieving and vagrancy, is preserved in Kipling's characterisation of loafers. Yet his fascination with these drifters also endows them with a certain transgressive desirability. In 'Letters of Marque', he highlights their potential for embarrassment; but it is an embarrassment that is expressive of a populist dislike of bureaucracy and anger at the concessions made to Indian society. Loafers in 'Letters' are the *Doppelgänger* of the 'hat-marked castes' – the district officers and 'bridge builders' – whose duty and servitude is at the heart of official imperial mythology. Loafers animate the other side of the colonial identity by voicing an aggressive megalomania; in contrast with what they see as a policy of 'extreme scrupulousness' in handling native affairs, they would advocate a policy that 'made [people] . . . sit up' (Kipling, 1919: 181, 198). The 'politics of loaferdom' is a candid brutality which 'sees things from the underside where the lath and plaster is not smoothed off' (Kipling, 1914: 201). If loafers are a lost generation, whose decadence, hedonism, and lack of principles make them morally reprehensible, their politics of unrestrained self-gratification points to a different brand of government. To be a loafer is to have no illusions about the 'civilising mission' or the white man's burden. Carnehan has no qualms about blackmailing the nobility of the Central Indian States for 'hush' money; he bemoans the Residents' interference in his attempt to extort money in the Princely States: 'the Residents finds you out, and then you get escorted to the Border *before you've time to get your knife into them*' (Kipling, 1914: 202 [my emphasis]). In 'Letters of Marque', the loafer remarks with conviction, 'there's enough money in India to pave Hell with if you could only get at it'; a 'hundred and fifty millions you could raise as easy as paint, if you just made these 'ere Injians understand that they had to pay an' make no bones about it' (Kipling, 1899: 198). 'Bummers, landsharks, skirmishers for their bread', loafers' knowledge of the underside of administrative life is privileged in Kipling's text as a 'truth' which is held albeit in an underhanded fashion. Despite his disavowal of the 'brutal cruelty' of the loafer's view as the 'babblings' of a drunken vagrant in 'Letters', the narrator's sneaking approval can be seen in the 'unscientific expression' left behind of 'a people wrapped in cotton-wool and ungettable'.

Typically, Carnehan and Dravot's vision of Empire-building reflects a loafer's view of Empire as the acquisition of territory through sheer will and military hardware. Boasting that they can build an alternative 'Sar-a-whack' in Kafiristan, they load camel bags with rifles and travel to the north disguised in native costume. Native disguise in Kipling's stories, as argued in the previous chapter, functions as an indicator of transgressive knowledge or empowerment; 'The Man Who Would Be King', is no exception to the rule. Here native costume signifies the loafers' lack of inhibition in crossing moral and social boundaries for their own ends; for Dravot in particular, it also denotes an intimate knowledge of native affairs – a knowledge that is put to devastating effect in his quest to be king. Knowledge and power are twinned in a revealing sequence where Dravot, proud of his ability to be 'complete to the native mind', breaks his disguise. Dravot momentarily drops the guise of the mad priest to direct the frame-narrator's hands to rifle butts under his camel bags, 'twenty of 'em . . . and ammunition to correspond, under the whirligigs and the mud dolls'. On arrival in Kafiristan, they easily overwhelm the native population, '[picking] them off with rifles before they knew where they was' (Kipling, 1914: 225). The loafers' audacity culminates in Dravot's installation as tribal God and King.

AN ALLEGORY OF EMPIRE?

The very title of Kipling's short story, 'The Man Who Would Be King', leads readers to expect a parable with an easy moral. It begins with the frame-narrator's elucidation of a moral precept that prefaces the narrative of kingship, 'Brother to a Prince and fellow to a beggar if he be found worthy'. Addressing readers directly as if to reply to the question of merit, he offers to tell the story of his strange association with loafers and their tale of sovereignty: 'I once came near to kinship with what might have been a veritable King and was promised the reversion of a Kingdom – army, law-courts, revenue and policy all complete'. Subsequent anecdotal references to historical kings confirm that the issue of real or worthy sovereigns remains the fable's central concern.

But the main protagonists of the tale do not, in any ordinary sense, represent the conventional material of worthy monarchs. At best, Carnehan and Dravot seem to be audacious but likeable 'overreachers' in their quest for personal and political power. Yet the question of how seriously one is to treat the story of these men who would be kings is a question that all critical interpretations of the story have to address. Louis Cornell encourages us to see the story of the two loafers as a straightforward parable of Empire. Carnehan and Dravot are men who personify both the patriotism and ambition of the colonial enterprise. He argues,

Dravot and Carnehan recapitulate the British conquest. Like Clive and the great generals who follow him, they prove that a disciplined native army, provided with effective weapons, is a match for a much larger force of untrained tribesmen. Like great Anglo-Indian administrators, they find the land divided by petty rulers: they put an end to internecine war, establish the Pax Britannica, and win the support of the tribesmen who prefer subjection to anarchy.

(Cornell, 1966: 163)

Cornell cites Kipling's letter to Edward White in support of his interpretation. Kipling is quoted as writing, 'men even lower than Peachey and Carnehan [*sic*] made themselves kings (and kept their kingdoms, too) in India not 150 years ago'; yet Kipling also goes on to give the story the status of myth arguing that 'all "King" tales of that kind date back to the Tower of Babel' (Harbord, 1961: 359). If the story of Carnehan and Dravot is to be treated as a founding legend, what kind of myth is it? Cornell's argument solves none of the problems of interpretation. To wit, are these men really kings? And if they are kings, what kind of kings are these men and what kind of kingdom do they possess? Can we trust the frame-narrator or does his involvement with the characters cloud his responses? Strategically, what is missing from Cornell's estimation of the tale is an assessment of the story's complex frame. The story of Carnehan and Dravot is narrated to the journalist frame-narrator by Carnehan. The story's narrative frame courts alternative interpretations – is the story true, an instance of the frame-narrator's proximity to veritable kings, or is the story false, and the product of the fevered imagination of loafer or frame-narrator.

One of the obvious difficulties for an interpretation which has this story as an unproblematic allegory of Empire-building lies in the status of Kafiristan and its inhabitants. The people of Kafiristan are introduced early as sharing the same racial group as the natives of England. Carnehan and Dravot's attempts at finding more information about the country which they seek to conquer unearth some surprising facts. Carnehan's researches result in a surprising find, 'Blow Bellew! . . . this book here says they think they're related to us English' (Kipling, 1914: 214). Later, his description of the tribes in question builds on this connection: 'They were fair men – fairer than you or me – with yellow hair and remarkable well built' (Kipling, 1914: 225). This link between the natives of Kafiristan and

244

Englishmen is kept up throughout Carnehan's story of their rise and fall. Dravot's inaugural speech as Grand-Master and king repeats the impression of racial commonality: 'I know you won't cheat me because you're white people – sons of Alexander – and not common, black Mohammedans' (Kipling, 1914: 234). Furthermore, when planning the expansion of his empire, Dravot refers to his subjects as English. The full irony of this parable of Empire is apparent in his ravings:

> 'I won't make a Nation,' says he. 'I'll make an Empire! These men aren't niggers; they're English. Look at their eyes – look at their mouths. Look at the way they stand up. They sit on chairs in their own houses. . . . Two million people – two hundred and fifty thousand fighting men – and all English! They only want the rifles and a little drilling.'
>
> (Kipling, 1914: 236)

Carnehan's story is the tale of two vagrants who attempt to build an Empire through discipline; their version of discipline and character-building turns on educating the white natives of Kafiristan on how to drill in formation. Is 'The Man Who Would Be King' a parody of Empire? Re-reading the tale again and again, I am certain that the manic humour which envelopes these two tramps pokes fun at the pomp and glory of the British Empire. The irreverent image of Empire-building as consisting primarily of rifles and stiff parades reads more like a practical joke than a founding legend. J. M. Barrie's summary of the short story as the tale of two 'stone-broke' scamps 'who, as they can get no other employment, decide to be kings' (Green, 1971: 81) treats Kipling's tale as a mischievous joke. Given the rigid class distinctions of the Anglo-Indian world (and its metropolitan counterpart), James Harrison and Tim Bascom's question is a serious one; they ask whether these two men representing the 'scum of Anglo-Indian society' (who yet seek to civilise the sons of Alexander) are Kipling's idea of a joke (Bascom, 1987: 170, 173). As Harrison puts it, 'Can Kipling be scurrilously parodying the British acquisition of India?' One could, of course, hold both views simultaneously; one could, for example, read the story as a narrative which stages the imperial scenario with breathless impudence, but also takes the edge off its boldness through a pleasurable and comic characterisation of the two loafers' antics. Cornell's reading would more or less fall into this category. Yet, I would suggest, a more literal and less pleasurable reading may also be found if one reads Kipling's tale as a parody of imperial mythologising.

The problem may be resolved in part if we could distinguish between real and false kings. But the text offers us a bewildering array of kingships and kingdoms. There are real Rajput kings and princes who rule over the exotic and mysterious Native States of 'unimaginable cruelty'. There are European kings 'on the other side of the world' who when viewed from the distance of Anglo-India are less real than the *zenana*-mission ladies, mad inventors, colonels passed over for promotion, and zealous missionaries who fill the columns of the Anglo-Indian newspaper. The original allusion to royalty in the first paragraph of the tale is itself ambiguous – 'But, today, I greatly fear that my king is dead, and if I want a crown I must go and hunt it for myself'; we do not know the dead king's identity nor what kind of king he was; neither do we know what kind of kingdom he possessed. The confusion between the kings that matter and the kings that do not, between what is real and important, or what is unreal and unimportant – exacerbated by the monotony, heat and India's distance from Europe – creates a surreal atmosphere. I would suggest that this confusion is deliberate; for the question of the veracity of Carnehan's story (which cannot in any case be verified) then pales in comparison to the compelling power of his tale and its effect on the frame-narrator.

TRANSFERENCE: PARABLE OR PARODY?

The frame-narrator is crucial to the manner in which a narrative trap is set for the reader. The frame-narrator's role within the narrative structure of the story encompasses two very distinct spheres of reference: the prosaic world of nineteenth-century reality and the epic and fabular world of the two loafer–kings' adventures. The frame-narrator occupies both the position of story-teller and listener; he is the figure to whom Carnehan directs his story and the figure that mediates Carnehan's story. For some readers, his location within the historical reality of nineteenth-century British India facilitates a better acceptance of what would otherwise be the incredible achievements of two loafers. For others, his specific contribution lies in the complex framing of the story, enabling an allegorical reading. As Tim Bascom argues, the improbability of the story is softened by the narrative frame which lets us commit ourselves to the telling of the tale, if not its actual content. Yet it is the narrator's presence in the historical world of Pax Britannica that makes the Kafiristan empire seem less real, 'prompting us to view it parabolically' (Bascom, 1987: 162).

Bascom's article is an exemplary reading of 'The Man Who Would Be King' as a parable of a vicarious desire for power. He argues that a secret desire for power links readers to Dravot via the frame-narrator, who is as eager to listen to Carnehan's story as we (presumably) are to his. Like Marlow in Conrad's *Heart of Darkness*, the frame-narrator paves the way for our vicarious entry into the fictional world by functioning as our narrative surrogate. Bascom asserts, '[most readers by definition are much too thoughtful and controlled to act on their desire for domination,] Dravot offers us the satisfaction of seeing our desires fulfilled while at the same time . . . [keeping] us safely distanced from the action, protected from the consequences' (Bascom, 1987: 166). The text's manipulation of symbols supports such an interpretation. Freemasonry functions within Kipling's story as an organising principle that brings order to the chaos of the warring tribes; it becomes a metaphor for Empire and the civilising mission – the process of restoring order, law and discipline. But while Bascom is right about some of the interpellative effects of 'The Man Who Would Be King', his argument pays little attention to why readers should share Carnehan, Dravot and the frame-narrator's desires. I propose, instead, to direct more attention to how this 'truth' is rendered convincing. Rather than assert that the 'truth' of domination is the hidden kernel of the story that interpretation uncovers, I would argue that this compelling 'truth' is really only produced retroactively, after our initiation into the transferential structures (teller/ listener) of the story. It is the text's transferential structures that encourage a reading of the tale as one of Pax Britannica.

The frame-narrator is positioned in relation to the two loafers as an intra-textual listener of their story; his reading position – one of attentive fascination – is a position that the extra-textual reader is encouraged to replicate. The frame-narrator listens to Carnehan's story just as we read his account of it. But Carnehan also catches the frame-narrator in a transferential relationship, because he embodies for the frame-narrator the subject who is presumed to know (the realpolitik behind Empire), the subject that 'knows' the frame-narrator's desires. The frame-narrator attracts our identification because he initiates and expresses our desire for more knowledge about the loafers, who are presented as the object of fascination.

The relationship between the loafers and the frame-narrator cannot be characterised as disinterested. Concerned about the fate of the two loafers at the hands of Native Princes, he informs the authorities of their presence in Rajasthan. He does not turn them away when they appear in his office but allows them access to his library. More importantly, the narrator, Carnehan and Dravot are all brothers in the Mother Lodge; masonic allegiances bind the narrator firmly to the loafers' narrative and their brand of myth-making. The frame-narrator's first meeting with Carnehan marks his fascination quite clearly; Carnehan's presence in the 'inter-mediate' train carriage, which holds only travellers 'most properly looked down on', catches his eye. The frame-narrator finds himself in instant rapport with Carnehan; we are told that 'he was a wanderer like [himself]' with stories to tell of amazing things seen and done in 'out-of-the-way corners of Empire' (Kipling, 1914: 201). The loafer's politics of opportunism are shared by the frame-narrator: '"if India was filled with men like you and me . . . it isn't seventy millions of revenue the land would be paying – it's seven hundred millions . . ." I looked at his mouth and chin [and] . . . was disposed to agree with him' (Kipling, 1914: 201). Later, the frame-narrator's initial response to Dravot partakes of the same veneration that Carnehan has for his companion. If Dravot's face, described as 'great and shining' identifies him as a special figure, it is also the first in a series of messianic references that accrue to the visionary figure of the red-bearded loafer (even though it is Carnehan, not Dravot, who is crucified).

The main meeting between Carnehan and the frame-narrator shows that the latter is caught in transferential identification. His absorbed silence on hearing Carnehan's strange tale of his efforts in Kafiristan reflects his affective involvement. He readily agrees with Carnehan's request for an audience; he steadies the loafer's straying mind with references to their past associations in order to overcome Carnehan's narrative blockages. Story-teller and listener are intimately bound. Carnehan's entreaty – 'Keep looking at me, or maybe my words will go all to pieces. Keep looking at me in my eyes and don't say anything' – is met with the frame-narrator's response: 'I leaned forward and looked into his face as steadily as I could. He dropped one hand upon the table and I grasped it by the wrist' (Kipling, 1914: 222). In the exchange of looks the frame-narrator, mesmerised by Carnehan's narration, prompts him for more information:

> The punkah-coolies had gone to sleep. Two kerosene lamps were blazing in the office, and the perspiration poured down my face and splashed on the blotter as I leaned forward. Carnehan was shivering, and I feared that his mind might go. I wiped my face, took a fresh grip of the piteously mangled hands, and said: – 'What happened after that?'
>
> (Kipling, 1914: 247)

By positioning Carnehan as the subject who possesses knowledge or a secret worth unveiling, the frame-narrator imbues the loafer with narrative authority in a chain of displaced desire. Bascom remarks that by identifying with the loafers, we let Carnehan (and by implication Dravot) act as our character surrogates, and they become figures that express our covert desires. But Bascom's reading begs the question why Carnehan/Dravot should be privileged figures that command attention; the question of how their alleged knowledge is linked with desire is ignored. Carnehan's knowledge is not separate from the frame-narrator's desire but, in Bascom's reading, neither is the frame-narrator's knowledge separate from the critic's desire. As Peter Brooks points out, story-telling relies on the transferential relation between speaker and listener and this relies on desire as much as 'truth'. In a particularly revealing passage, Brooks links meaning and knowledge to desire through narrative:

> Narrative truth, then, seems to be a matter of conviction, derived from the plausibility and well-formedness of the narrative discourse, and also what we might call its force, its power to create further patterns of connectedness. . . . Calling Lacan as a gloss to Freud, one could say that narrative truth depends as much on the discourse of desire as on the claims of past event. The narrative discourse – like the discourse of analysis – must restage the past history of desire as it exercises its pressure toward meaning in the present. The past never will be recollected at all except insofar as it insists on continuing to mean, to repeat its charge of affect in the present.
>
> (Brooks, 1994: 59)

The transferential relationship is first and foremost founded on the axis of desire. But the subject does not really possess knowledge; he is perceived to have knowledge simply by virtue of being a subject of desire, or where desire is focused. Slavoj Žižek's work on the temporal loop of narrative analysis foregrounds the retroactive nature of transference. Žižek argues that 'truth' (that the subject is presumed to know) is an illusion; 'it does not really exist in the other, the other does not really possess it, it is constituted afterwards, through our – the subject's – signifier's working'. Yet it is a 'necessary illusion', a misrecognition, for 'we may paradoxically elaborate this knowledge only by means of the illusion that the other already possesses it and that we are only discovering it' (Žižek, 1989a: 56–57). Žižek puts a different twist on Brooks's more optimistic understanding of dialogue between narrator and narratee in the transferential dynamics of story-telling by introducing ideology into the equation. In Žižek's re-reading of Althusser through Lacan, the dynamics of transference are linked to ideological interpellation; in his estimation, transference marks the point of 'attachment' that produces ideological knowledge inscribed retroactively; it is 'the point of attachment that links his very desire to the resolution of that which is to be revealed [that is to say the 'truth' of ideology]'.

It is only after the double inscription of colonial desire that Bascom's observation of the narrator's silent participation in the fantasy of kingship rings true. The frame-narrator facilitates such a reading, but he also requires the listener's transferential identification in order to activate meaning – as opposed to a competing reading which might see in Carnehan's tale a literal parody of Empire, or the comic hallucinations of an insane man.[1] In order to read the tale of loafers as the parable of men who would be kings, that is to say, in order to activate the allegorical or parabolic meaning of Kipling's tale, one must have already given in to the colonial fantasy of power and domination. Bascom's words, 'if we let him act as our subject character', hinge on an ideological and fantasmatic interpellation. Surely the moral of the tale is not that the silent participation of the narrator and sympathetic reader is a *universal* desire for power and domination but that such a dream (or nightmare) is peculiar to colonialism – and one which is to haunt the very image of the colonial civil state. To help us locate one final set of transferential relations that repeat colonial desire across listeners and tellers, we must make a distinction between Carnehan and Dravot, and scrutinise closely the manner of Carnehan's narration.

THE GREAT GAME

Dravot and Carnehan's characters are more sympathetic and likeable when compared with their earlier prototype in 'Letters of Marque'. The loafer in Kipling's travels in Rajasthan appears to be unnaturally obsessed with the alleged wealth and deviousness of the Princely States. In contrast to the normal practices of colonial governors and British Residents, the Rajasthan loafer would be ruthless with his collection of revenue: 'I'm a pauper, an' you're a pauper – we 'aven't got anything hid in the ground – an' so's every white man in this forsaken country. But the Injian he's a rich man. . . . if you send half a dozen swords at him and shift the thatch off his roof, he'll pay' (Kipling, 1899: 182–183). Philip Mallet is correct to observe that the softening of the loafer's portrait in 'The Man Who would Be King' is achieved by excluding much of Carnehan's and Dravot's past and by excluding much of the paranoiac and exploitative characterisation of the Rajasthan loafer.

Dravot and Carnehan make attractive characters because they insist on taking an anarchic, impudent and cynical view of the colonial status quo. Their actions are predicated primarily on the thrill of a prank and the audacity with which they perform their various hoaxes for personal profit. As long as they remain in a position of relative powerlessness, their madcap schemes for exploiting situations and peoples can be viewed with indulgence. It is when Dravot and Carnehan are able to amass a store of rifles and ammunition that the context and reception of their gaming should change. But the text, in fact, records no such change.

Dravot's intervention in the Kafiristan tribal wars is told in more or less the same language and manner of his previous madcap schemes. His decision to aid the aggressors rather than the victimised is purely arbitrary; no reason is supplied by Carnehan who is simply recorded as saying, 'Says Dravot, unpacking the guns – "This is the beginning of the business. We'll fight for the ten men"'. Whilst in their relatively impecunious state, these men's scrapes amount to nothing more than minor irritations for all concerned; but on acquiring the fire-power needed to subdue hostile territory, their actions have devastating consequences. Yet Carnehan's third-person narration betrays little change:

> he fires two rifles at the twenty men, and drops one of them at two hundred yards. . . . The other men began to run, but Carnehan and Dravot sits on the boxes picking them off at all

ranges, up and down the valley. Then we goes up to the ten
men that had run across the snow too, and they fires a footy
little arrow at us. Dravot he shoots above their heads and they
all falls down flat. Then he walks over them and kicks them,
and then he lifts them up and shakes hands all round to make
them friendly like. He calls them and gives them boxes to
carry, and waves his hand for all the world to see as though
he was King already.

(Kipling, 1914: 225)

Carnehan's narration registers no visible difference between the
severity of the present situation and the previous schemes the
loafers engage in. His language is kept at a purely descriptive level
and proceeds by substituting one action for another in an accumu-
lative series of deeds that is devoid of any emotional or moral
response. Words such as 'drop' and 'picking them off' function as
euphemisms for killing and are in keeping with the deliberately
anti-climactic and prosaic account of events. Carnehan's distanced
account of their participation in the war reads more like stage
farce than historic imperial battle; the description of event is
aligned more with music hall or vaudeville than with historic
battles staged to conquer real kingdoms. Carnehan's deadpan
narration gives the story of loafer-kings its curious sense of
absurdity and fabular timelessness. It also imparts to the story a
relentless logic and reality. J. H. Millar records his impressions in
a review of 1898, 'the reader, falling more and more under the
master's spell, is whirled along triumphantly to the close. No time
to take breath or to reflect, so impetuous and irresistible is the
torrent' (Green, 1971: 208).

Mallett's observations on Carnehan's narrative viewpoint are
pertinent. Carnehan tells his story with little or no interjections
from the frame-narrator; Carnehan's tale is also told without any
moralising comment. Framing Carnehan's story in this manner
means that readers have access to Dravot only through Carnehan's
perspectival limits of 'scams' and tricks: 'Dravot is seen only . . . in
terms of his personality, and the only [intra-textual] moral relation
in which he stands is his relation to Carnehan, his friend and his
fellow in their enterprise' (Mallet, 1989: 104). Hence, Carnehan's
limits are the parameters of the story's transferential frame; identification is effected only through Carnehan's viewpoint as loafer.
Because Carnehan provides the story's only moral perspective on

Dravot, the latter is presented as morally reprehensible only within Carnehan's own frame of reference (Mallet, 1987: 104).

If Dravot's actions are reprehensible, they are also recuperable, for the text's use of Carnehan as focaliser means that any crime Dravot commits can be redeemed; in his friend's eyes, 'he [Dravot] can atone for his flaws by admitting them and magnanimously offering to die alone' (Mallett, 1989: 104). Such an atonement within the story's narrative structure helps elevate Dravot's stature from that of a misguided fool to that of a tragic hero. By the close of the tale, Dravot has acquired the virtues of self-knowledge and dignity. Because the narrative excludes the experiences of the natives of Kafiristan, their interpellation of Dravot as God and King is read not as (Carnehan's and) Dravot's desire inscribed retro-actively (the product of transference) but as a fulfilment of prophecy/fate. Furthermore, the natives of Kafiristan function as the object lesson for Dravot's overreaching ambition. They remind him of his humanity, and enable him to die with dignity. 'The Man Who Would Be King' may be read as a parable of Empire with a moral difference: Empire becomes the means by which men may discover themselves. Mallett remarks, 'on these terms, what counts is not what the white man offers the subject peoples, but [that they] are the occasion for him to learn self-mastery and loyalty and what are sometimes embarrassingly called the masculine virtues' (Mallett, 1989: 106). What Kipling's 'The Man Who Would Be King' contains is a parable within a parable. If the inner parable offers a moral lesson in 'masculine virtues' or a moral truism in vicarious excitement, such readings are predicated on the act of transmission, where the reader enters into the transferential space; if the story 'has "taken hold", the act of transmission resembles psychoanalytic transference' (Brooks, 1994: 51). But the story in question is one told by a loafer noted for his confidence tricks and imaginative presentations of himself 'for a few day's food' (Kipling, 1914: 201). There is perhaps a more substantial link between loafer and journalist-narrator than simply that of Freemasonry. To adopt Conrad's metaphor, the meaning of the story lies not inside, like a kernel, but outside. Carnehan's story proves to be a powerful one in terms of the effects it produces on the frame-narrator, but perhaps Carnehan's story (and its effects) also provide an analogy for Kipling's story (and its effects). In this reading, not only is the frame-(journalist–)narrator's position identical to Carnehan's, but Kipling's own position as writer is identical to Carnehan's; both

Kipling and Carnehan are ever in search of a new situation or new trick to play on their listeners. For part of the frame-narrator's avowed function as a journalist in the text is to record curious and unexpected incidents of Anglo-Indian life; the frame-narrator spends his time in search of a good story to report to his readers. He finds such a story in Carnehan's fantasmatic account of his adventures in Kafiristan. What 'The Man Who Would Be King' offers is a parable of story-telling: the colonial text as a hoax – a 'scam' – pulled off by enterprising vagabond story-tellers. Kipling's fascination with the figure of the loafer represents the artist as petty thief who steals and trades in stories of other people's lives. The interface between story-teller and journalist is clearly worth scrutiny.

THE IMPERIAL STORY-TELLER

The preface to *Life's Handicap* records a conversation between a native story-teller, Gobind, and the author–narrator of the series of short stories that follows. Gobind, whose tales were 'true but could not be printed in an English book', is firmly located within the oral traditions of story-telling as opposed to the narrator's avowed role as *kerani* or writer. He is likened to the native bazaar craftsman 'speak[ing] straight to men and women' and performs his stories within the locale of communal and stable agrarian societies. Gobind advises Kipling the narrator–writer:

> Tell them first of the things thou hast seen and they have seen together. Thus their knowledge will piece out thy imperfections. Tell them of what thou alone hast seen, then what thou hast heard, and since they be children, tell them of battles and kings, horses, devils, elephants and angels, but omit not to tell them of love and such like.
>
> (Kipling, 1897: ix)

Robert Kellogg argues that story-tellers thrive on the creation of an alternative heroic world to the ordinary real world of their listeners. Odysseus or Boccaccio's narrators 'keep alive heroic desires when they cannot be acted out in actual circumstances'. Kellogg suggests that the framed narrative is one method of keeping alive story-telling's archaic and magical functions: 'we readers know that there are not more heroes, demons, saints, magicians, or gods left in the world; but it comforts us mightily to know they exist in stories'

(Bascom, 1987: 163). Benjamin's alternative homage to the archaic and magical properties of story-telling is captured in the figure of the travelling journeymen: 'in it was combined the lore of faraway places, such as a much-travelled man brings home, with the lore of the past, as it best reveals itself to natives of the place' (Benjamin, 1973: 85). Benjamin contrasts the communal aspects of story-telling with the solitary sensation of the novelistic experience driven by print technology – 'the story-teller takes what he tells from experience . . . his own or that reported by others. And he in turn makes it the experience of those who are listening to his tale' (Benjamin, 1973: 87).

Sir Walter Besant, a contemporary critic and novelist, perceived Kipling as essentially a story-teller; he emphasised the marvellous and magical which the traveller as story-teller is privileged to convey, and the communal and experiential knowledge that is passed on from story-teller to audience. Kipling, the narrator of colonial desire, acts as the privileged point of transference:

> Kipling . . . knows the world – especially the Anglo-Saxon world – the world of our empire and the world of the American republic. He is one of those thrice blessed who have not only received the gifts of observation and of sympathy – the gift of story-telling with the dramatic instinct and the power of selection and grouping – but he has obtained the gift of opportunity; he has lived in the lands where there are still adventures and the adventurous . . . where there are still unknown mysteries of hills and forests; he has found mines of material diverse and new and marvellous, and he has worked these mines as they have never been worked before.
>
> (Green, 1971: 254)

Besant even describes a performance in which Kipling, as frame-narrator–journalist, told the story of 'The Man Who Would Be King'. I have no evidence that such a performance happened but Besant's description confirms my version of the powerful transferential relation between story-teller and listener that is inscribed within some of these tales:

> While that story was told, there was not heard in the whole of the vast audience a sound, a whisper, a breath. In the dead silence it was received; in the dead silence it concluded – in a dead silence save for the sigh which spoke of a tension

255

almost too great to be borne. Perhaps that sigh might be taken for applause. Perhaps the story-teller himself took it for pleasure.

(Green, 1971: 255)

Kipling was on occasion not adverse to promoting this version of his writing self. Late in life, he presented himself as the imperial legend-founder, the man 'afflicted with the magic of the necessary word' whose task it is to write the record of his tribe:

all it suggests is that the man with the Words shall wait upon the man with achievement, and step by step with him try to tell the story of the Tribe. . . . When it is done this is the literature of which it will be said, in due time, that it fitly represents its age.

(Kipling, 1928: 6–7)

Kipling's *Recessional*, written in 1897, is a hymnic call to the nation not to forget the duties of British 'dominion over palm and pine' (Kipling, 1969: 328). Benita Parry calls Kipling 'an exemplary artist of imperialism' whose 'homilies on the development of character in the metropolitan population, hymned in one of the verses as adherence to a code of Law, Order, Duty and Restraint, Obedience, Discipline', and whose 'projection of the white race as the natural rulers of a global space' worked towards the 'fabrications of England's mysterious imperialist identity and destiny' (Parry, 1988: 61–62). His *Puck* stories may be seen as attempts to create a mythic-text of the British Empire, which produces the figure of the child at the centre of its narrative enchantment. After all, Kipling's children are no ordinary children, they are the heroes and heroines who will inherit the duties, power and responsibilities of the whole of the British Empire.[2]

OR THE ARTIST AS LOAFER?

We are used to describing Kipling as the imperial story-teller or the preeminent bard of Empire, but I also hope to show an alternative portrait of Kipling, and one indebted more to journalism and its quest for novelty. For what is equally apparent in his early texts is a journalistic flair for the dramatic potential of a good story. The Anglo-India stories, many later collected in anthologies such as *Plain Tales* and *Life's Handicap*, were published as newspaper fiction (literal 'turnovers') and included impressionistic and fragmented, specular bit-part sketches of native life. His narratives often employ the persona of journalist–narrator as the narrative correspondent: the man-on-the-spot who relays information for a reading audience. While his narrative persona is not always objective or distanced from the events that unfold, his function within the narrative is akin to journalistic mediation and interpretation of news. In 'The Return of Imray' and 'The Mark of the Beast' his presence serves to verify the authenticity of strange affairs and to mediate their experience for readers. In 'The Strange Ride' and 'The Man Who Would Be King' he comes across unusual incidents, which he (re)stages for readers' benefit. In 'The City of Dreadful Night' and 'To be Filed For Reference' his nightly exploration of parts of the native city yield tableaus of native and colonial lives. In this respect, his narrator is often a petty pilferer or loafer, either stealing bits of other people's lives or stories of their lives to fashion a novel story.

Kipling's narrator is usually a journalist who has an affinity for the underside of official life. In 'The Man Who Would Be King', his narrator classifies himself as a 'wanderer and vagabond' whose occupation sanctions his experience of things in 'out-of-the-way-corners of Empire'. The epigram which prefaces the tale – brother to a beggar and to a prince – indicates not only 'the right sort of king' but his worth as a writer. While it is dangerous to equate the frame-narrator with Kipling, there are passages in 'The Man Who Would Be King' which are lifted directly from Kipling's record of his own travel experiences in the Princely States. On assignment for the *Pioneer* in Rajasthan (which resulted in 'Letters of Marque'), he describes himself in a letter to his cousin Margaret Burne-Jones in similar terms as his frame-narrator. He describes himself as having 'railed and rode and drove and tramped' and 'slept in King's palaces or under the stars' with natives in 'desolate wayside stations'.[3] Diverse experiences contribute to the narrator's authority; 'wonderful and awful things' experienced during the journey become fodder for his writing. Kipling's early years as a journalist in India show a marked fascination with peripheral figures and experiences outside the pale. To return to the Burne-Jones letter quoted earlier:

Underneath our excellent administrative system; under the piles of reports and statistics; the thousands of troops: the doctors: and the civilian runs wholly untouched and unaffected the life of the peoples of the land . . . immediately outside of our own English life, is the dark and crooked and fantastic; and wicked: and awe-inspiring life of the 'native' . . . . I have done my best to penetrate into it and have put the little I have learnt into the pages of 'Mother Maturin' – Heaven send that she may grow into a full blown novel before I die. My experiences of course are only a queer jumble of opium dens, night houses, night strolls with natives; evenings spent in their company in their own homes (in the men's quarter of course) and the long yarns my native friends spin me, and one or two queer things I've come across in my own office experience.[4]

This passage contributes to the myth of Kipling as a great mediator of native culture. His knowledge is imaged as comprehensive and covers not only the everyday official life of the administrator but also its hidden native counterpart. The contact is illicit and vaguely sexual; but the underworld with its 'dark, crooked and fantastic' forms and stories provide the source and inspiration of his tales. The most compelling image that emerges from this description of his nightwalks is an image of the artist as loafer or flaneur. The artist walks through Indian streets in the same manner as the Baudelairean flaneur strolls along the pedestrian mall of the Parisian city, taking in the sights, or as a Dickensian nightwalker on his slumming expeditions in London. India yields a similar magic-lantern of familiar and phantasmagoric images.

There is a touch of the romantic and the bohemian in Kipling's (descriptions of his) expedition. Kipling speaks of how 'little an Englishman can hope to understand [these natives]': 'I would that you see some of the chapters in Mother Maturin and you will follow more closely what I mean'. Here, then, is the contradictory move-ment in Kipling's project. His task is both to mystify and to reveal native life for all to see. Mother Maturin is Kipling's unfinished (lost) novel about the 'unutterable horrors of lower class Eurasian and native life'; it is said to have been gleaned from his own 'experiences' in India. The Orientalist influence of the French Symbolists, the romantic heritage of decadent artists and the literary influence of Dickens may have contributed to the novel but, as a result of family disapproval, the novel was never published. But there is more than a glimpse of this aspect of Kipling's persona in his relation to the underworld of Lahore City away from departmental life. In a letter to his ex-editor Kay Robinson, Kipling writes:

> I hunt and rummage among 'em; knowing Lahore City – that wonderful, dirty, mysterious ant hill – blindfold and wandering through it like Haroun-al-Raschid in search of strange things. . . . the bulk of my notes and references goes to enrich a bruised tin tea-box where lies – 350 fcp. pages thick – my Mother Maturin. The novel that is always being written and yet gets no furrader. . . . heat and smells of oil and spices, and puffs of temple incense, and sweat, and darkness, and dirt and lust and cruelty, and above all, things wonderful and fascinating innumerable. Give me time Kay – give me seven years and three added to them and abide the publishment of 'Mother Maturin'. Then you shall sit down in your gas-lit, hot water pipe warmed office, at midnight, and shall indite a review saying that the book ought never to have been written.[5]

The letter is built on a series of contrasts: dirty/clean, magical (strange)/rational, sensual/sensible (ordinary, safe), dangerous/ 'gas-lit, hot water pipe warmed office' which depict experiences outside the English official world. 'The House of Suddhoo', 'The Gate of Hundred Sorrows', 'The City of Dreadful Night' (two versions) and 'To Be Filed For Reference' are all obsessed with journeys into the native quarter and with meeting figures who know it well. I will comment here only on the short story 'To Be Filed For Reference', because it deals directly with the aesthetics of loaferism that we have been discussing.

'To Be Filed' is the very last tale to be included in the first book-form collection of his short stories, *Plain Tales From The Hills*. The narrative recounts a meeting with a loafer who has gone native. Formerly an Oxford man, McIntosh Jellalludin is now a dissolute drunk, who is married to a native woman 'not pretty to look at'. As a literary aesthete turned 'Mussulman', he is also, the narrator records, 'the most interesting loafer that I had had the pleasure of knowing for a long time' (Kipling, 1898: 302). The narrator's nocturnal visits to his loafer friend are a form of education. McIntosh Jellaludin's mind was a 'perfect rag-bag of useless things', a hybrid list of classical quotations, literary knowledge, native customs and languages. But it is precisely this hybrid world which attracts the narrator's attention and it is McIntosh Jellaludin's knowledge of native customs that the frame-narrator covets for his

own artistic ends: '[that] he had his hand on the pulse of native life
. . . was a fact. . . . As Mohammedan *faquir* – as McIntosh Jellaludin
– he was all that I wanted for my own ends. He smoked several
pounds of my tobacco, and taught me several ounces of things
worth knowing' (Kipling, 1898: 303).

McIntosh Jellaludin's claim on posterity lies in a big bundle of
papers, 'all numbered and covered with fine cramped writing',
which he calls, in the manner of the Bible, 'the Book of McIntosh
Jellaludin'. The bundle of papers is an account of the loafer's
knowledge and experience of India: 'showing what he saw and how
he lived, and what befell him and others . . .'; this text, like all
romantic visionary texts, is described as being 'paid for . . . in seven
years' damnation'. A literary child of two or more cultures, the book
(described by the loafer as 'my only child') will be the lost gospel
of British India. Strickland's legendary knowledge of things native
will pale in comparison. McIntosh dies exhorting the narrator to
publish it: 'do not let my book die in its present form. . . . Listen
Now! I am neither mad nor drunk! That book will make you
famous' (Kipling, 1898: 309).

Is it stillborn or still to be born? McIntosh's book is also the book
of Mother Maturin, 'being also the account of the life and sins and
death of Mother Maturin'. The narrative of 'To Be Filed For
Reference' ends on a note of ambiguity. It is stillborn because the
child who is a product of two cultures must be a sterile hybrid and
because Strickland, the wise policeman and expert on native life
and custom 'thought the writer an extreme liar'. But McIntosh
Jellaludin's book is still-to-be-born because by the close of the story,
'Mother Maturin' has yet to be published. The references to
McIntosh Jellaludin's 'Mother Maturin' matches what we know of
Kipling's own unpublished novel; his own descriptions of the
content of his '350 fcp pages' of writing kept in a tea tin matches
the narrator's descriptions of the loafer McIntosh's book.

Kipling's book contains 'all things wonderful and fascinating
innumerable' and was to show his 'hand on the pulse of native life'.
Kipling's 'Mother Maturin' by all accounts seems to have been as
contentious and provocative a piece of work as McIntosh Jellaludin's
book. In a letter to his Aunt Edith Mcdonald on July 30 1885,
Kipling describes the early drafts:

> Further I have really embarked to the tune of 237 foolscap
> pages on my novel – Mother Maturin – an Anglo Indian

episode. Like Topsy it 'growed' while I wrote and I find myself now committed to a two volume business at least. Its not one bit nice or proper but it carries a grim sort of a moral with it and tries to deal with the unutterable horrors of lower class Eurasian and native life as they exist outside reports and reports and reports. I haven't got Pater's verdict on what I've done. He comes up in a couple of days and will then sit in judgement. Trixie says its awfully horrid: Mother says its nasty but powerful and I know it to be in a large measure true.[6]

At this time, the manuscript exerted a powerful hold over Kipling, who describes it as an 'unfailing delight', and his own writing at a 'stage where characters are living with me always'. Mrs Hill, a close friend of Kipling in India, read parts of the earlier work and describes the story as that 'of an old Irishwoman who kept an opium den in Lahore. She married a civilian and came to live in Lahore – hence a story how government secrets came to be known in the Bazaar and vice versa' (Carrington, 1970: 423). The seedier side of Indian and Anglo-Indian urban life in all its 'unutterable horrors' is part and parcel of Kipling's poetics of decadence; the book is 'nasty but powerful'. When Kipling returned to London in the nineties, the novel was still unfinished. Kipling's letter to his former editor Kay Robinson, written in a bout of depression, speaks of his frustration at London's literary scene and his desire to return to India as an Anglo-Indian writer. 'Mother Maturin' is again invoked as a book that would launch his literary career.[7]

'To Be Filed For Reference' does not belong to the original 'Plain Tales' series of stories in the *Civil and Military Gazette*; it is also placed at the end of the anthology. Hence, 'To Be Filed' gestures towards the significant new novel that Kipling hoped to publish in the near future. Yet 'To Be Filed' contains a coda disclaiming authorship. The disclaimer is strategic, given the negative reception of his unfinished novel. In this light, one may be forgiven for taking McIntosh Jellaludin to be a *Doppelgänger* of the respectable journalist of the text. McIntosh Jellaludin, the loafer gone 'fantee' must be disavowed in order to preserve the integrity of the narrator's colonial identity. But Kipling's disavowal coexists with his avowal; it is present, for example, in the transferential relation between journalist and loafer.

In one of his last essays, Freud discusses fetishism's dual and contradictory attitudes towards external reality, and its effects on subjectivity (Freud, 1964). He argues that the contrary dynamics of avowal and disavowal produces a 'splitting of the ego': 'everything has to be paid for in one way or another, and this success is achieved at the price of a rift in the ego which never heals but which increases as time goes on' (Freud, 1964: 275–276). I would argue that in this context, Kipling's contradictory attitudes towards 'Mother Maturin' result in a splitting which is *repeated* in the conflict between the respectable journalist and the disreputable loafer. It is the unstable doubling of the loafer/journalist–author that results in the joke which closes 'To Be Filed': 'If the thing is ever published, some one may perhaps remember this story, now printed as a safeguard to prove that McIntosh Jellaludin and not myself wrote the Book of Mother Maturin. I don't want the *Giant's Robe* to come true in my case' (Kipling, 1897: 310).

The case of McIntosh Jellaludin is interesting because it reminds us that there is a side to Kipling's story-telling other than that of imperial bard and visionary, who was responsible for some of the 'founding legends' of Empire. In this final tale of *Plain Tales*, and in my reading of some of the early short stories, Kipling also emerges as flaneur–tramp, whose inquisitive and often deliberately voyeuristic gaze uses others for his own ends. Kipling's early collections consist of a rag-bag of different stories. The two sides are part of one whole. The narrator's occupation enables him to take up a privileged position as collector of experiences; it allows him to function as a sympathetic ear for local gossip and to traverse racial and class boundaries in search of a good story. As both listener and teller of the tale, he is free from the network of social taboos which keep him within the strict boundaries of Anglo-Indian society. His voyeurism is parasitic on the society he moves in and out of and his position as writer and journalist sanctions such voyeurism.

Kipling as imperial story-teller offers both the magic and enchantment of the Indian story and its voyeurism; Edmund Gosse's reference to Kipling as 'the master of a new kind of terrible and enchanting peepshow' with readers that 'crowd around him begging for "just one more look"' (Green, 1971: 108) captures the spirit of his early work. Gosse's comment also hints at the spirit of commerce which informs the trade in stories and lives. Kipling's acknowledgement of his occupation as journalist–writer is an acknowledgement of the market forces and commodity relations which characterise the literary scene in the late nineteenth century.[8] The journalist–writer's response to Gobind's advice in the preface to *Life's Handicap* underscores a commercial awareness:

in regard to our people they desire new tales, and when all is written they rise up and declare that the tale were told better in such and such a manner ... Nay, but with our people, money having passed, it is their right; as we should turn against a shoeseller in regard to shoes if these wore out. If then I make a book you shall see and judge.

(Kipling, 1897: x)

John Rignall asserts a close relation between the flaneur and the commodity culture of the nineteenth century by highlighting the 'significant affinity' between spectator and reader (Rignall, 1992). Not only are both spectator and the realist novel products of the commercial culture of the nineteenth century, but 'the novel, itself a commodity, presents in the figure of this observer an image of the very consumer on whom it depends' (Rignall, 1992: 4). Sara Suleri's is perhaps the most perceptive comment: writing about *Kim* she observes that Kipling's genius lies in his 'apprehension of the applicability of journalism to imperial narration'. For journalism revels in novelty and the text's youthful celebration of novelty and its successive 'montage of autonomous moment' is a major part of its picaresque attraction (Suleri, 1992: 111, 112). The same might be said for Kipling's short fiction; in displacing the figure of the traditional story-teller for that of the *kerani*, *Life's Handicap* and *Plain Tales*' juxtaposition of short stories – 'collected from all places, and all sorts of people' – produces an entertaining timeless montage of other worlds. Chronology, Suleri argues, is always a thorny issue for the 'story of empire' and imperial narratives display both coyness and discomfort when dealing with 'their situatedness' within history. 'To name the present tense of history is of course to turn to journalism ... in the story of journalism, history is perpetu- ally novel and necessarily occurs in the absence of precedent.' In Kipling, we have a 'brilliant literalization of the colonial moment' where 'empire confronts the necessary perpetuation of its adoles- cence in relation to its history' (Suleri, 1992: 111).

CONCLUSION

Throughout this book, I have described how the trope of the mirror may offer a useful way of reading the representation of other cultures because the activity of forging cultural identities seems to take place in relation to the dialogic construction of Otherness. Psychoanalysis has provided the terms of the debate; between the mirror and the signifying chain, we have an indication of how desire, identification and fantasy are set in motion. For in entering the Symbolic, the order of language and culture, the subject 'forfeits' the possibility of wholeness. All subsequent relations and activities will be directed at filling this gap. Fantasy is the psychic formation for filling this lack. Fantasy provides the subject with a desiring position and a narrative to dramatise desire. Nowhere is fantasy more potent than in the dynamics of identification; as Silverman argues, 'the *mise-en-scène* of desire can only be staged', in other words, by 'drawing upon the images through which the self is constituted' (Silverman, 1992: 5). Identification is not only grounded in vision and visual images but is also activated discursively, in so far as it is based on a point of address.

Haggard's early African romances are based on a narcissistic identification with Zulu or the prototypical African, which re-stages an imaginary moment of empowered masculinity amidst current anxieties of cultural and imperial decline. His narratives draw on the contemporary discursive use of the body as a metaphor for literary, national, physiological, psychological and moral health. Haggard himself participated in debates about urban poverty and racial degeneration and in the critical controversies over the literary status of romance. His advocacy of romance, his praise of frontier life and his romanticisation of Zulu culture is a reaction against what he saw as *fin-de-siècle* decadence and enfeeblement.

Haggard's narratives are consistently nostalgic or elegiac; his ideal vision of society travels back consistently to a pre-modern period modelled on feudal lines in *Allan Quatermain*, or to a vicarious participation in 'primitive' societies in his Zulu romances.

Kipling's output was so prolific and his range of stories so wide that critical assessment of his literary achievements must come to terms with a writing career that spans five decades and three continents. My assessment of Kipling is necessarily much more modest and is fuelled by a desire to trace the narrative and historical twists and turns of some of his early work as a journalist. Also, I have limited myself to Kipling's portrayal of Hindu and Muslim culture in India in order to develop the overall theme of colonial alterity and the politics of identification.[1] Kipling's early Indian prose is based on a more ambivalent identification with both Hindu and Muslim Indians, and is perhaps more the product of colonial Anglo-Indian culture than imperial British culture. Consequently, Kipling's early stories are more difficult to place solely within the context of metropolitan Britain. Stories like 'Beyond the Pale', 'The Gate of Hundred Sorrows' and 'To Be Filed For Reference', and travel narratives like 'The City of Dreadful Night', show a kinship with *fin-de-siècle* romantic decadence and pessimism. 'The City' also echoes some of Dickens's journalism and satire, and utilises the investigative paradigm of urban slum writing and employs some of its stark images.

Where Haggard's writing accentuates the imperial frontier's presentation of a heroic and romanticised masculinity, Kipling's early stories highlight an Indian landscape which is filled with reminders of her historic achievements and a hybrid urban space that mimics London. If Haggard's stories are based more on a narcissistic appropriation of Zulu culture, Kipling's early Indian stories show the instability of the colonial mirror which might reflect images of self terrorised by its own reflection or images of the Other that threaten the sanctity of the self. Kipling's ambivalent identification can also be located in imaginary figures like Strickland and Kim whose knowledge and feeling for the host culture sets them apart from the ordinary Anglo-Indian; firmly ensconced as policeman and spy, their transgressive excursions are linked irrevocably to the maintenance of colonial power. In characterisation, Kim comes closest to Haggard's imperial appropriation of Zulu culture and marks the changes in Kipling's writing as he moves from colonial to imperial artist. An analysis of the whole text lies outside the scope of this book but it is worth registering, perhaps, that the text of *Kim* is different from Kipling's early Indian work in so far as the text seeks to purge anxiety, fear and conflict from the encounter between Anglo and Indian. Unlike Strickland, who thrives on conflictual relations, Kim is friend to all the world. Hence adjectives of conciliation and syncreticism are often used about *Kim*; in the words of Angus Wilson, 'other books . . . [are] marred by aspects of his social ethic . . . [but] none of these is present in *Kim*' (Wilson, 1977: 185).

The status of both writers is tied to their allegedly authoritative and knowledgeable representations of Africa and India. Haggard's early African fiction attempts to appropriate the mythic space imputed to Zulu cultures through re-writing the history and culture of Zululand, while Kipling speaks of trying 'his best to penetrate' cultures that 'an Englishman can [little] hope to understand'. In Kipling, we find instances of a character who is likened to an anthropologist in that he is depicted as having knowledge of the 'native' world which far exceeds that of ordinary people. Figures like Strickland, Kim and Dravot move in and out of the Indian world as easily as changing clothes; they are both the source of fascinating stories of exotic and strange terrains and are presented as figures on which the transferential dynamics of colonial story-telling are built. I have argued that for Kipling, there is an unmistakable awareness of the narrative dynamics between speaker and listener that produces the authoritative persona of both the one who crosses cultural boundaries and also the narrator who mediates their stories. Authority and knowledge are invested in the story-teller–narrator by virtue of narrative mediation. Narrative mediation is built into the structure of stories like 'The Mark of the Beast', 'The Return of Imray', 'In the House of Suddhoo', 'Beyond the Pale', 'To Be Filed for Reference' and 'The Man Who Would Be King' either through an observer or through a character–narrator who mediates his own or someone else's story. In the last three stories, the narrator is a figure who meets or knows of characters who transgress cultural boundaries and who himself knows something of the thrills of the venture; knowledge and excitement are generated through the transferential dynamics that occur between speaker and listener. Kipling's narrator-persona is represented as one who has a good eye for what makes an interesting story, and in this respect, Kipling's stories owe much to his experience as a journalist.

Although Haggard's stories do not possess the self-conscious awareness of some of Kipling's work, they do invoke the same transferential paradigm, albeit in a much simpler manner. Haggard's manifesto for romance is based on a claimed kinship with folktales, medieval epics and sagas. Lang's praise of Haggard's fiction was based on his powers of story-telling and his ability to create a good 'yarn' to charm young boys, 'cattle drivers' and 'jaded' literary critics (Lang, 1888: 500). Haggard's fiction is characterised by a re-creation of a narrator–story-teller, usually Quatermain, who addresses readers directly and imparts the story of past adventures. While perhaps not as self-conscious as Kipling's or as textually sophisticated as Joseph Conrad or Henry James, Haggard's fiction relies on a persona (often the character Allan Quatermain) *telling* the story of his adventures, or a narrator who acts as mediator between story-teller and listener. In *King Solomon's Mines*, the character–narrator is depicted as the author of the narrative which he dedicates to 'all the big and little boys who read it'. While his story exists imperfectly in printed form (Quatermain offers apologies for his 'blunt way of writing'), the narrator tries to recreate the immediacy of the story-telling. This is done by addressing the reader directly; both in the preface and within the tale, the narrator takes into account the presumed reactions of his audience. As with *King Solomon's Mines*, the sequel, *Allan Quatermain*, is written in the first person interpellative. In this story, the direct relation between Quatermain and reader is sustained through the fictional frame of the diary, and is supplemented by a fellow character, Henry Curtis, after the narrator's death. It is then finally framed by the brother of Curtis who receives the manuscript. In the transition of the manuscript from one character to another, the veracity of the document is assured and secured.

In Haggard's historical romance *Nada the Lily*, the narrative mediations are made across cultural boundaries. The tale is a written account of a story told by an African magician, Mopo, to a white trader in the final nine days of the Zulu's life. Readers are encouraged to believe the account of Zulu history in *Nada* because it is not the white trader's story but Mopo's. If the truth of such stories is tied to the impressions of the hearers of the tale, the sincerity of the story is vouched for by the white trader's assertion that Mopo seemed to relive his experiences in the telling of the tale; the trader remarks, 'it was the past that spoke to his listener, telling of deeds long forgotten, of deeds that are no more known'.

Nada the Lily begins and ends with the death of Mopo. The written historical romance of Zulu destruction is contingent on the silencing of the Zulu subject. In Kipling's stories, if the colonial story is more of an ambivalent struggle with Indian voices, the status of the narrator is enhanced for the struggle. His stories also incorporate a canny manipulation of narrative to seduce readers into a colonial representation of desire. Kipling and Haggard's identifications with the Other of India and Africa produced complex, contradictory and ambivalent stories of empire; they also produced powerful forms of representational dispossession that parallel the dispossession of Empire.

NOTES

INTRODUCTION

1 I am indebted for this expression to Peter Stallybrass and Allon White (Stallybrass and White, 1986).
2 An exception, in the case of Kipling, is *Kim*, published in 1901. I have included *Kim* because it makes a useful comparison to Kipling's Strickland stories and because it was based on a novel that Kipling wrote during his years as a journalist in India.
3 For a definition of the distinction between the specular 'other' and the Symbolic 'Other' in Lacanian psychoanalysis, see Fuss, 1994, and Wright, 1992.
4 Haggard's actual readership would, of course, have far exceeded the figures for his book sales. Walter Besant estimated that only about 400,000 families out of a population of over 40 million would have had enough income to purchase new and expensive books (though Haggard's novels, priced at 6s, would probably have attracted more buyers) (Keating, 1989: 405–408). Thus while it is not possible to ascertain the exact number and nature of Haggard's readership, it is probable that a very broad cross-section of the population did read his fiction. There is also evidence that this readership extended to the working classes, as may be glimpsed from Lady Florence Bell's study of an iron-works community in North Yorkshire (where the average household income per week was often below £4). Of the 200 families in her survey, 16 households had read sea-faring stories, tales of adventure and travel, wild escapes and romances; 'Mrs Henry Wood seven times, Shakespeare twice, Dickens twice, Marie Corelli once, Miss Braddon once, Rider Haggard once'. Haggard's popularity is apparent from library subscriptions; for example, George Gissing in a letter to his sister in July 1887, complained that Mudie had ordered 2,000 copies of *Allan Quatermain* as opposed to a mere 85 of his own novel *Thyrza* (George Gissing, *Letters of George Gissing* (London: Constable, 1927)). Similarly, John Barrie was to object to the libraries' 2,000 copies of *Allan Quatermain* in the absence of a single copy of Hardy's *A Pair of Blue Eyes*. Exasperated at Haggard's popularity, Barrie remarked, 'Saddest is the fate of Mr Stevenson, for Mudie's subscribers read "Kidnapped"

when all the 2,000 copies of "Allan Quatermain" are out' ('Gavin
Ogilvy', *British Weekly*, August 5, 1887).

5 Again, there are some exceptions to the rule; for example, 'Beyond the
Pale' and 'To Be Filed For Reference' appear for the first time in *Plain
Tales*.

CHAPTER 2 THE DOMINION OF SONS

1 For an analysis of gender in the preponderance of pastoral fantasies
in militaristic and authoritarian cultures see Klaus Theweleit, *Male
Fantasies II* (Oxford: Polity Press, 1989), p.67.

2 As Lorna Duffin notes, the perfect lady as 'perfect symbol of status' was
the image of 'conspicuous leisure and . . . consumption'. Her status
gave her 'no purposeful activity but rendered her progressively more
and more useless' and reinforced her incapacity and disablement
(Delemont and Duffin (eds) 1978: 26). Elsewhere the argument linking
femininity and invalidism/death may be found in Gilbert and Gubar,
1984. They write, 'the aesthetic cult of ladylike fragility and delicate
beauty – no doubt associated with the moral cult of the angel-woman
obliged "genteel" women to "kill" themselves . . . into art objects: slim,
pale, passive beings whose "charms" eerily recalled the snowy, porcelain
immobility of the dead. . . . Whether she becomes an *objet d'art* or a
saint, however, it is the surrender of her self . . . that is the beautiful
angel-woman's key act, while it is precisely this sacrifice which dooms
her both to death and to heaven' (p. 25).

3 In Eve Sedgwick's exploration of the political and psychological
tensions between male homosocial desire and homophobia in the
novel *Edwin Drood*, she uncovers a 'de-individualizing, relatively universal Gothic critique of the organisation of male desire' and poses a
question of narrative stability: 'If it collapses the rigid, vulnerable
structures of Jasper's relations to the man and the woman he "loves",
can it stop short of Crisparkle's deeply congruent ones?' Sedgwick's
answer is in the affirmative – the 'jagged edge of a racial faultline across
the novel's plot and setting facilitates that coarse [visible *and* arbitrary]
halving' of the good/bad bond. In my analysis of the male homosocial
community of black and white men in the adventure narrative,
Sedgwick's jagged line of race applies. Race, after all, refers to whole
groups of people; in enacting the marginalisation of women in these
homosocial (not 'homosexual') bonds, Haggard's narratives are
careful to insist on a *temporary* romance between individual people
which deliberately obscures the wider politics of race and sexuality,
nation and colonialism. See Sedgwick, 1985.

CHAPTER 3 MIMESIS OF SAVAGERY

1 As David Welsh reports, the franchise system deliberately ruled out
voting by black peoples. Only those who had immovable property of
£50 or more, or could rent property at £10 a year were entitled to vote;

NOTES

as a black African, one also needed to profess Christianity. In May 1865, the franchise bill was submitted to the Legislative Council to be enacted as Law 11; voters were required to have at least 12 years residence in Natal, seven years' exemption from customary or native law and the usual property qualifications under the 1856 charter. They were also required to have a certificate testifying to good conduct and loyalty by three Europeans, which was to be endorsed by a Justice of the Peace, among others, who was to 'declare that he had no reason to doubt the truth of the information contained in the applicant's certificate and that the voters who signed it were "credible persons"' (Welsh, 1971: 63).

2 The concept and phrase is taken from Taussig, 1987. Taussig's study of the semiotics of terror among the stories of the primitivity of the Putumayo Indians, and the 'epistemic murk' generated by colonial lore, observes a strategic congruence between the 'savagery attributed to the Indians by the colonists' and 'the savagery perpetrated by the colonists in the name of ... civilization'. Taussig's analysis of the colonial representation of Putumayo cannibalism and barbaric practices goes beyond mere projection. It includes the introjection and transformation of the real through image-making: 'And what is put into discourse through the artful storytelling of the colonists is the same as what they practised on the bodies of Indians' (Taussig, 1987: 134). My point with regard to native law is that the status and position of Secretary for Native Affairs was rendered real by an incorporation of what was in part understood, and what was in part projected, as native despotism.

3 'Natal Report of the Expedition sent by the Government of Natal to install Cetywayo as King of the Zulus, in Succession to His Deceased Father, Panda', February 6, 1875, British *Parliamentary Papers* LII, 1878–9. Norman Etherington also makes this point in Dumins and Ballard (eds), 1981.

4 See for example, Robert James Mann, *The Zulus and Boers of South Africa* (London: Edward Standford, 1879) and *The Zulus – By an Ex-Colonial Chaplain* (London: Chapman and Hall, 1879).

5 May 28, 1861: Letters received Natal 1 D25a/233 1860–67, SPG Papers, Rhodes House Library (Oxford). Alice and Ann MacKenzie were both missionary helpers in Southern Africa. From the letter alone, it is not possible to ascertain which of the sisters wrote of the incident between Shepstone and Cetshwayo.

6 See note 3.

7 Story-telling accrues narrative power through its presentation as a death-bed confessional; as Walter Benjamin notes,

> a man's knowledge or wisdom ... is the stuff that stories are made of ... [it] first assumes transmissible form at the moment of his death ... suddenly in his expressions and looks the unforgettable emerges and imparts to everything that concerned him that authority which even the poorest wretch in dying possesses for the living around him. This authority is at the very source of the story.
> (Benjamin, 1973: 94)

271

8 I am indebted to Benita Parry for this expression (Parry, 1988).

TRANSITIONS

1 See Martin's excellent overview of the representation of Zulu culture (Martin, 1982).
2 Anderson himself argues that there is a fundamental 'incomparability of empire and nation' in 'English official nationalism'. His point here is that the restrictive ideology of Englishness does not allow for the incorporation of the peoples that are in all respects culturally English and that *anglicisation* works as a definition that excludes rather than includes colonial subjects from the imagined nation that is England (Anderson, 1983). My point is the corollary of Anderson's; I would argue that the Anglo-Indian community is distinguishable from the imagined community of England because its cultural identity is predicated on separation and exile.

CHAPTER 4 THE COLONIAL UNCANNY

1 The phrase originally signified the country outside Dublin under colonial rule.
2 The narrative does occasionally fall over itself in its hurry to impart the cautionary tale; for example in the middle of Trejago's affair with Bisesa we encounter the following: 'Who or what Durga Charan was, Trejago never inquired; and why in the world he was not discovered and knifed never occurred to him till his madness was over, and Bisesa . . . But this comes later' (p.163). By offering information ahead of the story's internal time sequence, Kipling's story imparts a sense of urgency in the telling of the tale. One could, alternatively, decide that the mistaken use of the *boorka* as a form of disguise indicates Kipling's lack of knowledge, despite the narrative's authoritative pronouncements on Indian customs: why does Trejago wear Muslim female attire to enter a Hindu quarter of the city to court a Hindu woman? Yet such a question may not have been relevant for contemporary British and colonial readers, as it presumes an intimate knowledge of Hindu and Muslim culture. My response would be that in order for the fabular structure to work, the reader must and in all probability will be carried by the narrator's assumption of authority.
3 The fear of castration is the counterpart to the racist and colonial fear of having one's women raped. Its anxieties are both present and exorcised in the lynching of the native body.
4 Mark Paffard argues that the audience for *Plain Tales from the Hills* was located in the 'smoking-room set', pointing out that Andrew Lang and other contemporary critics reviewed Kipling's short stories for a male readership (Paffard, 1989: 45).
5 Knowledge of the forbidden native city and 'object-letters' is something both the narrator and Trejago share. Only experience of the Oriental

world of passion – Trejago's 'dearer, out-of-the-way life' – brings fulfilment. But the authorial exposition, in order to establish its privileged vantage point must also have traversed the boundaries outside its ideological lesson. The narrator parallels Trejago; both have access to forbidden fruit. Both know the references of the text – Jitha Megji's *bustee*, Amir Nath's Gully that 'ends in a dead-wall pierced by one grated window'. Both know where Bisesa resides in the native city. Is the narrator trustworthy? 'Beyond the Pale's trade in structural ambivalences and contradictions makes the text an unstable one.

6 For an account of a different but related series of problems between narrative authority and modern ethnography see Clifford, 1988, chapter one.

7 See for example Watson and Kaye (eds), 1868, which was prepared and initially distributed under the auspices of the colonial authorities.

8 In 'Letters', the 'voice of the city' is differentiated carefully from the political voice of the 'main roads'; the latter can always be trusted to oppose the colonial.

CHAPTER 5 THE CITY OF DREADFUL NIGHT

1 See Abul JanMohamed's reworking of Fanon's theorisation in Jan-Mohamed, 1985. He writes 'The dominant model of power – and interest-relations in all colonial societies is the manichean opposition between the putative superiority of the European and the supposed inferiority of the native . . . the manichean allegory [is] a field of diverse yet interchangeable oppositions between white and black, good and evil, superiority and inferiority, civilization and savagery, intelligence and emotion, rationality and sensuality, self and other, subject and object' (p. 63).

2 I am indebted to John Rignall for this phrase; see Rignall, 1992.

3 The piece on Lahore is found in Kipling, 1897 and the longer piece of writing on Calcutta is found in Kipling 1899a.

4 For an account of Kipling's views of the late century artistic movements see Robert Caserio, 'Kipling in the Light of Failure' in Bloom, 1987.

5 For an alternative critical lineage for Kipling see Arata, 1993, and Sullivan, 1984.

6 The small section in 'The City' on the Eurasian community shows an obsession with unmasking the Eurasian body as only 'appearing' to be English.

7 See Wurgaft, 1983, for the debate between the Punjab tradition (the West, periphery) and the Bengal one (centre, East). The closest parallel to this in the narrative is the construction of the captains of the merchant navy. They conform closely to the 'bronzed, black-moustached, clear-speaking Native Calvary Officer . . . exist[ing] unnaturally in novels, and naturally on the Frontier'. Their marginal existence at sea and at the fringes of the state makes them the parallel of the Frontier Man which Kipling upholds as the very model of 'civility'.

CHAPTER 6 THE COLONIAL MIRROR

1 My understanding of the body and how body-image is crucial to the establishment of human subjectivity is heavily indebted to Elizabeth Grosz's excellent work on the body in psychoanalysis, notably Grosz, 1990. Also see her 'The Body' in Wright, 1992 and *Jacques Lacan: A Feminist Introduction* (London: Routledge, 1990).

2 Freud's definition of the uncanny, which develops the semantic reverberations of the word *heimlich* to *unheimlich* emphasises the ambivalence of the term. His notion of uncanny 'doubling' which touches on alienation and primary narcissism is invoked in Bhabha's politicised conception of mimicry.

3 See Mackenzie, 1984 and Jackie Bratton, 'Theatre of War: the Crimea on the London Stage, 1854–5' in David Bradby *et al.*, 1980.

4 Sara Suleri's remark that Kipling's genius lies in his 'apprehension of the applicability of journalism to imperial narration' is a telling reminder of Kipling's debt to journalism. For journalism revels in novelty and the text's youthful celebration of novelty and its successive 'montage of autonomous moment' is a major part of its picaresque attraction. Suleri also argues that such a wilful 'abnegation of chronology' is congruent with a more generalised colonial disavowal of history as development, maturity and independence. The colonised society is allowed 'neither the precedent of the past nor the anticipation of the future'. See Suleri, 1992.

5 Walter Benn Michaels' analysis of the contemporary racial inflection of culture and cultural identity poses the problem succinctly: 'to be a Navajo you have to do Navajo things, but you can't really count as doing Navajo things unless you already are a Navajo' (Michaels, 1992: 655–685). Kim's early socialisation does not make him any less white; Sahibness is not a matter of cultural behaviour but of cultural identity. The narrator's insistence on making such a distinction inscribes a racial fault-line exactly where one would presume its disappearance.

6 The tradition of disguise is much in evidence in detective, police and 'spy' fiction of the same period: Holmes has antecedents in William Godwin's *Caleb Williams* and Eugene François Vidocq's *Mémoires*.

7 Stocking, 1982, especially chapter 3.

8 Lack might refer to earlier divisions, for example, the child's discovery that s/he is not the exclusive desire of the mother that s/he wishes to be. Accordingly, Oedipal castration anxieties are inscribed retroactively onto these fundamental divisions. In Lacan, the phallus breaks the duality of the mother–child relation by introducing a third term which disrupts its imaginary plenitude; this break grants the child access to the symbolic (and social) world but only under the sign of desire: 'what we meet as an accident in the child's development is linked to the fact that the child does not find himself or herself alone in front of the mother, and that the phallus forbids the child the satisfaction of his or her own desire, which is the desire to be the exclusive desire of the mother' (quoted in Rose, 1986: 32). Victor Smirnoff's analysis of fetishism concurs: 'the relation between mother, child, and the phallus is changed through the function of the *symbolic*

father, the author of the law. The phallus as a signifier becomes the *signifier of desire* (Victor Smirnoff, 'The Fetishistic Transaction' in Lebovici and Widlocher, 1980: 30).

Current re-reading of Freud and Lacan makes the point that lack is fundamental whilst attempts to express this lack are historical and culturally circumscribed. Kaja Silverman for example follows Lacan's premise that lack and division is the condition of subjectivity and that in entering the order of language and culture, the subject 'forfeits' 'any future possibility of wholeness' (Silverman refers to this as 'symbolic castration'). All subsequent relations and activity – especially fantasy – will be directed at attempting to fill this hole or gap. Silverman also argues that the 'fiction' of the ego papers over lack; it is a fantasmatic attempt to 'compensate for symbolic castration'. Slavoj Žižek's work is similar to Silverman's in this respect; Žižek also argues that the lack or gap which the phallus signifies is overlaid on the divisions of self and Other (the mirror stage) and is the condition of/for language. In the resolution of the Oedipal complex, the child takes on the phallus (having it) which positions him as subject/under patriarchal law. But by giving up *being* the phallus, he is also subjected to loss and division; the phallus which promised much turns out to be a fraud. See Silverman, 1992, and Žižek, 1989a.

9 Silverman argues for a careful differentiation between the laws of language, kinship structure and family ideology so that the absence of the penis is not the only way to signify lack.

10 Silverman goes along with the classic Freudian account of fetishistic substitution as a warding-off of the fear of castration, albeit at the cost of further splitting the male fetishist's own identity. But she reads Freud against the ideological grain to turn his account of castration inside out. She argues for a more primary tale of disavowal where the penis emerges as the primary fetish. If the child's entry into culture is premised on being positioned within the signifying chain of lack, the phallus/penis complicity is a disavowal achieved through a projected transfer of castration onto the female subject, where it is signed as the absence of the penis. Silverman argues one can read in Freud's account of disavowal a case of projection where the 'unwanted feature of self' causing anxiety is relocated in another. Whereas in Freud disavowal is posited as 'male defence against *female* lack', it is really a defence against what is in the final analysis *male* lack (Silverman, 1992: 45–47). The penis/phallus conflation sutures lack for the male by investing biological differences with a projected sexual division of the haves and have-nots and the symbolic circulation of all they entail.

11 Letter to Margaret Burne-Jones dated November 28, 1885; *The Kipling Papers* (11/6–7), University of Sussex Manuscripts.

CHAPTER 7 LOAFERS AND STORY-TELLERS

1 See for example, Drandt, 1984.

2 See J. S. Bratton, 'Of England, Home and Duty: The Image of England in Victorian and Edwardian Juvenile Fiction' in MacKenzie, 1988, for an analysis of the child and the imperial ideal.

3 Letter to Margaret Burne-Jones dated January 25, 1888. Kipling's letters to his cousin are found in *The Kipling Papers*, University of Sussex Manuscripts, Box 11, File 6–7.
4 Letter to Margaret Burne-Jones dated November 28, 1885, *ibid.*
5 Letter to Kay Robinson April 30, 1886, *ibid.*, Box 17, File 25.
6 Letter to Edith Mcdonald, *ibid.*, Box 11, File 10.
7 Letter to Kay Robinson dated April 30, 1886, *ibid.*, Box 17, File 25.
8 See Keating, 1989 on literary agents, author's contracts, royalties and book pricing, the Net Book agreement, periodical fiction, libraries and book sales. Keating's book is the single most comprehensive study of the business of letters within the context of the late nineteenth and earlier twentieth century.

CONCLUSION

1 Some of Kipling's work, like Haggard's, also draws attention to the dynamics of male identities which are predicated on national and imperial regimes. Geoffrey Searle, for example, charts Kipling's affiliation with the National Efficiency movement and assesses stories such as 'The Army of a Dream' which promote military conscription as a means of fostering a spirit of national unity (Kennedy and Nicholls, 1981). Lewis Wurgaft and Shamsul Islam, in looking at stories of soldiers and district officers, present a version of Kipling which draws heavily on masculinist and authoritarian structures (Wurgaft, 1983; Islam, 1975). In a similar vein but at a tangent to critics like Islam and Wurgaft, Ann Parry's analysis of Kipling's reception by the Victorian periodical press argues that contemporary reviewers sought to emphasise the masculinity of his work and its glorification of England's superiority (Parry, 1985: 254–263).

BIBLIOGRAPHY

Dates in square parentheses indicate original publication.

Abrams, M. H. (1971), *A Glossary of Literary Terms*, New York: Holt, Rinehart and Winston.

Allen, Charles. (1975), *Plain Tales From the Raj*, London: André Deutsch and the BBC.

Althusser, Louis. (1971), *Lenin and Philosophy and Other Essays*, London: New Left Books.

Altick, Richard D. (1957), *The English Common Reader: A Social History of the Mass Reading Public 1800–1900*, Chicago: University of Chicago Press.

—— (1973), *Victorian People and Ideas*, London: J. M. Dent and Sons.

—— (1978), *The Shows of London*, Cambridge, Mass.: Harvard University Press.

Anderson, Benedict. (1983), *Imagined Communities*, London: Verso Press.

Anderson, Warwick. (1992), 'Medicine as Colonial Discourse', *Critical Inquiry* 18, pp. 506–529.

Arata, Stephen. (1993), 'A Universal Foreignness: Kipling in the Fin-de-Siècle', *English Literature in Transition* 36(1), pp. 7–38.

Arendt, Hannah. (1951), *The Burden of Our Time*, London: Secker and Warburg.

Arnold, David. (1979), 'European Orphans and Vagrants in India in the Nineteenth Century', *Journal of Imperial and Commonwealth History* 7(2), pp.104–127.

—— (1987), 'Touching the Body: Perspectives on the Indian Plague 1896–1900', *Subaltern Studies* 5, pp. 55–90.

—— (1988), *Imperial Medicine and Indigenous Societies*, Manchester: Manchester University Press.

Bakhtin, Mikhail. (1984), *Problems of Dostoevsky's Poetics*, Manchester: Manchester University Press.

Ballhatchet, Kenneth. (1980), *Race, Sex and Class Under the Raj*, London: Weidenfeld and Nicholson.

Barker, Francis, Peter Hulme, Margaret Inversen and Diana Loxley. (1982), *Europe and its Others*, 2 volumes, Colchester: University of Essex.

277

Barratt-Brown, Michael. (1974), *The Economics of Imperialism*, Harmondsworth: Penguin.

Barry, William. (1890), 'Realism and Decadence in French Fiction', *Quarterly Review* 17, pp. 57–90.

Barthes, Roland. (1973), *Mythologies*, London: Paladin.

—— (1975), *S/Z*, London: Jonathan Cape.

Bascom, Tim. (1987), 'Secret Imperialism: The Reader's Response to the Narrator in "The Man Who Would Be King"', *English Literature in Transition*, pp.162–173.

Bedarida, François. (1979), *A Social History of England*, London: Methuen.

Bell, Lady Florence. (1907), *At the Works: A Study of a Manufacturing Town*, London: Edward Arnold.

Benjamin, Walter. (1973), *Illuminations*, Bungay, Suffolk: Fontana.

—— (1983–4), 'Theoretics of Knowledge; Theory of Progress', *The Philosophical Forum* 15(1–2), Fall–Winter, pp.1–40.

Bennett, Tony. (1988), 'The Exhibitionary Complex', *New Formations* 4, Spring, pp. 73–102.

Bettelheim, Bruno. (1988), *The Uses of Enchantment: The Meanings and Importance of Fairy Tales*, Harmondsworth: Penguin, [1975].

Bhabha, Homi. (1983), 'The Other Question', *Screen* 24, November–December, pp.18–36.

—— (1984), 'Of Mimicry and Man: The Ambivalence of Colonial Discourse', *October* 28, Spring, pp.125–133.

—— (1985), 'Signs Taken For Wonders', *Critical Inquiry* 12, Autumn, pp.144–165.

—— (1988), 'The Commitment to Theory', *New Formations* 5, Summer, pp. 5–23.

—— (ed.) (1990), *Nation and Narration*, London: Routledge.

Bird, John. (1965), *Annals of Natal 1495–1845*, volume 1, Cape Town: C. Struik.

Bloom, Harold. (ed.) (1987), *Rudyard Kipling's Kim*, New York: Chelsea House Publications.

—— (1987), *Rudyard Kipling*, New York: Chelsea House Publications.

Bolt, Christine. (1971), *Victorian Attitudes to Race*, London: Routledge and Kegan Paul.

Booth, Michael. (1981), *Victorian Spectacular Theatre 1850–1910*, London: Routledge and Kegan Paul.

Bradby, David, Louis James and Bernard Sharriat. (1980), *Performance and Politics in Popular Drama*, Cambridge: Cambridge University Press.

Brantlinger, Patrick. (1985), 'Africa and the Victorians', *Critical Inquiry* 12, Autumn, pp.166–222.

—— (1988), *Rule of Darkness: British Literature and Imperialism 1830–1914*, Ithaca: Cornell University Press.

Bratton, J. S. (1981), *The Impact of Victorian Children's Fiction*, London: Croom Helm.

Brooks, Peter. (1984), *Reading for the Plot: Design and Intention in Narrative*, Oxford: Clarendon Press.

—— (1994), *Psychoanalysis and Storytelling*, Oxford: Blackwell.

Buchan, John. (1947), *Prester John*, London: Thomas Nelson and Sons, [1910].

—— (1946), *Greenmantle*, London: Thomas Nelson and Sons, [1916].

Buck-Morss, Susan. (1986), 'The Flaneur, the Sandwichman and the Whore: The Politics of Loitering', *New German Critique* 39, Fall, pp. 99–140.

Bullough, Vera. (1976), *Sex, Society and History*, New York: Science History Publications.

Burgin, Victor. (1990), 'Paranoiac Space', *New Formations* 12, Winter, pp. 62–73.

Burke, Kenneth. (1962), *A Grammar of Motives and A Rhetoric of Motives*, Cleveland, Ohio: Meridian Books.

Burton, Sir Richard. (1893), *A Personal Narrative of a Pilgrimage to Al-Madinah and Mecca 2 volumes*, London: Tylston and Edwards.

—— (1924), *Selected Papers on Anthropology, Travel and Exploration*, London: A. M. Philpot.

Byam, W. and R. G. Archibald. (eds) (1921), *The Practice of Medicine in the Tropics*, Volume 1, London: Henry Frowde and Hodder and Stoughton.

Cambridge History of the British Empire (1961), ed. J. Holland Rose, A. P. Newton and E. A. Benians, Cambridge: Cambridge University Press.

Carrington, Charles. (1970), *Rudyard Kipling*, Harmondsworth: Penguin, [1955].

Cawelti, John and Bruce Rosenberg. (1987), *The Spy Story*, Chicago: Chicago University Press.

Chapman, Rowena and Jonathan Rutherford. (eds) (1988), *Male Order: Unwrapping Masculinity*, London: Lawrence and Wishart.

Clark, Robert. (ed.) (1985), *James Fenimore Cooper: New Critical Essays*, London: Vision Press.

Clifford, James and George Marcus. (eds) (1986) *Writing Culture: The Poetics and Politics*, Berkeley and Los Angeles: University of California Press.

Clifford, James. (1988), *The Predicament of Culture*, Cambridge, Mass.: Harvard University Press.

Coetzee, J. M. (1988), *White Writing*, New Haven, Conn.: Yale University Press.

Cohen, Morton. (1960), *Rider Haggard: His Life and Works*, London: Hutchinson.

—— (1965), *Rudyard Kipling to Rider Haggard*, London: Hutchinson.

Cohn, Bernard. (1983), 'Cloth, Clothes and Colonialism: India in the Nineteenth Century', unpublished paper, *Cloth and the Organization of Human Experience Symposium*, Troutbeck, Armenia, New York, September 28th–October 5th.

—— (1989), 'Cloth, Clothes and Colonialism', in Annette Weiner and Jane Schneider (eds), *Cloth and the Human Experience*, Washington: Smithsonian Institute Press.

Coleman, F. M. (1897), *Typical Pictures of Indian Natives*, Bombay and London: Times of London.

Colls, Robert and Philip Dodd. (1986), *Englishness*, London: Croom Helm.

Comaroff, John and Jean Comaroff. (1992), *Ethnography and the Historical Imagination*, Boulder, Col.: Westview Press.

Conan Doyle, Arthur (Sir). (1950), *The Lost World*, London: Pan [1912].

—— (1986), *The Complete Illustrated Sherlock Holmes*, Ware, Hampshire: Omega Books.

Conrad, Joseph. (1963), *Heart of Darkness*, Harmondsworth: Penguin, [1902].

—— (1926) *Last Essays*, London: Dent.

Cornell, Louis. (1966), *Kipling in India*, London: Macmillan.

Cousins, Mark. (1989), 'In the Midst of Psycho-analysis', *New Formations* 7, Spring, pp. 78–87.

Coward, Rosalind and John Ellis. (1977), *Language and Materialism*, London: Routledge and Kegan Paul.

Cruse, Amy. (1935), *The Victorians and Their Books*, London: George Allen and Unwin.

—— (1938), *After the Victorians*, London: George Allen and Unwin.

Cumming, Sir John. (ed.) (1939), *Revealing India's Past*, London: The India Society.

Cunningham, Hugh. (1971), 'Jingoism in 1877–78', *Victorian Studies* 14, Summer, pp. 429–453.

—— (1981), 'The Language of Patriotism 1750–1914', *History Workshop* 12, Autumn, pp. 8–33.

Dabydeen, David. (1985), *The Black Presence in English Literature*, Manchester: Manchester University Press.

Darton, Harvey. (1982), *Children's Books in England: Five Centuries of Social Life*, Cambridge: Cambridge University Press, [1932].

Davis, H. W. C. (1926), 'The Great Game in Asia', *British Academy Raleigh Lecture on History*, 1926.

De Certeau, Michel. (1986), *Heterologies: Discourse on the Other*, Minneapolis, Minn.: University of Minnesota Press.

Delemont, Sara and Lorna Duffin. (eds) (1978), *The Nineteenth Century Woman: Her Cultural and Physical World*, London: Croom Helm.

Denning, Michael. (1987), *Cover Stories*, London: Routledge and Kegan Paul.

Derridà, Jacques. (1976), *Of Grammatology*, Baltimore, Md: Johns Hopkins University Press.

Dickens, Charles. (1899), *Reprinted Pieces*, London: Chapman and Hall.

Dickes, Robert. (1963), 'Fetishistic Behavior: A Contribution to Its Complex Development and Significance', *Journal of American Psychoanalytic Association* 11, pp. 303–330.

Dijkstra, Bram. (1986), *Idols of Perversity*, Oxford: Oxford University Press.

Dollimore, Jonathan. (1991), *Sexual Dissidence*, Oxford: Oxford University Press.

Douglas, Mary. (1984), *Purity and Danger: An Analysis of the Concepts of Pollution and Taboo*, London and New York: Ark, [1966].

Drandt, Manfred. (1984), 'Reality or Delusion? Narrative Technique and Meaning in Kipling's "The Man Who Would Be King"', *English Studies* 65(4), pp. 316–326.

Dumins, Andrew and Charles Ballard. (eds) (1981), *The Anglo-Zulu War: New Perspectives*, Pietermaritzburg: University of Natal.

Dunae, Patrick. (1980), 'Boy's Literature and the Idea of Empire 1870–1914', *Victorian Studies* 24, Autumn, pp. 105–121.

Dyer, Richard. (1987), *Heavenly Bodies*, Basingstoke: Macmillan.

Edwardes, Michael. (1967), *British India 1772–1947: A Survey of the Nature and Effects of Alien Rule*, London: Sidgwick and Jackson.

—— (1969), *Bound to Exile: The Victorians in India*, London: Sidgwick and Jackson.

Ellis, Havelock. (1933), *The Psychology of Sex*, London: Heinemann.

—— (1936), *Studies in the Psychology of Sex*, Volume 2, New York: Random House.

Ellis, Peter. (1978), *Rider Haggard*, London: Routledge and Kegan Paul.

Empson, William. (1950), *Some Versions of Pastoral*, Norfolk, Conn.: New Directions.

Etherington, Norman. (1984), *Rider Haggard*, Boston: Twayne Publishers.

—— (1981), 'Anglo-Zulu Relations 1856–1878' in Andrew Dumins and Charles Ballard (eds), *The Anglo-Zulu War: New Perspectives*, Pieter-maritzburg: University of Natal.

Fabian, Johannes. (1983), *Time and the Other: How Anthropology Makes its Object*, New York: Columbia University Press.

Fanon, Frantz. (1983), *The Wretched of the Earth*, Harmondsworth: Penguin, [1963].

—— (1986), *Black Skin, White Masks*, London: Pluto Press, [1967].

Felman, Shoshana. (ed.) (1982), *Literature and Psychoanalysis*, Baltimore, Md: Johns Hopkins University Press.

Fieldhouse, D. K. (1981), *Colonialism 1870–1945: An Introduction*, London: Weidenfeld and Nicholson.

Flugel, J. C. (1950), *The Psychology of Clothes*, London: Hogarth and the International Psychoanalytical Library.

Foucault, Michel. (1977), *Language, Counter-Memory, Practice*, Oxford: Blackwell.

—— (1979), *Discipline and Punish*, Harmondsworth: Penguin, [1977].

—— (1980), *Power/Knowledge: Selected Interviews and Other Writings 1972–1977*, Brighton: Harvester Press.

Freud, Sigmund. (1925), *Collected Papers IV*, London: Hogarth and the Institute of Psychoanalysis.

—— (1955), *The Standard Edition of the Complete Psychological Works of Sigmund Freud*, Volume 17, London: Hogarth and the Institute of Psychoanalysis.

—— (1964), *The Standard Edition of the Complete Psychological Works of Sigmund Freud*, Volume 23, London: Hogarth and the Institute of Psychoanalysis.

—— (1977), *The Ego and the Id*, London: Hogarth and the Institute of Psychoanalysis.

—— (1977), *On Sexuality*, Harmondsworth: Penguin.

—— (1982), *Civilisation and its Discontents*, London: Hogarth and the Institute of Psychoanalysis, [1930].

Frye, Northrop. (1957), *Anatomy of Criticism*, Princeton, NJ: Princeton University Press.

—— (1976), *The Secular Scripture*, Cambridge, Mass.: Harvard University Press.

Fuss, Diana. (1994), 'Interior Colonies: Frantz Fanon and the Politics of Identification', *Diacritics* 23(2 and 3), pp. 20–42.

Garber, Majorie. (1992), *Vested Interests*, New York: Routledge.

Gilbert, Elliot. (1972), *The Good Kipling*, Manchester: Manchester University Press, [1970].

Gilbert, Sandra and Susan Gubar. (1984), *Madwoman in the Attic*, New Haven: Yale University Press.

—— (1989), *No Man's Land II: Sexchanges*, New Haven: Yale University Press.

Gilman, Sander. (1985), 'Black Bodies, White Bodies: Towards an Iconography of Female Sexuality in Late Nineteenth Century Art, Medicine and Literature', *Critical Inquiry* 12, Autumn, pp. 166–222.

Girouard, Mark. (1981), *The Return to Camelot: Chivalry and the English Gentleman*, New Haven: Yale University Press.

Gloversmith, Frank. (ed.) (1984), *The Theory of Reading*, Brighton: Harvester Press.

Gopal, S. (1965), *British Foreign Policy in India 1858–1905*, Cambridge: Cambridge University Press.

Graham, Kenneth. (1965), *English Criticism of the Novel*, Oxford: Clarendon.

Gramsci, Antonio. (1971), *Selections from Prison Notebooks*, London: Lawrence and Wishart.

—— (1985), *Selections from Cultural Writings*, London: Lawrence and Wishart.

Green, Martin. (1980), *Dreams of Adventure, Deeds of Empire*, London: Routledge and Kegan Paul.

Green, Roger Lancelyn. (1946), *Andrew Lang: A Critical Biography*, Leicester: Edmund Ward.

—— (ed.) (1971), *Kipling: The Critical Heritage*, London: Routledge and Kegan Paul.

Gross, John. (1969), *Rudyard Kipling: The Man, His Work and His World*, London: Weidenfeld and Nicholson.

Grosz, Elizabeth. (1990), 'The Body of Signification' in John Fletcher and Andrew Benjamin (eds), *Abjection, Melancholia and Love*, London: Routledge.

Guy, Jeffrey. (1971), 'A Note on Firearms in the Zulu Kingdom with Special Reference to the Anglo-Zulu War', *The Journal of African History* 12(14), pp. 557–570.

—— (1979), *The Destruction of the Zulu Kingdom*, London: Longman.

Haggard, H. Rider. (1882), *Cetywayo and His White Neighbours*, London: Trubner.

—— (1887a), 'About Fiction', *Contemporary Review* 2, February.

—— (1887b), *Jess*, London: Smith, Elder and Co.

—— (1899), *A Farmer's Year*, London: Longmans, Green and Co.

—— (1902), *Rural England*, London: Longmans, Green and Co.

—— (1905), *The Poor and the Land*, London: Longmans, Green and Co.

—— (1915), *Allan's Wife*, London: Hodder and Stoughton, [1889].

—— (1926), *The Days of My Life*, London: Longmans, Green and Co.

—— (1931), *Allan Quatermain*, London: George Harrap and Co., [1887].

—— (1933), *Nada the Lily*, London: J. M. Dent and Sons, [1892].

—— (1940), *King Solomon's Mines*, London: Cassell, [1885].

—— (1979), *She*, London: Hodder and Stoughton/Coronet, [1887].

Haggard, Lilias Rider. (1951), *The Cloak That I Left Behind*, Ipswich: Boydell Press.

BIBLIOGRAPHY

Haley, Bruce. (1978), *The Healthy Body and Victorian Culture*, Cambridge, Mass.: Harvard University Press.

Hanson, Clare. (1985), *Short Stories and Short Fiction 1880–1980*, London: Macmillan.

Harbord, R. E. (ed.) (1961), *Reader's Guide to Rudyard Kipling's Work*, Volume 1, Kipling Society, Privately Published.

—— (ed.) (1963), *Reader's Guide to Rudyard Kipling's Work*, Volume 2, Kipling Society, Privately Published.

Heath, Stephen. (1986), 'Psychopathia Sexualis: Stevenson's *Strange Case*', *Critical Quarterly* 28(1 and 2), pp. 93–108.

Higgins, D. S. (ed.) (1980), *The Private Diaries of Sir Henry Rider Haggard*, London: Cassell.

—— (1981), *Rider Haggard: A Biography*, New York: Stein and Day.

Hobsbawm, Eric and Terence Ranger. (eds) (1983), *The Invention of Tradition*, Cambridge: Cambridge University Press.

Hollis, Patricia. (ed.) (1979), *Women in Public 1850–1900: Documents of the Victorian Women's Movement*, London: Allen and Unwin.

Houghton, Walter. (1957), *The Victorian Frame of Mind*, New Haven, Conn.: Yale University Press.

Howe, Susan. (1974), *Novels of Empire*, New York: Columbia University Press.

Husain, S. S. (1964), *Kipling and India*, Dacca: University of Dacca Press.

Islam, Shamsul. (1975), *Kipling's Law: A Study of His Philosophy of Life*, London: Macmillan.

Jacobus, Mary. (1986), *Reading Woman*, New York: Columbia University Press.

James, Louis. (1963), *Fiction For the Working Man 1830–1850*, Oxford: Oxford University Press.

—— (1973), 'Tom Brown's Imperial Sons', *Victorian Studies* 17, September, pp. 89–99.

Jameson, Fredric. (1981), *The Political Unconscious: Narrative as a Socially Symbolic Act*, London: Methuen.

JanMohamed, Abul. (1985), 'The Economy of the Manichean Allegory', *Critical Inquiry* 12, Autumn, pp. 59–87.

Jeal, Tim. (1989), *Baden Powell*, London: Hutchinson.

Jeffrey, Robin. (ed.) (1978), *People, Princes and Paramount Power: Society and Politics in the Princely States*, New Delhi: Oxford University Press.

Joshi, Svati. (ed.) (1991), *Rethinking English: Essays in Literature, Language, History*, New Delhi: Trianka.

Kanta Ray, Rajat. (1984), *Social Conflict and Political Unrest in Bombay 1875–1927*, New Delhi: Open University Press.

Katz, Wendy. (1987), *Rider Haggard and the Fiction of Empire*, Cambridge: Cambridge University Press.

Kaye, J. (1890), *History of the War in Afghanistan*, London: Allen Lane.

Keating, Peter. (ed.) (1971a), *Working Class Stories of the 1890's*, London: Routledge and Kegan Paul.

—— (1971b), *The Working Class in Victorian Fiction*, London: Routledge and Kegan Paul.

—— (ed.) (1976), *Into Unknown England 1866–1913*, London: Fontana.

283

—— (1989), *The Haunted Study*, London: Secker and Warburg.

Kemp, Tom. (1967), *Theories of Imperialism*, London: Dennis Dobson.

Kennedy, Paul and Anthony Nicholls. (1981), *Nationalist and Radicalist Movements in Edwardian Britain and Germany before 1914*, London: Macmillan.

King, Anthony. (1976), *Colonial Urban Development*, London: Routledge and Kegan Paul.

Kipling, Rudyard. (1897), *Life's Handicap*, London: Macmillan, [1891].

—— (1898), *Plain Tales From the Hills*, London: Macmillan, [1888].

—— (1906), *Puck of Pook's Hill*, Leipzig: Bernhard Tauchnitz.

—— (1907), *The Light that Failed*, London: Macmillan, [1891].

—— (1912), *Kim*, London: Macmillan, [1901].

—— (1914), *Wee Willie Winkle and Other Stories*, London: Macmillan, [1895].

—— (1919a), *From Sea to Sea: Letters of Travel*, Volume 1, London: Macmillan, [1899].

—— (1919b), *From Sea to Sea: Letters of Travel*, Volume 2, London: Macmillan, [1899].

—— (1928), *The Book of Words*, London: Macmillan.

—— (1937), *Something of Myself*, London: Macmillan.

—— (1969), *The Definitive Edition of Rudyard Kipling's Verse*, London: Hodder and Stoughton, [1940].

Kline, Benjamin. (1988), *The Genesis of Apartheid*, Lanham (Maryland) and London: University Press of America.

Krafft Ebing, Richard von. (1978), *Psychopathia Sexualis*, New York: Stein and Day.

Lacan, Jacques. (1977), *Ecrits: A Selection*, London: Tavistock.

—— (1977), *The Four Fundamental Concepts of Psycho-Analysis*, London: Hogarth and the Institute of Psychoanalysis.

Lang, Andrew. (1887), 'Realism and Romance', *Contemporary Review* 52, November, pp. 683–693.

—— (1888), 'A Dip in Criticism', *Contemporary Review* 54, October, pp. 495–503.

—— (1889), 'Alexandre Dumas', *Scribner's Magazine* 6(3), September, pp. 220–270.

—— (1891), *Essays in Little*, London: Henry and Co.

—— (ed.) (1893), *The True Story Book*, London: Longmans, Green and Co.

Laplanche, J. and J. B. Pontalis. (1983), *The Language of Psychoanalysis*, London: Hogarth and the Institute of Psychoanalysis.

Lebovici, Serge and Daniel Widlocher. (1980), *Psychoanalysis in France*, New York: International Universities Press.

Lee, Alan. (1976), *The Origins of the Popular Press in England 1855–1914*, London: Croom Helm.

Lenin, V. I. (1939), *Imperialism, the Highest State of Capitalism*, New York: International Publishers.

Lévi-Strauss, Claude. (1987), *Introduction to Marcel Mauss*, London: Routledge and Kegan Paul.

Lloyd, David. (1991), 'Race Under Representation', *Oxford Literary Review* 13(1 and 2), pp. 62–94.

London, Jack. (1903), *The People of the Abyss*, London: Macmillan.

Low, Gail Ching-Liang. (1989), 'White Skins/Black Masks: The Pleasures and Politics of Imperialism', *New Formations* 9, Winter, pp. 83–103.
—— (1990), 'His Stories? Narratives and Images of Imperialism', *New Formations* 12, Winter, pp. 97–123.
Ludlow, W. R. (1882), *Zululand and Cetewayo*, London: Simpson, Marshall and Co.
Lyall, Alfred. (1894), 'History and Fable', *Quarterly Review* 178, pp. 31–51.
—— (1895), 'Novels of Adventure and Manners', *Quarterly Review* 179, pp. 530–552.
McClure, John. (1981), *Kipling and Conrad*, Cambridge, Mass.: Harvard University Press.
MacDonald, Robert. (1986), 'Discourse and Ideology in Kipling's "Beyond the Pale"', *Studies in Short Fiction* 23(4), Fall, pp. 413–418.
McGrane, Bernard. (1989), *Beyond Anthropology: Society and the Other*, New York: Columbia University Press.
Macherey, Pierre. (1978), *A Theory of Literary Production*, London: Routledge and Kegan Paul.
Mackenzie, John. (1984), *Propaganda and Empire*, Manchester: Manchester University Press.
—— (ed.) (1988), *Imperialism and Popular Culture*, Manchester: Manchester University Press.
Macleod, Roy and Lewis, Milton. (eds) (1988), *Disease, Medicine and Empire*, London: Routledge.
Mallett, Philip. (ed.) (1989), *Kipling Considered*, Basingstoke: Macmillan.
Mangan, James. (1981), *Athleticism in the Victorian and Edwardian Public School*, Cambridge: Cambridge University Press.
—— (1985), *The Games Ethic and Imperialism*, Harmondsworth: Viking.
—— and James Walvin. (eds) (1988), *Manliness and Morality: Middle-Class Masculinity in Britain and America*, Manchester: Manchester University Press.
Marks, Shula. (1970), *Reluctant Rebellion: The 1906–8 Disturbances in Natal*, Oxford: Clarendon Press.
Martin, Sir James Ranald. (1861), *The Influence of Tropical Climates on European Constitutions*, London: John Churchill.
Martin, Samuel John Russell. (1982), *British Images of the Zulu 1820–1879*, Unpublished doctoral dissertation, University of Cambridge.
Mason, Philip. (1975), *Kipling: The Glass, The Shadow and the Fire*, London: Cape.
—— (1982), *The English Gentleman: The Rise and Fall of an Ideal*, London: André Deutsch.
Masterman, Charles. (1901), *The Heart of the Empire*, London: Unwin.
—— (1905), *In Peril of Change: Essays Written in the Time of Tranquillity*, London: Fisher Unwin.
—— (1909), *The Condition of England*, London: Methuen.
Mayhew, Henry. (1968), *London Labour and London Poor*, Volume 1, New York: Dover, [1861].
Meath, Lord. (1908), 'Have we the "Grit" of our Forefathers?', *The Nineteenth Century* 64, September, pp. 421–429.
Mendus, Susan and Jane Rendall. (eds) (1989), *Sex and Subordination*, London: Routledge and Kegan Paul.

Michaels, Walter Benn. (1992), 'Race into Culture: A Critical Genealogy of Cultural Identity', *Critical Inquiry* 18, Summer, pp. 655–685.

Miles, Robert. (1993), *Gothic Writing 1750–1820*, London: Routledge.

Miller, Jacques-Alain. (1988), *The Seminar of Jacques Lacan: Book I: Freud's Papers on Technique 1953–1954*, Cambridge: Cambridge University Press.

Mohanty, Chandra Talpade. (1988), 'Under Western Eyes', *Feminist Review* 3, Autumn, pp. 61–88.

Mohanty, S. P. (1989), 'Kipling's Children and the Colour Line', *Race and Class* 31(1), July–Sept, pp. 23–39.

Moore, W. J. (1874), *A Manual of Family Medicine for India*, London: J. and A. Churchill.

—— (1883), *A Manual of Family Medicine for India*, London: J. and A. Churchill.

Moore-Gilbert, Bart. (1978), *The Imperial Idea in Some Modern Fiction*, Unpublished MA dissertation, University of Durham.

—— (ed.) (1983), *Literature and Imperialism*, London: Roehampton Institute.

—— (1986), *Kipling and 'Orientalism'*, London: Croom Helm.

Morris, Donald. (1969), *The Washing of Spears: A History of the Zulu Nation Under Shaka and its Fall in the Zulu War of 1879*, London: Cape, [1965].

Moss, Robert. (1982), *Rudyard Kipling and the Fiction of Adolescence*, London: Macmillan.

Mulvey, Laura. (1975), 'Visual Pleasure and Narrative Cinema', *Screen* 16(3), Autumn, pp. 6–18.

—— (1981), 'Afterthoughts on Visual Pleasure', *Framework* 15–17, Summer, pp. 12–15.

Neale, Steve. (1979–1980), 'The Same Old Story', *Screen Education* 30–34, Autumn/Winter, pp. 33–37.

—— 'Masculinity as Spectacle', *Screen* 24(6), pp. 2–17.

Nelson, Cary and Lawrence Grossberg. (1988), *Marxism and the Interpretation of Culture*, Urbana and Chicago: University of Illinois Press.

Neuburg, Victor. (1977), *Popular Literature: A History and Guide*, Harmondsworth: Penguin.

Novak, Max and Edward Dudley. (eds) (1972), *The Wild Man Within*, Pittsburg: University of Pittsburg Press.

Nowell-Smith, Simon. (1958), *The House of Cassell, 1848–1958*, London: Cassell.

O'Day, Alan. (ed.) (1979), *The Edwardian Age: Conflict and Stability 1900–1914*, Hamden: Archon Books.

Oldershaw, Lucien. (ed.) (1904), *England: A Nation*, London: Brimley Johnson.

Orel, Harold. (ed.) (1983), *Interviews and recollections I*, London: Macmillan.

Orwell, George. (1960), *Critical Essays*, London: Secker and Warburg.

Owen, Roger and Bob Sutcliffe. (1972), *Studies in the Theory of Imperialism*, London: Longman.

Pakenham, Thomas. (1982), *The Boer War*, London: Futura.

Parr, Henry Hallam. (1880), *A Sketch of the Kaffir and Zulu Wars*, London: Kegan Paul.

Parry, Anne. (1985), 'Reading Formations in the Victorian Press: The

Reception of Kipling 1888–1891', *Literature and History* 11(2), Autumn, pp. 254–263.

Parry, Benita. (1972), *Delusions and Discoveries*, London: Allen Lane.

—— (1983) *Conrad and Imperialism: Ideological Boundaries and Visionary Frontiers*, London: Macmillan.

—— (1987) 'Problems in Current Theories of Colonial Discourse', *Oxford Literary Review* 9, pp. 26–58.

—— (1988), 'The Contents and Discontents of Kipling's Imperialism', *New Formations* 6, Winter, pp. 49–63.

Phillips, C., H. C. Singh and B. N. Pandey. (1962), *Select Documents on the History of India and Pakistan Vol IV: The Evolution of India and Pakistan 1858–1947*, London: Oxford University Press.

Pick, Daniel. (1989), *Faces of Degeneration*, Cambridge: Cambridge University Press.

Pinney, Thomas. (1986), *Kipling's India: Uncollected Sketches 1884–1888*, Basingstoke: Macmillan.

Platt, Kate. (1923), *The Home and Health in India*, London: Baillière, Tindall and Cox.

Pollock, Griselda. (1988), 'Vicarious Excitements: *London: A Pilgrimage* by Gustave Doré and Blanchard Jerrold 1872', *New Formations* 4, Spring, pp. 25–50.

Poole, Adrian. (1975), *Gissing in Context*, London: Macmillan.

Porter, Bernard. (1975), *The Lion's Share: A Short History of British Imperialism 1850–1970*, London: Longman.

Pratt, Mary. (1985), 'Scratches on the Face of the Country', *Critical Inquiry* 12, Autumn, pp. 119–143.

—— (1992), *Imperial Eyes*, New York: Routledge.

Praz, Mario. (1970), *The Romantic Agony*, Oxford: Oxford University Press.

Propp, Vladimir. (1958), *Morphology of the Folktale*, Bloomington: Indiana Research Centre in Anthropology.

Racinet, Albert. (1988), *The Historical Encyclopedia of Costume*, London: Studio Editions.

Raskin, Jonah. (1971), *The Mythology of Imperialism*, New York: Random House.

Ray, Rajat. (1979), *Urban Roots of Indian Nationalism: Pressure Groups and Conflict of Interest in Calcutta City Politics 1875–1939*, New Delhi: Vikas Publishing House.

Read, Donald. (1982), *Edwardian England*, London: Croom Helm.

Ridley, Hugh. (1983), *Images of Imperial Rule*, London: Croom Helm.

Rignall, John. (1992), *Realist Fiction and the Strolling Spectator*, London: Routledge.

Robinson, Ronald and John Gallagher with Alice Denny. (1981), *Africa and the Victorians: The Official Mind of Imperialism*, London: Macmillan, [1961].

Rosaldo, Renato. (1989), 'Imperialist Nostalgia', *Representations* 26, Spring, pp. 107–122.

Rose, Jacqueline. (1984), *Peter Pan and the Impossibility of Children's Fiction*, London: Macmillan.

—— (1986), *Sexuality in the Field of Vision*, London: Verso.

Ross, Revd J. (1854), *The Parish of St James with Pockthorpe* [pamphlet].

Royal Commission on the Sanitary Conditions of the Army in India, (1863).

Russell, William. (1860), *My Diary in the Years 1858–9*, 2 Volumes, London: Routledge, Warne and Routledge.

Rutherford, Andrew. (1965), *Kipling's Mind and Art*, London: Oliver Boyd, [1964].

Said, Edward. (1978), *Orientalism*, London: Routledge and Kegan Paul.

—— (1987), '*Kim*, the Pleasures of Imperialism', *Raritan* 7(2), Fall, pp. 27–64.

Saintsbury, George. (1887), 'The Present State of the Novel', *Fortnightly Review* 42, Sept, pp. 410–417.

Sandison, Alan. (1967), *The Wheel of Empire*, London: Macmillan.

Schiebinger, Londa. (1993), *Nature's Body*, Boston: Beacon Press.

Schilder, Paul. (1970), *The Image and Appearance of the Human Body*, New York: International Universities Press.

Schreuder, D. M. (1980), *The Scramble for South Africa 1877–1895*, Cambridge: Cambridge University Press.

Searle, Geoffrey. (1971), *The Quest For National Efficiency*, Oxford: Basil Blackwell.

Sedgwick, Eve Kosofsky. (1985), *Between Men: English Literature and Male Homosocial Desire*, New York: Columbia University Press.

Seltzer, Mark. (1992), *Bodies and Machines*, New York: Routledge.

Shanks, Edward. (1940), *Rudyard Kipling*, London: Macmillan.

Shannon, Richard. (1984), *The Crisis of Imperialism*, London: Paladin, [1974].

Shaw, Valerie. (1983), *The Short Story: A Critical Introduction*, London: Longman.

Shelley, Percy Bysshe. (1988), *Shelley: Poetical Works*, Oxford: Oxford University Press.

Showalter, Elaine. (1987), *The Female Malady*, London: Virago, [1985].

Silverman, Kaja. (1992), *Male Subjectivities at the Margins*, New York: Routledge.

Smith, Sheila. (1980), *The Other Nation*, Oxford: Oxford University Press.

Solarides, C. (1960), 'Development of Fetishistic Perversions', *Journal of American Psychoanalytic Association* 8, April, pp. 281–311.

Spivak, Gayatri. (1986), 'Imperialism and Sexual Difference', *Oxford Literary Review* 8 (1 and 2), pp. 225–239.

Springhall, John. (1977), *Youth, Empire and Society*, London: Croom Helm.

Stallybrass, Peter and Allon White. (1986), *The Politics and Poetics of Transgression*, London: Methuen.

Stedman Jones, Gareth. (1971), *Outcast London*, Oxford: Oxford University Press.

Stevenson, R. L. (1948), *Treasure Island*, London: Collins, [1883].

—— (1925), *Memoirs and Portraits*, London: William Heinemann.

—— (1977), *The Strange Case of Dr Jekyll and Mr Hyde and Other Stories*, London: J. M. Dent and Sons, [1886].

Stocking, George. (1982), *Race, Culture and Evolution*, Chicago: University of Chicago Press.

—— (1987), *Victorian Anthropology*, New York: Free Press.

Stoller, Robert. (1975), *Sex and Gender II: The Transexual Experiment*, London: Hogarth and the Institute of Psychoanalysis.

Stott, Rebecca. (1989), 'The Dark Continent: Africa as Female Body in Haggard's Adventure Fiction', *Feminist Review* 32, Summer, pp. 69–87.

Street, Brian. (1975), *The Savage in Literature*, London: Routledge and Kegan Paul.

Studlar, Gaylyn. (1988), *In the Realm of Pleasure: Von Sternberg, Dietrich and the Masochistic Aesthetic*, Urbana and Chicago: University of Illinois Press.

Suleri, Sara. (1992), *The Rhetoric of English India*, Chicago: University of Chicago Press.

Sullivan, Zoreh. (1984), 'Kipling the Nightwalker', *Modern Fiction Studies* 30(2), Summer, pp. 217–235.

Tanner, Tony. (1983), *Adultery in the Novel*, Baltimore: Johns Hopkins University Press.

Taussig, Michael. (1987), *Shamanism, Colonialism and the Wild Man*, Chicago: University of Chicago Press.

Theweleit, Klaus. (1987, 1989), *Male Fantasies I and II*, Oxford: Polity Press.

Thompson, F. M. L. (1963), *English Landed Society in the Nineteenth Century*, London: Routledge and Kegan Paul.

Tompkins, J. M. S. (1959), *The Art of Rudyard Kipling*, London: Methuen.

Troup, Freda. (1975), *South Africa: A Historical Introduction*, Harmondsworth: Penguin.

Turner, Victor. (1977), *The Ritual Process*, Ithaca, NY: Cornell University Press.

Van Wyk Smith, Malvern and Don Maclennan. (1983), *Olive Schreiner and After: Essays of South African Literature in Honour of Guy Butler*, Cape Town: David Philip.

Vicinus, Martha. (1977), *A Widening Sphere: Changing Roles of Victorian Women*, London: Methuen.

Viswanthan, Gauri. (1990), 'The Beginnings of English Literary Study in British India', *Oxford Literary Review* 8 (1 and 2), pp. 2–25.

—— (1990), *Masks of Conquest*, London: Faber and Faber.

Watson, John Forbes. (1867), *The Textile Manufactures and Costumes of the People of India*, London: W. H. Allen and Co.

Watson, John Forbes and John Kaye. (1868–1875), *The People of India*, 8 Volumes, London: India Museum.

Weeks, Jeffrey. (1981), *Sex Politics and Society*, London: Longman.

Weintraub, Joseph. (1975), 'Andrew Lang: Critic of Romance', *English Literature in Transition* 18, pp. 5–20.

Welsh, Alexander. (1971), *The City of Dickens*, Cambridge, Mass.: Harvard University Press.

Welsh, David. (1971), *The Roots of Segregation: Native Policy in Colonial Natal 1845–1910*, Cape Town: Oxford University Press.

Widdowson, Peter. (ed.) (1982), *Re-reading English*, London: Methuen.

Wiener, Martin. (1981), *English Culture and the Decline of the Industrial Spirit 1850–1980*, Cambridge: Cambridge University Press.

Williams, Raymond. (1985), *The Country and the City*, London: Hogarth, [1973].

Wilson, Angus. (1979), *The Strange Ride of Rudyard Kipling*, London: Granada.

Wollen, Peter. (1987), 'Fashion/Orientalism/The Body', *New Formations* 1, Spring, pp. 5–33.

Wolseley, Garnet. (1888), 'The Negro as Soldier', *Fortnightly Review* 44, December, pp. 689–703.

Woodruff, Charles. (1905), *The Effects of Tropical Light on White Men*, New York and London: Reloman.

Wright, Elizabeth. (1984), *Psychoanalysis and Criticism*, London: Methuen.

—— (ed.) (1992), *Feminism and Psychoanalysis: A Critical Dictionary*, Oxford: Basil Blackwell.

Wurgaft, Lewis. (1983), *The Imperial Imagination: Magic and Myth in Kipling's India*, Middletown, Conn.: Wesleyan University Press.

Yeo, Eileen and Stephen Yeo. (eds) (1981), *Popular Culture and Class Conflict 1590–1914: Explorations in the History of Labour and Leisure*, Brighton: Harvester Press.

Younghusband, Capt G. J. (1890), *Frays and Forays*, London: Percival.

Žižek, Slavoj. (1989a), *The Sublime of Ideology*, London: Verso.

—— (1989b), 'The Undergrowth of Enjoyment: How Popular Culture Can Serve as an Introduction to Lacan', *New Formations* 9, Winter, pp. 7–29.

INDEX

Page numbers in **bold** denote major section/chapter devoted to subject

acclimatization 17, 28–9, 192
Africa: creation of Locations in 7, 68, **71–5**, 83; image of an 'inflicted continent' 29–30; need for imperial paramountcy in 80–1; subversion of chieftain authority 80, 84; version of pastoralism in 39–42; *see also* Natal
African(s): exhibitions of 25–8, 30; *see also* Zulus
Allan Quatermain 4, 6, 17, 64, 65, 66, 83; bonding across racial divide 61–2; dissatisfaction with modern society 37; exclusion of foreigners policy 82–3; gendering of nature as female 48; Masai description 51–2; narrator 267; pastoral idyll 37–8, 265; women in 47
Allan's Wife 40–2; colonial fantasy of virgin territory 40–2; dedication in, 42–3, 44, 45, 46; gendering of nature as female 48–9; pastoralism 38–9, 42–3; women's link with primitivity 62–3, 64
Amber 144, 154
Anderson, Benedict 108
Anglo-Indian community: alienation experienced by 108, 110, 118, 122, 141–2; conflict with Britain 109; disavowal of in 'The City of Dreadful Night' 189–90; division into two halves in colonial city 158; importance of newspapers to 108; in 'Letters of Marque' *see* 'Letters of Marque'; paranoia over native threat to 114–15, 158–61; *see also* colonial city
Anglo–Zulu War 81, **90–103**, 104; Haggard's representation of 96–100; heroism seen through Zulu warriors 55–9, 93, 95–6; origins 90–1; reporting of in family weeklies 55, 90, 91–5
anthropology 2, 24–5, 31–2, 72
Arata, Stephen 235
Arendt, Hannah 36
Arnold, David 29, 241
'At the End of the Passage' 155

Baartman, Sarah 23
Baden-Powell, Lord 53–4
Balfour, Andrew 29
Bascom, Tim 120, 245, 246–7, 249, 250
Bengalis 175, 177; depiction of babu in 'The City of Dreadful Night' 178–80, 182, 185–6
Benjamin, Walter 2, 255
Besant, Sir Walter 255
'Beyond the Pale' 115, **130–5**, 136;

Biesa's mutilation as projection of Trajago's castration 133–4; desire for Other 135; focus on inter-social not intra-social relations 125, 134; as moral fable 130–2, 135; narrator 134, 136; questioning of Trejago's sexuality 132–3

Bhabha, Homi 1, 124, 147, 181, 193; and colonial identity 196–7, 198–200; on pleasure/unpleasure 3, 114; racial fetishism 224–6

Birdwood, Vere 164

black body *see* body

body: and clothes 227 *see also* cross-cultural dressing; colonial **24–30**; and cult of masculine Christianity 19–20, 60; cultural **30–5**; and degeneration 17–18, 19; functions as 13; gendered **21–4**; heroism of white man seen through black 58–60; identification and racial **195–200**; imaging of black as idealised counterpart for white reader 6, 62; linking of mind and 19; mirrored 193–5, 197; nudity of black against clothed white 54–5, 59–60; principle of healthy 13, 19–20; projection of physicality by black 60; sexualisation of black 53–4, 55

body image 192, 193–4, 195, 196, 227

Boondi 136, 138–9, 140; Palace of 153–4

Booth, Michael 206

boy(hood) 7, 238; 'anthropology' of 31, 33; building of character 20–1; link with colonialism 44–5; link with imperialism 36; and pastoralism 44–6, 75; and romance 32, 33, 45–6

Brantlinger, Patrick 114

Britain: fear for vulnerability of 13–14; importance of Empire to 14; *see also* England

'Bronckhorst Divorce-Case, The' 216, 217, 230

Brooks, Peter 134, 231, 249

Buck-Morss, Susan 172

Burgin, Victor 196

Burke, Kenneth 43

Burne-Jones, Margaret: Kipling's letters to 233, 257

Burton, Sir Richard 3, 209–10

Calcutta 191; division of spaces in 182–3; importance to Britain 175; system of administration 176–7; *see also* 'City of Dreadful Night, The'

Canning, Lord 106, 107

cantonments 158–60

Carlyle, Thomas 19

Carrington, Charles 5, 7, 169

Cetshwayo 75, 89; coronation 84, 87–8; depicted in *Illustrated London News* 91–2; meeting with Shepstone 86, 88–9

Cetywayo and His White Neighbours 4, 68, 81

Charter Act (1833) 107

Chelmsford, Lord 99, 101

childhood *see* boy(hood)

Chitor 150, 154

Christian masculinity 19–20, 60

'City of Dreadful Night, The' (1885) 168, 171–2

'City of Dreadful Night, The' (1888) **156–90**, 257; disavowal of contemporary Anglo-Indian society 189–90; hostility towards Bengali babu 178–80, 182, 185–6; hybrid contamination 187–9; imitation of Calcutta as London 8, 156–7, 171, 173–4, 181, 187, 191, 194; narrator 174, 177, 182, 184–5; native quarters in 181–2, 183, 185; prostitution 186; role of policeman in 182, 183, 184–5; similarity to Dickens 183–4; undermining of Calcutta's local government proceedings 177, 178–9

'City of Dreadful Night, The' (Thomson poem) 168–9

Civil and Military Gazette (*CMG*) 4, 7
Clifford, James 135
clothes *see* costume
Cohn, Bernard 105, 107, 144
Coleman, F.M. 204
colonial city **158–68**, 191; cantonments 158–60; depiction of native quarters in 'Typhoid at Home' 166–7; establishment of culture through anxiety of contagion 162–4; native city seen as danger to health of 158–61, 162–3; picture of decadence in *The Light That Failed* 169–70; versus native city 165; *see also* 'City of Dreadful Night, The'
colonial identity 191, 193, 196–200
'colonial uncanny': meaning of 114
Comaroff, John and Jean 29
Conrad, Joseph 45, 50, 113, 247
Contagious Diseases Acts 159
Cornell, Louis 243–4
Cornwallis, Lord 105, 176
costume: and acclimatisation 192; effect on body schema 227; and knowledge 220–1; participation in metamorphosis 219–20; Victorian indulgence of exotic 192, 203, 204–5, 206–7; *see also* cross-cultural dressing
cross-class dressing 219–20, 236–7
cross-cultural dressing 192; and the black body 54, 60; in Burton's *Pilgrimage* 209–11; and cross-class dressing 219–20; empowerment and 54, 230, 227–8, 232–3; and fantasy 220, 227, 232; in *Kim* 192, 200, 202–3, 207–9, 230; and Lawrence of Arabia 228–9; linked to espionage 209; in narrative 232; need for proclamation of white identity in 211, 212–15, 220, 230; and racial fetishism 223–6, 227, 232; and Strickland character 192,

216–17, 218, 230; and surveillance 218, 223; and Trejago character 133; voyeurism 223; *see also* transvestism
cross-dressing, sexual *see* transvestism
Cunningham, Alexander 145
Cuvier, Georges 23, 24

Darwin, Charles 22, 23, 63
Days of My Life 67
degeneration, urban 15–16; link to body 17–18, 19; theory of hereditary 17
Departmental Ditties 5
diamond boom 79, 83
Dickens, Charles 185; attack on parish government 177–8; 'On Duty with Inspector Field' 16, 183–4; similarity to Kipling 183–4, 265
disease: Anglo-Indian's fear of from natives 114–15, 158–61; establishment of culture through anxiety of 162–4; preoccupation of early colonial medicine 29–30
disguise *see* cross-cultural dressing
Diver, Maud 109, 141
Dollimore, Jonathan 22
Douglas, Mary, *Purity and Danger* 162, 163, 165
Dufferin, Lord 106

'Earthmen from Natal' (exhibition) 25–6, 28
East India Company 104–5
Edwardes, Michael 108
effeminacy, and corruption of manliness 20, 21, 22, 93
Empson, William 43
England: concern with urban poverty 15–16; pastoralisation of 18; urban degeneration 16–17; *see also* Britain
environmentalism: and race 16–17
Etherington, Norman 89
ethnography 2

ethnology 24, 25, 31
exhibition, of Africans at St George Gallery 25–8, 30

Fabian, Johannes 24, 72
Fanon, Frantz 156, 165, 193, 195, 196–7, 227–8
fantasy 39, 264; and cross-cultural dressing 220, 227, 232; division between reality and 2, 8–9
Fantis 30
femininity: body politic articulated against concept 21; gendering of nature 48–50; link with invalidism 34, 49, 270n; and primitivity 23–4, 62–4; and separate spheres ideology 22–3; *see also* women
fetishism: Bhabha's reading of 224–5; defined 223–4; Freud's theory 224, 225, 261–2; racial **221–6**, 232; sexual 225, 226
Firminger, T. 161
folklore 31–2, 35
Foucault, Michel 148–9, 183
Freud: on ego 193, 197; *heimlich/ unheimlich* 114; theory of fetishism 224, 225, 261–2
Frye, Northrop 42, 46
Fuss, Diana 196

Garber, Marjorie 226, 227, 228
'Gate of the Hundred Sorrows, The' 171
Gibbon, Edward 19
Gilman, Sander 23
Godwin, George 219
Gopal, S. 106
Gosse, Edmund 121, 223, 236, 262
gothic 113–14, 115; Kipling's use of 114, 191; use of in describing Native States in 'Letters of Marque' 137, 148, 149–50, 151–4
Graphic, reporting of Anglo–Zulu War 90, 91, 94, 96, 102
Green, Martin 96, 98
Greenwood, James 219
Grosz, Elizabeth 194–5

Guy, Jeffrey 89, 95–6

Haggard, Henry Rider 109; ability to portray Zulu culture 5, 6, 9, 90; background 3–4; 'boy' in fiction of *see* boy(hood); on Britain's declining fortunes 14; on colonial policy in Natal 68, 69–70; critical assessment 264–5, 266; defence of violence in novels 32–3; gendering of nature as female 48–50; gift of savagery 5, 85; narrative mediations 267; and pastoralism 7, 18–19, 39–40, 265; popularity 6; presentation of heroic masculinity through romanticised image of Zulu 7, 35, 96, 104, 264–5; preoccupation with justification of white presence in Africa 42; readership 269n; representation of Zulu battles 96–100; romance in writings of 46–7, 267; and Shepstone 4, 66–7, 87–8; storytelling 85, 267; *see also individual titles*
Haley, Bruce 34
Harrison, James 245
Hastings, William 104, 105
health: and body 19–20; concern for in Anglo-Indian community 158–61; concern for urban poverty and degeneration 15–18; *see also* disease
heroism 50; seen through bravery of Zulus 55–9, 93, 95–6
Holmes, Sherlock: similarity to Strickland character 192, 215, 216, 218
homoeroticism 53, 55, 61
Household Words (Dickens) 178
Hughes, Thomas 19

identity 191, 193; and colonial fantasy 264; and colour 196; formed through self–Other trajectory 193–5; Lacan's definition 194; Lacan's mirror

stage 193–4, 195, 197; and the racial body **195–200**
Ilbert Bill 180
Illustrated London News: reporting of Anglo-Zulu War 90, 91–3, 95, 96, 99, 100–3
In Black and White 5
India 29, 104–8, 143; archaeological survey 107, 144–5; British relationship with customs and traditions 107, 143; discouragement of British settlement in 107–8; growth of British stake in 175; modernity and past 144–8; occupation of 104; Orientalist and Anglicist phases of rule 104–5; policy of goodwill towards Princes 106–7, 143–4; Queen's proclamation (1858) 105–6; *see also* Anglo-Indian community; Calcutta; 'Letters of Marque'
Isandhlwana 58, 59, 91

Jaipur 136, 146
James, Henry 34
Jess 4, 38, 51
Joshi, Svati 105

Kanta Ray, Rajat 175
Kellogg, Robert 254
Kemp, Sandra 127
Keswick, J. 180
Kim 6, 8, **200–15**, 233, 235, 239, 265; characterisation of 213–14, 239, 265; crisis of identity at heart of 214; critical acclaim 201; cross-cultural disguise 192, 200, 202–3, 207–9, 230; function of costume 202–3, 207, 209, 215, 220; insistence on white colonial identity 211, 212–15, 220, 230; link of knowledge to power 233; story 200–1; purging of conflict from Anglo-Indian encounter 266; transferential structures 231, 237
King, Anthony 108, 158

King Solomon's Mines 4, 47, 55, 83; battle scenes 96–8; and boyhood 32; character–narrator 267; critical acclaim 5; critique of colonisation 76–8, 77, 81–2; feminisation of landscape 49–50; publication 6; reclamation of moral status in treasure discovery scene 78–9; story 39; Umbopa/Curtis doubling 59–60, 60–1; women's link with primitivity 63;
Kingsley, Charles 19, 33
Kipling, Rudyard 35, 113, 127, 191; ability to cross cultures 5, 235–6, 237, 258; attack on municipal government in India 175, 176, 177, 178–9; background 4; critical acclaim 5, 235–6; critical assessment 265–6; dual heritage 170; early decadent years 169; intended audience 109; and journalism 4–5, 256–7, 263, 266; knowledge of native underlife 166–7, 171, 172, **233–7**, 239, 258, 259, 266; narrative persona 257, 262, 266; popularity 7; rise to literary fame 5; similar to Carnehan in 'The Man Who Would Be King' 253–4; similarity to Dickens 183–4, 265; as storyteller 239, **254–6**, 262; task to mystify and reveal native life 258; theme of Anglo-Indian insecurity 115; and unpublished novel 'Mother Maturin' 258–9, 260–1, 262; use of gothic 114, 137, 191; *see also individual titles*
knowledge: and costume 220–1; link with power 233, 243

Lacan, Jacques 224; definition of transference 231; and lack 274–5n; mirror stage 193–4, 195, 197
lack 224, 225, 229, 232, 233, 274–5n
Lahore: depicted in 'The City of

Dreadful Night' 171–2; depicted in 'Typhoid at Home' 166–8

Lang, Andrew 5; defence of romance 31–2, 33; on Haggard 84–5, 267; on Kipling 125–6, 235–6

Laplanche, J. and Pontalis, J.B. 225, 227, 231

Lawrence, T.E. 3, 228–9, 230

'Letters of Marque' 8, **136–47**; alienation of Anglo-Indian community 141–2, 143; anxiety of colonial authority 115, 147–8, 154–5, 156; architecture as India's legacy 145; contrast between urban metropolis and original native lifestyle 140–1; contrast of globe-trotter character with Anglo-Indian narrator 142–3; depiction of Engineers of Princely States 139–40; difficulties with Anglo-Indian identity 137; history of Rajasthan 144; loafer in 242, 251; and modernity of Princely States 146; narrator's persona of globe-trotter and pioneer 138–9; narrator's phobia of native bodily contact 137–8, 151–2; Palace of Boondi 153–4; Tower of Victory 151–2; travel sketches 136; use of gothic in describing Native States 137, 148, 149–50, 151–4; vacillation between modernity and past 137

Life's Handicap 254, 256, 262–3

Light That Failed, The 169–71

Lloyd, David 196

loafer(s) **238–53**; artist as 256–63; definition 241; hostility towards by Anglo-Indians 241; Kipling's characterisation 241–2; in 'Letters of Marque' 242, 251; politics of 240–3; relationship between journalist and 261–6; representation of 238–9; in 'To Be Filed for Reference' 259–60, 261; *see also* 'Man Who Would

Be King, The'

Locations: creation of in Africa 7, 68, **71–5**, 83

London: Calcutta as imitation of in 'The City of Dreadful Night' 8, 156–7, 171, 173–4, 181, 187, 191, 194; depicted in Thomson's poem 168–9; Lahore as double of 171–2; literary attacks on bureaucracy of 177–8

London, Jack 219–20

Longman, Charles 85

Ludlow, W.R. 30

Lyall, Alfred 32, 33

MacDonald, Robert 131, 132

MacKenzie, A. 88–9

Mallet, Philip 251, 252

'Man Who Would Be King, The' 8, **239–54**; attractiveness of loafer character 251–2; conflicting interpretation over parable or parody of Empire 240, 243–6, 253; Dravot's actions seen only through Carnehan 252–3; frame-narrator in 244, 246–8, 250, 254, 257; function of native disguise 243; loafer's politics 242; narration of Carnehan 250, 252–3, 253–4; relationship between loafers and frame-narrator 247–9, 250, 253; story 240–1; text as hoax 239, 251, 254; transferential structures 247–50, 252–3

Mangan, J.A. 21

manliness *see* masculinity

Manor, James 109

'Mark of the Beast, The' 115, **125–30**, 217, 230, 257; balance between reality and fantasy 126; Fleete's transformation into beast 127, 128; polarising of East and West 126–7; story 126; white man's transgression from civility to barbarity through torture of Silver Man 126, 128–9

INDEX

Marks, Shula 69, 72
Marshall, Alfred 17
Martin, Sir James 28
masculinity: boyhood and culture
of 33; changing ideal of 60; and
cult of muscular Christianity
19–20, 60; desire to build up by
youth movements 30–1;
effeminacy and corruption of
20, 21, 22, 93; Engineers of the
Princely States as emblems of
140; formation of English
through romanticised image of
Zulus 7, 21–2, 35; and imperial
authority 126; and primitivity
35; seen as natural
characteristic of British race 20;
and Zulu warfare 96
Mason, Philip 201
Masterman, Charles 15, 17
Maudsley, Henry 17–18, 23
Mayhew, Henry 15
Mearn, Andrew 15–16
Meath, Lord 20, 21
Mhlontlo 82
Miles, Robert 113–14, 115
Mill, J.S. 177
Millar, J.H. 252
mimicry: discourse of 181, 199
'Miss Youghal's Sais' 216–17, 230–1
Moore, William 28, 161
Moore-Gilbert, Bart 7, 108–9, 118
Morris, Donald 86
'Mother Maturin' 258–9, 260–1,
262
Mughal empire 104, 105, 107
Mulvey, Laura 44

Nada the Lily 4, 90, 267–8;
distribution figures 6; function
of women in 47–8; Shepstone's
investiture of spirit of Shaka
86–8; story-telling 85–6; vision
of savagery 85, 87; Zulu battle
scenes 97–8, 99–100
narrator: Kipling as 172, 257, 266;
privileged status of in
Haggard's texts 51, 53;

transferential relationship
between listener and 237,
249–50, 267–8; see also
individual titles
Natal 40, **67–75**; Haggard's view of
colonial policy in 68–9, 69–70;
policy of segregation with
creation of Locations 68, 71–5;
native law 71, 72, 73–4;
settlement of by British 67;
subversion of tribal authority by
British government 72–5, 84
Native Princely States 137, 143–8,
149–50, 151–4
nature: communion between man
and 40–1, 42; gendering of as
female 48–50
'Negro as Soldier, The' (Wolseley)
21–2, 30
novel of manners 33, 34

'On Duty with Inspector Field'
(Dickens) 16, 183–4
O'Pray, Michael 9
Orientalism 2–3

Parr, Capt. Henry 58–9
Parry, Benita 201, 207, 256
pastoralism **37–50**, 75; African
39–42; and boyhood 44–6, 75;
and England 18; ideal in *Allan
Quatermain* 37–8, 265; need to
reproduce in foreign lands
26–40; suited to poetics of
Empire 43–4; versions of **42–7**
Pick, Daniel 17–18
*Pilgrimage to Al-Madinah and
Meccah* (Burton) 209–11
Pinney, Thomas 108
Pioneer 4, 90
Plain Tales from the Hills 5, 109,
134, 259; see also individual titles
Platt, Kate 161
policeman: role of in Kipling 8,
182, 183, 184–5, 192, 238
Pollock, Griselda 185
pollution 162, 165, 168, 187
Poole, Adrian 113, 168
Pratt, Mary 43, 135

297

INDEX

Prester John 55
primitivity 24, 35, 76; and
femininity 23–4, 62–4; link with
folklore movement 31–2, 35;
and masculinity 35;
reconstituted through image of
noble savage 53, 62;
romanticising of healthy 30;
violence modelled on 32–3
prostitution 24; feared source of
contagion 159, 186
psychoanalysis 191, 193, 223, 227,
231, 264
Puck stories 256

race, reasons for diversity of 28–9
racial environmentalism 16–17
racial fetishism **221–6**
Racinet, Albert 203, 206
Rajasthan 115, 137, 143–4, 146
Ramasubban, Radhika 160
realism, genre of 33, 34
reality, division between fantasy
and 2, 8–9
Recessional 256
'Return of Imray, The' 115, **121–5**,
217, 257; alienation 122;
colonial vulnerability 121–2;
Imray's murder 123; tension
between master and servant
124–5
Ribeiro, Aileen 206
Richard, E.P. 182–3
Rignall, John 263
Robinson, Kay 4, 5, 234, 235,
258
romance: and aristocracy 46; and
boyhood 32, 33, 45–6; Lang's
defence of 31–2; representation
of manly and healthy British
morality 34; transformation of
gothic into imperial 114;
violence as part of 32–3
Rome, ancient 19
Rosaldo, Renato 44
Rose, Jacqueline 45, 46
Ruskin, 'Of Queen's Gardens'
22
Russell, W.H. 163, 165

Said, Edward 2, 195, 211
Schilder, Paul 195, 227
Schreuder, D.M. 69
scouting movement 21, 31, 53
Seeley, John 20
Seltzer, Mark 30
sexuality 22; and black body 53–4,
55
Shanks, Edward 201
Shannon, Richard 169
Shaw, Valerie 120–1
She 4, 6, 64–5; link between
women and primitivity 63–4
Shepstone, Sir Theophilus 3, 69,
84; authority of 74, 89–90, 99;
dedication to in *Nada the Lily*
86, 87; and Haggard 4, 66–7,
87–8; influence of 66–7;
invested with spirit of Shaka
86–9; setting up of Locations in
Natal 71–3, 74
Silverman, Kaja 8–9, 228–9, 264
Singh, Jey 144
'slumming' expeditions 218–19
Southern Africa *see* Africa
Spencer, Herbert 23
Stedman Jones, Gareth 16, 17
Steevens, G.W. 163
Stevenson, Robert 5, 32, 33;
Treasure Island 45
Stocking, George 24–5, 223
Stoller, Robert 229
story-teller 239, 266; Kipling as
239, **254–6**; transferential
dynamics 249, 250
'Strange Ride of Morrowbie Jukes'
115–21, 125, 257; benevolent
image of imperial rule 119;
Dass character 118–19; fantasy
and reality in 119–20, 126;
Jukes's transition from civility to
brutality 116, 117, 118; tale of
Anglo-Indian insecurity 115–18;
use of narrative frame 119–21
Strickland, character of **215–21**,
239, 265; desire of native
culture 217; and disguise 192,
216–17, 218, 230;
empowerment of 230–1, 232;
familiarity with native life

216–17, 231; narrator and 231, 237; similarity with Sherlock Holmes 192, 215, 216, 218
Suleri, Sara 221, 263

Taj Mahal 145
temporal distancing 75–84
Thomson, James 168–9
'To Be Filed for Reference' 171, 230, 256, 259–60, 261
Tod, Colonel James 143
Tompkins, J.M.S. 201
Tower of Victory 151–2
transvestism 226, 227, 229
travel writing 2, 115, 135–6, 140
Treasure Island 45
'Typhoid at Home' 166–8

Udaipur 141
Under the Deodars 5

venereal disease 159
violence, Haggard's defence of 32–3

Ward, Thomas 236
warfare, Zulu: Haggard's sexualisation of 98–9; and masculinity 96; *see also* Anglo–Zulu War
Watson, John Forbes 133, 220–1
Welsh, David 73
Wilde, Oscar 22
Williams, Raymond 169
Wilson, Angus 266

'Without Benefit of Clergy' 131, 132
Wolseley, Garnet 20, 21–2, 30, 93
women **21–4**, **47–50**, 63; Anglo-Indian 164; and association with nature 48–50; black women as symbol of sexual promiscuity 23–4; division between man and 22–3; in Haggard's adventures 47–8; and invalidism/death 34, 49, 270n; Meath attack on modern 21; and primitivity 23–4, 63–4; replacement by black man as man's object of affection 62; in *She* 64–5;
Woodruff, Charles 28–9

Zam-Zammah cannon 212
Žižek, Slavoj 193, 198, 250
Zola, Emile 34
'Zulu Kaffirs, The', exhibition 25, 30
'Zulu War Dance, A' 76
Zululand 67, 68, 81, 90
Zulus 44, 104; against Prince Imperial 55, 56–7, 58; depicted in *Nada the Lily* 85–90; English heroism seen through bravery of 55, 58–60; four decrees at Cetshwayo coronation 84; mobilisation of 95–6; and portrayal of masculine heroism 7, 21–2, 35, 93–5, 96, 104, 264; romanticising of healthy primitivity of 30; *see also* Anglo–Zulu War